Money for the Cause

CONSERVATION LEADERSHIP SERIES
Sponsored by the
River Systems Institute at Texas State University
General Editor, Andrew Sansom

Money for the Cause

A COMPLETE GUIDE TO EVENT FUNDRAISING

Rudolph A. Rosen

*Fundraising art and illustrations
by Katie Dobson Cundiff*

Foreword by Andrew Sansom

TEXAS A&M UNIVERSITY PRESS
College Station

© KATIE-DIDS! ORIGINALS, INC.

Library of Congress Cataloging-in-Publication Data
Rosen, Rudolph A. (Rudolph Albert), 1952–
Money for the cause : a complete guide to event fundraising /
Rudolph A. Rosen ; fundraising art and illustrations by Katie
Dobson Cundiff ; foreword by Andrew Sansom.—1st ed.
p. cm.—(Conservation leadership series)
Includes index.
ISBN–13: 978-1-60344-693-8 (book/hardcover (printed case) :
alk. paper)
ISBN–10: 1-60344-693-1 (book/hardcover (printed case) :
alk. paper)
ISBN–13: 978-1-60344-752-2 (ebook)
ISBN–10: 1-60344-752-0 (ebook)
1. Fund raising—United States—Management. 2. Charities—
United States—Finance—Management. 3. Nonprofit
organizations—United States—Finance—Management.
I. Title. II. Series: Conservation leadership series.
HV41.9.U5R674 2012
658.15′224—dc23
2012016411

Contents

Foreword

I FIRST MET RUDY ROSEN when he was working in Georgia as a senior official of America's largest conservation organization, the National Wildlife Federation. I convinced him to come to Texas and direct all fisheries and wildlife management programs for the Texas Parks and Wildlife Department. To this day, I believe it was one of the best decisions I ever made.

At that time, now more than twenty years ago, the department, generally beloved in Texas, was embroiled in scandal involving the transfer of wild animals to the ranches of politicians and other influential folks. Despite the growing realization that more than 95 percent of the wildlife habitat in Texas is located on lands owned by private citizens, the department had not created an aggressive program to help them protect it. There were other pressing problems in the department that also demanded attention. Into this milieu stepped Dr. Rosen, who immediately engaged his colleagues and the constituencies they served with a professional, science-based, and modern approach that fundamentally changed the department's fish and wildlife programs for the better and set the agency on a course that has persisted to this day.

Inevitably, and bolstered by his success in Texas, Rudy went on to become the director of the Department of Fish and Wildlife in Oregon, where he served in the cabinets of two successive governors. He later was named executive director of Safari Club International and served as director of operations of Ducks Unlimited. In these capacities, he has emerged as one of the most successful fundraisers in the American conservation movement.

And fundraising is a principal challenge of our movement. Today, thousands of non-profit organizations across the nation indicate that environmental and conservation issues are all or part of their mission and each is dependent on the generosity of the rest of us in order to support their efforts. So it is fitting that in the inaugural volume of a new and exciting series in conservation leadership we focus on *Money for the Cause*. As the global population continues to exponentially grow and the oceans, atmosphere, and habitat of our planet become more imperiled, the non-governmental sector must be prepared to take an increasingly active role in defense of the earth and its resources. These pages provide one pathway to an ever more essential ingredient in the fight: financing.

Today, Rudy is back in Texas, helping to fund vital efforts to understand, preserve, and interpret our water resources for the benefit of future generations while sharing his wisdom and experience with so many who are struggling each day to pay the way.

—ANDREW SANSOM
General Editor,
Conservation Leadership Series

Acknowledgments

A THIRD OF THIS BOOK was written almost ten years before the last two-thirds, giving me plenty of time to accumulate people to acknowledge. Time also blurs details of events—fundraising and otherwise. Thus it is no accident I now thank Steve Comus and Travis Cundiff. They were present at many of the events serving as stories in the book and made sure I had my facts straight. I apologize for any slight nuances between my memory and what others may recall. Steve also reviewed the text and that is particularly meaningful because he has probably written and published more about high-dollar fundraising events than anyone else in history. I also thank Alan Wentz, a mentor and thorough reviewer of this book who has spent more years observing fundraising events than I ever will. Many others have mentored or helped me along the way in fundraising, including Andy Sansom, who so graciously wrote the foreword to this book, Larry Schweiger, Charlie Shaw, John Jensen, Peter Hunter, Pat Johnson, and Rebecca O'Connor. Special thanks go to Charles Leigon, a dear friend and colleague whose patient encouragement to write helped renew my interest in finishing this book.

I also am grateful for the partnership with Shannon Davies, Louise Lindsey Merrick Editor for the Natural Environment of the Texas A&M University Press. Considerable work goes into birthing a book. Shannon's friendship, help, and encouragement made the work go smoothly.

Special thanks go to Katie Cundiff, a phenomenally talented artist whose work has made this book a visual feast of fundraising art. But even more significant, many of the works displayed on the pages that follow have been used to raise funds by many organizations serving many causes.

Finally I thank my "in-house" reviewers. My wife, Jackie, dutifully read every word, several times, and helped edit. She also provided substantive content in areas of event arrangements, such as food service, site selection, accommodations, and negotiations which are her areas of expertise. My "lucky" daughter Julie, now an attorney doing some nonprofit practice, helped review and contributed to sections of the book covering legal matters. Julie is a dedicated advocate of greening fundraising events, and along with my other daughters, Laura and Shelly, regularly volunteers to help raise funds for worthy causes.

Money for the Cause

Introduction

Standing near the former president of the United States was a tall, handsome African dressed in a blaze of traditional Maasai red. Barely 20 years old, the young man was the son of a chief and in time would become a chief in his African homeland. But he was not with the former president because of politics or tribal status. He was a student whose education was being funded at a leading university in South Africa by members of the audience. He was among the "motivational elements" assembled at this international nonprofit organization's premier fundraising event where more than 15,000 members had assembled for four days of fun and fundraising.

At one of the event's several formal dinners, to be followed by a major auction, members heard the young African speak of his dedication to the cause of wildlife conservation. They listened intently as he told of his commitment to take what he had learned from members of the organization during his visit and go back to his country to use his new knowledge as a leader. The members were enthusiastic and renewed their commitment to fund education of young Africans at African universities.

Later the former president spoke, introduced by a celebrated former general of the US Army. This was yet another of many attractions driving $8 million in revenue orchestrated by the host organization over the four-day event. The people who came gave. Many received something of value in return by bidding at the auction and playing raffles, while others simply gave to the cause. When they returned home, many members worked to hold their own local fundraisers. They duplicated the banquet/auction/show format at events in their own communities. They raised money and funded favorite causes locally, as well as helped fund the inter-

national organization's conservation, humanitarian, and education work in the United States and throughout the world.

TIME AND AGAIN, a simple fundraising formula is duplicated. Each time it will be a success when done right. It will work in good financial times and bad. Money for a cause will be raised. Fundraising events range from elite affairs in large cities, where black tie and gown definitely are not optional, to the "meat and potatoes" banquet auctions and backyard barbecue fundraising events held in thousands of small towns in rural America. This book covers them all, describing methods adaptable to any situation and illustrating basic through advanced techniques that both novice and veteran event planners can duplicate to raise net revenue to fund important mission-related work of nonprofit organizations, large and small.

Let's Get Started

This book is primarily about fundraising through events that include auctions, raffles, games of skill and chance, food and drink, photo opportunities, merchandise sales, exhibits, tours, and entertainment as the main attractions and key sources of net revenue. All these activities can be part of a successful fundraising event. The examples, theories, and techniques described apply to virtually any fundraising event where attendees are offered opportunities to contribute to a cause, but not everything in the book will apply to all events. Choosing which to use in a given situation is discussed at length, because the mix of fundraising activities—for example, many or few, low dollar or high—determines ultimate net revenue raised for an organization's basic operations and mission work. In this book I explain how using a major event as a centerpiece for fundraising can allow first-time event planners to succeed and experienced event planners to multiply their best efforts of the past. I will also reveal tricks and trappings of planning and holding financially successful events.

An organization need not hold an event to successfully raise money, but this book will explain how to use an event as the centerpiece of an annual repertoire of fundraising that will produce high net revenue. Volunteers and staff of nonprofit organizations can deliver spectacular results for a worthy cause in good economic times, and generous results in times of economic downturn, by hosting a well-organized, well-run event.

Does $8.3 million raised at one event sound possible? This is the amount raised during an annual four-day event for which I was responsible as executive director of a nonprofit organization. But this event was much more than just an auction or a grand banquet. It was a series of auctions, raffles, exhibitions, educational seminars, and breakfast, lunch, and dinner extravaganzas followed by even more spectacular auctions. Another organization I helped manage held nearly 5,000 auction-raffle events each year. The events were successful because they followed a tested formula that involved making fundraising and event management decisions based on objective criteria, business planning, close attention to expenses, and teamwork.

Many readers may find greatest value in this book's description of actual fundraising techniques, but the fundraising event is an elaborate affair where everything attendees see, hear, smell, and do once they enter the event site affects the outcome of giving, and thus net revenue, to the host organization. Therefore, this book covers all aspects of the fundraising event, along with several advanced techniques to further enhance fundraising.

What I see most often at fundraisers are highly competent staff and volunteers incompetently running fundraising events. Anyone can act incompetently if he or she doesn't have the knowledge, experience, or training to act otherwise. This book provides a comprehensive base of knowledge to those very competent, dedicated people who are passionate about a cause and willing to spend their time and energy raising money to achieve a goal that will benefit society. Given all the time, talent, and energy that go into event fundraising each year, isn't it about time to channel this time, talent, and energy most effectively and efficiently?

Fundraising Is Not for the Faint of Heart

I explain fundraising events by focusing on an auction-event format and its many variants, add-ons, and extremes. Groups of all descriptions and economic status use this form of fundraising. It can offer huge net revenue, but due to significant costs of staging an event, the host can assume considerable financial risk. A $100,000 fundraising event is a total failure if it raises $100,000 but costs $100,000 to hold. Whether an event raises $100, $100,000, or $1 million, only net revenue (revenue earned after all expenses are paid) counts toward funding an organization's mission. This book focuses the reader's attention on event planning and management techniques that raise net revenue and truly fund organizations and their missions.

Money raised goes to every imaginable charitable cause, drawing people from every walk of life and belief. Events range from formal black tie to casual. Locations vary from the fanciest hotels to public park ramadas. Rooms range from chandeliered ballrooms to rescue mission basements. Food varies from five-course international gourmet excursions with sherbet to cleanse the palate, to just plain meat, potatoes, and a slice of bread with butter.

All the information in the book is relevant to fundraising events, but not all information is relevant to all events. Covering the widest range of events, providing considerable detail, and giving multiple examples to cover differences in types of organizations and events are intentional objectives of this book. Readers will need to pick and choose the information that is most relevant to their own organizations and event planning goals. Readers can dive deep into details or gloss over them as suits their needs. The principles, practices, and tricks to staging net-revenue-producing events are the same, regardless of event size. The scale of events may differ; the financial risk may vary; the number of bells, whistles, and add-ons may be more or less; but best practices are what they are.

Good planning, sound financial management, use of well-instructed team-oriented volunteers, techniques to acquire donations, and so on all remain similar if not identical regardless of event size or

the host's fundraising objectives. Using sound techniques provides a ready pathway to success. There is no difference between a big or small event when it comes to the things that matter most in achieving peak performance or creating a financial disaster. Key to event planning is determining what an event should focus on based on attributes of the organization's membership, mission, and expected attendees. Deciding which fundraising activities to exclude is just as important as which to include. This book provides guidance on doing just that.

Planners' biggest challenge may be resisting the temptation to overcomplicate the planning process: there is no need for elaborate solutions in event planning where simple ones will do. The intensive planning and analysis exercises described in this book will help in designing the perfect small "members-only" event, but the depth of coverage of all the minute aspects of hosting an effective high-net-revenue event provides equal value to planners working to host large events where attendees' interests, willingness to spend, and other information relevant to event planning is not well known. Such events may carry the greatest risk to an organization, but well planned and managed, these same events may offer the highest potential net revenue.

Any one nonprofit organization is different from any other. Differences are reflected by the desires and interests of the members, dedication to different causes, and different economic situations of members. Event fundraising must take into account the host organization's members' interests, expectations, needs, wants, and financial capacity to contribute to the organization. The event planner must tailor the event to the audience. In describing fundraising, I account for this diversity by using many examples and suggestions.

What will work for one group may not work for another. Although this may seem obvious, examples of mismatched fundraising are not hard to find. These are the events where a group expecting caviar is offered mini-dogs on a stick, and where a group expecting red-hot barbecue finds salty fish eggs on water crackers. But it's not just the food that tips the scale. It is in every aspect of event planning where careful tailoring of the event to the donors' expectations, lifestyle, and capacity to contribute is vital to success. Even entertainment is important. So choose carefully. A string quartet playing classical music will simply not do, no matter how accomplished the musicians, when the crowd wants country. One kind of music is not better or worse than another, only different.

Successful fundraising requires exceeding the expectations of potential contributors in all respects. Site, time of day, day of year, food, entertainment, raffle prizes, ticket prices, drink service, access, auction items, public exposure, and on and on—all are more or less important, but any one item can become critically important if ignored or mishandled, with the criteria for ultimate judgment solely in the hands of the event attendee. Sometimes less is more when seeking to enhance net revenue. Remember that all activities, add-ons, entertainment, extra food items, decorations, and much more carry added costs. Some carry revenue potential, such as fundraising activities, while others are pure costs. Even when items are contributed, for example, a member donates decorations, there is a cost to someone that might result in forgone revenue to the organization in the long run, because that someone may have just as readily donated the equivalent value in cash to the organization.

It's a Real Circus in There!

A good analogy to a well-run auction event is a well-run circus. There is something for everyone, and the goal is for everyone to have fun. Something is always going on to see or do. The circus has its center ring and the main event. The gala auction event has its auction, always held on center stage. The event's main attraction is the live auction.

An effective auction unfolds like a stage play, with a cast of actors and an audience. Auctioneers, spotters, runners, and models work together to present exciting visual imagery of the auction items. Just as high-flying circus performers dazzle from above while clowns below involve the audience, auction players tantalize bidders with descriptions and testimonials from the stage while players on the event floor directly engage bidders. The actors in this

stage play involve the bidders and onlookers in an intense drama of rapid-fire bidding and entertaining competition. Side conversations are held with bidders and then repeated for all to hear. Models carry wearable fashion items or jewelry to bidders to "try on." A rideable "green" electric lawn mower zooms between tables as bidders vie with each other to win it. A big motorcycle onstage is started with a roar. Bidders are pitted against each other, but always in a fun way. It is a grand play, in motion and in the round, because everyone, literally everyone, becomes part of the play.

Around the center ring of a circus are side acts. At the event the side acts are fundraising opportunities, such as bucket raffles and silent auctions under way when the center ring is silent. The circus midway has an arcade with its games and exhibits. So does a full-feature fundraising event have its own brand of arcade games of skill and chance. People who go to a circus are enticed to spend a little here, play a game there, take a chance at three-for-a-dollar, and so on. A well-run event has workers who know how to entice attendees to spend as they duplicate the circus barker's call to play. The circus has its other attractions, many of which are free and add to the excitement. Food of various descriptions and things to buy are available.

The circus sounds like a friendly, fun place, and it can be, but don't be fooled. Everything about the circus is geared to enticing the person who enters the gate to part with his or her money. Even "free" attractions are mere enticements to draw the crowd into paid attractions. So it is with the event fundraiser. Silent and live auctions, raffle boards, bucket raffles, games, and merchandise sales booths are all there for one reason only: to entice attendees to part with their money.

An event may be hosted by a charitable organization, but the event itself is not charity. The event is fundraising! The work of event planners needs to be geared to enticing people to come who have money to spend, offering attendees a dazzling array of opportunities to spend money, and convincing them that spending money is exactly what they should do. That's what a fundraiser is all about. Doing event fundraising right is what this book is all about.

2

Why Hold an Event?

I had just completed a strategic planning process involving board members and staff, and the president had finished studying the strategic plan. He was not one to read a lot or put up with much process. He usually knew what he wanted and was known for getting things done, regardless of what might stand in the way. The plan included a series of goals, objectives, and actions to turn the organization around. Turnaround was among reasons I was hired. Problems left unsolved, lack of professional management of personnel, legal action against the organization, underperforming fundraising, bickering among staff and volunteers, and worse plagued the organization. The plan dealt with these problems.

So I asked the president, "Where do you want to start?"

He replied, "We need to do them all."

I agreed and added, "We can't do them all at once, there is too much to do, and some things need to be done before we can start others."

He was insistent. "All are important; we need to do them all and do them all now."

He was right. So was I. All needed to be done. But we could not do them all at once. Some had to be done first, or at least done fast. Otherwise, the organization would further decline. My challenge was to initiate and complete the actions that were most critical to enabling the organization to ultimately complete all the actions, because the president was absolutely right. All were important, and all needed to be done. My choice was obvious, and it involved a decision-making process I had used in previous turnaround work. My approach was to solve the problem that needed to be solved first. It may not have been the easiest or hardest to solve, but after its solution, it became possible to solve the next most troubling problem.

Here's a good example of this process in action. I had been appointed head of a government agency that was at odds with state elected officials, a situation that was causing a host of problems for the agency. The first job to tackle was the political instability experienced by the agency. To solve the political situation, my staff and I took action to establish better relationships with elected officials. Solution of the second problem, a lack of funding stability, depended on establishing political stability because elected officials controlled the agency's appropriations. With political stability would come political support needed to gain appropriations for the agency. After solving those two problems, we could pick and choose what to solve next since most other problems could be addressed through greater appropriations.

That progressive process was also applied in implementing the strategic plan described earlier. After the president declared he wanted everything done first, we proceeded to take on the one problem that would provide the greatest stability to the organization, which then allowed us to take on the next problem. What would provide the organization stability? For that organization at that time, a dependable, increasing funding stream would provide a period of stability during which we could make needed changes.

The organization had a successful annual event based on an auction and consumer trade show, but multiple problems were affecting revenue and growth potential. Dealing with problems relating to planning and managing the event was the first and most important step in moving the strategic plan forward. An initial step was dealing with staffing problems. After that, staff and volunteers worked together to take corrective measures and adopt policies that created fair and open practices, in particular for donors. The result was an immediate affirmative response by vendors, donors, and attendees. Within three years of corrective action, gross revenue from the event doubled to more than $8 million. Long before that point, we had progressively worked through the other goals and objectives of the strategic plan, all helping drive similar increases in financial measures and operating ratios in other aspects of the organization's business. The key to building the organization was first creating a dependable (and increasing) annual funding base driven by a well-managed, full-feature auction-event fundraiser.

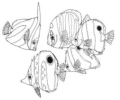

IN THE PREVIOUS EXAMPLE the key to success was to solve the problem that would lead to the solution of all other problems. For many, maybe most, nonprofit charitable organizations, success starts with a secure, stable, annual funding base. The well-planned, well-managed annual fundraising event can provide that funding base and change the fortunes of an organization. Nonprofit organizations hold events to raise funds because such events work. However, they may not work equally well for all organizations or under some conditions, so this chapter explores the event from the perspective of an organization attracted to the idea of holding an event and provides insight to answering the question, "Should we, or shouldn't we?"

Even though all organizations can use event fundraising to their advantage, it may not be the most cost-effective and time-efficient way for some organizations to raise money. Some simply do not have staff or volunteers willing to put in the time and effort necessary to effectively conduct a major event. This book provides information, instruction, and hints useful to planners of events for any organization, but no book can substitute for the time and motivation needed to develop functional teams, create viable event plans and budgets, market an event, or do any of the many other things required to host a successful event. Failure to properly plan and manage a major event risks the good name and finances of an organization. A successful event can turn an unknown, struggling organization into a celebrated powerhouse for social and environmental change.

Let's Hold an Event!

The reason to host an event is to earn significant net revenue for an organization and its cause. Money raised by event fundraising is particularly attractive to nonprofit organizations because use of the money is unrestricted, unless the event was expressly held

to raise money for a specific program or project and
donors were told funds would be restricted to a particular purpose. Unrestricted funds from events
can be used for general administration and management of the organization or anything else related to
the purposes of the organization. Many donations
to nonprofit organizations are restricted by donors,
so having flexibility in how funds can be used is of
great value to a host organization's staff and leadership.

Additional reasons to hold an event include
having fun, introducing new people to an organization, gaining community exposure, and generating
excitement for a cause. But there are easier ways to
have fun, less risky ways to earn money, and less
costly ways to get community exposure for an organization and its cause. Sidebar 2.1 lists compelling
reasons to host a major auction-based fundraiser.

Efforts by volunteers and staff in planning and
holding a fundraising event can be a lot of fun and
offer huge advantages to the host organization.
Media exposure, attendance by personalities, and
the prospect of an event becoming the "must-attend"
affair on everyone's social calendar are enticing to
host organizations' leadership. For volunteers, life-
long friends are made in the course of planning and
holding events. For some members of host organizations, being a volunteer becomes part of how they
are seen in the community and how they see themselves helping promote a cause. They take action to
make social or environmental change through their
work on events that fund a mission. Volunteerism is
often passed on to relatives and children. For many
volunteers, working on events truly is a family affair.

My wife and I attended a statewide auction event
planned by staff and volunteers that was a fundraiser
serving the added purpose of recognizing the efforts
of volunteers from throughout the state who had
hosted events in their own communities during the
preceding year. At our table was a couple, longtime
volunteers for their local event, accompanied by
their teenage daughter. Both husband and wife had
been chairpersons for their local event committee
in past years, but they were there because of their
daughter's achievements. Helping Mom and Dad
plan and hold events from the time she could walk

Sidebar 2.1. **Nine Good Reasons to Host a Major Event**

1. The leadership is seeking to raise money from people who are not already contributing members.
2. The leadership wants to introduce new people to the organization's mission and make money while doing so.
3. The organization has a large membership, and the leadership wants to bring members together at one location on a regular basis to conduct business, have fun, and raise money.
4. Membership is large and highly dispersed geographically, and the leadership wants members in local communities to get a chance to meet each other and work together to support the organization and its mission. In this situation, local members organize, plan, and hold auction events in their communities.
5. Members are not generally philanthropic but have special interests that can be turned to fundraising advantage by holding events that offer auctions, raffles, and games featuring specialty merchandise, services, and vacation trips that members desire.
6. Members enjoy social interaction with each other.
7. The leadership wants to increase the organization's profile in the community.
8. The leadership wants to raise funds that are unrestricted, which means money raised can be used to fund basic organization operations and administration or accomplish a specific work program, mission-related objective, or capital project.
9. The organization has a ready supply of volunteers and/or staff who can effectively plan and conduct auction events that are fun and earn high net revenue.

and talk, this young woman had grown up a volunteer for the organization. She had just chaired her
first major auction fundraising event and was to receive an award. She was being honored not because
she was so young but because the event had met
high standards and achieved fundraising goals that
topped several categories of fundraising in statewide
competition with nearly 100 other events held in the
state by more than 70 event committees that year.
The committees had raised more than $1 million.
Her parents were bursting with pride. The young
woman was also very excited and told us how much
she enjoyed being a volunteer and helping the cause.
She was about to go off to college where she wanted
to host an event on campus to fundraise for the organization.

If event workers are effective at soliciting full
donations for most or all of the items used in an

event's fundraising activities, if the items are effectively marketed before and during an event, and if event expenses are tightly controlled, the host organization can receive incredibly high revenues after all expenses have been paid. For some organizations a single well-run and well-attended event held annually can provide a solid base of funding for the organization's programs. This can ensure a sound future for the organization and a well-earned sense of accomplishment for the organization's leadership, staff, and members.

There May Be an Easier Way to Raise Money

Many people love to attend fundraising events because events are so much fun. Many of these same people are also members and officers of nonprofit organizations. It's no surprise when those event lovers say they want their organization to host an event, too. And why not? Everyone knows events are fun and "all the other charitable organizations" host events. So members, officers, and staff (if there are any) get together and agree to host an event. That's it. The desire to have fun and do what others do becomes the basis for forging ahead. These emotional drivers substitute for strategic and business planning, objective evaluation, and number crunching. "Let's have an event," is the one and only agenda item for the meeting that gets the ball rolling. We're going to have an event. Now what?

Although it may take some time, event planners eventually will face reality: a major fundraising event is a lot of work involving many people who must have considerable time and talent to invest in the event. There can be serious logistic challenges and financial liabilities even when experienced event planners are involved. If event planners are ill prepared for the job because of a lack of skills, knowledge, and experience, the risk of failure can increase considerably. This book was written to help leaders of nonprofit organizations raise significant funds in good economic times and bad but not to entice would-be event planners to take on a task well beyond their ability and create financial hardship for the host organization when an event costs more

than it earns. Sidebar 2.2 lists reasons an organization should consider alternatives to a major auction event for raising funds.

When considering event fundraising, also consider alternative ways to raise funds that may have less financial risk, are easier to plan, and do not require as much staff and volunteer time. Make this evaluation before committing an organization to its first major fundraising event. Evaluate as objectively as possible the capacity of the host organization to guarantee a sufficient number of attendees having sufficient disposable income to reasonably ensure fundraising success if meeting planners do a reasonably competent job of hosting the event. Concentrate on identifying who can be relied on to attend the event. Event planners may even want go to the extreme of writing down names of people who will come to the event (and spend money). If the result is a long list, then maybe an event is a truly viable option. If the list is short, then the expected attendees had better be wealthy if the event is intended to deliver high net revenue. How much money will attendees be expected to spend? Use the business-plan model in chapter 5 to do a hypothetical financial evaluation of costs and revenues. Consider this a "risk-evaluation" exercise, because events all carry

> **Sidebar 2.2. Six Good Reasons to Strongly Consider an Alternative to Major Event Fundraising**
>
> 1. The host organization has no individual(s) willing to serve (or capable of serving) as a chairperson (or co-chairs) who will organize and lead an event planning and management team.
>
> 2. No staff or volunteers are willing to work as a team and put in the time and effort necessary to effectively conduct a major event.
>
> 3. Staff or volunteers are willing to act as workers if assigned simple tasks, but none are willing to develop a business plan and take leadership roles to guide planning and managing the event.
>
> 4. The organization does not have a clear mission or purpose to motivate giving.
>
> 5. A donor base readily gives cash or other direct gifts if and when asked.
>
> 6. The membership has no interest in meeting with each other for social, business, or fundraising purposes.

some level of risk. Is it reasonable to expect the event will be profitable?

If the objective assessment of attendance shows the only people that can reasonably be expected to attend are the host organization's officers, event planners, and a smattering of the organization's members, all of whom are already making regular donations to the organization, then there is a much easier and less costly alternative to raise the same amount of or more money than by holding an event. That more effective and efficient alternative is to just ask each anticipated participant to give donations to the organization directly in lieu of holding a major event fundraiser. Base the amount of the request on a frank discussion with all potential donors. Tell them about the proposed event. Ask them how much money and how much time they expect they would spend helping organize the event and how much money they would probably spend during the fundraising event. Let them know a direct donation is tax deductible, whereas contributions to an event may not be, or may be only partially deductible, provided the host organization is a qualified charitable organization. They can keep the answer to themselves if they feel uncomfortable sharing this information. But then ask them to add up the time and money they would spend on the event and just contribute the monetary equivalent directly to the organization. As a result the organization can save huge amounts of time and up-front expense on hosting a major fundraising event, avoid all risks, and make as much or more net revenue than if an event were held. This is possible because the direct donations will have much less associated cost; thus, there is no expense cutting into revenue raised. If the host organization's leadership or staff are uncomfortable asking for donations in such a frank manner, then the same leaders and staff will be doomed when asking for the quality and quantity of donations, underwriting, and contributions necessary to conduct a high-net-revenue-producing auction event.

To summarize, if an event brings together only the same people who would donate the same amount of money to an organization with or without an event, then the consequence of the event is to greatly increase the cost of raising the same amount of money from the same people, leaving the organization with much less net revenue and a huge outlay of staff and volunteer time. Creating a visual picture that helps would-be planners make the right decision really comes down to solving a very simple arithmetic problem. It is amazing how many otherwise very smart people fail to pass this simple test and hold poorly planned, underperforming, costly events. The events may be fun, but is the objective fun or fundraising?

*Event Fundraising Requires a
Lot of Asking for Donations*

Event fundraising is complicated in many ways. It is not an activity to undertake lightly, and those who do undertake it had better be comfortable asking other people to make donations. The successful event involves simultaneous fundraising by many of the host organization's volunteers or staff asking many people for several different kinds of donations, with much of this taking place long before the event begins.

By the end of an event, most "donations" are subject to at least two levels of solicitation, marketing, and administrative-financial tracking: (1) Event workers solicit many or all the items used in an event's auctions, raffles, games, and giveaways. Someone from the host organization asks a donor for a donation of cash, services, or hard goods. Even cash donations routinely used to buy items for auction or raffle come as a direct result of an "ask" by someone. (2) Event attendees are then solicited to come to the event; once they arrive, they are solicited to buy tickets for raffles, enticed to play games of skill and chance, offered opportunities to bid for items, and otherwise solicited to spend money to benefit the host organization and mission.

Thus, at a minimum, two solicitations for each item used at an event are required before the host organization receives any revenue. There are also usually many items that need to be handled, tracked, and financially accounted for over the

course of the event, as well as subsequent steward-
ship of the donors and buyers.

Event Fundraising Carries Continued Risk of Liability

Finally, unlike events where people just pay an
admission price, full-feature auction events create a
continued liability for the host organization. Many
auction or raffle items, services, and trips "come
back" to the host organization, as service providers
fail to provide promised services, merchandise isn't
what it was claimed to be, and trips are not as advertised. Whereas savvy event planners take steps to
reduce risk of liability, unsatisfied auction and raffle
buyers come back to the host organization and seek
amends. Even given proper disclaimers and advance
notice, these buyers require care and consideration
because they are also the organization's members
and supporters. Many services or vacation tours sold
at auction and awarded in raffles may not be completed for a year or more after the auction ends. The
auction event is unique in producing this continuing
liability, ending sometimes years after the event.

Check the Numbers: Can You Afford It?

Later in this book event planners are urged to develop business plans for events, which includes developing a budget (see chapters 5 and 18), because
auctions can be very costly to hold. My reason for
mentioning business planning and budgets now is
to emphasize that events must be carefully planned
to earn net revenue. If planners cannot work out an
event budget that logically allows for that, they need
to find some other way to raise money.

When planners do not pay attention to costs, an
event can fail financially and create financial harm
to an organization. Many costs are obvious to the
host, but there are also hidden and contributed
costs. For example, if volunteers were paid minimum wage for their time and this was added into
event costs, most events would probably lose money.
Fortunately, volunteers don't get paid and their cost
of time can be ignored. But for organizations that
have paid staff who work on helping plan and stage

events, there is a direct and calculable cost of this
work. This cost should be added into the event budget as an expense. Many organizations fail to include such costs in the event budget and continue
as if the cost of staff were irrelevant. They assume
that staff have to be paid anyway, whether they work
on an event or something else. Volunteers and officers often place pressure on staff to put long hours
into event work. Such costs are hard costs of staging
an event and a direct payout of revenue by the host
organization. They must be accounted for along with
all other costs in evaluating an event's financial success or failure. Staff could be using their time (and
revenue of the host organization) doing other types
of fundraising or accomplishing mission-related
work. If staff are being paid anyway, responsible
financial planning and accounting require an organization employing staff to properly account for their
time.

There are probably many events that would be
canceled as a result of cost outweighing revenue if
all costs of holding the event were considered. If an
event will cost an organization more than it raises,
what then? The organization should consider raising
money a different way or change the way in which
it plans and holds an event so the event really does
make significant net revenue.

Can We Get Help?

Besides this book, is there help available for an
organization that wishes to host an event? Yes, services are available. Fundraising and event service
providers can provide help with specific needs, such
as planning and negotiating catering, or providers
can supply complete fundraising and event services.
It is likely planners will turn to service providers for
some aspects of event planning and for services at
the event itself. Using service providers and negotiating services are topics covered in several chapters of this book. The best time for professional consulting help is at the early planning stage. At that
point, groundwork for an effective event can be laid,
with expert advice. The planning team can then
move forward with confidence. Should questions
arise, the consultant can be asked questions or regu-

larly scheduled meetings can be held as a check on progress.

An organization can also employ an event management service to professionally manage the event, from A to Z. Here no volunteer help may be used, or volunteer involvement may be minimal and menial and only during the event itself. Full professional management of an event creates significant expense to the host organization. It also deprives the organization of the contributions of volunteers, but it may be the only alternative for some organizations if volunteer help is unavailable or unreliable. A variation of this "full-service" approach to professional event fundraising is the involvement of a fundraising team or service provided by the parent entity of organizations having chapters or affiliates. Regardless of such convenient assistance, the most effective fundraising in terms of excitement and net return often comes in those organizations' chapters and affiliates that do fundraising entirely on their own, with all planning and other work done by volunteers.

One other point needs to be made here: beware those who claim they can come into the picture the day of the event and, for a fee, supervise and increase the success of a fundraising event. Besides the expense of such help, last-minute organizing is makeshift at best. A well-run fundraising event is planned over time, jobs are assigned and completed, preparations are made, and people who have worked together in planning assemble on-site for the big event with a well-understood game plan and a familiarity with each other as a result of months of working together. If event planners are panicked enough to feel they need to pay for last-minute help by outsiders, then they probably failed to properly plan in so many areas that no person coming in at the last minute can really straighten out the mess. It is just added expense on top of what is likely going to be a financial failure anyway. Save the money and let someone else plan next year's event. Or read this book and do it right next time.

To ensure an optimum financial return to the host organization, conduct fundraising event work to the greatest degree possible by volunteers. Of course, this depends on volunteers having the time, skills, and motivation to do a good job. There are exceptions to relying on volunteers. For example, a professional auctioneer should be employed for major live auctions, regardless of the skills of volunteers and staff. Other examples and options are provided where professional help should be considered. Also, when the host organization employs professional staff, then paid staff should be involved in event planning, but only to the extent necessary to support volunteers. If volunteers can be successful on their own, then staff should step aside.

Get Another Organization to Host the Fundraiser

In this book the term "host organization" is used to refer to the nonprofit organization that an event will benefit. The host organization's staff and volunteers are responsible for planning and conducting the event in all respects, such as donating or overseeing acquisition of auction merchandise, renting the auction room, obtaining catering, paying deposits, printing of tickets, holding the auction and associated raffles, and so on. The host organization, its staff, and volunteers are legally liable for any problems that may happen in connection with the event.

The host organization reaps the financial rewards of the event or suffers financially if the event fails to produce net revenue. This is generally the case, but it is not uncommon for one organization to play event host for another organization. Sometimes the two organizations are connected, possibly by a common board; for example, an organization may have split into two cross-supporting entities: a charitable entity recognized under Section 501(c)(3) of the IRS Code and a social advocacy entity recognized under Section 501(c)(4). The social advocacy organization may host an event that supports the charitable entity. For the host group or organization to attract attendees seeking tax-advantaged giving, any donated funds must go directly to an organization qualified as a "charitable organization" under Section 501(c)(3) of the IRS Code. Sometimes the organizations are separate, but one benefits by helping the other. For example, an organization dedicated to medical research can hold an event at which all checks are written to another nonprofit entity, such as a hospital. Some events are held by organizations not qualified to accept tax-deductible contributions. (See chapter 21 for information on tax deductibility of event donations and purchases.)

For an organization unable to conduct event fundraising effectively, working with another organization that is better equipped to do so can be very effective and provide the advantages of holding an event without the need to invest time and labor. An example of an organization unable to effectively host an event is one that has too few members or its members simply do not have the time to plan and hold an event. In establishing such an arrangement, it is important to clearly define the roles and responsibilities of each organization and determine exactly how expenses and any net revenue will be handled.

That's No Fundraiser

Sometimes organization executives or volunteer leaders may say they want to have a big event because they want to recognize people who have been generous to the organization or they want to just have a fun event for members. But, oh, by the way, they will also say they want to raise money. My suggestion is pretty straightforward in such cases. If an organization's leadership wants to recognize people or have fun, then by all means they should do so and do it well. But if it's fundraising they really want, they make a mistake pretending a fundraiser is anything but a fundraiser. They risk losing the trust of attendees and future fundraising if people come to an event expecting one thing but experience another.

There is nothing wrong with holding a raffle or selling a few logo items at a fun event or recognition dinner. The problem arises when an advertised fun activity or recognition dinner is instead a ruse to get attendees into a situation where they can be strong-armed into making big donations. When attendees perceive they have been invited to a fundraiser in disguise, they lose faith in the organization. When people perceive that the advertised purpose of an event was really a ruse to gather them to be squeezed for money, the next "real" fundraising event staged by the same group or organization is likely to fail. People who attended the earlier "bait-and-switch" event may consider that they have already given and may be less likely to attend or, if they do, participate halfheartedly.

My suggestion is, do not mix event or activity types. Sure, raise a few dollars at fun activities, but save the real fundraising for advertised, true fundraising events. Getting squeezed for money is what a fundraising event is all about. Use the circus example, where every sight and sound beg for money. Use every means and method to raise funds. Squeeze until they squeak. They may give more or less, but no one is upset about being solicited for money at a real fundraiser. The only way attendees can be disappointed or lose faith with the host organization at a fundraiser is if they don't get asked to donate money and never hear about the wonderful work to be done by the organization with the money raised.

Failure Is Possible

I have heard event planners say they can't understand why some organizations' events do so well but events held by other organizations in the same city do poorly. They say that they and other event planners do everything they can think of to imitate the successful organizations' events. They do this year after year, and it never seems to work. They are frustrated and confused by event fundraising, yet they continue to hold events and seek secrets for success because they see other organizations thriving on event income. They ask what they are doing wrong.

Although it's impossible to give specific answers to such questions without analysis of the events, I typically advise event planners to stop trying to imitate events held by the successful organizations and instead plan events for their organization and their members. The successful event planners have created events that work well for their organizations' members and missions. It's up to event planners for all those other organizations to do the same for their organizations. Each organization is different from any other. Members are different, their economic situations are different, and so is the cause they celebrate. Event planners must take differences into account and tailor each event to the audience.

Some people continue to do the same thing, over and over, expecting each time to get better results and then, amazingly, are surprised when the results are no better than last time. So it is with fundraising. The past is prologue to the future. Success or failure is likely to be repeated in fundraising if the same thing is done year after year. The best predictor of future success is past success. If it worked well before, do it again if similar successful results are desired. If better results are desired, make adjustments to what worked well before, based on a rational evaluation of past results and actions. If a fundraiser is a failure, one can almost ensure a repeat poor performance by repeating the formula for failure. While this may seem obvious, it's a lesson some event planners never seem to get. Perhaps it's pride, per-haps it's a lack of objective analysis of performance, or perhaps it's just an inability to lead change.

If last year's successful formula doesn't yield the same good results the following year, make adjust-ments in the future. Analyze the results. Look for extenuating circumstances; after all, if the local high school football team made it into the playoffs and the playoff game was held the same evening as the event, it's likely anyone with high school–aged chil-dren may have been sidetracked. Don't ignore the obvious. Keep what seems to work, and adjust what doesn't after careful assessment of results. There are patterns to follow in fundraising. Find what works, and follow that up, expanding and improving. When trends, tastes, or conditions change, quickly adjust and adapt, following the new pattern to success.

3
The Secret to Successful Event Fundraising in Good Times and Bad

The economy cycles from good to bad and so does fundraising success for organizations that fail to discover the secret to successful event fundraising in good times and bad. One such organization helped pioneer effective auction-event fundraising techniques and, in so doing, built one of the largest nonprofit wildlife habitat conservation organizations in the nation. But when the economy faltered, their fundraising did, too. This organization failed to use more recession-proof techniques in auction-event fundraising discovered by other organizations with similar missions. Top-level staff responsible for event fundraising in this organization aggressively prevented anyone from bringing in ideas from outside their ranks. The only ideas for recovery had to be theirs and theirs alone.

Although their auctions always carried some "recession-proof" items, staff analyzing fundraising success just didn't seem to understand the difference between fundraising in good times and bad. The organization's auctions were loaded with items people didn't really need, and probably didn't want. These items produced decent revenue during good economic times, and even in the worst of times the items sold. I ascribe that to the dedication of the organization's supporters and volunteers who, in their desire to shore up the organization, felt they had no option but to bid on items they really didn't need or want. But there are only so many people willing to do that and for only so long, even in good economic times. So attendance, dollar spent per attendee, and revenue started a long downward slide that accelerated as the economy declined.

Then an amazing business decision was made. Production of most of the items was outsourced to the nation's biggest foreign competitor in an attempt to reduce cost of manufacture. The result was auctions and raffles stocked with the same kinds of items, but many items were now of lesser quality and all carried the name of a foreign producer. Attendees at the organization's events were presented with lower-quality items for which they still had little or no use. Now produced at the cost of sending American jobs overseas, foreign manufacturing stickers on each item reminded event attendees why America is losing jobs.

The cost of the auction items was never at issue to event attendees. The problem was auctions and raffles filled with too many knickknacks for the shelf or wall that had little or no value to attendees, regardless of price. The organization's event revenue continued to decline, tugging at the entire organization's financial future.

WHEN PEOPLE ENTER AN EVENT, they may initially arrive with purely social reasons in mind. Many come because they are invited by friends, but within seconds of entering they are presented with an assortment of opportunities to donate to the organization. They have no choice in what prizes a raffle may offer or the merchandise and services up for auction, but their level of interest in buying raffle tickets or bidding ultimately depends on several factors. For many attendees, the most important of these factors is whether they want the item being raffled or auctioned. The secret to a successful auction-event fundraiser in good times and bad is to present attendees with merchandise or services that they truly want or need and can afford (when offered at auction). But there is a catch. To successfully apply this secret, the host must create an effective setting for fundraising. An event must offer so much fun and excitement that absolutely "everyone" must attend. With everyone packed into an event filled with fundraising items they want or need, a fundraiser is perfectly positioned for spectacular success.

I was fortunate to lead an organization that had discovered this secret to effective fundraising. The basic concepts were in place by the time I arrived, and I claim no part in discovery. I do claim recogniz-

ing the fundraising power of offering items to attendees that bring their bidding and raffle ticket buying to a fever pitch. We were able to capitalize on presenting attendees just the right items and services. The result was continuously increasing fundraising success, even through changing economic times.

The early leaders of the organization did no objective analysis or complicated business plans to discover the perfect auction and raffle items. Instead, they just stocked the organization's auctions with goods and services they personally wanted or needed. Members joined the organization to raise funds for a common cause. Those who came to the organization's events had similar interests, wants, and needs, which made for exciting and profitable auctions and raffles. Attendees all arrived with one thing in common—they wanted or needed the same things. Such commonality of interest among members is not unusual in membership-based nonprofit organizations.

The Right Stuff Further Defined

There are several characteristics that make an item a winner at auctions and raffles in good times and bad—they are items and services that event attendees want or need, but there is more to it than that.

Only Found Here

In the case of the organization last mentioned, early planners of the organization's events brought merchandise and services to auction that were also hard to find or expensive, particularly for individuals seeking to acquire the items or services on their own. An example is wildlife-related adventure travel at a time when such travel was expensive and there were few providers. With the buying power created by the organization's auctions and associated consumer trade shows, such travel opportunities were brought directly to the organization's members.

Where attendees are presented with merchandise or services that are hard to acquire outside an organization's event, the items can drive high bidding at auction and strong raffle ticket sales. But making a wanted or needed item "easy to acquire" is just an added characteristic that creates extra revenue potential by boosting bid price or sale of raffle tickets. Offering attendees a difficult-to-obtain item will be of little value at an event if no one wants or needs it. For example, if attendees are offered a difficult-to-obtain bottle of imported wine that no one wants, then the wine's rarity is of no value.

Consumability

The next characteristic is "consumability." Consumable items are merchandise and services that are used soon after event attendees receive them, and then the same or similar items are desired or needed again by the time of the next event. It is these consumable items that sustain high-net-revenue fundraising year after year, regardless of the economic situation.

Vacation trips fit into this category. So do services that are used and either are needed again by the next event or were so wonderful that everyone hears about them and wants them when auctioned again at the next event. Spa treatments, restaurant gift certificates, flower arrangements for Valentine's Day, coolers full of lobster, and a gourmet meal cooked in the winner's own kitchen by a local chef are all items won in one year that are normally used by the time the next event takes place. These examples are generally items people typically want, or in the case of items like Valentine's Day bouquets and spa treatments, may be "needed" by many attendees for special occasions. Why not get that very special gift at the auction held by your favorite charity?

An item needed by an attendee may do well at auction once if it's not a consumable. If needed by a different attendee at the next auction, it may do well again. But if an item is consumable, such as an oil change for a car, any attendee who bids on it at one event is likely to bid on it again next time, even if he or she won it at the previous event. Finding these consumable items wanted and needed by attendees year after year ensures continued success regardless of the economic situation.

Wants and Needs Change with the Times

The gap between what people need and what they want expands and contracts as personal financial conditions shift. This can generally be tied to overall economic conditions, but if attendees all come from the same local community or one economic sector, conditions that specifically affect the community or sector will matter most. Finances are a relative matter. Financial conditions affect a person's willingness to bid on items, whether it's a multimillionaire who is left with a mere million dollars in assets because of a decline in stock values or an hourly worker who has a job but is worried about continued employment. What a person may want versus what he or she may actually need will draw closer together as one's financial situation or the perception of it declines. Wants and needs will ultimately merge as one's financial situation degrades to the point where only basic needs can be afforded.

For example, I may want a high-priced sports car, but I also need a minivan to comfortably transport my five family members. In good economic times, I may be able to afford both what I want and what I need, so at my organization's annual event I bid on and win a fabulous sports car. In poor economic times, I may still want the sports car, but what I really need, and now have no choice but to want, is the minivan. If I go to an event and a sports car comes up for auction, I won't bid on it. However, if a minivan comes up at the auction, and I need to replace the one I have, I will most likely bid.

The key is to know the attendees' needs and wants. For instance, when attendees come from an area where there are large lawns and gardens to maintain, a riding lawn mower may make a great auction or high-value raffle item. But what if the local economy is in shambles? While many attendees may want a new riding mower, in tough economic times the old mowers may get repaired until times get better. It may be difficult to receive a reasonable bid price for a riding mower. But the lawn-and-garden theme may offer fundraising ideas that can work in good times and bad. For example, in areas where mulch is a landscaping staple, bags of tree bark or mulch will be needed each year, poor economy or not. The old lawn mower may last another year, but the old mulch won't. Many attendees will want and need mulch. Auction off bags of mulch for flower beds and a pile of fertilizer (delivered to the home of the buyer, of course) for the vegetable garden. Someone attending the event will need it—guaranteed.

Never-out-of-style items that event attendees need or want should constitute a large percentage of auction items and prizes offered at fundraising events even in the best of times. In the worst of times, these kinds of items should be the only items offered by the host organization seeking the highest achievable net revenue.

This does not mean the value of items must be lowered during tough economic times. Even at an auction where most attendees have modest incomes, some may be in the market for high-value items, such as a new minivan. If the type of vehicle several attendees need is available for auction, it is likely to get bids or attract raffle ticket sales. When such a vehicle is partially donated by a local car dealer and a reasonable reserve price set, the host organization takes no risk in putting it up for auction. Risk is further reduced if event planners know of people who will be attending that have large families and need a new minivan.

THE SIMPLE IDEAS described in this chapter need to be kept in mind while reading the remainder of the book. While the fundraising ideas are simple, setting the stage for the perfect fundraising event requires considerable skill, knowledge, caution, and effective teamwork. It is anything but simple. There is considerable financial risk to the host organization if not done well. The rest of this book describes how to successfully implement the now revealed secret of effective event fundraising in both good times and bad.

4

Organizing for Success

This is a tale of two fundraising legends, each located in a coastal state but a continent apart. Both worked for chapters of the same organization. East and West, the chapters for which our legends worked thrived. With the blessing and oft-stated awe of chapter leadership, these two individuals assumed full responsibility for the annual fundraising events. Year after year, our legends managed the events from A to Z. Both worked hard and were successful. But that's where the similarity ended.

Our legend in the East took control of the event in the most literal sense imaginable. He chaired every committee. He did every job he possibly could by himself. And in the few instances in which an activity was assigned to another, our legend chose his closest friends. Each assignment was divided into the most minute division of labor. The workers were expected to report progress or completion to our legend, then await the next assignment. There was no question that this was the legend's fundraiser.

This was not so much an "iron-fisted" sort of control as it was tradition, which began in the formative stages of the chapter when our legend was inexperienced in fundraising and found himself assigned responsibility for the new chapter's fundraising event. He had little or no help in those early years. He felt he had no choice but to do it all. Because the event was small, the expectations of chapter members were modest, and no one else wanted the responsibility, he worked alone. He learned to run the event by on-the-job experience. His way was the way—the only way—he learned to do the job. Over time he became one with the fundraising event in the eyes of chapter members and people in the local community. The event was even known as his event and unofficially carried his name.

Although the chapter had hosted the fundraising

event for nearly two decades, the only member of the chapter who had accumulated any event management experience during that time was our legend. The chapter's leadership could not conceive of a time when our legend was not "in control" of the event. And if something happened to him, all believed they would suffer financially without our legend's esteemed leadership.

On the other side of the continent, our legend in the West took a different approach. There was no question about who was in control of the annual fundraising event. He was, but instead of personally performing all work, he shared responsibility among many. The sharing was so complete and the preparation so thorough that at the fundraising event, many attendees must have wondered what role our legend played. After all, our legend seemed to just wander around, while others worked busily. He was humble about his role and praised the work by others. His work had been completed well in advance of the event. But should a problem arise, our legend was immediately on the scene helping his workers find solutions. Once problems were solved, he went back to standing around as others managed the event. Those others accumulated the experience and praiseworthy attention of attendees who enjoyed seemingly flawless events, year after year.

Our legend saw his responsibility clearly. He was the organizer, facilitator, coach, recruiter, strategist, orchestrator, and on-site consultant. He recruited and assembled a group formed for the express purpose of holding the fundraising event. He delegated responsibility and let members of the event team take center stage. Our legend shared his knowledge, and members of the group shared theirs, all around. The novices learned from the experienced as the event team was forged and honed to a fine edge over time. New people were always welcome, and jobs were available for all who wanted to work and learn. Changes came with new ideas and new people. The chapter's leadership could not conceive of a time when our legend was not "in control" of the event. And if something happened to him, all believed they would do well in all respects, even without our legend's esteemed leadership.

ONE-PERSON EFFORTS can succeed and an organization's fundraising event can make money, but only for a time and up to a certain level. With a single person doing all tasks, event growth and fundraising potential are limited. In addition, one-person fundraising efforts create a formula for disaster should something happen to that person. Major event and auction-based fundraising is a team effort. There is just too much to do for one person to be successful over the long term and once an event begins to grow. Members of a well-formed event team bring a variety of skills and experience to accomplish the varied tasks involved in hosting a successful event. This chapter describes how to strategically assemble a planning and management team that will raise money for a nonprofit organization.

Creating an Event Timeline

Even though each event is unique, the sequence of planning and management activities is similar. Figure 4.1 displays a typical generalized timeline for event planning and management and makes reference to specific chapters in this book that cover these activities. For annual or recurring events, some work is continuous throughout the year, such as maintaining the event Web site and generating publicity, although such activities will increase in importance and activity level as the date of the event nears.

Timelines for first-time events should begin at least a year before the event. Events held annually may establish a set pattern based on year-to-year experience. This enables planners to reduce the length of the planning timeline by employing the same service vendors in succeeding years, holding the event at the same site, using the same set of policies and procedures, and so on, saving considerable time and volunteer or staff effort.

Assigning Event Functions and Jobs

Key functional areas of work that need to be covered at an event are listed in sidebar 4.1. Also listed are example job titles and responsibilities.

These functional areas of work can be made more

Action	Chapter	Time to Event Date								
		>12 Month	12-9 Month	8-6 Month	5-2 Month	1 Month	1 Week	1 Day	Event	+1 Week
Evaluate if organization can host a successful event	2, 3	■	▨							
Select event chairperson, organize planning team	4	▨	■							
Select and reserve the event site; develop business plan	5, 7, 8	▨	▨	■						
Develop event policies, procedures, security and emergency plan	6, 21, 20		▨	■						
Negotiate detailed terms for the event site	7, 8		▨	■						
Select and secure entertainment, auctioneer, MC	10, 15, 24		▨	▨	■					
Select and secure catering and remaining services (e.g., security, tent, seating)	7, 8, 9, 12, 15, 20, 22		▨	▨	■					
Develop event program; address liability matters	6, 11, 20			▨	▨	■				
Determine mix of fundraising activities, acquire raffle, auction and gift merchandise	13, 18, 19			▨	▨	■				
Sell admission, invite guests	14				▨	■	■			
Secure required permits	20				▨	■				
Train event workers: reception, receipts, auctions, raffles, etc.	6, 13, 14, 15, 16, 17, 19, 20, 22				▨	■				
Generate publicity	12				▨	■	■	■		
Obtain event sponsorships, underwriting	14				▨	■				
Print event (auction) program, auction bid sheets, buyer's agreement forms	6, 15, 16, 21					▨	■			
Assemble auction and raffle items, prizes, display materials	15, 16, 18, 20						■	▨		
Event set-up: raffles, arcade, auctions, registration, payment, prize pick-up	6, 15, 16, 17, 20, 22							■	■	
Hold a rehearsal	19							■		
Hold event, accounting, safe deposit of receipts	6, 15, 16, 17, 18, 19, 22								■	
Evaluate results and thank all who helped	23									■

FIGURE 4.1. Event planning and management timeline.

Sidebar 4.1. **Event Functions**

Functional area	Example title	Example responsibilities
Leadership	Event chairperson and team leaders	Select volunteer workers, make job assignments, carry out overall event planning and management, send invitations to VIPs, develop program, and make announcements; select or approve master of ceremonies, auctioneer, caterer, and entertainment
Finance	Treasurer	Carry out accounting, banking, payments, collections, credit card management, financial planning, event budget development and management, event audit, and reporting of financial results
Arrangements	Arrangements chairperson	Secure and negotiate event location, accommodations, meals and refreshments, entertainment, audiovisual services, hospitality, lighting, security, and set up event room
Publicity and event marketing	Publicist	Arrange for promotion, press, social networking using technology, public service announcements, editorials, press conferences, radio, television, community relations, internal announcements, and photos
Fundraising	Fundraising chairperson	Solicit prizes and event merchandise for auctions, games of skill and chance, and raffles; during the event, oversee auctioneers, spotters, and raffle sales, execute auction and raffle, and arrange prize displays
Registration	Registrar	Arrange for ticketing, Internet-based registration, on-site check-in, attendee records management, and membership sales
Sales	Merchandise sales store manager	Sell the host organization's mission-related and "logo-identified" merchandise at the event
Sponsorships	Development chairperson	Arrange for sponsorships; foundation, corporate, and individual donations; and sale of ads in event program
Education	Education chairperson	Promote organization projects and mission

or less inclusive, meaning the number can be reduced or increased by splitting or consolidating areas on the list. For example, one could divide the function of "fundraising" into several subcategories, such as auctions, sponsor solicitation, and raffles, with a person or team assigned to cover each area. One person may also work within more than one functional area. For example, "leadership" is listed as a functional area, but team leaders will also conduct work in other functional areas.

Within the functional areas, individual work assignments are made. Work assignments are the jobs, or specific work responsibilities, assigned to individuals. Event planners can create job descriptions or, less formally, write out or verbally deliver work assignments. Each function may involve one or many jobs to be completed. Many people working together over an extended period may be required to complete some jobs; a single person working for only a brief period may complete others.

Work assignments or jobs can be expanded to allow more people than actually needed to be involved. This may be done for the simple reason of offering maximum opportunity for volunteer involvement in the event. Getting members involved in an organization's activities enhances member retention and the likelihood of giving. Involvement of many members in the annual fundraiser also provides a ready field of candidates for future leadership roles in the fundraiser and other activities of the organization. For a membership-based organization, there is no such thing as too many event volunteers. Volunteers (and staff) will not get in each other's way if work assignments are well planned and work proceeds in an orderly manner, with all involved respecting the roles and responsibilities of each other.

The functions list presented in sidebar 4.1 is a guide. It provides an overview to help event planners picture the scope of work necessary to stage an event and visualize how to organize the volunteer and staff workforce. The following discussion describes in detail how the event's top leadership can match jobs that need to be done with available volunteers and/or staff.

Forming Management Teams

Organizations hosting fundraising events usually form work groups, often called teams or committees, around the functional areas and responsibilities of planning and managing the event. The groups may be called groups, boards, work parties, panels, squads, or other names customary for the locality or organization. Most important is that work be logically and fairly divided among volunteers (and staff if relevant). In this book, the terms "committee" and "team" are used interchangeably to depict the staff and/or volunteer work groups that form the backbone of event planning and management.

Heading the work groups are team leaders or committee chairs. Co-leaders may share responsibility for a committee or team of workers. Organizations that have paid staff typically share leadership responsibility for committees between a staff and volunteer leader. Sometimes staff serve as advisers to the volunteers. It is common for the staff co-leader to take on the true leadership role, particularly when the staff member has professional-level expertise in the functional area of work. If there are no staff, volunteers take on all duties. Team leaders often form subcommittees to further divide responsibilities and jobs among workers. Here subleaders or subcommittee chairpersons may be assigned various leadership roles to plan and manage the event.

Event planners must use care, show sensitivity, and pay attention to detail in the means used to allocate leadership responsibilities and jobs among workers. Decisions about who leads a committee or who works with whom can be overwhelmingly important. Such decisions can be made through group processes during early planning meetings. This can help ensure that event workers see that decisions directly affecting them are made in a fair manner. Making decisions through group dialogue can also help build a feeling among event workers that they are helping make important decisions, thus creating a sense of inclusion. Event planners, and in particular the event chairperson and key committee chairs, need to stay in close contact with workers and be ready to make adjustments, provide motivation, and maintain momentum from the beginning through the end of the event.

Assigning Volunteers and Staff Jobs

The list of functions helps guide assignment of jobs to staff and volunteers who will work as members of the event planning and management team(s). Jobs come from the various functional areas of work. Jobs vary somewhat by the size and nature of the event and are divided among workers. Large events featuring many different fundraising activities, meals, and entertainment will require more jobs be done than at smaller events. Both large and small events can be successful. Both require staff and volunteers who will deal with the same functions listed in the sidebar, but the smaller event will require fewer specific jobs. Both can be managed by the same number of people. If the number of people is large, individuals working on the smaller event might share many of the jobs. If the number of people working is small, people working on the larger event will take on multiple jobs.

Since there are many kinds of events that can be hosted by many kinds of organizations having many kinds of memberships and organizational structures, it follows that there is no single, standard way to organize staff and volunteer workers for a fundraising event. This chapter describes general functions, responsibilities, and jobs and offers ideas on how to organize workers. This can provide a starting point for first-time event hosts or guidance on making improvements to ongoing event planning efforts. An organization hosting a fundraising event will gain experience over time, as long as that experience is recorded and passed on from planning team to planning team, and then that experience is used to make year-to-year improvements.

Work can be divided among staff and volunteers in multiple ways. One way is to create subteams or committees based around the several functional areas of work. For example, a team leader and team members can be assigned responsibility for all aspects of the fundraising function. This can be further broken down into additional subteams, such as one for raffles, one for games, and one for auctions. Several teams and subteams are most effective for large events and for organizations with a large number of volunteers who want to get involved. This provides a simple way to accommodate many people who are seeking substantive and distinct roles. Host organizations may find it useful to have separate teams working in at least the following functional areas of event planning and management: arrangements, fundraising (raffle, auction, and games), and publicity. On the day of the event, a separate setup team may be assembled to ready the room and fundraising items. For the period of the event itself, separate registration and money-handling teams may also be formed.

When selecting workers, whether to lead a team or to do a specific job, try to match people with work assignments that fit their skills, experience, and ability. For example, given a choice of two volunteers, one who is a certified public accountant (CPA) and the other a professional caterer, the CPA would probably serve better in the position of event treasurer. The caterer would probably better serve as chair of the arrangements team.

If an organization's membership is diverse, it may be possible, given a little digging, to find people whose professional backgrounds fit skills needed for event management. But it's not just people with professional backgrounds who may provide critical skills. A college student may bring much-needed new technology-based social-networking skills into the mix of activities that create publicity and solicit people to attend an event. Simply ask volunteers what they can do best to help. Often the chair is faced with various jobs that need to be done and a group of willing but otherwise "unskilled" workers. The chair simply makes assignments. Some of the more complicated jobs from the standpoint of skills are often performed by people who have no qualifications other than being asked to do the job by the chair or subchair of the event team.

Challenged by matching many jobs with volunteers or staff having varying skills and ability, pick the best, most reliable workers for the most financially critical tasks and tasks creating the great-

est risk of liability for the host organization. Then, work through available jobs, assigning volunteers with more modest skills and less experience. Finally, assign the least-skilled workers to do those jobs creating the least risk of liability or financial impact should a problem arise. These workers may gain enough experience in one year to train them for jobs having a higher level of responsibility in following years.

Jobs

Within the functions are various responsibilities that can be broken down into a series of jobs. The jobs can be assigned to volunteers and staff, if available. For an organization that employs staff, responsibility for many of the jobs will be set by staff employment responsibilities. Volunteers provide assistance to staff and fill in where there are no staff responsible or available.

A single person may perform numerous jobs, as many of the jobs will not be performed simultaneously. For example, solicitation of auction items is always done in advance of the auction. A person working on auctions may be responsible for soliciting auction items from merchants in advance of the auction and, once finished with that job, will be free to do other jobs in the area of auctions. That same person can be assigned responsibility for setting up the silent auction table the day of the auction. Then during the event the person can take on yet another auction-related job, for example, serving as an auction spotter.

Example jobs in various functional areas of responsibility are detailed in the following sections to help event planners visualize the scope of responsibilities, jobs, activities, assignments, and options for effectively allocating available volunteers and staff. This is not a complete list, as the list of jobs will vary by event.

Event Chairperson

The chairperson for the entire event is responsible for planning and managing all aspects of the event, including supervising the activities of team leaders, subteam leaders, team members, and other workers. Assign this responsibility to a single person. Here, when the event chairperson is described, reference is to the working chair. Some organizations hosting a fundraising event may identify a well-known local personality or celebrity as "honorary" chairperson for the event. This is a great way to add credibility or entice members of a particular crowd to an event, but such chairpersons rarely are expected to do any of the real work in planning, setting up, or managing an event. The honorary chair simply lends his or her name and endorsement. This can be extended even further by creating an entire event committee composed of honorary members. Although in some instances an honorary chair and members do substantive work, an organization is well served by selecting an event chair and event committee members who are firmly committed to working hard, long hours to make the event a success.

Sometimes the organization president or board chair is named event chairperson. This usually sets up the same situation as naming a celebrity honorary chair. In either case, the named event chair is almost always more figurehead than worker. Regardless of what the event chairperson is called, that one person who will oversee the event must be an actual worker, be committed to the job, and have sufficient time to do the real work of chairperson. This should be someone with prior involvement in fundraising events if possible. Regardless of the amount of experience a person may have, the event chair also must have leadership skills. Sidebar 4.2 lists ten top attributes of a successful event chairperson.

THE EVENT CHAIR'S JOB

The event chair has the job of soliciting people to volunteer for work and appointing workers to leadership positions, such as the treasurer, publicist, and fundraising chair. The event chair is responsible for the overall planning of the event and making sure there is coordination among teams and subteams. This person should solicit active participation in planning by all other leaders and any members of the event workforce the chair sees fit to in-

> Sidebar 4.2. **Top 10 Attributes of a Successful Event Chairperson**
>
> 1. *Sets the tone.* Be inclusive and provide support to the entire event team.
>
> 2. *Sets the plan.* Lead the event planning effort, follow the plan, and modify the plan as needed.
>
> 3. *Sets the pace.* Establish deadlines and keep team members on track.
>
> 4. *Establishes communication.* Communicate regularly with everyone on the team; ensure that all members of the team communicate readily and often with each other, including by e-mail, telephone, and meetings.
>
> 5. *Establishes lists.* Make and distribute a list of volunteer and staff workers that includes everyone's name, e-mail address, and phone numbers; make sure everyone knows who is working on the event and how workers can get in touch with each other.
>
> 6. *Sets the goals.* Assign challenging yet obtainable goals to members of the team as work progresses.
>
> 7. *Sets the example.* Do not ask someone to do something that you are not willing to do yourself. This does not mean do it all yourself. Be the first one at meetings. Leaders must also be workers. Be prepared. Follow through. Attend all team meetings. Use praise.
>
> 8. *Acts as coach.* Nurture, develop, and train team members. You can use this book to help educate team members, but not everyone will read it or relates well to "paper training." Many people learn by doing. Create a large team, which provides a training ground and event chairs for the future. Once people are trained, they will be more able and likely to accept leadership roles.
>
> 9. *Pays attention to detail.* Maintain focus on priorities but give appropriate attention to the little things that can make the difference between success or failure. Let team members deal with the minute details.
>
> 10. *Delegates responsibilities.* Delegate for effective and efficient coverage of all event tasks. The event chairperson cannot do it all. A successful event is the result of many large and small actions taken by many people.

clude. The more involvement by staff and volunteers during the early planning process, the more support the chair is likely to get from the workers later on. The chair should develop an event business plan, with primary assistance from the event treasurer and leaders of the other functional work groups. Development of the business plan is discussed in chapter 5, but this is a good time to note that the business plan requires input and involvement of staff and volunteers working in each functional area, as their assessment of event expenses and revenues will form the basis for the budget and financial forecasting in the business plan.

The event chair's responsibilities may vary depending on the authority granted by the host organization's leadership. Although a president, executive director, or chairman of the board may delegate responsibility for an event to an event chairperson, such delegation may be conditioned on meeting certain requirements or constrained by limitations on authority. For example, the event chair may be told whom to select for other leadership posts, what type of event to hold, when the event will be held, whether to have refreshments and a meal, whom to have as entertainment, and so on. This may ease or further complicate the job of event chairperson, depending on the motives and understanding of event planning among those involved.

In an ideal situation, the event chair is authorized to hold an event based on a set generalized plan or concept agreed upon in advance by the host organization's leadership, including input from the event chair. That plan or concept may be based on past event experience (the event is the "same" every year), a strategic-planning or business-planning process, or the outcome of reading this book or retaining an adviser. The concept or business plan provides a base for the event chair to begin planning details of the event. Thus, one of the earliest jobs of the event chair is to undertake the event planning process. This may include strategic planning and operational planning, or just operational planning if the strategic planning has already been completed. The operational plan provides the step-by-step details of holding the event. It can include work assignments, timelines for completing various jobs, specific items desired to solicit for auction use, and so on. Part of the planning should be development of the event business plan. Operational planning can be included in the business plan, or the business plan can be developed separately.

Before starting the detailed planning process, the chair should solicit workers and appoint team leaders responsible for the functional areas that will be covered in the course of planning and holding the event. The leaders will form the planning team. The chair should use discretion in determining how to divide responsibility for work in all the functional areas of event planning and management among available volunteers and, if available, the organization's paid staff. Sidebar 4.1 lists examples of responsibilities in the various functional areas of the event. How responsibilities are divided and formed into work assignments among event workers will differ from event to event based on the size and complexity of the event and the number and experience levels of staff or volunteers available to help.

Work of the event chair involves overall oversight of management of the event from A to Z, including the following:

- Motivating and recognizing the efforts of event workers
- Holding progress meetings with staff and volunteers
- Coordinating the efforts of all workers on all aspects of the event
- Making sure all jobs get done
- Keeping the host organization's leadership informed of progress
- Assuring proper financial controls are in place and the event complies with all laws
- Developing the program with assistance from the fundraising and entertainment chairs
- Selecting and managing the master of ceremonies
- Maintaining the overall pace of the event
- Organizing event activities, including having the program drafted and printed and issuing invitations to VIPs
- Making sure there is proper protocol shown to major donors and sponsors
- Hiring (or recommending hiring to chief executive officer) the auctioneer(s), raffle sales models, entertainers, and other paid workers

After the event, the chair's job continues, as there should be at least one follow-up meeting to discuss the success of the event and collect information from workers about improvements that can be made, experiences, remaining items to complete, outstanding expenses, follow-up fundraising opportunities, and so on. The chair has a responsibility to report to the host organization's leadership by providing an evaluation of the event. A written report should make available useful information to planners of the host's next fundraising event. The host organization's leadership should evaluate how well the event chair performed. If the event chair performed reasonably well and will not be repeating as event chair, the host organization should seek to capitalize on that experience during at least the next following event by having the chair serve as an adviser to the next event planning committee.

THE MARK OF A SUCCESSFUL EVENT CHAIRPERSON

The greatest testament of a job well done by the event chair is to have nurtured a workforce that truly and totally manages the event so that the chair has nothing to do but stand by at the event, ready to assist if a complication should arise. The successful event chair observes and gives ready praise to committee chairs, subcommittee chairs, and all the event workers as they go about their jobs, confidently and flawlessly, managing all the details of the event. After all, why would the successful event chair have anything to do, having delegated assignments to a well-trained, highly motivated workforce of volunteers and staff? As the successful event chair receives praise from host organization leaders and event attendees, the chair responds by directing the praise to the event workers. Yes, the truly successful event chair's work is done by the time the event starts.

Treasurer

The treasurer is responsible for the financial management of the event, including developing the budget, authorizing payment of expenses, keeping financial records, setting up and managing the event cashier's booth or payment center, supervising the event's financial management team, participating in developing the business plan, and completing a final accounting of expense and revenue. Exact jobs assigned to the treasurer will vary, based on how the host organization is organized and administered. The ideal candidate is an accountant or other finance professional. If no volunteers with such experience are available, event planners should seek a person who is good with numbers, detail oriented, well organized, and highly trustworthy.

If the organization has paid professional staff, including a paid chief financial officer, then many of the responsibilities of event treasurer will fall to professional staff. If the organization has no professional staff, or if staff have not been legally assigned financial responsibility by the organization's board of directors, then the event treasurer may be assigned substantial financial responsibility. If the event is managed apart from the host organization, the treasurer is responsible for opening and managing a checking account; accepting revenues and deposits (banquet ticket sales, cash donations, auction and raffle sales, etc.); issuing receipts; paying bills; making arrangements for credit card payments, event payment booth, and service contracts; using generally accepted accounting procedures; and complying with all tax and other financial laws. If the organization has no paid professional staff, at least two signatures, including the treasurer's, should be required on all payments or commitments for payment, such as checks and contracts for services.

Since many organizations that hold fundraising events have special tax status, the treasurer should become aware of the tax status and be supplied with the organization's IRS recognition letter and nonprofit corporation Employer Identification Number for use in banking and other financial transactions. In states where raffles are regulated under special gaming rules, the treasurer's job will also include purchasing, tracking sales revenue, and managing legal requirements for raffle tickets. The treasurer will make financial reports to the event planning committee and the host organization's leadership, as well as approve a final financial report.

The treasurer should have at least two helpers. Prior to the auction the treasurer or helpers will manage a cashier's booth where they will receive payment from registering attendees and administer credit card transactions. During and after the auction they will receive payments for raffle tickets sold, game revenue, auction revenue, and other cash, check, or credit card receipts for auction items. Other responsibilities during the event include making sure proper auction receipts are given to successful bidders and proper records of payments are kept.

Arrangements Chairperson

The arrangements chairperson is responsible for creating the perfect environment for the fundraiser, including dealing with all aspects of location, furnishings, accommodations, food and refreshments, entertainment, and security. To divide the work into manageable assignments, the chairperson generally forms a number of work teams and appoints co-chairs or subcommittee chairs. Activities such as setting up the event room and making sure all aspects of arrangements go as planned during the event usually require many volunteers. The ideal candidate is a person with a professional background in the hospitality industry. If no volunteers with such experience are available, event planners should seek a person who is well organized, detail oriented, adept at supervision, and able to work with a wide variety of service providers.

Although the size and complexity of the event will determine the level of work and number of workers necessary to do an adequate job, several job assignments are common to all events: finding and securing the location; selecting menus, negotiating food and refreshment prices, and making sure food, refreshments, and service are as promised during the event; reserving overnight accommodations; securing and properly arranging appropriate furnishings, such as tables, seating, stages, lighting, podiums, and display stands for auction and raffle items; acquiring adequate sound, lighting, and projection systems and testing them immediately before the event starts to make sure all are working properly; and arranging for adequate security and making sure security workers are doing their jobs during the event (see chapters 8 and 9).

Publicist

The publicist manages external and internal marketing and publicity for the event. External efforts are those that publicize the event through media not controlled by the host organization. Externally directed effort is generally intended to reach out to people not already associated with the host organization. Internally directed publicity and event marketing materials are sent directly to the host organization's members and placed in the host's magazines, newspapers, Web sites, and social media. New technology-based social networking can work both internally and externally to an organization's membership, as such networking may be spread among individuals having their own "networks" of friends not tied to any formal membership lists held by organizations. The ideal candidate is a person with a professional background in public relations, advertising, media, marketing, sales, or social networking. If no volunteers with such experience are available, event planners should seek a person who is enthusiastic, dependable, adept at pitching ideas and writing compelling stories, and able to effectively meet and engage people in discussion.

The publicist is the chairperson of the event publicity and marketing committee. But if the host organization has paid professional staff, this function and any work ordinarily handled by a publicity and marketing committee may be completely handled by the host's public relations staff. The publicist may also obtain the assistance of paid or volunteer professional help through an advertising or public relations agency. It is sometimes possible to receive such help as a public service or at a reduced rate. When there are no paid or volunteer professionals helping, the publicist has a long list of jobs to do.

The publicist is responsible for planning and executing the publicity and marketing campaign; developing the event Web site or the section in the host organization's Web site that markets the event; generating technology-based social networking and Web presence; creating and placing marketing materials, including posters and advertisements; producing and placing news releases, public service announcements, editorials, and advertisements in newspapers and on radio and TV; staging press conferences; managing community relations; inviting and hosting members of the press and photographers at the event; creating media and marketing kits; and promoting event attractions, such as famous entertainers and personalities (see chapters 10 and 12).

Fundraising Chairperson

The fundraising chairperson is responsible for developing and staging the fundraising opportunities of the event. Net revenue from the event turns on the success of these fundraising opportunities. Success or failure of fundraising can depend on the skill and experience of the fundraising chairperson in planning and managing fundraising activities and supervising the teams of workers assigned to fundraising.

Given a need for a certain level of expertise, what defines a good fundraising chair? Having some professional fundraising experience in the mix would be ideal, but unfortunately there are few bridges between fundraising and typical professions of people who are members and volunteers of nonprofit organizations. After all, most professional fundraisers already work directly for nonprofit organizations to raise funds for the employing organization. When such organizations host an event, the job of fundraising chairperson is made easier by the readily available professional. The host's paid professional staff can supply the skills and expertise to ensure event fundraising activities are designed to be effective. The volunteer chairperson helps the professionals by managing the large volunteer workforce needed to stage a fundraiser. This division of labor and responsibility can work well, especially when the volunteer chairperson appreciates the importance of employing professional experience and capitalizes on that experience.

Occasionally a professional fundraiser will volunteer to help an organization, but organizations not fortunate enough to find such volunteers or unable to employ a professional fundraiser have to make do with volunteers who may not have professional credentials. In this case event planners will need to search among volunteers to find a good fundraising chairperson. A starting point is to consider individuals who have served competently on event planning and management committees for past events. Also consider people who have volunteered to raise funds before. The fundraising chairperson's job may be less about technical knowledge of fundraising methods and more about managing a large workforce seeing to the event's many different fundraising opportunities. A good fundraising chair is willing to learn and experiment, adept at seeking and using input from others, and good at supervising and delegating responsibility and has a drive to succeed and a can-do attitude.

The fundraising chair generally divides workers among several subgroups, each focusing on a different fundraising opportunity. For example, the fundraising committee can have a subcommittee for each of the following areas of fundraising: main live auction, silent auctions, raffles, and games of skill and chance. Workers in each of these subgroups can further divide the work, for example, by creating separate teams to manage all aspects of each different raffle and of each separate game of chance and skill.

Work by the fundraising teams begins early in the event planning process and continues to the end of the event. As an example, consider the progress of work required to offer a 20-prize vacation getaway raffle board: the raffle-board team will solicit donation of 20 vacation getaways as prizes, obtain raffle tickets that meet state and local standards for raffles, build (or have built) the prize display board, set up the prize display at the event site (or assist the arrangements team in having it set up properly), sell or arrange for the sale of raffle tickets at the event (perhaps also an additional sale in advance of the event), and oversee the drawing and awarding of prizes. Sometimes these same jobs are divided along slightly different lines. For example, a separate work group can be assigned responsibility for solicitation of prize merchandise. This allows the work groups to focus their efforts even more narrowly.

Registrar

The registrar is responsible for all aspects of registering attendees for admission to the event, tracking all registration information, and dealing with membership matters if the organization is membership based. The ideal candidate is a person who is well organized, is detail and customer oriented, and has some experience managing information using databases or social networking.

The registrar generally has several assistants during the event to help with on-site registration but may have dozens of workers helping sell tickets in advance of the event. The following are typical duties of the registrar; however, if the host organization has paid professional staff, some of these duties will generally be done by staff: designing and having tickets and other registration materials printed; assembling and supervising the workforce that will sell tickets in advance of the event (or devising other effective means to sell tickets, such as by mail, e-mail, an event Web site, or social networking); responding to questions from people interested in attending the event; keeping track of ticket sales; managing on-site ticketing and registration; controlling admission at the event door in association with security workers; ensuring that all attendees provide full contact information; assisting the treasurer collect payment from auction winners; assuring proper registration of any specialty items awarded that require legal verification of ownership transfer (such as vehicles and firearms); selling and managing on-site membership services; and managing and maintaining all attendee registration and event-related membership information.

The registrar also helps design and promote any "early-registration" incentives. The registrar would probably work cooperatively with others on the event planning and management team on early registration. For example, if the early-registration incentive is a raffle with a merchandise prize, the incentive could be developed jointly with the fundraising chairperson. Or the registrar could work in cooperation with the arrangements chairperson if the desire was to provide special seating or table placement to all or "winning" early registrants.

Merchandise Sales Store Manager

Sale of the host organization's mission-related and "logo-identified" merchandise at an event is an option for organizations having such merchandise (see chapter 17). The merchandise sales store manager is responsible for designing and building (or having built) the merchandise sales booth and then selling the host's merchandise at the event. But the job need not depend on existing merchandise. Organizations having no regular line of merchandise or products appropriate for sale at an event can have special merchandise made to order or produced on consignment for sale at an event. Arranging for such merchandise is the responsibility of the store manager. The ideal candidate is often found relatively easily among volunteers for work at charity events. For this job a person with a background in wholesale purchasing of dry goods or retail sales of consumer goods is a good fit.

Development Chairperson

This function may often be included in the duties of the event or fundraising chairperson, but it is considered a separate function here. Having a development chairperson is appropriate if host organization planners want to emphasize major cash gifts and direct donations apart from contributions associated with prizes or services made at fundraising events. These cash gifts may be directly or indirectly connected to the event, but the donor receives no prize or substantive service in return. This is a major donation. It is a direct contribution to the host organization with no goods or services received in return, which means the gift may be tax deductible if the IRS recognizes the host organization as a charity. The donor may receive recognition at the event and in the host's publications, and sometimes there are added benefits with no monetary value, such as special seating at the event.

In all cases the event is what provides the development chairperson the "excuse" to make the solicitation. Specific jobs of the development chair will vary depending on the opportunities provided by the host organization to solicit major gifts apart from the event's auctions, raffles, and games. One job is to solicit donors to underwrite portions of the event to reduce the host's expense, not to "replace" funds that would otherwise be received. Underwriters may be called sponsors, benefactors, patrons, or supporters. Examples of underwriting are a gift of cash to pay the host's costs for acquiring prize merchandise, a gift to cover the cost of a major speaker or entertainer, a gift to cover the cost of decorations for the event hall, and food and drink. The host organization would otherwise bear these expenses, reducing net revenue. Admission price or other charges to attendees should not be reduced as a result of such donations. If that were to be done, the gift would have no net value.

Another job is to identify potential future major donors to the host organization by doing research using the attendee list. Another is designing and managing a patron's activity at the event, that is, anyone who underwrote a significant portion of the event and any of the host organization's top patrons. This could be an opportunity to meet with a featured speaker or, if there is a celebrity performance, a backstage opportunity to meet the performer. These are low- to no-cost opportunities for the host organization's very special donors. This chairperson could also subtly solicit underwriters for upcoming fundraising events. Finally, the development chair should seek to draw potential major donors closer to the organization by using the opportunity of the event.

The ideal candidate has social and business connections to individuals in the community and beyond capable of making sponsor-level donations or offer underwriting. If no volunteers with such experience are available, event planners should seek a person who is socially adept and able to effectively meet and engage people who are financially able to make sponsor-level gifts and who own or manage businesses.

An event provides the perfect opportunity to invite someone who may make a connection to the cause and become a significant contributor. The chair can make an invitation through direct contact or through various networking or social-media avenues. The event provides the development chair an opportunity to introduce a potential donor to officers, staff, and patrons and also to show off education materials and other good works of the host.

I have heard numerous discussions among event planners about the need to reduce costs of admission, and talk often turns to getting a donation to cover some of the expense. Getting someone else to foot the bill for a bloated or poorly budgeted event is not the solution to poor performance. The key is to plan and build a budget for the event that returns an acceptable projection of net revenue (see chapters 5 and 18). From that point, the savvy planner aided by a skilled development chairperson should find ways to add revenue without adding to expense. One way is to solicit gifts that cover direct costs without reducing revenue, the number-one job of the development officer.

Education Chairperson

Nonprofit organizations holding fundraising events all have a story to tell. This story describes the mission and work of the organization. It is the education chairperson's job to get this story across to event attendees and coordinate with the staff and volunteers who will be working at the event to have them do their part in getting the story out. The ideal candidate for the job of education chairperson is someone with a professional background in education, marketing, media, or advocacy.

Research shows the primary motivation for charity supporters to attend fundraising events is a personal connection to the cause, but the same studies caution that attendees are mostly not interested in long speeches. The education chairperson is responsible for the strategic placement of educational materials and messages. This is done by providing the workers, entertainers, master of ceremonies, and auctioneer short sound bites about the mission and work of the organization and then briefing them on how to use these education bites. The chair should then make sure these subtle education messages are used. In addition, the education chair should build video or projected visual images of the host's work, design and have printed posters for strategic placement, place informational materials on dining tables, and outfit and manage an education materials and information booth at the event. Besides providing a central distribution point for educational materials, this booth can be a site for signing up volunteers for mission-related volunteerism.

Outsourcing the Event

It is not unusual to hear new event planners after a few weeks of work say, "This event sounds like a lot of work; can't we get someone to do it for us?" Event planners may consider hiring an event management team instead of doing it on their own. There are a few jobs that can, and in many instances should, be done by experienced professionals if possible. That may mean paying for services (or getting professional volunteer help). Hiring a highly skilled auctioneer and merchandise models can increase net revenue well beyond cost. A paid publicist may obtain media coverage that would be impossible to obtain otherwise. Design and maintenance of the event Web site may need to be done by a service provider. An event consultant to advise the planning and management committee may be a good strategic investment as well, but complete outsourcing of an event may not be cost-effective.

Hiring people to plan, manage, and work all jobs at an event has several pitfalls; for example, the cost of these services may outweigh the gain in net revenue. After all, the reason charitable organizations are able to make money on fundraising events is that volunteers do most (or all) of the work. The jobs requiring the greatest number of workers in advance—advance ticket sales, soliciting prize merchandise, and tending to the various booths and activities at the event and during an event—are not those requiring highly skilled or experienced event workers. Hiring people to do all these jobs would be expensive, and volunteers can do just as well. Event-savvy attendees expect to see a charitable organization's members doing volunteer work at an event. This legitimizes the event's charitable nature.

Surveys show supporters expect the bulk of their expenditures at an event to go to the mission of the organization, not to pay people to do things the members of the organization acting as volunteers can do for themselves. Paying for a professional auc-

tioneer, caterer, performer, Web site designer, or armed security guard is something attendees can understand, because of the skill, experience, or licensing required to do those jobs. It is quite another matter for the host to be seen paying for workers to tend games of skill and chance, pick up auction bid sheets, run payment sheets between bidders and cashier, and perform other jobs almost anyone can do.

In some instances hiring most or all of the event workers makes sense, such as big events where net revenue of hundreds of thousands or millions of dollars is expected, where the event is being staged at an exquisite location and extraordinary attention to detail is required, and where there is an expectation among attendees that every aspect of the event is run "professionally." For example, if there are games of chance involving cards, attendees expect professional-level card dealers, not the members of the Saturday afternoon bridge club dealing the cards. Some host organizations can pull off such events on their own without help; others may be better off leaving it to professionals. Given an event that promises a truly high revenue potential, a very favorable event efficiency is readily possible even with the expense of a professional workforce. It is all a matter of keeping expense low relative to revenue. For most charitable organizations, however, that means nearly all event jobs should be filled by volunteers or existing staff, with exceptions noted elsewhere in this book.

Building Tomorrow's Event Team Today

Event planning and nurturing event workers are a continual process for organizations that fundraise from year to year. An event may be one of a kind, but if any fundraising event follows, it is likely many of the same people will be involved in planning and managing the next event, and planning and managing the one after that. A systematic approach to continual growth and improvement is maintained by effectively using the growing experience of past event workers, planners, and managers.

This involves continually improving and reinvigorating event planning and management performance by using the growing skills and experiences of the staff and volunteers, plus refreshing the core workers. New event volunteers are continually sought, and as many as possible are recruited for each event as an avenue for growth and innovation. They are invited to work at the event and invited to planning meetings with the team with which they will be working. Good workers at one event become subteam leaders for the next. If a worker proves to be a good leader, the person may be made a team leader at the next event.

Unfortunately, some organizations neglect to bring new volunteer workers along. Maybe the leadership invites members to volunteer as event workers but then fails to move them into leadership spots once the new volunteers gain experience. In such organizations, people in event leadership spots remain in those spots, event after event, year after year. This happens either because the host organization leadership is satisfied with the status quo or because no one is willing to give up a volunteer job he or she is accustomed to holding. This is not a good situation. Even the premise that leadership is content with the way an event is run should be unacceptable, as there is always room for improvement.

New workers need to be found, invited, and involved in event planning, management, and leadership as a means to circumvent complacency and rejuvenate the event team. Occasionally, volunteers seem to come out of nowhere, but most often new volunteers need to be actively sought and encouraged to volunteer. Any organization that is complacent about growing new event leaders may remain stagnant for a very long time.

PART 1

Learning the Basics

5

Event Business Plan

I recently attended an auction-event fundraiser where I was told a story similar to many I had heard before. An executive director of a nonprofit organization told me of a colleague in charge of an annual auction event that typically raises about $125,000. The organization holding the event was small, so $125,000 in event revenue sounded like a successful event to me. He said his colleague was frustrated with the event, because the net proceeds were only about $30,000 and the event was a lot of work. It was obvious why the event planner was frustrated. Spending $95,000 to raise $125,000 is not a very efficient way to raise money for a nonprofit organization.

Poor management of expenses at an event breaks faith with attendees who believe they are giving money that goes to the mission-related work of the host organization. Attendees took $125,000 out of their wallets and gave it to the organization during the event. They surely thought the dollars they spent would help the organization hosting the event. Instead, most of the money raised was used to pay expenses of holding the event.

I was told the entertainment at the event cost $15,000. For a $125,000 event, $15,000 for entertainment is unconscionable, unless the event is centered around that entertainment, which was not the case in this instance. Consider the event starts out with a fundraising efficiency of only 88%, just accounting for the cost of entertainment alone. Add to that all the other costs, and the "event efficiency" percentage will drop much lower.

AN ASSESSMENT OF "event efficiency" is one of the key tools in event planning. This is a ratio that measures the cost of the event against revenue raised. It provides a direct measure of the efficiency of fundraising, thus provides a quantitative objective measurement of fundraising success. For the event in the example, with expenses of $95,000 and only $125,000 raised, the event efficiency was 24%. Another way to express this efficiency is to say the organization spent $0.76 to raise each $1.00 at the event.

Event Efficiency

During the process of building the event business plan, the projected event efficiency should be computed. This is an estimate that can be used as a key planning tool. It presents an objective basis for making adjustments in expense and revenue in the business plan and provides a means to communicate to members and attendees the efficiency, or effectiveness, of fundraising.

The event planner in the example probably did not build an event business plan or address event efficiency. That is too bad, because year after year, patrons of this organization have spent dearly at the annual event. They were surely thinking they were helping fund the work of the organization, only to have the money they spent go into the pockets of entertainers and other paid providers of services for the event. Only $30,000 of the $125,000 raised went to fund the mission. If the organization's paid staff were involved in planning the event, and I believe they were, their time was probably not counted toward the cost of putting on the event (staff costs are often ignored in developing an event business plan). It is possible the fundraiser actually cost the organization more money than was raised after adding the cost of staff time into the overall cost of the event.

After each auction event, actual event efficiency should be computed using actual results from the auction. This actual event efficiency provides a useful fundraising statistic that can compare auction event to auction event, and year to year, by giving an objective measurement of fundraising success be-

tween auctions, between years, and over time. It is not the only measure of success, but the percentage expense to revenue is one of the most objective and easiest to understand.

Computation of Event Efficiency Percentage

The event efficiency percentage is simple to compute. Add up the costs, and subtract the total from total revenue to get net revenue. Then divide net revenue by total revenue, and multiply the result by 100.

$$\text{Revenue} - \text{cost} = \text{net revenue}$$
$$(\text{Net revenue} \div \text{revenue}) \times 100 = \text{event efficiency}$$
percentage

If the event efficiency is 72%, for example, event planners can report to the organization's board of directors that the event was 72% efficient. A 100% efficient event is one with no expense to balance against revenue. Another way to state the efficiency is the cost to raise a dollar at the event. If event efficiency is 72%, the cost is $0.28 to raise $1.00. Still another way to state the efficiency is the amount raised per dollar spent. In this example, the amount is $3.57 raised per $1.00 spent. No matter how it is expressed, event efficiency provides a ready means to communicate event success for any given event, compare the efficiency of one event to another, and compare an event from one year to the next if the event is an annual undertaking.

The Measure of Success

The acceptable level of efficiency depends on the nature of the event and the planning objectives of the host. In the example in which the event had $125,000 in gross revenue against $95,000 in expense, anything above 30% efficiency would probably be a welcome improvement. However, most organizations would be well advised to demand an efficiency considerably higher than 30%. An efficiency of at least 70% is attainable for most organizations that depend on volunteers to host the event and that seek full or partial donation of event merchandise.

Small events raising only a few thousand dollars

should have a high efficiency. When there is little money raised, even minor expenses can cut deeply into event efficiency and must be controlled. Costly entertainment, whiz-bang Web sites, and fancy surroundings are less an expectation at small events, so some expenses are easier to control for small events than for large events. For small events where full food service is involved, a low efficiency can be purely a function of food-related costs versus revenue earned. This may be entirely acceptable if food service is the prime attraction of the event. So event efficiency alone may not provide the whole story, but it still offers a ready means to measure and compare year-to-year success.

The mission of the host organization also influences the range of acceptable event efficiencies. Social service and religious organizations should always seek high efficiency ratios, as there is less expectation among attendees for extravagance. An efficiency well below 70% may be perfectly acceptable if the objective of the host is met in the course of the event. Although achieving a low efficiency may not be an objective, some events are simply costly and considered by the host reasonable in the course of doing an event. As an example, some events are intentionally extravagant. Others have high fixed costs (such as holding the event at an "exotic" location) that are considered unavoidable. The objective of any organization in this situation is to use the extravagance or costly option as a means to increase fundraising success. However, there can be a limit.

There is only so much money that an organization can take out of a room from a limited number of people, in a limited amount of time, and with a limited number of fundraising opportunities. Organizations that use business planning understand these costs in the context of the overall fundraising event and often put this into perspective with the organization's overall budget and its many funding sources.

The Business Plan

It is not always a simple matter to predict the price an item will bring at auction. Yet knowing how much money an auction will raise is one of the most

basic considerations in deciding whether to hold an auction event in the first place. After all, no organization holds a fundraising event to lose money, at least not on purpose. There is a guessing and praying game that is played out at auction after auction. Invariably when I am at events and speak to people involved in planning, discussion turns to auction items and what they expect—hope and pray—an item will bring. For the premier items, we discuss who among the attendees is likely to bid and where the bidding will end. Sometimes planners will discuss auction items with potential bidders in advance of an auction. Planners watch these prospective bidders and may even help the bidders stay attentive to the progress of the auction up to the point of auctioning the premier item. Many times that most anticipated bidder gets sidetracked or leaves the auction before the premier item comes up for bid.

In one instance, three bidders present at a large auction were known as collectors and were presumed by meeting planners, which included me, to be interested in an item that could bring nearly $100,000 in the auction. It's always necessary to have two bidders bidding against each other to increase bid amounts, but having at least three bidders is ideal, so this appeared to be an ideal situation. All three bidders had arrived at the event, and as the auction progressed, all appeared to be enjoying themselves. There was considerable discussion about who might bid the highest. When it came time to auction the item, only one of the bidders was in the room, and that person did not even bid on the item. We had no idea why none of the three anticipated bidders bid on the item. We presumed they wanted it. We presumed wrong.

The host organization received a lower final bid than expected. Event planners misjudged the chain of events. It is difficult to predict what people will do, and forecasting what people will spend at an auction is particularly challenging. Consider that event planners are seeking to foresee what people will spend on items they are not required to buy and probably don't really need. Sometimes a bidder's inattention or departure is intentional. Other times it is just a matter of happenstance. Maybe the three bidders in the story had no interest in the item, or maybe they were just distracted by other matters. Event planners need to consider that attendees and bidders have minds of their own, are easily distracted, and may not do as planners hope. After an item has been auctioned off, I have listened as the person who was expected to bid on an item was asked why he or she did not bid. Most often the answer is just a shrug, accompanied by "I don't know."

Not only is it hard to predict bidding on any particular item in advance but it can be even harder to determine why people bid the way they do. People are unpredictable and may not give truthful answers when asked about their participation in an auction. They may consider that if they told the truth about their failure to bid, or their minimal bidding, their answers would be taken as rude, insensitive, or insulting to the host. A common reason why people may not bid is that they are in some financial difficulty but do not want others to know. There are many reasons to avoid answering, and being asked such a question probably makes event attendees feel somewhat uncomfortable. Getting to the truth can provide crucial information for planning subsequent auction events, but it may be impossible to get to the truth. It is no wonder event planners often have such a hard time projecting auction-event revenue, but it can be done.

Collecting, Analyzing, and Using Information

I was employed by an organization that held almost 5,000 events each year and would repeatedly raffle and auction off the same types of items at events in different parts of the country, in big cities, in medium-sized towns, and in rural areas. Staff had the means to develop accurate event statistics. Year to year, many of the auction items were similar enough to be considered virtually identical. So, during any given year, high, low, and average bids for identical items were recorded. Over the course of many years, bid amounts for items were recorded. Included in record keeping was corresponding information, such as location and number of attendees. These records allowed staff to compute statistical averages and make comparative evaluations. The average price at auction for various kinds of items was known, and as more similar items were auctioned off, more data allowed more accurate estimates of expected average final bid amount, high and low final bids, and so on.

With that kind of information comes an ability to use quantitative data in the development of business plans for auction events. Where events also include identical or similar raffles, games of chance, silent auction items, and so on, those items and activities can be evaluated as well. Over the course of many events, this information provides the basis for powerful statistical evaluation. Event-to-event and year-to-year information becomes a truly functional financial planning tool. Although not many organizations hold multiple auctions offering the same merchandise and services at auction and in raffles, any organization can conduct year-to-year evaluations with a little forethought and record keeping. Such record keeping can form the basis for continually improving event business planning.

Ending an Event with Net Revenue

The goal of every fundraising event is to end with net revenue—the amount of money left over after all event expenses are paid. The business plan is a tool that event planners can use to plan and manage an event's expenses and revenues. A business plan itself does nothing, but use of such a plan will help event leadership manage the financial outcome of the event. This helps event planners achieve maximum net revenue or otherwise target costs and revenues. There are various ways to build a business plan, ranging from a simple list of expenses and revenue projections sketched out on a single piece of tablet paper to a lengthy, multitiered financial spreadsheet and accompanying detailed written plan of every penny to be spent and every nickel to be raised. Either approach may work well. In general, it is not the complexity, detail, or length of plan that determines its value to planners. Instead, it is how well planners are able to use the plan to estimate expense and revenue through the process of planning.

A short and simple plan, involving no more than addition and subtraction of a few numbers, can be dead-on in predicting event success (or failure) if the estimates of costs and revenues are dead-on. On the other hand, a highly complex and excruciatingly detailed plan, in which the most minute expense is listed and revenue is painstakingly estimated for every conceivable aspect and angle of fundraising, can be incredibly off the mark if the estimates of cost and revenue are inaccurate. This truly is a process that follows the rule "garbage in, garbage out." The business plan, no matter how simple or complex, is only as good as the assumptions of cost and revenue. Getting those assumptions as close to actual as possible is the key to sound business planning. The process used to create a business plan provides a means for event planners to do just that.

Creating the Business Plan

An auction event can make money for the host organization or lose money if expenses are greater than the amount of money earned. The most basic business plan for an event simply provides an estimate of money that will be earned or lost. The bare-bones plan lists all expenses and the revenue. All projected expenses are added together, and all projected revenues are added together. Total expense is then subtracted from total revenue. The result will be either net revenue earned, if the number is positive, or the amount of loss if the number is negative. The purpose of doing a business plan is to determine ahead of time, as accurately as possible, the result of this simple addition-and-subtraction equation.

The business plan and planning exercise discussed here may not be the same as a plan an MBA might create for a new business. Instead, this is a more simplified version of planning, where our objective is simple: develop a plan for an auction event that should result in net revenue after all expenses of the event are taken into account. It provides a means to objectively look at what is planned for the event, test different event options, make adjustments, and in so doing keep adding or subtracting costs and revenue sources until planners have a

reasonable and business-like evaluation of cost and revenue projections for the event. This provides an objectively based estimate of what the organization can expect to earn from the event.

Using the Business Plan as a Predictive Model

For the reader looking for a more technical explanation of the business plan, think of it as a prediction model with multiple variables. The variables here are (1) categories of costs (e.g., food service, event-room rental, prize merchandise, printing) and (2) categories of revenues (e.g., event registration fees, sponsorship donations, silent auction proceeds). The business plan—call it a model—can be used to test how changing one or more variables affects other variables in the model. The model can help planners identify costs, establish revenues, and help identify what to change to meet financial objectives. The business model can be used to figure out how changes to cost and revenue will affect the financial outcome of the event.

By building such a model, planners are forced to think of and list all the costs and revenues. This is important in figuring out what to charge for various items because the event host doesn't want to learn of a cost after it is too late to make sure it can be covered by revenue. Once all cost and revenue sources are set into the equation, planners can easily determine, as an example, how much can be spent on food given a set fee for event registration.

Here is a simplified look at how the model may be used. If event registration is set to include the cost of food service, then revenue to account for food service costs must be contained within the "event registration fee" revenue variable. It will only be one component of the registration fee, but it is a component that can be changed because food is not a fixed cost. The variable "food-service expense" can be modified by choosing among various meal options. For example, an evening meal can be a five-course, full-service steak and lobster dinner or it can be serve-yourself salad, spaghetti, and meatballs off a buffet line. Both will fill up diners, but the first option costs more than the other, making the point that the variable "food-service expense" can be varied. Other expenses may be fixed, such as event-room rental, so that goes into the model as a fixed cost, along with all the other fixed, variable, and estimated costs.

Putting It All Together:
Expense and Projected Revenue

The business plan is put together well in advance of an event. Prior years' experience is a crucial element of business planning, as records of costs and revenues of past events help planners narrow estimates of expense and revenue at subsequent events. Costs are known, proportional to attendance, or estimates. Revenues are usually estimates. The best predictor of a future cost or revenue is cost and revenue experienced during past events. Even if all sources of expense and revenue are not known, listing what is known provides a point from which to start the business plan and evaluation of costs and revenues. Expense categories are generally easily listed, as are sources of revenue. These display what planners initially plan. Sidebar 5.1 lists typical broad categories of expense and broad sources of revenue.

Some expenses may be directly associated with a source of revenue, such as the cost of printing raffle tickets, while other expenses, such as rental of the facility, are a fixed cost not associated directly with any one source of revenue. Putting all of this into a business plan forces planners to do a financial evaluation using this initial information. Some expenses are known. As a start in building a business plan, list these costs. For example, rental of the facility may be a set fee, not open to negotiation or change. Rental fees for public facilities are often set. Known expenses can be listed as fixed base costs. This provides a solid expense floor.

Other expenses can be estimated with varied accuracy. These expenses may be dependent on other estimates, such as the number of people who will attend and dine. For example, rental cost of tables and chairs may be a set fee per table and chair. However, the number of tables and chairs that must be rented may be unknown, because that number will be dependent on the number of attendees. Plan-

---

Sidebar 5.1. General Categories of Expense and Revenue

Expense
- Food and drink
- Entertainment
- Printing
- Facility rental
- Table, chair, and other rental
- Auctioneer
- Event models
- Cash purchase of prize and auction merchandise and services
- Advertising
- Security
- Credit card processing
- Audiovisual services
- Staff salary and payments to paid event workers
- Recognition to donors, sponsors, underwriters, volunteers, and staff

Revenue
- Main raffle
- Roving raffles
- Silent auction(s)
- Event registration ticket sales
- Sponsor and other direct cash donations
- Games of skill and chance
- Main live auction
- Food and drink sales

---

ners often have a good idea of how many people will attend an event, which is a consideration that drives many estimates of cost. Some events are so popular that attendance is limited to a set number. As long as the event is fully attended, estimates of costs dependent on number of attendees can be very accurately estimated. More often attendance is estimated.

It is also possible that the number of tables and chairs can be varied to meet budget or other considerations. Many events do not involve all attendees sitting down at tables all at once. Other events, for example, where a dinner is served, will require the hosts to provide chairs and tables for the total number of expected attendees. Planners need to consider their requirements for tables and chairs, and those requirements can then be used to estimate the total cost of table and chair rental based on how many attendees planners anticipate will attend and require tables and chairs. When all factors are considered, the cost of tables and chairs may still be an estimate, but planners will usually come close to actual costs given the close examination of such costs required in developing the business plan.

Predicting the Unpredictable Expense

Some expenses are difficult to predict, and these expenses can create unpleasant surprises for the event host. This is a category of expense that planners need to treat conservatively. In other words, it is better to overestimate a potential expense and be pleasantly surprised if the expense turns out to be lower than estimated than to underestimate the expense and be shocked when the expense is much higher. Unexpected expenses can undermine an otherwise successful event. Examples of expenses that are difficult to estimate include the potential need for temporary shelter (tent) should the weather turn bad for an outside event, and the need for additional security should attendees express concern about the location of parking at an event at night downtown in a big city.

Many of the categories listed in sidebar 5.1 are overly broad for planning purposes and will need to be broken down into more detailed categories for accurate estimates of cost and revenue. Event planners may try to anticipate each invoice and purchase and each conceivable source of revenue. That may be an excessively detailed approach, but the level of detail in planning lends to the level of confidence in the business plan. As an example of greater detail, sidebar 5.2 provides a more involved look at the costs of printing and associated sources of revenue.

Some of the costs of printing are minimal, such as printing costs for silent auction bid sheets and winning bidder contracts. These materials are used in limited quantity and can be printed using a home computer and desktop printer. Other printed materials, such as programs and raffle tickets, are more expensive and may have to be printed on higher-grade printers or by professional services. Some items, such as raffle tickets that do not require specialized printing, can be purchased preprinted. However, raffle tickets may carry a high cost, as many states have legal requirements for tickets used in "gaming." Breaking down the general cost category into individual components, addressing the cost of each component, and then adding up these costs provide an accurate assessment of the overall cost of printing for the event. This is among key purposes of building a business plan—to enable planners to conduct an accurate accounting of anticipated costs.

Stretching the Utility of a Business Plan

Building a business plan for an event forces planners to conduct an accounting of all projected expenses and all projected revenues. It is simple to then expand the scope of planning to include a description of tasks such as how revenues will be raised, who will be assigned responsibility for various jobs, and so on. From the list of expenses, planners can make job assignments and create timelines and deadlines for action in completing jobs. For annual or recurring events, some jobs will continue throughout the year, such as maintenance of the event Web site.

Continuing with the example of costs for printing, each item represents a printing job or purchase that needs to be attended to by someone. For each job, there is a deadline for completion. For example, the absolute deadline to have raffle tickets in hand is the point in time the event starts. Even though that is the true deadline, it is always best to complete such tasks well ahead of an event. Waiting until the last minute to complete even simple tasks such as buying a roll of raffle tickets can have serious consequences to fundraising if the job is bungled and there is no time to recover. Failure to have legally acceptable raffle tickets in time for the event would

Sidebar 5.2. **Cost and Revenue Associated with the Example Expense Category of Printing**

Expense category of printing	Related revenue sources
General raffle tickets	General raffle
Printing or purchase of bucket-raffle tickets	Bucket raffle
Advance and auction programs	Silent and live auctions
Bidder number card	Live auction
Event tickets/receipts	Event registration
Auction-item receipt	Silent and live auctions
Silent auction bid sheets	Silent auction
Advertising placards and other advertising	All sources
Banners for display during the event	All sources
Advance registration materials—mailings	Event registration
Printing of invitations	All sources

result in a complete failure to earn whatever amount the raffle was projected to raise. Many jobs can and should be performed well before the absolute deadline.

Level of Detail in a Business Plan

The business plan enables a considerable depth of planning, but it is up to planners to decide how detailed they want to make the plan. It can be highly inclusive or just focused on financial aspects of the event. In the course of working through the business plan, planners can make assignments and set deadlines for completion of assignments. But not all the jobs to be filled hosting an event are associated with specific costs, as is printing. For that reason many jobs do not "show up" as a cost during business planning. The level of detail in a business plan can be expanded to include all aspects of an event, but it is first and foremost a tool to evaluate the financial picture of the event. The business plan can be used to determine how much to charge for raffles, food service, games of chance, and any other activities or actions to raise revenue. Or planners may use a less detailed plan, evaluating just the broad categories of cost and revenue. The strength of event business planning is dependent on using enough detail to manage the overall event in a financially efficient and effective fashion—no more and no less.

Tables 5.1 to 5.3 provide a variety of examples of how a detailed evaluation of costs and game options can be used to determine the amount of money to pay for prizes (expense) and charge (revenue) in a game of chance. For the examples, a game will feature chances to pull a prize-bearing rubber duck out of a water-filled tub. This is called a game of chance because each rubber duck pulled from the tub carries a certain level of chance that the rubber duck pulled bears a prize. There are many ways to structure the game, but what is the best way? That is a subject for discussion among event planners as part of the business planning process, as there are cost and revenue options to evaluate. An option that meets the needs and desires of planners of one event may not meet the needs of those planning another. For example, pricing and prize options will

be different when using the rubber-duck game at a family-oriented event where the game will be played by children than when using the game at an event where it will be played primarily by adults. The rubber-duck pull is a versatile game, so it provides a good example for the discussion that follows.

Examples of Revenues from a Rubber-Duck Pull

Let's start with 50 rubber ducks floating in a water-filled tub, with each duck offering a chance at a prize. Following are a number of options, discussion of strategy of each option, and an example of using the business planning technique to evaluate expense and revenue potential for each, all focused on just this one game of chance.

Table 5.1 displays revenues from the rubber-duck pull where there is a total of 50 ducks and every duck provides the player with a prize. In this example, the game is one that can be played by all ages but here is oriented to children, so the prizes are items desirable to children and, as is customary for games oriented to small children, a prize is awarded for every play. The game can be varied to make it attractive to various age groups.

Although this evaluation of costs may look acceptable and could lead event planners to add this game to the event, the evaluation of costs and revenue ignores the expense of setting up the game. Setup costs include the cost of rubber ducks, table rental, tub, and display materials. If setup materials such as the rubber ducks and tub are already available at no cost, then there is no added expense and table 5.1 displays an accurate accounting of expense and revenue. Either way, in determining the cost and revenue, all expenses need to be considered.

Table 5.2 shows the same analysis with all expenses considered. This changes the picture event planners see, and the potential financial outcome changes markedly. In addition, planners need to consider that not all ducks may be pulled, yet all prizes must be purchased and available in the event all ducks are pulled.

One situation in which all ducks may not be pulled occurs if the grand prizes are selected early

Table 5.1. **Example revenues from a rubber-duck pull**

Prize	Number	Expense per prize ($)	Total expense of prizes ($)	Revenue per duck ($)	Total revenue ($)	Net revenue ($)
Pencil	40	0.10	4.00	2.00	80.00	76.00
Duck whistle	5	2.00	10.00	2.00	10.00	0.00
Duck coloring book	3	4.00	12.00	2.00	6.00	−6.00
Small stuffed duck	1	10.00	10.00	2.00	2.00	−8.00
Large stuffed duck	1	15.00	15.00	2.00	2.00	−13.00
Totals	50		51.00		100.00	49.00

NOTE: There are 50 ducks, and each duck provides the player with a prize. Players pay $2.00 to pull a duck.

Table 5.2. **Example revenues from a rubber-duck pull**

	Number	Expense per item ($)	Total expense ($)	Revenue per duck ($)	Total revenue ($)	Net revenue ($)
Prizes						
Pencil	40	0.10	4.00	2.00	80.00	
Duck whistle	5	2.00	10.00	2.00	10.00	
Duck coloring book	3	4.00	12.00	2.00	6.00	
Small stuffed duck	1	10.00	10.00	2.00	2.00	
Large stuffed duck	1	15.00	15.00	2.00	2.00	
Other expenses						
Ducks	50	0.79	39.50			
Tub	1	donated	0.00			
Table rental	1	4.50	4.50			
Display materials	1	3.65	3.65			
Totals			98.65		100.00	1.35

There are 50 ducks, and each duck provides the player with a prize. Players pay $2.00 to pull a duck. All expenses are considered.

in the game and subsequent players are made aware of this. Without the higher-level prizes to attract players, interest in the game may falter. Planners need to consider this in setting up the game and evaluating costs. One method to address the effect of early awarding of the highest-level prizes is to associate a raffle with the game. This will work for games where the objective is not to provide an actual prize with each play (each duck pulled) and can be done in two ways. The first is to associate the game with the event's main raffle. In this scenario varied numbers of raffle tickets or ticket packages would be used as prizes in the duck pull. The second option is to use the game as the platform for a dedicated raffle.

NOTE: *Some states or local regulations may prohibit giving away raffle tickets under certain circumstances. Games of chance are regulated in a highly variable fashion, so use of raffles and handling of raffle tickets must be consistent with state and local requirements.*

The rubber-duck pull can serve as a ready platform for a dedicated raffle. A game used to conduct a dedicated raffle is one in which the entire game is focused on delivering chances (raffle tickets) to players for a raffle unique to the game being played. Raffle prizes are displayed at the location of the game. In the case of the 50 rubber ducks, pulled ducks provide players varying numbers of raffle tickets. These tickets then go into the raffle unique to the rubber-duck pull. The raffle tickets are drawn for the grand prizes when all ducks are pulled or at a set point in the event, regardless of how many ducks are pulled.

Table 5.3. **Example of a rubber-duck pull used to support a dedicated raffle with two grand prizes**

	Number	Expense per item ($)	Total expense of items ($)	Revenue per duck ($)	Total revenue ($)	Net revenue ($)
25 ducks, 1 raffle ticket	25	0.00	0.00	2.00	50.00	
15 ducks, 2 raffle tickets	15	0.00	0.00	2.00	30.00	
5 ducks, 5 raffle tickets	5	0.00	0.00	2.00	10.00	
3 ducks, 10 raffle tickets	3	0.00	0.00	2.00	6.00	
2 ducks, 25 raffle tickets	2	0.00	0.00	2.00	4.00	
Expenses						
Roll of 500 raffle tickets	1	3.00	3.00			
Small stuffed duck	1	10.00	10.00			
Large stuffed duck	1	15.00	15.00			
Rubber ducks	50	0.79	39.50			
Tub	1	donated	0.00			
Table rental	1	4.50	4.50			
Display materials	1	3.65	3.65			
Totals			75.65		100.00	24.35

There are 50 ducks. The two grand prizes are a small and a large stuffed duck. Players pay $2.00 to pull a duck. All expenses are considered.

Since the raffle tickets drawn at the end of the game determine who gets prizes, players are not appreciably affected by the success of players that come before them. Table 5.3 shows an example of a dedicated raffle having two grand prizes: one small and one large stuffed duck. Raffle tickets are a negligible expense, so the number of raffle tickets won by pulling ducks has little effect on cost of running this game. Cost is dependent on the actual cost of the dedicated raffle prize(s), which in this case totals $25. If the raffle prize(s) is donated, then that expense is also negligible.

Revenue is dependent on the total number of rubber ducks pulled. Because there is no appreciable change in cost to the host from increasing or decreasing the number of raffle tickets used in the game, there is no financial advantage to removing ducks from the pool after a player chooses a duck. By returning played ducks to the pool, players always have a chance at pulling rubber ducks that yield the highest number of raffle tickets. There are two added advantages of returning ducks to the pool after play: (1) it allows for an unlimited number of times players can play this game, and (2) it allows the host to reduce the number of ducks that need to be purchased to play the game, which reduces the "capital" cost of the game itself. This option is displayed in table 5.4.

Because ducks are returned to the pool after play in this option, it is no longer possible to determine total revenue if all ducks are played, as there are an unlimited number of plays available to potential players. In some previous examples, for comparative purposes it was assumed all 50 ducks would be pulled. That assumption is not relevant in this option. Instead, event planners must consider how many players (ducks pulled) this option will draw in determining revenue potential. Thus, for comparative purposes, if 50 ducks were pulled, the host would receive $48.05 net revenue. If 100 ducks were pulled, net revenue would increase to $148.05.

Perceived versus Real Value

Now let's really ramp up the "value" of the prize for pulling a winning duck. Prizes cost only $10 and $15 in the previous examples. Instead of providing a stuffed animal as a prize, what if the grand prize is a framed original print from an early edition of *Birds of America* by famed waterbird artist John James Audubon? How much would it cost per chance to pull a rubber duck now? Not only would each duck have to carry a significant cost to the player but the spread between the cost of the art and revenue from playing the game would have to be considerable to

Table 5.4. **Example of a rubber-duck pull used to support a dedicated raffle with two grand prizes**

	Number played	Expense per item ($)	Total expense of items ($)	Revenue per duck per pull ($)	Total revenue ($)	Net revenue ($)
15 ducks, 1 raffle ticket	Unlimited	0.00	0.00	2.00	?	
2 ducks, 2 raffle tickets	Unlimited	0.00	0.00	2.00	?	
1 duck, 5 raffle tickets	Unlimited	0.00	0.00	2.00	?	
1 duck, 10 raffle tickets	Unlimited	0.00	0.00	2.00	?	
1 duck, 25 raffle tickets	Unlimited	0.00	0.00	2.00	?	
Expenses						
Roll of 500 raffle tickets	1	3.00	3.00			
Small stuffed duck	1	10.00	10.00			
Large stuffed duck	1	15.00	15.00			
Rubber ducks	20	0.79	15.80			
Tub	1	donated	0.00			
Table rental	1	4.50	4.50			
Display materials	1	3.65	3.65			
Totals			51.95		?	?

An unlimited number of ducks may be pulled. The two grand prizes are a small and a large stuffed duck. Players pay $2.00 to pull a duck. All expenses are considered, and the ducks are returned to the pool after being pulled.

realize the potential net revenue warranted by such a grand prize.

But what if it is possible to offer what is perceived by attendees as truly grand prizes at no additional cost? No, this is not about having grand artworks donated for use in rubber-duck pulls. It is about offering prizes of great perceived value. Examples of this include a high-value package of tickets for the grand raffle. Let's say the grand prize for a duck pull is a $100 book of raffle tickets. The cost to the host is nearly nothing. Consider the prize could be increased to a $500 package of raffle tickets, $1,000, or even $10,000 worth of tickets. In all cases, the actual cost to the host would be nearly nothing. The perceived increase in value to players would be considerable. Of course, there is a reasonable limit and a strategy to creating grand prizes in this fashion.

Such prizes need to be reasonable in relationship to price per play and prizes elsewhere at the event, and respectful of the perceptions of people who pay full price for identical or similar raffle ticket packages. Raffle ticket buyers must not get the feeling their chances of winning raffle items are appreciably altered as a result of disproportionately large numbers of raffle tickets being offered as prizes on what they might perceive to be trivial games. Here, offering $10,000 in raffle prizes for a rubber-duck pull would probably not be appropriate, at least not at $2 per duck. However, if the rubber-duck pull was used as a main raffle venue and each duck pull cost $200 instead of $2, and ducks were replaced upon each pull, $100 in raffle tickets for low-level prizes and $1,000 or more for higher-level prizes should be perfectly acceptable to attendees.

6

Programs, Policies, and Procedures

Each year, two or three weeks from the date of the auction, the chapter auction chair would call to request a staff member to help organize the auction. The chapter had developed the habit of waiting until the last minute to start work on the auction. Planners would panic and call the parent organization for help. To date, they had been getting that help. And they probably would continue to get it as long as the chapter's leadership continued to beg the parent organization's volunteer officers. The volunteers always caved in to the request, and staff were sent to the rescue. The help had been needed when the chapter was just starting out. Staff had been hired for the purpose of getting chapters on the path to holding effective events and raising money, but this chapter was no longer new or needy.

I started a field fundraising support service as part of one of my earlier jobs. Once established, field service staff were on call to help the 250 or so chapters worldwide raise funds at their events. Most of the existing chapters were already solid performers, so the real added value of the field staff was in starting new chapters. Staff gave help where needed. The idea proved effective—get a chapter going on a sound footing by assisting in the first and maybe second fundraiser and then provide occasional support if necessary thereafter. Local chapter fundraising revenue rose by 89% in three years as this service geared up.

These chapters were successfully using many of the techniques mentioned in this book, and some were pioneered there. Among keys to success was an established set of policies and procedures by which auctions were run and to which the chapter's event planners were held accountable. These were the standards that established the credentials of the chapters to raise *funds and created consistency in how they did so. They were published for all to see.*

A PRINTED OR ONLINE advance event program and printed auction program provide important information intended to help potential attendees and market the event and its fundraising. Some events feature their own Web site and additional Web presence through profiles on social-media sites. Descriptions of auction items and values should be included to entice people to attend, but in addition to marketing materials, the programs and Web sites should include information that helps establish the authenticity and professional nature of the event, the auction, and the host organization. Such information includes auction and bidding rules, as well as a set of bidding instructions to help people who are new to auctions bid with confidence or to refresh the memory of seasoned auctiongoers. In addition, the host organization's event policies and procedures should be listed in printed programs and online materials. This serves as a legal notice to bidders and binds the host organization to a set of rules. These help guide both bidder and host organization in addressing any problems that may arise in a fair and consistent manner. They serve to establish the authenticity of event and host. Such printed and online materials are an essential ingredient in a well-planned, well-managed auction event. Chapters 20 and 21 provide additional details and example materials essential to establishing sound event policies and procedures.

Advance Program

An advance program lists and describes auction items, raffles, and all the other exciting, fun activities of the event. This program goes to all potential attendees. It is among primary "invitations" pro-

---

Some example language suggested in this chapter has been adapted from policies and procedures of Safari Club International (SCI), with permission, including sample language on bidding instructions and sales.

> **Sidebar 6.1. Items to Include in an Advance Program and Event Web Site**
>
> - Invitation to attend from the host organization president or featured personality who will be in attendance
> - Statement about the host organization and its membership
> - Statement about the charitable cause that will be aided by funds raised—the mission of the host organization and objective of the event
> - Registration information and ticket prices
>   - Time, place, hotel accommodations, and other logistics of attendance, such as parking availability
> - Information about sponsorship and purchasing a table for group attendance
> - Early-bird registration, raffles, prizes, ticket discounts, bring-a-friend offerings, and so on
> - Program of events, including dining options if offered, and descriptions of raffles, auctions, games, and entertainment
> - Special attractions, including notice about any well-known personalities who will attend (such as sports heroes, movie stars, and high-profile politicians), and perhaps photos of the personalities and a short biographical sketch
> - Testimonials by well-known personalities regarding contributing to the cause by attending the event
> - Live auction preview, including a description of each auction item; illustrations, photos, or video of auction items; text description; item value; and any restrictions or special considerations
> - List of auction policies and procedures
> - Host organization advertisements for membership, product sales, upcoming meetings, and events
> - Paid advertisements from sponsors

vided to potential attendees. This is usually sent by mail or e-mail to lists maintained by the host organization of its members, potential donors, and potential event attendees. It also may be sent to people meeting certain criteria from a list purchased by the host organization from list-service companies. The advance program can also be published in its entirety or in installments in the host organization's newspaper, magazine, and newsletter and on its Web site. Event Web sites can feature an interactive auction section where photos and video of auction and raffle items can be viewed. Sidebar 6.1 lists items to be included in an advance program.

The advance program and any associated social-media marketing materials should be designed to invite and entice people to attend the event. Advance materials should convey a sense of fun and excitement. They need to explicitly state that the event will be an enjoyable way to participate with friends and neighbors, community leaders, or business associates in helping contribute money to a worthy cause. The program (or highlights from it) can be published in local newspapers or on community Web sites. Auction items can be featured on Web sites supporting video. Sponsor advertising can be used to reduce or wholly cover publication and distribution costs of the advance program.

The central focus of the advance program should be on the items to be presented at the live and silent auctions. This "auction preview" section showcases the best of the best and gives attendees a good idea of what will be available. Items to be used in major raffles can also be advertised in this special fashion. Value of auction items and mention of the donor should be displayed in addition to tantalizing descriptions or video of the items in online media. Such descriptions of auction items generate excitement, while photographs and video help paint a vivid picture of the merchandise, service, or activity. Figure 6.1 provides an example page from an advance program showing descriptions for three typical auction items.

For example, if describing a catch-and-release fishing trip for marlin, a photo of people having fun on board a fishing boat with one person hooked up to a marlin breaking the surface in the background would immediately attract attention and entice people to read the details. Text details can include length of the fishing trip, port of departure, amenities on board, and level of accommodations in port. For a work of art, a written description of the work and a brief biography of the artist should accompany a photograph of the item. Text should be kept reasonably short; the key is for visual imagery and accompanying text to paint an alluring picture.

Instructions to Bidders

It is important for the organization to provide instructions on how to bid at an auction to all bidders, regardless of how experienced attendees may be or may believe they are. Brief instructions should be printed in the auction program and listed on the event Web site. When a host organization makes an effort to provide bidders with rules, it also reduces risk of liability should a bidder register a complaint or have a dispute.

Some attendees may be new to auctions but would like to participate, and many others who have attended auctions in the past may have acquired bad habits. Although it is up to the auctioneer and spotters to help bidders bid properly, in the heat of an auction, bidders, spotters, and the auctioneer can make mistakes. Most mistakes are the result of bidders not understanding what is going on during the bidding process and losing track of the bid sequence and last amount bid. Mistakes can cause frustration among bidders and result in disputes. Sidebar 6.2 provides sample instructions to bidders that can be printed in the auction and advance programs.

If an auctioneer detects that the audience is new to auctions, prospective bidders can be referred to the written instructions in the auction program. In addition, the auctioneer can give a quick onstage lesson in how to bid and how to understand the special language of the auctioneer. Such an onstage lesson should be planned in advance if the event organizers anticipate that a large number of attendees will be new to live auctions. This lesson should be staged as a planned activity and listed as such in the program. A good auctioneer will use a little showmanship in giving this lesson and will add to the fun of the event. Such lessons may result in more aggressive, faster bidding and help reduce the chance of a problem during the auction. For this reason, some auctioneers advise a short auction lesson in advance of bidding at any charity auction.

Auction Program

The purpose of the auction program is to provide information that promotes bidding, thanks contributors, and provides bidders information that will be helpful if a portion of the purchase price may be tax deductible (see chapter 21 for detailed information about tax deductibility of items offered at events).

No. 23. Original Art Work

Original Oil Titled "The Old Kettle"
by Ruth E. Rosen

24"x18" framed in antique wood

Donated by the artist, Ruth E. Rosen works primarily in oil and acrylics. Her work has been displayed in fine homes and galleries throughout the country. Concentrating on still life and sailing themes, Rosen is a frequent contributor to help raise funds to aid in the fight against stomach cancer.

Value: $2,000

No. 24. One-of-a-Kind Theme Piece

Desert Hare Metal Designer Handbag
by Dry River Designs

From the renowned metal works design firm, Dry River Designs, comes this year's featured theme item. Displaying a whimsical rendition of the object of this year's Fundraiser for Desert Life, the endangered desert hare, this one-of-a-kind metalwork handbag is made of recycled antique ceiling tin. Dry River Designs is also a frequent contributor to our efforts to promote protection of desert life and hopes their contribution of this year's featured item will help protect all the desert's precious reptiles.

Value: $150

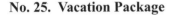

No. 25. Vacation Package

Trek Into the Remote: Namibia
Compliments of African Desert Adventures

Visit one of the most remote places on earth in this 10-day trip for two to the starkly beautiful deserts of Namibia. Not for the faint of heart, this trip includes a hot air balloon ride over Sossusvlei, a climb to the top of the world's highest sand dunes, and hikes through lava fields, wind sculpted rock gardens and primeval dry river gorges. A 2-day 4-wheeler tour of the Naukluft Mountains will go through some of the most scenic mountain terrain on Earth. You will see wildlife such as gemsbok, springbok, ostrich, meerkats and the rare Burchell's zebra.

Included is airfare from New York, all accommodations and morning and evening meals while in Namibia. Ample time will be provided for shopping and sightseeing in the quaint port city of Swakopmund, shopping at the curio market in Okahandja, and touring the bustling Namibian capitol, Windhoek.

Tour the Skeleton Coast Park, site of innumerable shipwrecks, and the world-renowned Etosha National Game Park, located one-day's travel north of Windhoek for additional fees.

Value: $8,500

FIGURE 6.1. Example page from an advance program showing descriptions of auction items.

Sidebar 6.2. **Instructions for Bidding at Live Auctions**

- Anyone who is a registered attendee may place a bid on any item in accordance with the rules of bidding.
- The auctioneer or an announcer will announce each auction item, in turn, stating the number of the auction item and describing the item. The item will then be displayed onstage, projected on-screen, or displayed in some other highly visible fashion. The auctioneer will begin bidding by either stating a minimum required bid amount or asking for an opening bid.
- Bids shall be allowed on only one auction item at a time, and auction items will be placed for bid in sequence at the discretion of the auctioneer. While an effort will be made to place items for auction in the order in which they are listed in the program, circumstances may require altering the sequence. Thus, bidders must be alert to changes in the order in which items are offered for bidding. Each item will be announced by auction-item number and a description of the auction item. In addition, each item will be displayed as it is auctioned. Please watch the stage and screen displays for current information.
- If a minimum opening bid amount is required, the auctioneer will ask for an opening bid of that amount or higher. A required minimum bid is the least amount that the *Host Organization* will accept for the auction item. If the minimum amount is not offered by a bidder, the auction item will be withdrawn from the auction.
- If no required opening bid amount is announced, then the auctioneer may ask for an opening bid or may suggest an opening bid amount. In either case, a bidder may open with an amount of his or her own choice.
- Bids increase in increments as bidders bid, with the amount of increment at the discretion of the auctioneer or by action of bidders.
- Auctioneers may seek a reasonably high opening bid and reasonably high incremental bid amounts to help expedite bidding. The auctioneer will state the amount that is currently being sought from bidders. This is called the "asking bid." Auctioneers will help bidders keep track of bidding by repeatedly stating the current amount already bid and the "asking bid."
- Bids are placed by gaining the attention of the auctioneer or a spotter and stating the amount the bidder wishes to bid or by accepting the auctioneer's current "asking bid." The auctioneer or spotter may ask bidders to hold their bidder number card aloft so that the number can be seen and bidders clearly identified. It shall be the responsibility of bidders to gain the attention of the auctioneer or spotters. Spotters and the auctioneer shall make every effort to identify bidders, but spotters and the auctioneer shall not be held liable in any way for missing a bid.
- Upon successfully completing a bid, the bidder will be acknowledged by the auctioneer and the amount bid will be repeated by the auctioneer. Until a new bid is received by the auctioneer, the current highest bidder will continue to be recognized by the auctioneer along with the amount of the last bid. If no subsequent and higher bids are received, the last highest bidder will be acknowledged by the auctioneer and the final amount bid stated clearly.
- In the event of a dispute regarding bids, the auctioneer's decision shall be final.
- Immediately upon completion of bidding on each item, the winning bidder will be met by a runner who will present a "buyer's agreement" to the bidder. This agreement will contain a description of the item, the item's value, and the final amount bid. The winning bidder is required to sign this form, which is a binding agreement that acknowledges the buyer's intent to purchase the item at the agreed-upon price. The buyer will receive a copy of the agreement and shall make payment at the cashier's booth or payment center prior to leaving the auction room *or according to other arrangements acceptable to Host Organization*. Once payment has been received, the item may be picked up from *auction item pickup location* or arrangements may be made at time of payment for shipping the item.

The program lists all auction items in the order they will be auctioned and also provides attendees the full schedule of activities at the event. It also provides instructions to bidders and lists auction rules, disclaimers, and policies. Item descriptions used in the advance program can be repeated in the auction program, but illustrations are no longer needed, because the real items will be on display throughout the event. Illustrations or photographs can be used as on-screen displays during the time the item is being auctioned.

Donors of auction items are given prominent recognition in the program. This should include mention of the donor in any additional displays or video descriptions of auction items. Event underwriters and sponsors, corporate donors, volunteer helpers, and staff should also be acknowledged in the program. The auction program can be handed to attendees when they arrive at the event or enter the auction room. Programs can also be placed at table settings and at strategic locations in the auction room. Format of the event and configuration of the room will influence how and where attendees receive the program.

Display Auction Items

Because the event program provides a guide to auction items, it serves to market items during the course of bidding. It also provides attendees other important information, such as the schedule of activities. However, programs can be discarded, misplaced, hard to read if lights are dim, or be the subject of many other oversights that result in their never being used as the event host hopes.

Although a well-designed program may provide attendees with an excellent guide to the event, the event program should not be the sole source of information about auction items, activities, and the schedule during the event. In addition to descriptions in the program, auction items should be on display in advance of and during the course of the auction on the event-room floor or onstage. Additional display of auction items, along with a running schedule of events, can be projected on big-screen displays throughout the event, as well as during bidding. Where possible, floor displays and projected displays of auction items should include marketing materials, such as brief descriptions or video clips. These should be designed in a fashion appropriate for marketing a particular item to potential buyers, for example, a vacation trip, restaurant night out, or spa treatment.

All of this information should be posted on the event Web site. Pages containing information about auction and raffle items can be designed so that item descriptions, photos, and videos can be used during the event to display information needed by bidders or raffle buyers. Design of a Web site to enable such use creates added efficiency and simplifies the work of event planning team members responsible

for managing the raffles and auctions. Kiosks featuring Internet access can even be set up at an event to allow attendees to browse the section of the event Web site carrying information on raffle and auction items. Attendees can also access information about these items by using their own wireless devices.

Auction Policies and Procedures

The advance event program, auction program, and event Web site should include auction rules and bidding procedures. These policies and procedures for the live and silent auctions should be published in locations and in a fashion that makes it reasonably certain bidders will have seen them by the time bidding begins. The policies and procedures help guide both the bidder and the host organization to address in a fair and consistent manner any problems or disputes that may arise. Some will take the form of disclaimers. This information also helps establish the authenticity and professional nature of the event and auction.

The following sections list items to be covered in the policies and procedures, along with sample text.

Establish the Credentials of the Host Organization

This item explains the legal status of the host organization, its membership, and mission. Following is example language:

- *<Host Organization>* is a Section 501(c)(3), nonprofit charitable organization *<host organizations recognized under other sections of the IRS Code should make appropriate changes to this section> (see chapter 21 for information about IRS recognition of nonprofit organizations).* *<Host Organization>'s* purpose and mission are *<describe charitable purposes and mission here>.* *<Host Organization>* appreciates the support of our donors, members, and other supporters in helping to further our mission, programs, and activities. Auction revenue funds a large part of *<Host Organization>'s* budget for accomplishing our mission.

• *For organizations qualified as charitable by the IRS:* Items donated to <*Host Organization*> for use in auctions and amounts paid to <*Host Organization*> in payment for auction items may qualify as charitable deductions. <*Host Organization*> is a qualified charitable organization; however, tax deductibility of auction items varies, and some kinds of donations do not qualify for deductions. The buyer of an auction item may be eligible for charitable deduction for that portion of the payment that is over the item's fair market value. <*Host Organization*> does not provide tax advice to donors or buyers of auction items. Please refer to IRS Publication 1391, *Deductibility of Payments Made to Charities Conducting Fund Raising Events,* and consult your tax adviser.

• *For organizations not qualified as charitable by the IRS:* Items donated to <*Host Organization*> and amounts paid to <*Host Organization*> as part of the auction do not qualify as charitable deductions. <*Host Organization*> is not a qualified charitable organization; therefore, no portion of any auction donation or purchase is eligible for a tax deduction. <*Host Organization*> does not provide tax advice to donors or buyers of auction items. Please refer to IRS Publication 1391, *Deductibility of Payments Made to Charities Conducting Fund Raising Event,* and consult your tax adviser.

Establish the Auction Date, Time, and Schedule

General information about the event date and time is provided. This gives notice to potential attendees when auction activities will be held. For events lasing several days and during which several auctions will be held over the course of the event, list start and ending times of silent and live auctions. Following is an example in which three auctions at a single event will be held at a hotel on November 22, 2011.

1. "An Event to Remember"
Date: November 22, 2011
Location: <*hotel name and address*>
Nature Adventure Buff Live Auction

An after-lunch live auction will feature 20 local weekend getaway trips for nature and adventure buffs. This auction will be held at 1:00 P.M. at the <*hotel name, address, and the room name*>. Preview of auction items will begin at 12:00 P.M. in the Lakeview Dining Room.

2. "Let's Go Fishing" Silent Auction
A late-afternoon silent auction will feature rods, reels, and other fishing items. The auction will be held 3:00 P.M.–4:00 P.M. at the <*hotel name, address, and the room name*>. Preview of silent auction items will begin at 2:30 P.M.

3. Evening Live Auction
The event's most spectacular feature will be an evening live auction that will offer the bidder many unique and exciting vacations, art, and sporting merchandise. The auction will begin at approximately 8:00 P.M., immediately after the <*Host Organization*> charity dinner gala. Preview of auction items will begin at 6:00 P.M. in the Grand Ballroom.

Define Terms Unique to the Policies and Procedures

Define the terms unique to policies and procedures of the fundraising event. Following are sample definitions:

• The term "auction" refers to silent auctions and live auctions.
• The term "auction item" refers to silent and live auction items, raffle prizes, game prizes, door prizes, table prizes, and any other merchandise, real property, or services purchased or otherwise acquired at the event.

Establish Eligibility Requirements

Specify all special requirements, if any, for bidding or entry to the event. For example, sometimes only members of an organization are eligible to attend an event. Some state or local rules may require that all participants in raffles be members of the host charitable organization (see chapter 20 for additional information on special rules and regulations). If this is the case and raffles will be featured at an event, the host organization must require all attendees to be members. Following are examples of language describing special requirements:

- The purchase of an event entrance ticket *<and "meal" ticket if the auction will be associated with a meal>* is required for registration for the silent and live auctions. Only registered bidders may bid on silent and live auction items.
- Upon registration, all registered bidders will receive a unique bidder number used to identify individual bidders during the bidding process. When requested by the auctioneer or spotters, bidders must show their bidder number.

Establish Allowed Methods of Payment

Winning bidders should be required to pay for their items by the end of the event and be allowed to take possession of items only after having paid for them. Generally, winning bidders are directed to a payment booth, and auction items are picked up from a secure storage area. Receipts may require specific language for donors to receive charitable deductions, as explained in detail in chapter 21. Following is language that can be used to make this clear in the programs:

- Payment for auction items will be accepted at the cashier's booth, located *<location at the event site>*. The cashier's booth will be open for financial transactions from *<time>* to *<time>* on the day of the auction.
- Payment may be made by cash, check, or credit card. Checks should be made out to *<Host Organization>*. Visa, MasterCard, American Express, and *others* are accepted. A receipt for the purchase will be issued upon payment. This receipt will be required to obtain possession of the auction item and to remove the item from the auction room.
- Auction items may be picked up from *<location of pickup>*. All auction items must be paid for and picked up by *<time>*. No auction items

may be removed from the auction room without payment and a valid receipt.

Establish Shipping Policies

Winning bidders may not wish to transport auction items themselves. Some items are too large to easily transport in a personal vehicle. If attendees travel by air to an event, it is almost a requirement for the host organization to supply a shipping option. For these and other reasons, the host organization should establish a procedure for shipping auction items on behalf of winning bidders and provide a policy to cover the risk of liability for such service. For large events where many items may be shipped by auction winners, an independent shipper may be used to provide shipping services. Following is language to explain shipping policies:

- For convenience, boxing and shipping services will be available on-site to take care of packing and shipping auction items. *<Host Organization>* representatives will be available to provide an estimated cost for shipping and coordinate shipping arrangements for items purchased at auction.
- If shipping is needed, ask for help at the cashier's booth for direction to a representative of *<Host Organization>* who will assist in making arrangements. Prices for shipping will be based on dimensional weight, insurance, and destination. Form of packing will depend on the shipping requirements of the item to be shipped.
- Shipping insurance will be required for all items packed and shipped. All costs for packing, packaging materials, shipping, and insurance are the sole responsibility of the buyer. *<Host Organization>* assumes no responsibility for any damage or loss that may occur during packing or shipping.

Include a Statement about Responsibility for Taxes

Include a statement that auction winners are responsible for paying all applicable state and local sales and other taxes for items at time of purchase, and for any added taxes that may be applicable and due in the course of registering real property or in the course of a trip or using a service.

Provide Auction Bidding Procedures, Conditions of Sale, and Disclaimers

Host organizations acquire auction merchandise and services in various ways but usually have no role in designing, constructing, or manufacturing any of the merchandise or providing any of the services auctioned or raffled off at charity events. As a result, the host organization cannot allow itself to be held liable for items purchased at auction that do not work properly, for items that are defective, for items that are not as claimed by donors, or for services that are not performed as described by donors and as anticipated by buyers.

This section of the policies and procedures is designed to reduce the risk of liability to the host organization for those and many other possibilities that are among risks in conducting an auction event where many kinds of services and items are purchased.

- Bidders must be registered and present during the auction to be eligible to bid. A person who bids on behalf of another person is assumed the bidder and will be held responsible for payment in its entirety.
- All items auctioned are sold "as is." *<Host Organization>* assumes no responsibility for the validity of the descriptions, authenticity, or condition of any item donated for auction. *<Host Organization>* makes no warranty or guarantee, express or implied, regarding any property or service sold at auction including, but not limited to, any warranty of fitness for a particular purpose or merchantability. Values listed are not warranted by *<Host Organization>* for tax deductibility or any other purpose.
- All items auctioned (whether goods or services) have been acquired or obtained by *<Host Organization>* from third parties. The buyer acknowledges that auction items have not been inspected by *<Host Organization>*. No services auctioned

are to be performed by or will be performed by *<Host Organization>*.
- All auction items are sold "as is." *<Host Organization>* does not make or express any warranties or representation of any kind or nature with respect to auction items. Nor does *<Host Organization>* deem to have made any representation or warranty of the description, genuineness, attribution, provenance, or condition of auction items. No statement in the advance or auction program, or made at the sale, or contained in the bill of sale or invoice or elsewhere is, or shall be deemed to be, a warranty, representation, or assumption of liability by *<Host Organization>*. Any written warranties with respect to items purchased are those solely and expressly supplied by the manufacturer or donor of such items.
- By making a purchase of an auction item, the buyer waives any claim for liability against *<Host Organization>* for any personal injuries or damages to property that may result from the utilization of any item, real property, or services sold. If any action or claim is made against *<Host Organization>* by an individual, entity, or state, local, federal, foreign, or political body for any matter whatsoever arising from the use of the auctioned items, or any actions or parties conducting business with respect to the auctioned items, the donor and/or buyer will pay *<Host Organization>*'s attorneys' fees and costs and will hold *<Host Organization>* harmless from any judgments.
- By making a purchase, the buyer agrees that the auction and purchases made at the auction shall be governed in all respects, whether as to validity, construction, capacity, performance, or otherwise, by the laws of *<State>*, except as preempted by federal law, and that the venue for any and all actions, including litigation, mediation, and/or arbitration, shall be in *<County, State>*.
- If during a live auction, a final bid for an item is erroneously taken from two bidders, the bidding is closed to everyone except those two bidders. The high bidder acknowledged by the auctioneer shall be the buyer. The auctioneer shall have sole and final discretion to determine the successful bidder in any auction. At each live auc-

tion, there will be predesignated bid spotters in the audience, and it is the responsibility of the bidder to direct bids to the auctioneer or nearest spotter. The auctioneers and spotters will make every attempt to acknowledge all bids, but *<Host Organization>* is not responsible for any missed bids.

• After each item's sale (whether through a live auction, silent auction, or raffle), the successful bidder (buyer) will immediately sign a Buyer's Agreement. The Buyer's Agreement will be brought to where the bidder/buyer is sitting for review and signature. The bidder/buyer will retain one copy at that time. For silent auctions, the Silent Auction Bid Sheet is considered a Buyer's Agreement to purchase the indicated item. All signatures on the Buyer's Agreement and the Silent Auction Bid Sheet demonstrate that the bidder/buyer acknowledges that the agreement is a legal and binding contract to purchase the item at the accepted bid price. Any changes, deletions, or additions to the description printed on the Buyer's Agreement, which are agreed to by the buyer and an authorized representative of *<Host Organization>*, must be noted and signed by both parties in order to be recognized as part of the auction purchase.

• Successful bidders may, during or immediately following the auction, present their copy of the Buyer's Agreement to the cashier's booth, where they may pay by cash, check, or credit card. Checks should be made to *<Host Organization>*. Visa, MasterCard, Diner's Card, Discover, and American Express are accepted.

• All auction items purchased must be paid for in full before *<deadline for payment>*. Any auction items that have not been paid for by the close of the event will be subject to *<a penalty can be assessed on late payments, for example, "after 11 P.M., November 22, 2011, a 10% surcharge will be added to the winning bid and this total will then become the purchase price">*. Any items not removed by the close of the event and for which arrangements for removal have not been made will be shipped at buyer's expense to the buyer (winning bidder), who shall pay to *<Host Orga-*

nization> a 10% handling surcharge in addition to direct costs for packing, packaging materials, shipping, and shipping insurance. Any bidder/buyer who leaves purchases at the event does so at the buyer's own risk. *<Host Organization>* is not responsible for any item not removed from the event by the winning bidder/buyer.

• All sales are final. All tangible goods purchased at auction are subject to the current state and local sales tax rates. There will be no exchanges or refunds on items or services.

• *<Host Organization>* shall retain the right to withdraw any auction item for any reason at any time during the auction up to the point the Buyer's Agreement is signed.

• Unless otherwise indicated, all auction items that are services or trips must be used within one year of the date of purchase at auction. Dates and times for applicable services or trips are to be arranged at the mutual convenience of the donor and winning bidder/buyer.

• It is the buyer's responsibility to contact the donor regarding purchased items that are services or trips and to make all arrangements for dates, travel requirements, and any necessary applications or paperwork necessary for licenses, permits, visas, or other requirements. *<Host Organization>* is not, and will not act as, a conduit or agent between the buyer and donor. Although *<Host Organization>* has made every effort to ensure the quality of donated services and trips, it cannot, and does not, guarantee the satisfaction of either the donor or the buyer.

• The buyer's signature on the Buyer's Agreement or Silent Auction Bid Sheet signifies and guarantees that the buyer has read and understands the rules and regulations and accepts and agrees to completely abide by and be legally bound by all the terms conditions, rules, and regulations for the auction.

Special Items May Require Special Policies or Procedures

Some trips and travel may be subject to "value-added tax," "goods and services tax," or other charges. Often these taxes are due and payable before travel can be started. Other items or activities during the course of travel may be subject to sales taxes. The host organization should not assume responsibility for these fees and must establish a policy that makes all such fees the responsibility of the buyer. Auction winners of trips should be required to verify travel dates and requirements with the donor in advance of travel. Winners should specifically ask the donor about any additional costs for services and travel requirements.

Auction or raffle winners of motor vehicles may be subject to certain taxes, registration fees, and licensing. The host organization should not assume responsibility for any of these fees. If motor vehicles will be offered at an event, a policy governing such items should be included in the advance and auction programs.

Auction or raffle winners of firearms are sub-ject to certain requirements, the nature of which should be listed among policies and procedures and discussed with a federally licensed firearms dealer. Generally, purchasers or winners of firearms are subject to a background check through a federally licensed dealer, and firearms may be obtained only from a federally licensed dealer.

Some auction merchandise may be very old or subject to certain verification requirements or otherwise be subject to rules requiring documentation intended to ensure items have not been illegally obtained. Items in this category can be antiquities and animal products that may be made of or resemble currently legally protected species. Generally, legal possession is verified by accompanying permits. Sometimes such items should be verified with relevant authorities. The host organization must use caution when accepting donations and selling items subject to regulation.

7

Negotiating Agreements with Service Providers

On behalf of one organization I worked for, I signed about 1,500 contracts per year for various types of services received and rendered. In most of these contracts, at least one and often several clauses covered compensating or holding harmless one or both parties for any money one party would have to spend to defend against a lawsuit caused by actions of the other party. These were the indemnification or "hold harmless" clauses of the contracts.

The corporate attorney who reviewed contracts taught me a valuable lesson by pointing out that few of the contracts we received that had been initiated by other parties provided equal protection or mutual indemnification. The contracts were strictly one-sided in favor of the other party. The contracts may as well have read like this: "You pay me for anything you do that might cost me extra money, but anything we do that may cost you extra money, you pay for, too, out of your own pocket." I gained respect for the attorney, as his goal was to create a fair contract that did not allow one party to take advantage of the other. Contracts my organization initiated started out with indemnification clauses that provided equal protection to both parties.

When we received contracts that were one-sided, we attempted to negotiate equitable indemnification clauses. This often became a sticking point, as many service providers appeared unaware of just how unfair and disrespectful they were by bringing such contracts to my organization for signature. We were a nonprofit charitable organization working to restore the natural environment. Why should a service provider think we should pay to protect them and ourselves from their mistakes? How rude is that? Unfortunately, at times we had very little negotiating room. For example, many government contractors were particularly uncaring *about fair contracting. The only means to win some negotiations is to gain negotiating leverage.*

Here's an example of what that can mean. While working for a different organization, our annual conference and event commanded significant negotiating strength. We usually held the event in Reno, which is a fair-sized resort-oriented city that has a large convention facility and many large hotels. At that time our convention and other meetings that were held concurrently constituted the largest event held in Reno each year, with about 15,000 to 18,000 attendees. We drew a sufficient number of attendees to book a high percentage of sleeping rooms at the city's hotels and many of the large event rooms, including the entire Reno convention center. Our event provided us with incredible negotiating strength. The result was a conference that was of great benefit to Reno's local economy and to our members, who enjoyed many perks and discounts during our event.

We also occasionally held the event in Las Vegas, which has more meeting space and hotel rooms than anywhere else in the world. Despite the large size of our event, it was only a moderate-sized event for Las Vegas. Our negotiating strength was much weaker there than we enjoyed in Reno. We did not "fill the city." We didn't even come close.

"FILLING UP" A FACILITY OR, as my organization did in Reno, "filling up a city," is an effective way to gain negotiating strength for event planners. This is one of the negotiating techniques described in this chapter, but don't be intimidated. Even an event attracting only a few hundred attendees can generate serious negotiating strength at a mid-sized event facility hungry for business. Hosting an event will invariably bring an organization's event planners into contact with service providers. Whether the planners decide on a full-service event facility or a variety of independent providers to help stage the event, when agreement is reached, all involved parties should draft and sign a contract covering all

services. Chapters 8, 10, and 22 address contracting matters and service requirements. Planners must be sure contract language provides the host organization the services desired as well as protection if services do not meet expectations or if the service provider causes an incident that carries risk of liability. The following sections describe recommendations for contracts and negotiating tactics that will help event planners get the best, most protective agreements possible.

Start Early

In any negotiation, the party pressured for time is at a disadvantage. The deadline in event-services negotiations is set by the host organization when it sets the date the event will be held. That date will be provided to the service provider at the outset of the negotiation. By starting early, the person negotiating the services contract will know the event planner is not pressed for time. For instance, if negotiating for food service, an early start reduces pressure on the event planner and shifts pressure to the caterer, who will know the savvy event planner has time to move on to another caterer if not satisfied that an agreement can be reached quickly.

In any negotiation, ultimate power goes to the party with the ability to walk away from the deal. For the event planner, the only means to hold power to walk away is to have plenty of time to make a deal with an alternative service provider. That does not mean the caterer (or any other service provider) will be backed into a corner by such a tactic. Any service vendor can negotiate only so far, beyond which the vendor must walk away as a matter of good business. For the service vendor there is always a point at which price equals the service's true market value and the vendor's true cost.

Negotiate for Advantage

Food and food-service prices are highly variable considering the unique nature and requirements of the many kinds of catered functions. Facility rental is also variable, especially when renting event space at facilities where meetings and events are regularly held and where services in addition to bare room space are provided. Depending on the level of service desired at a facility, cost can vary greatly, with considerable flexibility available to facility managers.

But everything has a true cost; thus, there is always a base-level price at which cost of service equals price. There is also a "market price," which is the price people generally pay for the service. This is subject to more variation than actual cost and may vary by season, demand, and service provider. List prices are probably not the best guide to value, or "what it's worth." At best, list prices should be considered a starting point for discussion with a service provider and may be a readily available means to compare one provider to another. After all, how could a caterer set prices on a list when requirements from one catering job to another are so individual and variable? It is impossible; so why believe a price list presented by a caterer is anything other than an invitation to the buyer to pay the highest possible price? Displaying a price list is surely a profitable practice, as there are many buyers of catering or event-facility services who approach shopping for these services as they would shop for food in a grocery store—whatever is marked on the can or box is the price they pay. So why is purchasing catering and event-facility services any different from buying a dozen oranges, a box of soap, or an oil change for your car?

Catering is inherently a negotiable item because food and service can vary greatly. Menus can be modified throughout the negotiating process. At some point in negotiations the price of food service and its value will merge. At that point the negotiation can be deemed successful, and the event planner can move on to other aspects of a contract. It is the same for facility rental. Unless the facility is bare bones, such as a picnic ramada in a city park, usually a host of options are available to the event planner. Most large event and meeting facilities offer numerous event-related services, including catering, security, and secure parking. As a result, there is potentially a great deal of negotiating flexibility when dealing with event-site managers. This also applies to many other services event planners may desire, ranging from event Web site design to decoration design.

What is the key to effective negotiation when service cost and price can vary so greatly? It is knowing the actual approximate market value and actual cost of the service. As is common today when purchasing a car, buyers check dealer cost, then compare that to the sticker price and the prices people are actually paying (market price). Although it may not be possible to look up "dealer cost" and "market price" for catering and event-room services, some information may be available over the Web. This information is also available by speaking to others who have used a particular caterer or event facility before.

For example, there are numerous Internet-based services that offer discount hotel rooms and other similar services. Consider the negotiating advantage of knowing a hotel "sells" its rooms over the Internet for less than its facilities manager is willing to offer during negotiations with a nonprofit organization seeking to reserve and book an entire block of rooms. More to the point, by asking direct questions of the service provider and doing a little thinking and digging, the event planner can gain a good understanding of how much flexibility there is for negotiation with service providers. If one particular caterer is the best in town and the event will simply fail to attract the "right" crowd without using this exact caterer, then negotiating room is virtually zero. Only by the good graces of such a popular caterer will there be flexibility in pricing. Where there is no competition, price is set on the basis of demand: that is, the caterer gets what he or she demands.

Assuming there are several acceptable caterers offering varying pricing, price is set by base cost to the caterer and event planners' willingness to negotiate among caterers and willingness to accept a price. In such a situation caterers must be flexible, as it will be the most flexible caterer that gets the business, all other factors being equal. Another influence will be the amount of business each caterer is capable of handling at any one time. At any point when there is more demand than there are caterers to service that demand, the edge in negotiating goes back to the caterer. For example, the event host seeking the best deal may learn quickly to avoid holidays and other dates when there is high demand for catering. On the other hand, if the event planner is tied to a holiday as a traditional event date, there may be little negotiating room, but the savvy planner will understand that and book early to maximize what little negotiating room there may be.

Caterers may also offer other services. The event planner may be able to negotiate more aggressively when these services are desired. Such services could include the caterer making arrangements for rental of tables, chairs, and room decorations. Other expanded services could include entertainment. When entering negotiations for catering, the savvy event planner can investigate matters such as demand, services, seasonal variation, rates received by others, ease of working with the caterer, appearance of waitstaff, and many other factors to help provide an advantage in negotiations or selecting among caterers.

Negotiating with event-site managers is similar and requires an understanding of many of the same factors as negotiating with caterers, but since a full-service event site can offer such a wide range of services, flexibility may be considerably greater. In smaller cities, there may be few facilities in which to hold events. But that does not necessarily mean event planners lack negotiating room. There may be few locations in which to hold an event, but there also may be few sizable meetings to be held. There will usually be a prime time or season of the year when an event site is in greatest demand. The advantage in negotiating price and services during such times goes to the event-site manager. In smaller cities, event planners often get to know event-site managers, helping ease negotiations.

Negotiations for events scheduled during the "off season" may give the event planner more negotiating room, so flexibility in event date can provide a great advantage in negotiations. Planners need to weigh any disadvantages to an off-season location, such as lack of skiing at a ski resort in summer. In addition, fewer services may be available at any location where service providers are accustomed to catering to large crowds at a different time of the year. Following are several other ways to gain a negotiating advantage.

Take Advantage of One-Stop Shopping

Because event and meeting facilities vary in services provided, negotiating additional services along with the basic bare-bones event-room rental may provide added negotiating opportunity. Although it may be advantageous to self-cater or acquire third-party catering, skillful negotiating may result in a significant financial savings by having the facility provide virtually all services for an event. If the price is right and services adequate, this greatly reduces the work of the arrangements team. In this situation the meeting facility, such as a hotel or convention center, provides all services: event room, catering, security, audiovisual equipment, furnishings, decorations, sleeping rooms, auction models, bar service, parking or transport, and entertainment. Consider the greatly expanded negotiating room and added areas where the facilities manager can give or take. For example, the facility negotiator may initially add in cost for parking, but the only real added cost to providing parking space is if parking attendants are required. These added services can be deleted with little consequence to the facility's profit margin but provide the facility manager a range of potential revenue streams and event planners areas for negotiation.

Individual related services, such as security, entertainment, tent rental, and table and chair rental, are each subject to market price set by supply and demand. If demand is great and competition absent, the price may be fixed and high. If there is little demand and many alternative competitive vendors for a service, many options are available for negotiation where the ultimate price is limited only by the true cost of the service.

To have a wide range of options during negotiations, the event planner should compare services of many service providers against the one-stop services of the single event facility. The savvy event planner now has the flexibility to look at overall costs of all services combined and also consider the risk and expense of time taken to coordinate and negotiate among many service providers. The overall price offered by a full-service facility manager will probably have considerable flexibility built in and can be negotiated for savings. There may be times when a facility and all its services are in great demand. The facility manager knows that during such periods the facility will be booked at top dollar by one party or another. For an event planner seeking to book a facility and full services during peak demand, there may not be enough negotiating room to get real price concessions for the single event.

Become a Regular for a Better Deal

Even in situations where it appears the facility manager has no incentive or need to negotiate, there may be viable negotiating options, especially for a host organization that holds several events, meetings, or meal functions over the course of a year. These additional functions could include annual conferences with many attendees requiring overnight lodging, several board luncheon meetings, and a holiday flea market and may be held at times of the year the facility has little business. If the organization agrees to hold its other meetings at the facility, in addition to the event to be held at high season, the facility manager may be willing to give up a little during high season to book considerable additional business during a part of the year the facility might otherwise be empty. Facility managers compute various business statistics, including revenue per available room. It is a simple matter for a facility manager to evaluate a proposal for services over a set period and negotiate rates based on several events, meeting, and services. This is an effective negotiating option but only for an organization that can provide the facility an attractive amount of business.

Fill Up the Facility

For the organization that can provide a very substantial amount of business to a facility, regardless of season, everything is negotiable, as in the example at the beginning of this chapter. The event planner has enormous negotiating strength at the point when an organization hosts events of such a size that all rooms in a facility are booked and all the facility's services are used at full capacity. This may

sound like a negotiating tactic available to only the largest of the nearly 2 million nonprofit organizations, but it is not. Moreover, the tactic may not be available to large organizations, because employing the tactic is all about matching event size (needs) to available services. Even a small event, when attendees need overnight lodging, can fill a relatively small conference center and hotel. Consider the negotiating disadvantage if planners hold an event at a large facility when the facility is in demand and the proposed event will use only a fraction of the available room capacity.

The Contract

The final step in effective negotiation is the most important: when the negotiations end, make sure all negotiated points are clearly and accurately put in writing in a contract. In the event planner's drive to put on the best event for the lowest cost, negotiating price for services is all about attention to detail. Knowledge is power, and the more detailed the knowledge, the more powerful the negotiating position. The more detailed the contract, the more likely the planner's best efforts at negotiating the best price and service will result in actually receiving that well-negotiated deal. The remainder of this chapter is largely devoted to arming the event planner with the knowledge necessary to confidently understand and negotiate an event services contract. Sidebar 7.1 provides suggestions that will apply to just about any negotiating situation.

Contracts can contain confusing and one-sided clauses. The event host's negotiator must be capable of reading, understanding, and negotiating a contract that is fair and protective to both parties and delivers the services event planners expect. Following are a number of common confusing provisions and suggestions for dealing with areas of potential concern.

Indemnification or "Hold Harmless" Clauses

Service providers commonly offer one-sided contracts as starting points for negotiation. This one-sidedness is most evident in provisions that shift

Sidebar 7.1. Helpful Hints for Negotiating Service Contracts

- Know what you want, ask for what you want, watch out for what you don't want, and know what you can accept—all in detail.
- Do not make the mistake of believing a service vendor's standard contract must be signed "as is." This standard contract can be used as an initial starting point for negotiations or discarded completely at the outset but should never be assumed favorable to the event planner's interests.
- Set a deadline or schedule by which to complete negotiations.
- Start early, so negotiations can be ended if necessary with time to seek a different service provider.
- Be open to discussion, alternatives, new ideas, flexibility, and mutually beneficial compromise.
- Have options and alternatives. There is little or no room for negotiation if there are no options or alternatives, and both parties know it.
- Remain calm, show respect, listen, and be reasonable. Negotiations over event services are composed of a series of business decisions based on an understanding or appreciation of how each party is affected by points of discussion, so be business-like and make it a point to understand the details.
- Give and take. Negotiations are rarely one-sided, so it will probably be necessary to give on some points to receive on others.
- Document points of agreement in writing as negotiations progress.

- Seek guarantees or warranties for quality, completeness, and timeliness of services performed.
- Look for what is not in the contract. Ask if there are hidden charges for things not in the contract that might cost extra money. Negotiate the extras, and document the results in the contract.
- Don't assume contract details are correct or that the service provider's negotiator has studied the contract for errors. Confirm details.
  - Make sure the service provider's negotiator has authority to negotiate contract provisions.
- Get the price up front. If price remains hidden during negotiations with the service provider seeking to learn first what the buyer is willing to pay, remember that it is up to the service provider to name the price, because it is the provider selling the service.
- Establish and maintain a good relationship with the negotiator.
- Know what you want, but be double sure you know what you got before you sign, because all leverage and negotiating room ends when the contract is signed.
- Read, know, and understand what is in the contract. Really. Know what each provision means. Really know what each provision means exactly. Chapter 7 describes common provisions contained in service contracts, what they mean, and how the event planner can work to ensure such provisions are written to provide equal or mutually acceptable benefits.

liability for any and all problems to the event host. These provisions can be so blatantly unfair that the unwitting event host may sign a contract that makes it responsible for paying the cost of defending a service provider for causing harm to event attendees. An example would be a caterer whose contract would have the event host accept blame and the expense of legal defense for service of improperly cooked food that sickens attendees.

The example at the beginning of this chapter described the difficulty negotiating fair indemnification provisions. In practice it is important to ensure that indemnification works both ways. This is a big issue. Indemnification is relevant in agreements with all service vendors, not just with caterers and event-site providers. These vendors include printers, audiovisual service providers, decorators, and so on.

The goal is to ensure against being held liable for anything that anyone connected with the event may do that could result in injury or property damage. Thoroughly understand indemnification provisions. Resolve any concerns before signing the contract. If necessary, get professional legal help to understand or resolve this area of the contract. Obtain liability insurance, or confirm the level of coverage of existing insurance.

Even with liability insurance in place, an inequitable contract can create significant exposure to liability. There is more to negotiating indemnification provisions than just ensuring indemnification is mutually protective. What is indemnified or not is also important. For example, the contract could specify that the host organization is responsible for any and all actions of attendees while present on event-site property. Usually, the event site's own coverage for liability would take care of people doing harmful things on or to its property, but this clause in a contract shifts that liability to the nonprofit organization.

This kind of provision places the host organization in a position of having to compensate a service vendor for any loss it incurs, regardless of who causes the loss. But a nonprofit organization has no control over what attendees may do on an event floor, in the lobby of a hotel, or in a convention center's parking lot. Attendees may not even be members of the organization. And even if an attendee is a member, the organization can't control what that person may do. Insurance may well cover the organization's officers, staff, and even legitimate volunteers working at an event if they do damage in the course of their duties at an event, but members or nonmembers just attending are not likely to be covered should they do damage somewhere along the way to and from or at an event.

What kinds of situations are possible? Here are a few examples, each of which could result in lawsuits naming the organization. An attendee could accidentally start a fire in the lobby that harms another person and damages hotel property, rendering the hotel unusable for a period. A person providing a service during the event could run over someone in the parking lot. A person could start a fight and harm another. The host organization would not ordinarily be liable for such things if done by one of its supporters, but if the host organization signs an agreement making it liable, then the host organization may be held liable. Maybe the host organization's liability insurance will defend and cover the action, but maybe not. Avoiding such situations is much better than defending them. The host organization's planners should ensure the organization is not responsible for anything it does not cause or for any person it cannot control. The indemnification clauses of a contract need to be thoroughly addressed in the course of negotiations.

However, there may be rational and insurmountable reasons why a service vendor cannot agree to an indemnification clause that is mutually and equally protective, for example, in a case in which the service vendor is prohibited by law from signing a contract that could commit funds beyond the scope of the contracted service. Some government agencies receive appropriations approved annually by elected bodies, such as city councils, the state legislature, or Congress. Laws may require that only the elected body may approve certain expenditures of funds, and then only from year to year. Since indemnification covers an unknown cost that may take place well into the future, such provisions cannot be included in contracts with some government agencies. This can affect event planners, for example, if government-owned and -managed event facilities are used, as many conference and convention centers are. If a mutually protective indemnification is impossible to negotiate, the host organization's planners must make a business decision considering the risks associated with holding an event where there may be some liability beyond what might be faced at an alternative site.

Not What You Expected?

Event sites are toured, catering staff are interviewed, excursion buses are inspected, and many other matters are checked out well in advance to make sure everything will be perfect for the event. But when the day of the event arrives, the perfect site, impressive waitstaff, and impeccably clean buses are not as expected. Hotel renovation under way, new waitstaff not as good as the ones interviewed, huge crowds and noise at the event site, a bus not nearly as nice as the ones inspected? These are all part of the landscape for event planners. Attention to detail in review and negotiation of contracts and additions to contract language can help ensure what is expected of a service provider is what is received.

RENOVATION AND DETERIORATION OF FACILITIES

Partially completed renovations and construction activities in and around the event site can make for a less-than-appealing event location, including noise, dirt, and plenty of unwanted commotion. Property owners have a right to make their facilities look better, so what is an event planner to do? The savvy event planner first asks about the potential for such activity and then includes language in the contract requiring the event-site provider (1) to give notification of any construction ongoing at the time of the event, and (2) to take steps (these can be listed in detail) to minimize or mitigate disturbance to event attendees if such activity is under way.

But event sites in the middle of renovation may not be the only surprise for planners. Consider the event site that is booked two or three years in advance, but the site owner has failed to keep up the property. A facility that was once clean and fashionable may have fallen into disrepair and become dirty. The caterer who was quite fashionable when booked for an event could have fallen on hard times. The solution here is to negotiate language into the contract that specifies the event site, quality of dinnerware, condition of buses, and so on be in substantially the same or better condition or state of cleanliness (whatever the concern) as when the contract was signed. Although a contract can't force a service provider to keep up a property or service quality, by listing penalties in a contract for noncompliance with the previously suggested provision, the event host can establish an avenue for termination of the contract or a means to demand some amount of compensation.

QUALITY OF SERVICE

Another matter for negotiation and inclusion in a contract is quality of service. Here is an example. At an event disrupted by picketing labor unions, hotel workers were on strike and replacements were not as experienced as the regular workers, which created severe service problems. Event attendees were forced to cross picket lines to park and enter the event site. Event planners had not anticipated this when they booked the event site, but it affected all attendees. The savvy event planner should seek provisions in the contract that require the event-site manager or service provider to provide notification of impending strikes and specify what will be done to ensure services are substantially the same as contemplated when the contract was signed. This can be specified in the contract.

LABOR DISPUTES

But there is more to address in this example than just poorer-than-expected service. There is the matter of crossing picket lines. Some organizations have a mission of labor advocacy, or its members have great empathy for labor. Such organizations' members may be reluctant to cross picket lines. Some social advocacy organizations may even have board-adopted policies prohibiting staff from crossing picket lines for business purposes. For such organizations, a termination provision "in the event of labor dispute" should be negotiated.

ROOM CHANGES

Large facilities may hold several events and meetings at the same time. Contracts may include provisions that allow the site manager to reassign rooms to allow for accommodating as many different meetings and events at the facility as possible. At the outset of contract negotiations this may sound reasonable, but when an event planner chooses a room, that choice should be based on the number of attendees expected and specific space needs for the auctions, games, entertainment, catering, and displays. Fundraising events can have unique needs not well described by attendee head count alone. Important criteria can be turned upside down if an event is unexpectedly reassigned to a room different from the one the event planners chose. The room could be too large, too small, or in a shape that will cause difficulties. For this reason event planners should determine if a room change will create problems. For example, if all the event facility's rooms are the same size and configured identically, there will be little risk in signing a contract allowing last-minute room changes. If the event site may have only one room large enough to meet fire-code requirements for the number of people who will attend the event, reassignment of room is not an issue.

If reassignment of an event room could cause problems, planners need to reduce the potential for last-minute surprises. Thus, it is entirely reasonable to seek a contract provision that lists specific rooms for an event, with changes subject to mutually agreed-upon reasons. It is also reasonable to allow changing rooms, for example, should the specific room chosen for an event sustain damage and be in a state of disrepair at the time of the event. There needs to be an option for reassignment under a set of reasonable circumstances. That option may be payment of a penalty or use of another room. Such matters are subject to negotiation. But also consider that by locking in a specific room (or anything else in any contract), the event host may be restricted as much as the service provider, which could become an untenable position for the event host should plans need to be changed.

For example, advance ticket sales to an event may be so successful that the size of the event will be double that expected when the event facility was booked. The room selected may be too small, and now the event host needs to change the contract to accommodate the larger group. A contract needs to allow for reasonable changes as required by both parties yet allow for full accommodation of the event. Be specific about what those changes may be, price agreements, and the circumstances under which such changes are made. If the number of attendees rises or falls from that originally anticipated, size of room may have to change, but the size of the room ultimately used must also accommodate the planned fundraising activities.

UNWELCOME NEIGHBORS

In addition to making unexpected room changes, facilities capable of accommodating multiple events and meetings allow for the possibility of having unexpected and undesirable neighbors. It is common for contracts covering large events held at large facilities to include provisions specifying incompatible organizations or types of organizations should the event manager seek to book additional events or meetings at the same time as the contract holder's event. Where such provisions exist, organizations listed as incompatible would not be booked concurrently with the organization holding the contract.

A multiday event I was responsible for overlapped in the same facility for about a day with a pornography industry convention. This early part of our event was mostly attended by organization leadership, so by the time the large crowds attending my organization's event began arriving, the porn stars

and others in that industry had already departed. Although our organization's members who were there didn't seem to mind the short sharing of facilities, I can only imagine what it would have been like if our organization had been established by people with a religious or family-values mission.

It is not unusual to see two organizations with incompatible missions holding events side by side. After all, in many communities one or two large hotels may offer the only desirable meeting space. Large ballrooms are often divided to accommodate two or more events at once, and in many parts of the United States there is a weather-related season for events. This means a large percentage of organizations that regularly hold fundraising events or conventions will all book the limited number of event rooms at about the same time, making the presence of unwanted neighbors a very likely possibility. The most common situation, however, occurs when a raucous event takes place next to a meeting room filled with people trying to have a quiet, peaceful get-together. Too bad the solitude-seeking group didn't plan ahead with a contract barring a noisy fundraising event next door.

Contracts routinely specify incompatible types of organizations, but aside from types of organizations, just the mere presence of one or more events under way can cause added commotion or concern for security. Such potential for conflict warrants a provision in the contract that lays out expectations for exclusivity. If exclusive use of an event site is not possible, the contract may specify what would be acceptable or specifically unacceptable concurrent uses of the meeting site.

Added Taxes and Fees

Events are regularly booked in hotels, restaurants, and convention centers where prices for rooms, meals, and other services are subject to taxes and fees in addition to regular city and state sales taxes. These come in many forms and can add substantially to the cost of hosting an event. Here are some of the more popular add-ons: occupancy tax, convention center tax, tourism tax, hotel tax, recreation tax, hospitality tax, economic development tax, visitors bureau tax, and food and beverage tax. Although an event planner can do very little about the taxes that may be applied to a bill for services, the planner should take two steps during contract negotiations to clarify the impact of such added expense. First, have the contract specifically describe any taxes and fees that will be applied to contract prices for services and then list all prices "including taxes and fees." This will ensure no surprises when the host organization receives the final bill for services. Second, tax-exempt groups may be exempt from paying sales tax or some special taxes. The contract should recognize any special tax status of the organization, and prices in the contract should reflect applicable tax exemptions.

The Exclusion Clause

One little provision, either listed separately or hidden within a larger clause in a contract, can make all the reviewing, understanding, and negotiating a service contract just wasted effort: the "exclusion clause." It kicks out of the way some or all the protective clauses added into a contract by the savvy event planner. The exclusion clause reads something like this: "Notwithstanding any other provision, the service provider reserves the right to modify _____." Fill in the blank. It can refer to any part or parts of the contract. In particular it could refer to areas in which the event planner has carefully negotiated protective provisions, such as use of a specific room or a specific audio system with especially powerful speakers. With an exclusion clause in the contract, the service provider attempts to recapture ultimate control, rendering provisions included elsewhere moot. Carefully review a contract for such clauses, and have them stricken or narrowed.

Payment for Damages

Contracts may specify how damages are to be computed or may list specific amounts to be paid for specified damages should something go wrong and payment for damages is warranted. Try to have damages listed by specific amount to reduce the opportu-

nity for misunderstandings. The amount of payment for damages should be set on the basis of any actual financial estimated loss should an event be canceled or otherwise changed in a fashion that affects the service provider financially. Any amount beyond actual loss would equate to a penalty payment, which is not acceptable.

Usually contracts with service providers include a provision for payment of damages only to the service provider. Should the service provider cancel or significantly change services, the event host organization obviously could sustain damages. Therefore, when negotiating the contract, attempt to ensure that clauses covering payment for damages provide mutual protection and payment. Determining a host organization's projected loss is more difficult than determining loss to a service provider. But it can be done. The costs of finding and engaging an alternative service provider can be added up. It also may be possible to determine lost revenue of the fundraising event if the host organization has an established record in event fundraising and has kept detailed event financial balance sheets. Pursuing payment of damages to a contracting party, such as an event host organization, can become complicated and will probably require engagement of an attorney. However, if the matter is addressed effectively in the contract, there will be a record of intent to serve as guidance in any settlement or legal proceedings.

Termination and Cancellation Clauses and Force Majeure

Sometimes an event has to be canceled. Maybe the projected sale of 1,000 tickets used in developing the business plan was overly optimistic. Maybe the reason for fundraising was resolved and the basis for the event rendered moot. Maybe a blizzard shut down the airport for several days, stranding attendees en route. Maybe the hotel lost all of its meeting-room space due to a fire and canceled all events until the damage was repaired. Whatever the cause, someone has to pay. Pay for what and how much? In short, if one party suffers a financial loss as a result of cancellation, the party responsible for the cancellation may owe the other party some compensation. Resolution is the subject of termination or cancellation clauses in contracts.

These are important provisions to understand and, if necessary, negotiate to a point of mutual fairness. Cancellation of fundraising events to be held by nonprofit organizations is common. Less common are cancellations by event sites or service providers, but in today's economy, if an event-site manager can book a large conference over a long period at a much higher rate of profitability than a small fundraising event would yield, the manager could simply terminate the agreement with the event host. Without a termination clause there could be a fight for damages, but even with a sound termination clause, the site manager may be making a simple business decision by paying a penalty for canceling the small fundraiser in favor of the much greater revenue and profit of the larger, longer, higher-profit-generating conference.

Contracts with hospitality service providers often include very specific cancellation schedules or written statements about cost and condition of cancellation. For example, if the event attendees will be booking sleeping rooms at a hotel, the event host will usually reserve a "block" of rooms. The number of rooms in the block will be based on the number of attendees expected and number of nights they will stay. These rooms are reserved well in advance of the event. This block reservation usually then becomes part of the overall contract for services, or it forms a separate contract. This reservation ties up the hotel's rooms from being booked by others, so it is not surprising that hotel management would demand some compensation if room reservations are canceled at the last minute. Many contracts include a specific "schedule" listing the cost to the host organization of canceling a certain number or percentage of rooms by certain dates. This kind of schedule or written statement of consequence can also apply to early departure, in which case rooms booked are occupied but not for the length of time the rooms had been reserved.

The same system applies to booking catering services. Price and payment to the caterer are always based on the number of meals to be served to a certain number of people. There is usually a little flexibility built into the catering estimate, but as the event nears, caterers need accurate numbers so fresh ingredients can be obtained and meals prepared. If there are fewer people than expected, the host will still have to pay for the total number of meals listed in the contract, as the caterer's costs and expectations are based on the original estimate of diners. Depending on the contract, payment to a caterer may be adjusted based on how far in advance the caterer is informed of the need for fewer meals, but consider that the caterer is expecting to make a certain level of profit and accepts or rejects jobs based on anticipated revenue. For this reason, a specific schedule for cancellation is often included in contracts.

With a cancellation (or early departure) schedule both parties in the contract know the cost and conditions of cancellation. This schedule is an area for negotiation. Whether it is a detailed schedule or written statement about cost and condition of cancellation, such a provision should be included in a contract. Leaving the consequences of cancellation unclear is an invitation for potential problems. It is just too common for the number of attendees to differ from estimates, which commonly creates disagreements about payment to service providers.

Force majeure is a category of cancellation that addresses the situation in which neither party is at fault for the termination. The agreement between parties is terminated without liability. This provision comes into play, for example, when a natural disaster causes the cancellation. A qualifying provision would be a hurricane that forces evacuation of the entire area or a hurricane that renders the event facility uninhabitable until repairs are completed. There is room for argument in the case of force majeure provisions over timing, that is, what is the acceptable period of time within which this provision can be invoked given the date of the unintentional incident causing cancellation and the start date of the event? It is clear in the example of the hurricane that an event to start on the day the hurricane hits qualifies under this provision. But what about the situation posed by repairs to the event facility after the hurricane has passed? How much notice should the event planner be given if the facility will not be ready in time for the event? The hurricane caused the damage, but what if the facility manager thinks the facility will be repaired in time, the repairs drag on, and the event host receives notice one day before the event is to start that the facility is not ready? Getting such timing matters clarified, as well as definition of what constitutes force majeure, is open to negotiation (e.g., is a flu epidemic subject to force majeure?).

The general rule of thumb is that the bigger the event, the longer the interval between notification of an unintentional termination and the start date of the event. It is one thing to cancel an event involving a few dozen people on a moment's notice, but canceling an event involving 15,000 participants is quite another matter. The event host planners should insist on an equitable force majeure clause. If this is missing from the contract and the unexpected results in the host canceling the event, the host organization could wind up paying its own losses, the hotel's losses, and forgoing any anticipated net revenues if the event had been held as planned.

Our organization had booked an international event for more than 15,000 attendees, and the event facility was in the midst of renovation. When it became apparent to the facility manager that the facility would not be ready in time, we had no choice but to cancel the event there. This was done many months in advance, yet a 15,000-person international event is a very expensive undertaking for which event planners are working two to three years in advance and attendees make plans months in advance. Since there were no other event facilities in the city that could accommodate such a large event, we had to relocate to another city. The result was a heavy penalty payment to my organization that covered the added expense of relocating the event.

Termination clauses provide the means, manner, and consequences of termination and should cover and protect both parties. It may be necessary to negotiate this protection for the host organization and have it added into the contract. It is unlikely mutual protection is already part of a written

agreement first offered by an event-site or service provider.

Proof of Insurance, Limits of Liability, and Carrier

Information about insurance carried by the service provider must be included in all contracts. Make sure the contract is specific about the coverage. Require service vendors to append "Proof of Insurance" to the contract document as an attachment. Service providers should have substantial insurance with reputable carriers authorized to do business in the state in which the services are performed. Insurance should be at limits sufficient to cover risks of liabilities imposed by lawsuits and other claims. Coverage should insure claims that result from the services provided for under the contract, whether the services are provided by the party signing the contract or by a subcontractor or anyone else directly or indirectly employed or directed by either of them. Insurance should include coverage for the following:

- Claims under workers' or workman's compensation, disability benefits, and other similar employee benefit acts applicable to the services to be performed
- Claims for damages because of bodily injury, sickness or disease, or death of any person
- Claims for damage to the property of third parties
- Claims for damages insured by personal injury liability coverage that are sustained by a person as a result of an offense directly or indirectly related to employment of the person by the service provider
- Claims for damage because of bodily injury, death, or personal-property damage arising out of the ownership, maintenance, and/or use of a motor vehicle

Privacy Protection

Membership lists and personal information about supporters need to be protected. Although some organizations sell such lists to raise revenue, many organizations make protecting personal information a practice. So an organization hosting an event at a facility or using specific services, such as a publicity firm to mail or e-mail event invitations, may need to address use of personal information of members and supporters provided to service vendors. Any contracts for services in which member information may be provided to the vendor should include provisions protecting the information from sale or use for unintended purposes. Contracts should be specific about allowable uses of personal information and include penalties for misuse.

Freebies and Incentives

Event-site managers and other service vendors may provide incentives, discounts, or free services based on volume, spending, or other reasons. An example is an event site associated with a hotel that offers free or discounted hotel rooms if event attendees book a certain number of sleeping rooms. The event host may also qualify for free use of meeting and event space based on attendee use of associated hotel and restaurant facilities. The key is to ask what is available and how to qualify. Add relevant details to the contract.

PART 2

Creating the Perfect Setting

8

Site Selection, Rooms, and Setup

Here I was, head of an organization poised to raise well over $500,000 from the people filling the auditorium, yet I had only a conceptual image of what was to happen next. No one had ever seen it. There was no way to have seen it, because there was only one opportunity to do it, and now it was time. The president of the organization didn't have a clue what was going to happen, and he was starting to fidget. He would soon become upset. The invited guests were enjoying themselves—so far. Waitstaff were serving drinks, which was expected, of course.

I could hear the small talk starting. People were beginning to wonder what was going on. This event could be an absolute smash hit—at least in theory. We were assembled in an auditorium. Nothing was onstage. The nothingness was purposefully obvious. Looking onto the stage was like looking into a massive black hole. Nothing was in the seating area. Nothing was in the aisles. Nothing was anywhere and everywhere. A few people sat in the auditorium's seats, but mostly they stood in small groups in aisles and just waited in the emptiness.

Then it began. It was barely perceptible at first. Music. The theme from 2001: A Space Odyssey, Also sprach Zarathustra, *began. With sound from scores of speakers the music built until it rumbled through the room at untold watts of power. Then ever so slowly, from out of the immense nothingness that was the stage vague shapes began to arise. The entire auction room rose out of dark empty space. In it were dozens of formally uniformed waitstaff, bars, ice sculptures, fine artwork, displays of chocolate and fruit, a small orchestra, tables, coffee and gourmet tea stations, and displays of auction items having values of five figures and beyond. As the music grew into a deep thundering force, the world's largest moving stage rose to its full height—*

the stage was advertised as being large enough to hold a commercial jetliner. The invited attendees were caught in mid-motion as the scene unfolded. Awestruck, they watched. When the stage/room was in place and the rumbling music stopped, a small orchestra started to play and the crowd cheered.

Now that was an entrance. The display of auction items, refreshments, and entertainment literally materialized before the future bidders' eyes, as opposed to the usual circumstance where bidders walk into an event. With smiles and an enthusiasm that lasted the evening, the invited guests shifted position a few feet onto the stage-now-auction display. They were right where we wanted them.

SELECTION OF THE PROPER site for an event is critical to attracting donors. A location too fancy or too run-down can deter people from attending, depending on who is expected to attend. A location too far away or in the "wrong" part of town may limit attendance. Conference facilities offer turnkey services—for a fee. State park picnic sheds cut costs dramatically. Some facilities are simply "in" this year, while others are definitely "out." Free parking is always an advantage. Thus, site selection is important.

Location, decoration, and ambience of the event site influence who comes and can influence the level of fundraising that can be expected. Events held in expensive surroundings can demand a higher level of giving, assuming the attendees' capacity to give matches the surroundings. Overall raffle sales and auction bid-to-value ratios can be higher when the setting is more formal given a group of attendees who can afford the offerings in the first place. Event planners can precisely establish a desired mood with setting and decoration. An elegant hotel ballroom will endow an event with a different mood than a tent outdoors. However, a tent outdoors can be decorated to mimic a very elegant venue. Depending on where the tent is situated, for example, if it were set in a beautiful garden along the reflecting pool ad-

joining an elegant mansion, the tent setting could impart every bit as much elegance and ambience as a fine hotel ballroom.

Each auction event must be designed with anticipated attendees in mind. In some instances, especially in areas where attendees do not have high incomes, staging an event in an expensive-looking facility may not increase giving at all. In fact, it is more likely to inhibit spending if attendees feel the organization is spending too much money on a fancy facility. Event planners must carefully evaluate and understand how attendees will react to event-site details, understand the fundraising objectives of the host, and know the giving potential of people who will come and participate in fundraising. Using this and other information, skills, and experience, planners must select the event site, arrange it to the specifications of the event, and decorate it to the taste of the organization and attendees. This is the challenge faced by members of the arrangements team responsible for finding the perfect site and making it ready for the big event.

Choosing Location and Facility

Among the first actions in advance of an event is setting a date and time to hold the event. Determining the location and reserving the facility in which to hold the event are next. These actions should be completed many months or even years ahead of the event date. How far ahead depends on size of the event, availability of local acceptable event facilities, and the popularity of those facilities.

For regional, statewide, or national nonprofit organizations, choice of location can be a daunting task due to the many options available. Some organization's event planners have established a traditional location and facility for holding events, whereas others rotate locations based on where membership is concentrated. Still others seek out facilities offering competitive rates, with less thought given to location. Location needs to be chosen carefully, giving full consideration to availability of transportation and how weather may affect it, availability of facilities and cost, image or perception of location, safety, proximity to donors and prospective attendees, availability of entertainment or sports activities, and so on.

Organization planners in small cities and rural areas may have few options. Civic centers, social association lodges, and similar meeting halls may be the only facilities available with enough floor space. If the organization is local, or is a local chapter of a large umbrella organization, the location of the event is set by where the local organization or chapter is physically located, further limiting choices. Most fundraising in the United States is done locally, so choice of location may be relatively straightforward, limited to choices like "suburbs versus downtown" or "riverfront versus hilltop."

In small cities and rural areas, event attendees are familiar with all event facilities, because all events are held in them. The only alternative in small towns is to take the event outside by going to a park or similar outdoor location, holding it in the open or under a tent or covered ramada. Planners have an opportunity to create a more unique setting than may be available at the standing facilities, which may be confining and lack versatility. Weather will have a greater influence on attendance at outside locations than for inside locations with climate control, but it is impossible to avoid the detrimental impact of truly bad weather. Because of the limitations in small towns and rural areas, any local facility may be completely acceptable to all potential attendees. If any are not acceptable, the savvy event planner will know which are not just from being an observant community resident.

In large cities, the key to deciding where to hold an event can be a lot like buying real estate. It's all about location, location, location! And so it is with the real estate that houses an event: location is important. Some locations and event facilities are more attractive than others to people who frequent fundraising events. Some are perceived to be in safer areas than others. Some have convenient parking. Some allow attendees to avoid the hassle of inner-city traffic. Some have romantic views. Some are run-down, and others have just been remodeled. In a big city the event planner has a wide range of choices, from full-service convention centers and hotels, to local parks and vacant city lots.

But what location is best? It all depends, and it depends greatly. Even well-planned events can be a bust if the event is held in a substandard location or somewhere the kind of people the host seeks to attract simply do not go. There are two ways to approach deciding on the location and event facility.

1. This approach puts selection of location first. Planners decide which part of town, what type of setting, or what other general set of characteristics they want in the area where the event facility will be located. For example, event planners may want to hold the event in "the best part of town." That said, the next step is to find the perfect facility in that part of town. Planners may want to have the event near recreational opportunities, such as a ski slope in the winter or beach in the summer. Once location is set, planners look for acceptable facilities and seek the best value for price, with value including how well the event will "fit" into the facility.

2. This approach puts selection of facility first. Planners decide to hold the event in a particular facility or identify several facilities, based only on the characteristics of the facilities. This renders location of those facilities a secondary or irrelevant consideration. If planners decide there is only one facility in which the event can be held, negotiating leverage may be reduced greatly. How to address that is described in chapter 7.

Getting a rock-bottom deal from a facility manager on event-room rental may not be the best way to resolve the matter of event location and facility choice. It could be the worst possible deal in the long run if the location or facility is a mismatch with space and service requirements for the event, attendee expectations, ease of use, quality of service, or the planners' intended impression on attendees.

One indicator of the popularity of a facility or location may be how easily space can be booked. Popular event venues may charge a little more and require booking in advance. Event planners are delivered a not-so-subtle message when they learn one facility can be booked only a few weeks in advance whereas another must be booked two years in advance, but interpreting that message requires some added research. Just because an event facility is popular does not mean the facility's managers are easy to work with or accommodating to the special needs of an auction event. However, planners can easily investigate the popularity and ease of working with managers of one facility versus another because a great event facility will be the site of many events. Contact event planners from other nonprofit organizations that hold events at popular facilities. Also, consult members who are known to frequent charity events. Spend a little time in the facilities if possible. Take self-guided tours of event facilities, walk through kitchen areas and loading docks, and wander through meetings and receptions to look at service areas and watch how supervisors and workers behave.

If meeting facilities have professional staff to assist with event planning, planners ordinarily need only provide an estimate of the number of expected attendees to receive advice on facility space and special accommodations. But that advice may not be correct if the staff are unaccustomed to events featuring multiple fundraising activities and large live auctions. Full-feature fundraisers require more space than banquets or the simple dinner-auction. Events with numerous fundraising activities are distinctive with unique space requirements based on the number and types of fundraising activities, sales booths, entertainment, exhibit areas, and so on. A banquet facility's professional planning staff may not fully understand the space requirements for fundraising events. Space is needed for the head table, silent auctions, auction-item display, raffle tables, games of chance and skill, display of acknowledgment to donors, and any "advertising" space offered as part of donor agreements.

It is mandatory that event planners know what is needed in a facility to accommodate the event as planned. Select a facility that will handle the anticipated number of attendees and all event paraphernalia without the main event or live auction room feeling too crowded. Envision the facility set up for the expected number of attendees and all the anticipated fundraising activities. Imagine round tables, seating 8 or 10 diners. Picture table arrangement, tables for prize displays, ticket sales admis-

sion area, cashier's booth, merchandise sales area, stage, screen location, and so on. Draw a room diagram, fully loaded. If relevant, do this with the help of facility staff.

In large metropolitan areas, planners can likely find a facility having all the desirable features. The next challenge event planners face is linking such a facility to excellent catering, adequate parking, public transportation, low cost, easy access, proximity to attendees, and other attributes that may be desirable. Planning events in small towns and rural areas leaves planners with few choices, but since there are so few choices, selection is easily made—the right choice is usually obvious. With an understanding of what to look for and how to make adaptations, event planners will be in a good position to make sound choices.

None of the previous information is particularly relevant to planners working for host organizations that tie their annual event to a specific location associated with the organization. An example is an organization formed to support research at a hospital, and the hospital has a large cafeteria or auditorium where the event is always held. Nonetheless, such an organization may be able to boost event proceeds if it were held in a more substantial setting. Event planners can confidently do so by following the advice in this book.

Arranging for Success

Longtime organizers of a local annual auction-banquet fell out of favor with leadership of the parent organization and were told they were no longer allowed to fundraise under the organization's name. Thus it happens in the sometimes fickle world of volunteer-driven organizations that people can fall in and out of favor for any or no reason, even though this annual auction had been run honestly, faithfully, and efficiently for many years. It was among the parent organization's top auctions year after year.

I had not attended this particular annual event in the past but had attended other auction events held by the same group who had planned this one, and those other events had been first class. Thus, it was with considerable curiosity that I decided to attend the replacement fundraising event. I was led to believe it was being put on by a new group of volunteers. I was even more curious when I heard that one of the features of the new event was the shape of the room in which the event was to be held. The room was circular. It was a somewhat aged sports arena. Round arenas are great for boxing matches, theater-in-the-round, demolition derbies, and rodeos, but this was to be a fundraising auction.

This was definitely going to be a challenge for the new planning team, or so I thought. Circular rooms have no set front, back, or sides. Activities need to be set off in some fashion, and circular areas don't lend themselves well to that. An arena may be great for spectators in bleachers who can watch what's happening on the floor, but an auction involves everyone being on the floor. Event planners don't want spectators; they want active participants.

When I arrived, I found the space well arranged, with booths, activities, and work spaces lined up in front of the curving walls. There was a stage at one point along the wall and on-floor seating was typical with round tables each seating 8 to 12 people. Everyone had a good view of the auction stage, and the sound and other visual aids were as good as I have seen anywhere. This new planning crew knew what they were doing.

Out of curiosity I asked one of the leaders of the new planning group how they were able to cope so well with such a challenging event room. He said they had been doing it this way, in this same room for years, always with great success. At that point it became obvious to me that the people leading the new group had been members of the old group's work team. This was not their first event in the circular room. The old group's leadership had been ousted, but many volunteer workers remained true to the organization. They had learned well by performing their jobs in previous years, and here they were now leading the new event. Experience and time-honed testing had made this spot home to "their" event.

EVERY DETAIL OF THE auction room must serve to enhance fundraising and fix the attention of attendees on the auction stage during the live auction.

The room and its setup have an effect on bidders and the audience. Size, shape, height, lighting, table placement, stage location, entry, service entrance—everything should be evaluated and taken into account. The perfect room, in all respects, may be hard to find in big cities and may be impossible in small towns and rural areas. Innovative approaches to room arrangement may be needed when having to make do with what is available.

Elements of Room Arrangement

Hotel and event-facility management staff may provide advice on room arrangement as part of their job. A few may be knowledgeable about the basics of an auction room, but most probably will not. So it's up to event planners, generally members of the arrangements team, to work with facility managers to organize the room for maximum fundraising advantage. Event planners need to explain what they want as clearly as possible (this requires event planners' knowing what they want). It is the job of facility staff to respond with answers to questions about what can be done in the amount of space and configuration of the room.

This close interaction between facility staff and event planners in setting up a room is probably most important the first time a fundraising event is held in a particular facility. After the first time, planners and facility staff gain experience. Host organization event workers will learn how to make adjustments over time and will become less dependent on facility staff. Each time an organization returns to a location to hold an event, planning team members should seek the advice of volunteers and staff who were on past arrangements teams. Each year, event planners should explore new options by making adjustments and trying new ideas. Experiment to find improvement, but keep changes to a manageable level so it is possible to measure the direct result of a specific change.

For example, one of the basic elements of an auction event is the silent auction. Silent auctions are generally arranged in the main auction room along one of the side or rear walls. What if such an arrangement proved to be inconvenient because growth of the event placed greater requirements on wall space in the main auction room? This is a time to experiment. The silent auction could be held in an adjoining room. Maybe secure lobby space could be used. Perhaps a central, concentric configuration could work, where tables and displays formed into two concentric squares stage the auction to allow for better use of space.

REGISTRATION AND RECEPTION

A reception table where event workers register attendees should be set immediately outside the entrance to the room, if possible. If not, set it immediately inside the entrance. Everything else should be inside the event room or the event area if fundraising activities are being held outside. Attendee access to the event should be through a single entryway to control entrance, prevent attendees from coming onto the event floor without being registered, and allow for effective security. Attendees should be held at the reception area until they are fully registered. Strategic placement of the registration table can help control lines and processing during registration.

Another reason for having the registration area outside the main event room is to use "free" lobby or hallway space to provide maximum space in the event room for auction-item display, arcades, dinner tables, maneuvering space, and so on. Processing registrants can take up a large amount of floor space, because crowds and long lines can develop in front of the registration area. But registration lasts for only a short period, usually through the first hour or less of the event. A large amount of space dedicated exclusively to registration is wasted after that.

If there is no option but to bring registration inside the event room, once registration is over, this now largely empty space should be reused. One of the most effective ways to reuse the space is to convert it to space that receives heaviest usage toward the end of an event. It can be reset as space to process auction-item payment. Registration materials can also be maintained at the location in case there are late attendees, but resetting the bulk of space serves dual purposes, lends cost efficiency at the event, and keeps the area occupied so the event room continues to appear full.

NOTE: *Although the registration table should ordinarily be located outside the entrance to the event room, there is an exception. If the room is overly large for the event, including tables, arcade booths, exhibits, and so on, then the registration area should be located immediately inside the auction room. This will help give the room a more "full" appearance.*

TABLE ARRANGEMENT

Most often attendees are seated during the auction and other parts of an event, such as during meal service. Where to put tables and chairs then becomes a strategic decision, as they can take up considerable floor space. Seating can be in stadium bleachers, auditorium chairs, elementary school cafeteria chairs, folding chairs set in a circle on a neighbor's lawn, or at picnic tables. Some events are held outdoors, where bare ground provides the auction floor, and rocks or logs the seats. Although the varied possibilities can provide unique opportunities and challenges, most fundraising events make use of tables and chairs set in a room at a meeting facility, such as a hotel ballroom. Such settings provide meeting planners ideal opportunity to strategically arrange tables, chairs, and other furnishings so the site is comfortable for attendees yet organized for effective fundraising.

If the event is held in a single room, any meals are generally served at tables on the main live auction floor. Seating at dining tables then serves as seating for the live auction, which is often held immediately after meal service. Thus, setup for dining also serves as setup for the live auction, which makes dining table placement a matter of critical importance to fundraising. Even though a caterer or an event-facility's staff may provide excellent guidance on how to best set up tables in a particular room for the ultimate in meal service, what may be a superior arrangement for serving a meal may not be ideal for fundraising. Facility staff's goal may be to squeeze as many people possible into the smallest room possible, and the caterer's goal may be to arrange tables in a way that facilitates waitstaff access to and from food-service areas. Neither of these goals may support effective fundraising. Thus, the advice of the caterer or event-site staff may be useless, or worse yet, poisonous to fundraising. Success in fundraising is not dependent on creating the perfect setting for eating; it is dependent on creating the perfect setting for raising money.

The event planner needs to determine the best arrangement of stages, game booths, auction tables, display boards, registration, and cashier areas—in conjunction with dining tables—to enhance fundraising activities. Effective fundraising requires having sufficient space between tables where bidders are seated. Everyone seated needs a clear view of the auction stage and display screens. Auction models and spotters need clear access to all bidders, which means access to everyone seated at tables. Round-top tables seating 8 to 12 people are generally recommended because well-placed round tops almost guarantee access space between tables. Many event planners consider round tops the rule for events because in most rooms it is hard to arrange them so poorly that access is restricted. However, truly inept placement of a series of round tables can be as disastrous as tightly packed square or rectangular tables. Meeting planners must focus on an arrangement that meets a goal of free, comfortable access between and among tables, without tables being so far apart as to make people feel uncomfortable. Tables of any shape strategically placed can meet that goal.

Once event planners decide on room arrangement, they should make a drawing showing location and arrangement of tables, stage, displays, booths, and anything else that will be placed into the room. This drawing should be detailed, indicating approximate sizes of furnishings and measured positions in the room. The drawing should be signed and made part of the written agreement with the event-site manager and caterer.

SIZE OF ROOM AND FURNISHINGS

A meeting planner can be faced with a room that is shaped or sized in a way that makes arranging furnishings a challenge. A dinner-auction event I attended was held in an extremely large room, but there were only about 50 attendees. We were seated at round-top tables set for 8, but these tables easily could have seated 12. The seven or eight tables in the room were placed about equidistant from each other and from the walls of the room; neighboring tables were at least 20 feet apart. The stage was placed very near the wall at the front of the room, at least 20 feet from the closest table. This arrangement looked awkward and felt awkward to attendees. It's hard to determine how fundraising may have been affected, but the entire event had an odd feel to it. Each table of attendees seemed to be its own island, surrounded by a sea of carpet. Although the number of people was not really considered poor or unexpected attendance for the event, the combination of size of room and arrangement of room furnishings made the event feel like a failure to attendees.

How could the event planner have better accommodated the event in such an oversized room? The first step would have been to "wall off" a more appropriately sized portion of the room, perhaps by using attractive portable screens. If that option was unavailable, tightening table placement would have helped, along with focusing lighting in the area where the tables were located and darkening outlying areas. Some greenery, such as large potted plants or trees, could have been borrowed or rented (artificial or live) to help wall off unused areas. Between darkening unused parts of the room, using brighter lighting over the event area, and constructing "walls" of greenery, the mood would have been very different. The event area would have become a "room within a room" providing attendees a more intimate, comfortable setting for dinner and better seating for the auction. If darkening a portion of the room had not been an option, the greenery alone would have helped. Anything can be used as a barrier if necessary.

USING THE SAME SPACE TWICE

In a room too small, available space must be used efficiently, but there is only so much that can be crammed into an area that also must accommodate the activities of many people. The key is to manage timing of activities taking place so that two or more separate activities can share the same space over the course of the event. This may require resetting an area for a second activity or just removing a fundraising setup to expand open floor space. For example, the section of the room used to stage games of skill and chance can be reset once the games are over to accommodate additional tables and seating for the dinner and live auction. The area where a silent auction is held can be reset when the auction is over to accommodate a self-serve dessert station. The reception and registration area can be reset as the cashier's booth and distribution area for auction merchandise.

Timing of event activities becomes critical if parts of a room are to be reset to provide space for different uses. If the game area is to be reset for additional dining, games must end exactly as planned, and the area needs to be reset immediately. Workers need to be on alert to remove game booths and set dinner tables in place on time and quickly. This involves planning. All workers must know their roles. Furnishings for resetting need to be positioned and ready to move into their proper place. Resetting an area may look like a fire drill, but if workers know what to do, the switch can take place quickly, converting a multipurpose event floor into the setting for the next fundraising activity. Reusing space by resetting an area is a practical way to efficiently use small rooms or to better accommodate large numbers of attendees in large rooms.

Effective Fundraising Flow

For some inexplicable reason, people sometimes take on a herd mentality when traversing a room full of tables of auction items, arcade booths, raffle booths, exhibits, and other interesting things to look at. One person will follow the person in front, seemingly in a blind fashion. Followers go at the pace of all others and tend not to linger or vary from the pattern of the person immediately in front. Because interest level for one item versus another, or one activity versus another, varies from person to person, it is important for everyone to go at his or her own pace, exploring all the enticing auctions, raffles, and other items.

With a crowd lined up, one person behind another, it is natural for many people to remain in place. They may be uncomfortable breaking in or holding up the line. This can result in a person not seeing a fundraising item that would have been of interest, because someone was in the way. Another person may not have time to look carefully enough at an item or have enough time to bid on a silent auction item or to buy a ticket. Many people simply are shy and don't want attention turned to them, which they may perceive to be the case if they hold up the line. The line itself is just something that happens. It is not planned. Holding it up is of no consequence to anyone of any authority, but attendees may feel uncomfortable doing so. And the feelings and perceptions of the attendee guide his or her choices.

My advice about the herd syndrome is simple: break it up. Somehow break it up, because it is deadly. Use whatever means necessary, but in anticipation of facilitating a comfortable flow of the crowd throughout the event room, set up the room in a fashion that thwarts this follow-the-leader parade. At a minimum, avoid setting up the room in a way that encourages it. The distinguishing characteristics of arrangements that encourage this behavior are not clear, so I can advise event planners to watch for this behavior and in subsequent years make changes to arrangement of activities on the event floor and see what happens.

I once attended an event at which the arrangement of a room encouraged an extreme example of this syndrome. A herd processional took place in a small room just off the main auction floor. The silent auction was in the rectangular, rather narrow room. Along three walls and parts of a fourth were tables on which sat silent auction items. The herd adopted a door at one end along one of the long walls as the entrance, and on that same wall at the other end of the room was an exit door. There were no signs designating the entrance and exit; the crowd's movement made it obvious which was the entrance and exit. This was a parade to the extreme. People entered, moved along the tables, and went out the exit in a steady stream. Speed of movement was constant for the duration of the silent auction. I entered the stream, like the herd animal I had automatically become, moved along, and exited. People then formed up in line at the entrance to make another pass.

I am not particularly shy and usually don't have a problem being in someone's way, but in this instance I found myself not wanting to gum up the works. But I also wanted to take a better look at a few items, so I did what so many others were doing: I went around again. I noticed that people would make a pass, then make a second pass to take a second look at items or to very quickly write down a bid. It was quick. We just moved along at a constant pace. When attendees reached an item of interest, they wrote their bidding number on the bid sheet and moved on. People who bid on items continued to make this circuit by remaining in line, to protect their bid and bid again if needed. It was the darnedest thing. Attendees moving around in circles in this line were prevented from going elsewhere to play games or take part in whatever else was going on at the event. As many as half or more of the attendees were being held captive. This is the way the silent auction had been done for years. In this same side room, this curious continuous circular parade had been taking place year after year. It was a small community that loved their event. They raised money and had fun.

Negotiating

When an organization holds an event in a meeting facility, whether that facility provides full services or just meeting space, there are usually professional staff or a facility manager who will assist with event planning. At a minimum the staff or manager will work with event planners to develop an agreement or contract for services at the facility. Initial reservation of event space will often call for a written agreement. Sometimes an initial deposit is required, or a payment schedule is associated with this agreement. This early written agreement is a contract, although it may not be as detailed as a final contract, which may come later.

Depending on how the initial agreement is written, it may have more or less binding provisions. Event planners need to take the agreement seriously and understand what they have signed. Planners should negotiate mutually protective provisions, because this initial agreement may give the facility

manager the right to vacate the agreement on the simple basis of opportunity to rent the same space to a larger group that will more fully occupy the event facility (presumably providing the facility manager greater revenue potential). The agreement may not grant similar leniency to the event host to vacate the reservation should a better deal be offered by another facility (also see chapter 7).

In areas where there is competition for event and meeting space, giving reserved space away to another party may be common. In small towns, providers of event sites and services may have a limited number of events, so breaking an agreement to accept a larger group may not be of concern. Provisions to cancel the reservation may be as important to the host organization as the event-site manager. Sometimes event planners are uncertain of the host organization's intent to follow through on holding an event on a particular date, or at all. What if planning efforts bog down or few donations of auction merchandise are received? The key to negotiating an effective cancellation clause is knowing what is needed. If event planners are absolutely certain about the event date and site, the letter of intent should include the most binding language they can negotiate. However, flexibility to seek alternative event facilities or cancel a reservation makes better sense when there are uncertainties.

Event planners also lose some room for negotiating a final contract with event-facility managers if the reservation agreement includes heavy penalties for taking an event elsewhere. One way to clarify enforceability of an initial agreement is to make its provisions contingent on discussions and negotiations that will take place in the future, for example, when the final contract is developed with mutually agreed-upon event-room rates, catering prices, and so on.

Be Prepared to Negotiate

Many items will require discussion and negotiation between event planners and event-facility managers. If the facility offers a full range of event-related services, there may be an extensive menu of options to discuss. The final result of these discussions and subsequent negotiations will be a signed and binding contract for services with the event facility. Whether that contract is for a bare room or a turnkey event with all the trimmings, the work by event planners that goes into developing that contract is among the most demanding and intimidating aspects of making arrangements for an event. If services are needed but not obtained as part of an event-site agreement, those services will need to be contracted through negotiation with independent service providers or performed by the host organization's own workers.

Negotiations over the event room and event-related services are best done by people with experience in the hospitality industry. However, since there may be no person with such experience available to event planners, this book provides various guidelines. In conjunction with the guidelines please observe this disclaimer.

DISCLAIMER: *Negotiations over general contract provisions are often conducted by attorneys. I am not an attorney, and in making the recommendations in this chapter and elsewhere in this book regarding contracts, agreements, and negotiations, I am not representing anyone's legal interests. I am not claiming that anything stated herein is legally valid. Thus, I need to advise event planners to seek the assistance of counsel in any negotiation and before signing any legal document.*

Also see chapters 9 and 22 for suggestions on negotiating security and food services, and chapter 7 for general negotiation suggestions.

Set the Range of Services

Event planners must be specific in the contract. Discussions and negotiations, whether regarding room size, seating arrangements, table decorations, audiovisual equipment, parking, or security services, establish mutual expectations and price. The contract sets agreements in place. Goals for the event planner are to get the best value for price and reduce opportunity for misunderstandings. Seek

to lessen the likelihood that attendees will receive services that are substantially less than or different from what planners expect to be delivered by service vendors.

The contract will grant the host organization access to the meeting facility's common space and the specific rooms in which the event will be held. There will be specific conditions on use. Beyond that, specific services are almost always chosen and listed separately or as a package (listing a suite of services). This section of the contract will read almost like a menu from a restaurant. The level of detail should be such that it makes clear what the event planner really wants. For example, event planners may want free parking for attendees. But that may not be enough detail to preempt an event-facility manager's seeking a few extra dollars by requiring attendees to use a paid valet service to have cars parked in the free parking spaces the event planner so wisely negotiated. Here the planner did not get language in the contract that reflected exactly what was wanted, and the facility manager took advantage of a novice event planner.

Sidebar 8.1 contains a list of what to include in a typical full-service contract, services that are generally required or desired for hosting a fundraising event. Not all events will require all of these services. However, any required or desired services should be carefully discussed and negotiated in detail with service providers. Results of the agreement reached should be set in writing and signed by both parties. Event planners seeking to have the organization's volunteers provide services should seriously consider the capacity of the host organization to do so. Refer to chapter 20 for suggestions on reducing risk of liability to staff, volunteers, officers, and the host organization's assets.

Be Aware of Required Services

Event planners are often irked by outrageous charges demanded by contractors a host organization is required to use when holding events at large convention centers. In this case contractors are granted exclusive rights to provide specific goods or services. As part of a contract for use of the facility,

Sidebar 8.1. **Typical Content of the Facility Rental Agreement (Contract)**

Not all of the following will be relevant in all contracts. For example, an event where attendees do not require overnight lodging will involve a contract with fewer items to cover than those listed.

- Exact date, start, and end time of the event
- Provision for early setup and late takedown
- Number of attendees
- Diagram of room arrangement, including tables, stages, displays, and screens
- Name of supervising on-site facilities manager
- Requirements for security personnel and security measures to be taken inside and outside
- Conditions for obtaining electrical connections, including costs of electrician labor and electrical usage
- Audiovisual equipment to be provided, including equipment models, cost of equipment rental, and cost of operators
- Provisions to address medical emergencies, availability of medical responders, and on-site medical-response equipment
- Sleeping rooms
  - Complimentary rooms or conditions for acquiring complimentary or discounted room rates
  - Procedures for attendees to book rooms
  - Block room rates and cutoff date for receiving block room rates
  - Conditions and price for rooms reserved after block room rates expire
  - Allowance for early or late arrivals
  - Allowance for rooms booked before and after event dates
  - Allowance for departure prior to checkout date
  - Penalty or conditions for underbooking room block
- Costs of additional optional services, such as parking, valet, and recreational and health facilities
- Costs of additional required services and specific details of the service, such as security, electrical connections, and after-hours heating or cooling
- Costs of additional required fees, such as taxes or special assessments
- Conditions for price escalation and price guarantees
- Provisions for penalties in the event construction or other problems delay the event; that is, what happens if loss of the site or changes to the site harm the event
- Specific food, beverage, and bar service and how this will be provided (see chapter 9)
- Number of support staff and supervisors who will be on-site available to assist in the event of a facilities problem
- Clear statement of conditions allowing changes, additions, substitutions, cancellations, and special stipulations
- Specific responsibilities for cleanup and timing of cleanup
- Special considerations and provisions for attendees with disabilities
- Special arrangements for families traveling with children
- Special arrangements for pets
- Statement of compliance with laws, indicating that both parties will abide by prevailing laws
- Last date for changes for room requirements
- Function room guarantee or conditions that allow the facility manager to change function room
- Clear statement of force majeure
- Mutually protective indemnification clause
- Proof of insurance, limits of liability, and carrier
- Amount of deposit and payment schedule
- Refund and cancellation policy, including specific conditions or schedule for refund

event planners may be required to use such exclusive services while on the convention center's property. A contract may require the organization to hire in-house contract labor to do things the organization could easily do themselves, such as run an extension cord. Table setup, audiovisual service, candy on a table, security at entryways, plugs in a wall—all may be required to be performed by in-house contract or union labor.

With an exclusive contract and a requirement to use in-house or preferred vendor services, a lack of competition or alternatives guarantees no incen-

tive for providing prompt or quality services. This situation is not unique to big convention centers. Many hotels are no better. Outrageous prices forced on host organizations or event attendees allows an event-site manager to keep room rates low and make up for the low rates by charging high prices for hidden and required additional services.

This is a tactic similar to "loss-leader" ads in newspapers designed to get customers into a store, where they find only higher-priced items actually available. When an event facility is booked on the basis of low room rates and the event planner fails to ask about add-ons and required services, the host organization may find booking the event at the facility was not such a good deal after all. This is often noticeable in the area of food service, where food and beverages, such as a pot of coffee and tray of cookies, can be priced several hundred percent higher than cost; a pitcher of tap water placed on a meeting table may cost more than the finest bottled water; and items an event planner might assume to be free, such as electricity to a computer stand or use of a public address system, may cost hundreds of dollars. Price is whatever the preferred vendor has negotiated with event-site management. The contract states that use of in-house and preferred vendor services is mandatory. If there is a problem with the way something is set up, if work needs to be completed quickly, or if the price is outrageous, too bad. The host organization is stuck.

Can contracts be modified to avoid unreasonable in-house service costs? This is a tough one. Organizations can be stuck with such provisions. Any flexibility an event-site manager has to negotiate such matters may be controlled by contracts between event-site management and the service providers. The key to negotiating successfully is to know the limits of flexibility. When an event-site manager says there is no flexibility to negotiate, that may be the truth. But be cautious here, because the manager may be rewarded for requiring use of in-house services or preferred vendors. For example, there may be added revenue that goes back to the property owner when a preferred vendor is used. There will also be an advantage to the event-site manager having personnel familiar with the event site and known to the manager.

Here are negotiating tactics: Find out what is required and if there are alternatives. Get specific. Maybe the event-facility manager wants to require in-house services but is not contractually compelled to do so. For example, it may be possible to hire separate security guards but not separate caterers. There may be flexibility to use independent service providers by paying a surcharge or by agreeing to a charge for event-site staff to oversee the work of independent service providers. For the event planner seeking compromise, it may be necessary to offset concessions here with concessions on other matters for which there is greater flexibility. The manager may also be frustrated by the poor service and high fees of these service providers but may have no alternatives.

Event planners may also be surprised to learn of required services they did not even know they needed. For example, the facility may require on-site security personnel or standby medical responders, billed at an hourly rate for each hour the host organization uses the event site, with pricing set at a standard outrageous amount. Explore all possibilities. Asking tough questions may reveal that it is possible to use the host organization's own volunteers or outside contractors for certain services under certain conditions.

Hiring independent outside contractors or using volunteers can provide significant savings. One of the first questions to ask is if there are requirements to use in-house or preferred vendors, after which should come questions about extra charges for necessary services, such as electric connections and public address systems. The key here is to get all costs listed, clearly and openly. There should be no hidden costs. If the site is being booked one or two years in advance, it may be possible to set a cap on the price of in-house service or set a more reasonable price-escalation formula. If use of a particular event site means using in-house or preferred vendor services, the cost of all the additional and required services should be the subject of negotiation and added into the overall contract price for services as part the contract.

Holding Events at Sites outside the United States

Holding an event in a country other than the United States or Canada presents additional challenges for US nonprofit corporations. I was responsible for an organization that had members in more 80 countries and chapters in about 40 countries. Chapter members in many of those countries held fundraising events, but these were always planned and run by members who were citizens of the country where the chapter was located. Although the general trend or desire was to emulate the kind of fundraising conducted in the United States, the events were often very different from those held in the United States. The differences were a consequence of varied traditions (in some countries fundraising for charity was very much a foreign concept) and national rules covering money-raising activities.

Here is a sampling of issues that may arise for an organization hosting an event outside the United States. Food-service standards may differ, raising money may be regulated in odd ways, state controls over gaming activities such as raffles and games of chance may be difficult to understand, complying with rules governing gaming could be risky, legal liabilities may differ, laws governing disputes may differ, meeting-facility incentives differ, currency issues may arise, standards of language and translations in contracts may create liability, there may be differing standards for accommodating persons with disabilities that create compliance and liability issues, lax standards may not protect personal information, standards differ concerning security, and issues may arise with visas, passports, and other entry and exit matters.

When holding an event outside the United States, seek help from experts, including a person in the United States who regularly assists in staging events in the country where the event is to be held, and a person who is an event expert who resides in the event-site country. Rules, standards, traditions, and laws that govern and influence meetings and fundraising differ by country and from what a planner deals with in the United States. It is essential for event planners to seek competent help.

Even holding events in the United States that attract large numbers of attendees from other countries presents serious added challenges. Our annual fundraising event drew people from all of the countries where our members lived, including members who exhibited and sold goods and services at a trade show and who donated merchandise and services for auction. There were always problems getting goods into the United States, travel delays, and attendees denied exit from their country or US entry. There were also financial issues, because of exchange rates, and much more.

If large numbers of attendees from outside the United States are expected to attend a fundraising event, retain US counsel to assist with entry and exit problems and other emergencies involving the foreign travelers. Not much help can be provided to an attendee stranded in another country, but being prepared to give rapid assistance once a person reaches the United States can be the difference between a happy attendee or a very upset detainee.

9

Food Service

My staff in a regional office of a national organization had been holding a successful annual full-feature auction event for many years. The event was a great activity that pulled staff members together. It allowed individual staff to assume important leadership roles as volunteers outside their regular work duties. It was a modest-sized event, drawing about 120 people, but the net proceeds were always impressive. Among the features was a very good evening meal served family style that was usually dished up quickly, with large bowls and plates of food either on tables when attendees were invited to be seated for the meal or served immediately thereafter. It was enjoyable, taking little time away from fundraising activities.

The event planners did not consider the meal to be the central focus of the evening, but attendees occasionally mentioned having good food when commenting about what they enjoyed about the event. I suspect that subtle message about good food didn't register with event planners the year they decided to cut costs. One of the cost-cutting ideas was to reduce the expense of the meal, thus boosting net revenue. The notion was well meant, and members of the planning committee who were in charge of finding less expensive catering did what appeared to be a credible job locating a less expensive alternative.

Unfortunately, the lower-cost meal service did not go well. Maybe the caterer misjudged the help needed to serve or the amount of food required to feed the number of attendees. Or maybe the caterer simply undercut the service, skimping on quality and quantity to meet the bid price per meal. Either or both are possibilities, because service was slow and faulty, the quality of food was poor, portions were skimpy and served cold, and there was not enough food for everyone. The result was a lousy meal, if you were among the (un)lucky ones to get served, that affected the mood of attendees.

People grumbled about the food during the event, but most remarkable was the discussion among attendees long after the event. When asked about the event, people invariably mentioned the food was bad. Consistently, the key and often only thing people recalled about the event that year was bad food. Fortunately, the food that night was not as bad as it could have been. I don't recall anyone becoming ill. Poor-quality food is an unfortunate yet familiar feature at many events. National survey results indicate event attendees rate food low on the list of reasons they attend events. But for years, people had been coming to the staff-run event and enjoying good food. Poor food service in that one year set the organization up for failure, maybe not because the food was so bad but because it was so much worse than what attendees had expected.

Event organizers were aware of the disappointment and learned from the experience. The next year the former caterer was invited back, and attendees were treated to the standard of food and service they had previously learned to expect. During that meal I paid particular attention to the food and service and conducted my own totally unscientific analysis. After all, I was curious. I had gone through the year hearing grumbling about the previous year's food and had done some grumbling about it myself.

Were food and service truly great at the event held the following year? Not really. The food was just good but clearly much better than the cost-cutter meal the year before. It also marked a return to having the meal served "family style," which the attendees seemed to appreciate. It was not any better or worse than in the earlier years when this same caterer had built a reputation. People hadn't made too much fuss about the food one way or another during the many earlier years because it was just "good," not necessarily exceptionally good. But when event attendees were presented poor food, the reaction was immediate and long lasting.

The lesson here is that food can stay in the background as long as it's adequate to good. But however well intentioned the host, food and food service will not stay in the background if they are bad. Bad food can ruin an otherwise successfully organized and managed event.

FUNDRAISING EVENTS almost always feature some form of food and drink service. This may seem like common sense. After all, potential bidders and raffle ticket buyers need to be kept comfortable. Attendees cannot be expected to keep their mind on event activities if they are thirsty or hungry. They may leave the event to get refreshments. Maybe they will return, but even if they do, event planners have lost valuable fundraising time. Attendees leaving because there is no food or drink, because food is overpriced, or because the wrong kind of food is served would be particularly likely if the event were oriented toward families and children were present. If there is no appropriate food or drink on-site, once the kids become thirsty or hungry, families will leave. Event planners often give too little thought to the kind of food and drink to offer or to the level of service to provide. They may consider food and drink service more an inconvenient obligation than a fundraising opportunity or requirement.

To Serve or Not to Serve

When should food and drink be made available? Provide food and drink when and where needed to keep people happy and focused on the objective of the event—fundraising. At well-planned events, fundraising opportunities are set in motion immediately upon attendees' entry. As a result, if attendees are likely to be hungry or thirsty when they arrive, food and drink must be readily available when attendees arrive at the event site. An event starting on a weekday at 6:00 P.M. will probably be attended by many people coming directly from their places of work. They will be hungry when they arrive. Some attendees may not have eaten since breakfast. Sometimes a snack will be all that's needed at first, but if the event is longer than an hour or two and takes place during a normal meal time, heavier food is usually required to satisfy people. This need not be a full-service meal, but both quantity and quality of food need to be sufficient to keep attendees satisfied and their mind on participating in the fundraising fun.

If alcohol is available to attendees, then food needs to be available, too. Alcohol enhances the feeling of hunger. Alcohol served with no food available, especially if the event takes place at a time people are normally getting hungry, such as late afternoon, could cause attendees to leave the event in search of food. And it's not just an enhanced feeling of hunger that might drive attendees to leave. Alcohol can reduce attendees' inhibition to offend the host. Even though a person who has not had a drink but is hungry may remain at an event out of respect to the host, an attendee with a few drinks down the hatch who gets the munchies might just leave and say to heck with a host that's too cheap to set out a few nuts and pretzels. Therefore, if alcohol is available to attendees, whether through a cash bar or self-service refreshment table, some form of food needs to be made openly available, served directly to attendees, or sold on-site. If there will be no full food service, then serve hors d'oeuvres or snacks.

Menus and Meeting Attendee Expectations

Selecting the perfect menu and serving food quickly and flawlessly will keep attendees happy and well dispositioned to participate actively and generously in fundraising opportunities. Making this happen is where the magic of event planning comes into play. There simply is no way to advise event planners in a generalized fashion what kind of food and level of service will work best for each of the myriad events that takes place. There are examples in the following sections, but there is no substitute for knowing the audience. People who attend a fundraising event—an organization's members and supporters—have a preference. The job of the event planner is to figure out what that preference is and cater to it.

In moderately sized and large metropolitan areas, catering choices cover the full range of possible options for type of food and level of service. Food and service will also be somewhat linked to the location of the event and facility. People attending an event held in an elegant hotel will always expect finer dining and a higher level of service than attendees at an event held in a rescue mission's social hall. However, they will be equally pleased with the food and service in either situation, as long as their expectations for quality and service are met—or exceeded.

The choice of menu should also match the goals and objectives of fundraising. High-dollar fundraising may demand a more refined dining experience than an event seeking funding for new playground equipment. But even high-dollar events can get by with minimal offerings if that is part of the ambience the host organization is trying to create. For example, a nice barbecue at a board member's ranch, where grilled chicken is accompanied by sides of beans and a cob of corn, may be perfectly acceptable to people about to donate tens of thousands of dollars to a cause.

Options for level of food and service can be limited in small towns and rural locations. Some small towns may be blessed with a restaurant or social club that provides gourmet-level catering and service, but that is an exception. In small communities all events may offer a similar standard of food and service. People who frequent fundraising events in the community know the standard and are perfectly happy when they get what they expect.

The objective of planning for food and service is to meet the attendees' expectation for quality and quantity of food and the host's expectation for flawless and quick service—plus. The word *plus* means event planners should strive for meeting attendees' expectations, demanding a high level of vendor service, plus just a little extra. It can be little things, like asparagus in the late fall or a particularly attractive, high-standing chocolate dessert. Quick, efficient, and unobtrusive service with no surprises seems to work well. If the meal is to be served to diners, the host's planner should insist on having a few more waitstaff available than the caterer recommends. Those staff should be available in the event of a problem and "roam" with carafes of iced tea or coffee, ready to be of immediate service. Having a coffee cup refreshed or the bread basket refilled before having to ask is always a welcome surprise, even in the best of restaurants.

In locations where planners have a reasonable number of options, careful consideration of the prospective attendees should be standard practice. Food offers such a wide range of opportunity that it might take one or two events to get menus and service level just right. Food-service options also vary widely, with options limited sometimes by choice of location. With any option, however, quick, efficient, and unobtrusive service is the key, whether that service is self-service or attention by a full waitstaff.

Getting Food and Service Just Right

Food at an event need not be fancy if the event is not a fancy affair, but whether ordinary food will do or exotic and mysterious dishes best complement the event, the food needs to be of high quality. Even the fanciest of dishes will fail to impress if stale, limp, soggy, gritty, or worse.

Test food and food service of caterers by asking for samples. Even better than sampling food, go to an affair where the prospective caterer is serving food similar to what is being considered for the planned event. While there, in addition to sampling the food for taste, pay attention to how the food looks, how it is being served, how quickly food is served or buffet items replenished, how clean the service area is being kept, and how clean service personnel appear. If possible, ask the individual who contracted with the service vendor if the service and quality of food are satisfactory. Ask for references showing where the caterer has provided services similar to those being planned. Contact the references and ask questions about service, food quality, and overall experience working with the caterer.

Event planners may be tempted to seek catering services from a favorite restaurant. Some restaurants cater events and are very successful doing so, but catering for a large group at a location remote from a restaurant requires a very different approach to food preparation and service than serving a typical dinner crowd at the restaurant itself. Even when food is prepared in advance in a restaurant's kitchen, by the time it reaches an event site and is served, it

may present a very different dining experience than if it was served in the restaurant. Dishes that need to be served immediately upon preparation, such as many fish dishes, are especially prone to disappoint diners at events. There is also the matter of speed of service. Some restaurants serve quickly, but many do not and may not understand or even be able to accommodate the need for speed at a fundraising event. In fact, the idea of high-quality, speedy service may be an oxymoron in the minds of many restaurateurs.

The key to finding quality catering is to search for a caterer that provides quality service and food of the specific nature and for the specific number of attendees expected to attend the planned event. Insist on sampling menu items and confirming the caterer's capacity to deliver the food, drink, and service experience event attendees will expect. Don't make the mistake of assuming that a caterer who flawlessly serves impeccably designed and extraordinarily delicious hors d'oeuvres for a gathering of 10 can deliver the same-quality experience to a group of 500. But even a caterer who can deliver an unforgettable hors d'oeuvres service to that same crowd of 500 may be totally overwhelmed if a full three-course meal has to be prepared.

Have a Healthful Event

Choosing menu items to match the level of event and tastes of attendees is a given when working out details of food service. Event planners may also make a point to declare they expect food served to be of high quality. Once that is done, most event planners move on to other matters. They may never define what they really want in food and food service. For example, if the planner insists that the food-service contract specify that the caterer supply food of the "highest quality," what exactly does that mean? How will the caterer interpret quality?

With a little more work, the event planner can take steps to ensure there is a meeting of minds with the caterer about what constitutes high-quality food or any other detail of food, menu, ingredients, preparation, or handling. For a host organization with members who are focused on health and nutritional well-being, quality might be defined by insisting on organically grown fruits and vegetables and use of low-fat varieties of sauces and dressings served on the side. Another mark of quality might be an emphasis on using food from local producers or using fresh, never-frozen meats and fish. Such details, if important, need to be discussed with the caterer and written into agreements covering menu items and expectations for quality.

Give a Little Extra

The quality of food should not be so high as to lead attendees to believe that they are funding too much "party" and not enough charity. There is a fine line between too fancy and too plain at a fundraising event for charity. For example, food should be of a kind, and service at a level, that the donor "expects"—plus a little extra. "Extra" means affording a little something that provides an unexpected pleasure. This need not be, nor should it appear to be, an expensive or extravagant item or addition. In anticipating expectations, the event planner needs to consider that attendees expect the money they spend on the event to go to charity; therefore, the appearance of too much money going into food, facility, service, or anything else having a cost to the host organization can backfire.

The Need for Speed

Caterers may be well accustomed to luxurious dining affairs where a leisurely dinner is followed by after-dinner dancing. That sounds inviting and may be exactly what the caterer insists will be just perfect for the event. The savvy auction-event planner knows better. Fundraising comes first, and since the amount of time for the live auction may depend on getting meal service out of the way as fast as possible, food-service speed matters.

Instruct the caterer on the need for speed. Make speed of service a detailed part of the written agreement or contract, and add into this a requirement that service not only be as fast as possible but as unobtrusive as possible. If faster service costs a few extra dollars for additional waitstaff, it may be

among the best investments the host organization makes. An extra buffet line may cost a little extra, but consider the time saved as money earned on the fundraising floor. The alternative is fundraising opportunity forgone in a buffet line.

With a well-planned dinner, moving quickly and saving time, the fundraising opportunity per person is increased. When effort is made to accomplish this significant catering feat, there must be fundraising opportunities provided to effectively use this extra time. Lulls in an event break the pace and plunge a hot event into a bath of ice. Power fundraising requires a well-organized team. Everything must mesh together, and it can. Every minute attendees are in position to spend money counts toward bottom-line net revenue. Make every minute count.

Envision the well-served auction-event dinner as fine dining on steroids. Time spent dining is time stolen from fundraising. Sure, dining is important and plays a vital role in the fundraising event, but that role must complement fundraising. The best way to do that is provide the best food and refreshment possible at a pace that enables almost continuous fundraising action.

Self-Catering

Self-catering is an option for food and service that involves the organization's members or volunteers doing the bar service, cooking, and serving. This can be a potluck dinner where food is prepared in volunteers' homes and brought to the event site and served, or it can be a meal the organization's members themselves cook and serve on-site at the event if the facility has a self-service kitchen. Refreshment bars serviced by host organizations' volunteers are common at fundraising events. Although self-catering may sound like a great way to cut costs and serve good food and drink, local ordinances or regulations may require certain standards be met. For example, potluck dinners may be completely prohibited where members of the public are invited and admission fees charged.

Local ordinances covering food preparation and service often apply if food is served at functions where the general public is invited. These ordinances may require inspection and certification of food-preparation and serving areas and licensing of at least one person to oversee food handling, preparation, and serving of food. This licensing generally involves a person attending a training session on safe handling of food and then passing a test. This licensed overseer would need to be present throughout the event during food preparation and service and would be responsible for ensuring that safe food-handling requirements are followed. Inspectors generally have the right to inspect food handling at any event where the public is invited. Surprise inspections can take place.

Local ordinances may also require a specific permit be acquired to serve alcohol or food to the public, even if food preparation and service are done by a professional caterer and alcohol is served by a service vendor. Generally, if such permits are required and event planners have contracted for bar or catering service, the service vendors will assist in acquiring required permits. However, if the caterer should neglect to inform the host about permitting requirements, it will be the host organization, not the caterer, that receives the citation. Always ask the caterer if there are permits or requirements that need to be taken care of in advance of the event.

Ordinances may not cover activities held only among an organization's own members. A fundraising activity such as a church social where members meet at a local park and cook dinner over an open pit would not be regulated in the same fashion as the same church's members holding a fundraising event open to the general public where they serve food cooked over the same pit at the same park to non-members.

Food-Service Options

Event planners can choose from various options for type of food service. The following sections describe some of these choices.

Station Reception Service

Food is placed on tables ("food stations") at locations around a room. Attendees take what they want, when they want it. Food service can continue over an extended period, reducing the number of service staff needed. This method can have the added advantage of taking place at the same time fundraising activities are under way. Attendees can choose to participate in fundraising or enjoy their meal. However, if attendees take lengthy periods to eat, fundraising revenue may be decreased. One means to address this is to not provide full seating for the number of attendees. Provide instead a few small tables or high-top tables where people stand. Wherever there is food service, some seating should be available, because some people may have disabilities that require them to be seated while they eat. If the event is family oriented, children will need to be accommodated with seating. However, there are numerous ways to limit time spent eating by making it inconvenient to linger without making attendees uncomfortable. Attendees must be allowed to comfortably satisfy desires for food and drink, but consideration must be given to getting them back to participating in fundraising opportunities as quickly as possible.

Station Meal Service

Food is placed on tables or stations around the room and served for a limited period of time. Attendees serve themselves, or waitstaff serve at the stations, but diners proceed to stations at their own pace. Food items can vary by station, or all stations can contain the same menu of food items. There should be as many stations of large enough size as needed to allow quick and efficient service for the number of diners. Catering staff or volunteer servers must be diligent in keeping stations clean of spilled food, neatly arranging food items on the table, serving diners, and maintaining a supply of serviceware. Food needs to be protected against sloppy or unclean diners if self-served. This service option may be undesirable where children are allowed to self-serve at the same stations as adults. Children are prone to reach into serving trays with their hands, touch food, or take a food item and then put it back into a serving tray. Adults seeing this done by someone else's children can become disgusted and not eat. An option for this service method at family-oriented events is to have a separate children's serving area with menu items and portions selected specifically for children. A good caterer can assist planners in addressing such situations.

Buffet Meal

Food is served in bulk from heated or chilled service trays lined up on a table. Diners form a buffet line and move along the row of serving trays as they are served food or serve themselves. Multiple service tables and buffet lines can be in use at the same time. The number and size of service stations must be sufficient to quickly serve the number of people expected to attend. Nothing is more frustrating than waiting in a long service line for food, or waiting for your table to be called as other tables of attendees are finishing their food, having already made it through a buffet line. This is so simple yet often ignored by event planners. The general rule of thumb is to have at least one buffet service line per 50 diners. This "rule" assumes food trays remain adequately stocked for the duration of service.

Partial-Service Seated Meal

Some portion of the meal is served by waitstaff directly at the tables. This can be in the form of family-style service where each food item is delivered to the table in bulk service vessels, such as baskets, bowls, and large plates. Diners pass the bowls and plates around the table and take what they want. Another option is to have the main course and side items preplated and served directly to the diner. In this option, not all courses of the meal are served directly to diners. Salads can be conveniently placed on tables in advance of seating. Dessert can be located at dessert stations where diners can select items. This service option allows for faster service by waitstaff, because they only have to bring one item to the table while diners are seated.

Full-Service Seated Meal

The entire meal is brought to the table in courses by full-service waitstaff. This can be a simple meal or a meal with multiple courses, wine, and after-dinner drinks. The full-service meal typically involves several served courses and requires the greatest number of waitstaff and highest level of planning to accomplish successfully.

Reception Only

Receptions involve serving appetizers or other limited food offerings, sometimes in conjunction with open or cash bars. If alcohol is served, there should be adequate food service (see elsewhere in this chapter). Appetizers, snacks, fruit, and desserts are all possibilities. Food can be offered to attendees from trays carried around by waitstaff, placed on tables, or just offered at the refreshment bar.

Restaurant Sampler

Restaurants or catering services that regularly cater events bring food to the event and serve it to attendees. Service is usually set up at stations, each run by a separate restaurant or caterer. But food service can take place in any of the other usual ways, such as by roving servers for appetizer service, in buffet lines, or at a partial- or full-service sit-down meal. Food preparation for such events is generally done off-site, so food-preparation-area requirements are usually minimal. The event host generally has less control over types and quantities of food served, because this option is most often used when restaurants and catering services donate some or all of their services for the event.

Self-Catering Options

Members of the host organization or other volunteers prepare and bring food to be served at an event or prepare and serve food on-site. Although self-catering is an option for private events, and in particular small private events, food service for large events open to the general public where people pay for admission may require special certification of food handlers and inspection of food-preparation and food-handling facilities. Home kitchens, personal transport containers and serving vessels, and lack of food heating and cooling equipment in service areas make it unlikely that self-catering options will meet health and safety standards required for many events. In addition, even if health and safety standards do not apply, event planners need to consider the risk that home-prepared food may not have been handled properly. Even with food prepared by volunteers using on-site cooking facilities, there is always a risk of food-caused illnesses and diseases such as hepatitis being passed by poor food handling. Can the host organization take such risks, or is it better to pass the risks on to paid food-service providers? Options for use of self-catering include self-catering for all of the previously described formats. The following formats for food service are exclusive to self-catering.

POTLUCK

Attendees are asked to bring a hot or cold entree, dessert, or salad to be served at the event. Food service relies on food preparation and transport to the event by staff or volunteers of the organization.

BROWN BAG

Attendees bring their own food and refreshments. They do not share with others. From the standpoint of health, food safety, and risk management, this is the least risky self-catering option. Provided the event host does nothing to affect attendees' food, any problem with the food is the result of attendees' own negligence.

All About Alcohol

Full-service and self-service cocktail bars, kegs of beer, wine at dinner, and so on are standard fare at many fundraising events. Today in the United States so much attention has been focused on the problem of drunk drivers that the amount of alcohol served per person at events has decreased dramatically—

and with good reason. It would be tragic for a person to be harmed due to the negligence of a drunk driver leaving a charity event. Furthermore, court judgments have imposed heavy penalties on business establishments, organizations, and individuals who have served excessive amounts of alcohol to a person who then drove a vehicle and injured someone.

It is to the benefit of the host to be aware of any signs of drunkenness of attendees and make sure people who appear drunk are provided safe transportation home or are otherwise protected. Such protection also benefits others who could be hurt and reduces the risk of liability to the host. One method event planners have used to reduce risks to the organization is to serve alcohol only at cash bars, and only then where the cash bars are operated solely by and solely for the benefit of the business establishment housing the event, such as a hotel. Presumably, such establishments have policies and insurance to cover incidents involving alcohol. However, the host organization is immune neither to lawsuits that may be filed nor to the publicity in the aftermath of an accident. No charitable organization can afford to be saddled with blame for injury or loss of life because of a driver's drunken behavior upon leaving a charity fundraising event.

In the "old days" at many events open bars opened early and stayed open throughout the entire event. Drinks were served free and freely to attendees. The idea was that liquor loosened wallets. Of course, there was a limit. It was usually obvious when the limit was reached, for example, when attendees became too drunk to find their wallet. By that point, there were also often unintended consequences of drunkenness, none of which added much to an event's fundraising. It was time to refuse service when they reached the point of obnoxious intoxication, when they lost control of their senses. It was common to see alcohol-induced misbehavior, people passed out in chairs, and physical removal of disruptive people. This still happens today, but it is rare.

I no longer advocate wide-open, always-open, free drinks until attendees stagger away for fundraising events. Drinking to excess does not equate with free spending. In fact, the presence of even one obnoxious drunkard is likely to offend many attendees, causing them to feel uncomfortable and reduce their participation in the fundraising. People have become less tolerant of public drunkenness. It can ruin the fun that must be part of an event, leaving people with an unflattering opinion of the host organization.

Alcohol consumption can be controlled in several ways. Have a cash bar open upon arrival of attendees and through the early part of dinner only. Close the bar after that. Attendees who desire to have cocktails may do so freely for a set period at their own pace and expense, preferably using the alcoholic-beverage services of the facility to help defray risk of liability to the host organization. If the host is not making drinks, such as wine, available during the meal, holding the cash bar open during the early part of the meal allows people to "serve themselves." Cocktail waitstaff can be employed, but this may make alcoholic beverages more readily available. Here again, by providing this service only through the early part of the event and meal helps limit consumption and creates time between the last drink and the end of the event one to three hours later.

There are many organizations for which limiting alcohol may not be a ready option, given the nature of who attends the fundraising event. In such instances, use of designated drivers could avert disaster. For those organizations still holding events where everyone—attendees and hosts—use the event as an opportunity to drink, raise a few dollars, and drink some more, put in place a means to prevent intoxicated attendees from driving after the event. Have chartered or public transportation on standby, or have attendees stay overnight on-site.

Food and Drink Affect Event Revenue

The most important way food and drink may increase revenue potential may be the least obvious: food and drink help keep attendees on-site for the duration of the event. For this reason event planners should carefully consider the cost of refreshments or meals and balance cost of food service against the impact on attendance from charging attendees for refreshments or meals. Planners should also con-

sider options such as having food service underwritten or sponsored through donations or hosting. Food service is an integral cost of many events and needs to be treated as such in developing the event business plan.

The most obvious way money is raised from food and drink is through direct sale to attendees. Attendees can pay direct costs of food as they choose what to drink and eat at vending stands located at the event site. Admission tickets may include the cost of a meal, or a portion of the cost of food and drink, in the price. If food and drink are included in event admission, an attendee's spending on raffles, games, and other fundraising opportunities does not conflict with the less profitable spending on food and drink if purchased separately from admission.

The actual cost of food service should be known to the event planner, and the ticket price set accordingly. Some event planners use food and drink service to provide a source of net revenue, whereas others seek only to break even. Some planners may even purposely set admission ticket prices low and accept a net loss on food service but make up this loss in other ways. They use the "low" price of admission, which is advertised as including drinks and a meal, as a means to increase the number of people who attend. Cash bars and food concessions are common at events, but attendees often prefer the cost of food be included in the admission ticket. Well-fed and properly "watered" people are more likely to be happy and content. Having them in high spirits and well dispositioned toward the host is a definite plus when the real fundraising action begins. This can increase net revenue.

Good food served efficiently and without obvious blunder reflects well on the host organization. Conversely, poor food, undersized portions, and bad service will reflect badly. This is unfortunate, because problems with food and service may not be the actual fault of the host organization but of service vendors such as caterers. In the minds of attendees, however, the organization hosting the event will be held accountable. Poor food or service can adversely affect revenue. Dissatisfaction of any sort may be reflected in attendees' attitude toward fundraising activities, affect the length of their stay, and influence their decision to attend future fundraising events held by the host. Further, an influential individual dissatisfied with an event may influence others over the course of time to avoid a host organization's events. If one person is dissatisfied due to poor food or service, then others are likely to be as well. This can be a bad situation and one that is difficult to recover from quickly.

Should a food disaster occur that is truly the fault of no one—perhaps an oven was torn apart by an exploding soufflé—then tell the story. If the delivery truck carrying the beef Wellington had a flat tire, give progress reports as the meat is salvaged by air-rescue helicopters—whatever is necessary. Try to keep spirits up and thoughts off growing hunger. Let attendees know the truth: what happened was a fluke, and flukes happen. But don't ever make excuses for errors or problems with the caterer that result from the event planner's lack of diligence or poor judgment in selecting a subpar catering company. People who come to an event are usually savvy and not easily fooled by some buffoon who gets onstage and tries to pass the buck for his or her own poor planning.

The Meal Is Not the Event

Fundraising, not the meal, is the event, and all other activities lead up to and contribute to the fundraising, especially if there is a live auction. Even other fundraising activities should be designed to move attendees in the direction of the eventual, center-stage finale—the main live auction. Unless the event itself is designed around a gourmet theme (see chapter 24), food service and meals should be conducted in the background and with as much efficiency as possible. Here, efficiency is reduction of expense and increase in service speed. Every minute attendees spend in a buffet line or waiting on service is a minute away from fundraising activities. This is the reason that food service is so critical to the success of a fundraiser where a meal is served or where attendees will otherwise congregate at food- and drink-service points.

Speed of service is critical to keeping attendees in front of fundraising activities. Long, slow lines at drink-service areas keep bidders from seeing to their desired items at silent auctions or prevent them from playing games. It's common for an event host to save service costs by providing a single drink-service station instead of several. Attendees then spend considerable time in line for drinks, instead of in line to bid at silent auctions, buy raffle tickets, or play games of chance. Some event organizers will look at short or no lines at drink-service stations and see money wasted on service attendants or excess drink inventory. A savvy event organizer sees short lines as proof attendees are getting served quickly and moving back onto the fundraising floor.

Even though there may be some net revenue earned through charging attendees the price of a meal, a leisurely time consuming a meal will not add to revenue. It can and probably will subtract from net revenue. Buffet lines can use up precious fundraising time. Unless caterers can assure sufficient serving speed by providing multiple buffet lines and efficient replenishment, it may be best to avoid buffet service. The meal, including service, should take no longer than 30 to 40 minutes; a bit more time is acceptable if the meal is part of the planned objective and draw to the event, such as the lure of a truly elegant dining experience.

Spending a few dollars more for full-service table dining may result in as much as 30 to 60 minutes saved, if service is efficient. If it is not efficient, full-service dining can be a cash burner. Caterers must commit to employing sufficient serving staff to ensure speedy service. Even at very large events with several thousand attendees, it is possible for tables to be served nearly simultaneously. When people are seated, they arrive to tables set with salads, breads, and other starters. Some added service activities may take place for a few minutes, but not long after diners are seated, servers assemble and on cue, serve the second, or main course. They are ready, have plated meals stacked, and out they come, serving all tables almost simultaneously. Other courses follow in succession, with each timed, and each course served with precision. This can be done and it is not a luxury, especially for a large event. It is a necessity. And for large, high-dollar events, it is expected.

The Catering Contract

Unless the host organization holds a self-catered affair, it is likely members of the host's planning team will engage the services of a caterer either directly or indirectly, for example, by using an event site's services. Doing so will probably involve the host planners in negotiating and then signing a written agreement—a contract. Maybe a friend of the organization will provide catering services and no written agreement will be considered necessary. Of course, there is risk to that, but it is an obvious risk that needs to be discussed by the host's planning team and leadership.

If not using self-catering or receiving food service from a friend, the host organization's planners will most likely deal with a professional caterer, restaurant manager, or event-site food-service manager to arrange for food items and meals to be served at the event. In all these situations, a written agreement is standard practice in the food-service industry. Written agreements should be protective of both parties' interests. If a vendor of food services fails to present a written agreement or listing of services and agreed-upon costs, the event planners should insist that such an agreement be drawn up and signed.

One of the most intimidating aspects of contracting for food service is the negotiation over food items, type of service, and prices. Putting the results of that negotiation into a written agreement or contract may involve additional negotiations. Although it would make sense to expect the party paying for food service to be presented at the outset with a contract that favors the customer, just the opposite is ordinarily the case. Negotiations over a contract for food and drink service are best done by people with experience in the hospitality industry. Since there may be no person with such experience available to event planners, this book provides various guidelines. Please observe the following disclaimer.

DISCLAIMER: *Negotiations over general contract provisions are often conducted by attorneys. I am not an attorney and in making the recommendations in this chapter and elsewhere in this book regarding contracts, agreements, and nego-tiations, I am not representing anyone's legal interests. I am not claiming that anything stated herein is legally valid. Thus, I need to advise event planners to seek the assistance of counsel in any negotiation and before signing any legal document.*

Also see chapter 8 for suggestions on negotiating related services, such as event-site service contracts, and chapter 7 for general negotiation suggestions.

The contract is a document wherein event planners must be specific. Whether regarding menu items, cooking ingredients, dress of waitstaff, or how quickly people are to be served, discussions and negotiations establish mutual expectations and price. The contract sets all agreements into place. The event planner must work to reduce the opportunity for misunderstandings and increase the likelihood that attendees will receive services that the event planner envisions.

Specific menu items are almost always chosen and listed in the contract. This section of the agreement will read almost like a menu from a restaurant, but that level of detail may not be enough to make clear what the event planner really wants. For example, event planners may want a meal prepared to certain standards. The event planner may specify that the meal is to be kosher or vegetarian. But that may not be enough. Standards of preparation for kosher meals may be well understood, but that is not universally the case for vegetarian meals. So the event planner may wish to specify that no animal fats be used to prepare the meal or in any of the dressings served on the food or on the side. The contract is also the place to specify that only certified organically grown vegetables are used or that only locally raised beef be used if that is the desire and expectation of event planners. Consider how foolish the person planning the evening meal for the midwestern sheep growers' association would feel if the lamb served at dinner was produced in New Zealand.

Arrangements for the bar need to be set with the caterer or independent bartending service. Some event facilities insist on using in-house bar services. These can be expensive, but a cash bar is also a pos-

Sidebar 9.1. **Typical Content of the Written Catering Service Agreement (Contract)**

- Exact date, start, and end time of the event
- Number of attendees, with the number broken down as needed to clarify how many adults and children of different age groups will be served which food items and beverages
- Times at which food and bar service is to begin and end
- Diagram of room arrangement, including locations for food service
- Details of locations of food-service areas if different locations are used, including arrangement of food-service areas
- Pace (timing) of food service
- Overage or underage allowances
- Name of supervising on-site catering manager
- Cost schedule for waitstaff or other service staff to stay beyond contract time if the event runs late due to no fault of catering
- Provisions for penalties in the event catering problems delay or harm the event
- Specification of service type, such as buffet, station, or full service, along with details of that service, such as how many buffet lines or number of service stations will be used
- Snacks or hors d'oeuvres listed by item and price, number to be served, pace of service, and provisions for extras to be ordered on-site
- Refreshments, listed in detail by brand and price, including price of bottled and pitchered tap water
- Specification of each menu item, including special preparation or ingredient requirements
- Specification of special food needs, such as vegetarian, special diet, or kosher
- Cost per person or overall cost, if price fixed, including prices for adults and children, by age category
- Number of waitstaff, supervisors, bartenders, servers, and so on covering each category of catering staffing (Depending on type of service, staff requirements may be listed in different ways, such as staff per buffet serving line, staff per full-service dining table, staff per service station, staff per attendee, number of bartenders per bar, and number of roving waiters.)
- Dress of service staff
- Specification of serviceware, including dishes, glassware, and utensils (These can be identified and listed by brand as a means to guarantee a specific level of quality.)
- Specification of responsibilities for cleanup and timing of cleanup
- If catering is not being done in-house, specify the following:
  - Exact location of the event
  - The time catering is expected to arrive and time catering must vacate the event site
  - Where catering will set up service areas
  - Responsibility for providing tables and chairs, dinnerware, utensils, glassware, service-area tables and other food-preparation items, such as grills, ovens, and sinks
- Responsibility for catering equipment
- Schedule of charges for additional or fewer meals
- Last date for changes to the menu
- Start and end time for food service
- Statement of compliance with law, indicating that both parties will abide by prevailing laws
- Clear statement of force majeure, including a mutually protective indemnification clause
- Proof of insurance, limits of liability, and carrier
- Amount of deposit and payment schedule
- Refund and cancellation policy, including specific conditions or schedule for refund

sibility. Alcohol at fundraising events is covered elsewhere in this chapter. Bar service needs to be detailed in the written agreement. Be very detailed. Some of the points to cover include flexibility for the host to bring alcoholic beverages, corkage fees, number of bartenders, brands of bar setups, additional refreshment stations separate from bars or integrated, and brands (value, premium, or super-premium brands) of wine, beer, and liquor. Price needs to be negotiated, but in addition, specify any

"buy-back" allowances for unopened bottles of alcohol or mixers.

The more specific the details of food, preparation, and presentation in the agreement between caterer and event planner, the more likely that event attendees will get what was planned for them. Sidebar 9.1 provides a list of what to include in a typical catering-service agreement. Not all catering contracts will need to cover all of these services or points of consideration.

10

Entertainment and the Master of Ceremonies

Onstage, before an assembled group of 3,000, the organization's president appeared with a large talking bird on his shoulder. The president began to speak. The bird patiently waited its turn. Soon the president introduced the bird, and the two began a rehearsed routine. The president had been trained to make a few remarks in concert with the bird's tricks. It might have worked, too, had the responsible party placed the bird's treats into proper position.

While the president was clearly acting in his capacity as an unpaid volunteer, the bird was strictly working at prevailing bird union rates. No treat, no bird act. As the president tried to motivate the bird, the bird went on strike. It's hard to say if the routine would have been funnier with a cooperative bird, but everyone—except the bird and the president—enjoyed a good laugh.

There were a number of lessons learned that night, but the most important in relation to this chapter is that it pays to pay the entertainers, or at least pay attention to what they want, because you will probably get only as much as you pay for. Another lesson learned is that it is important to choose the entertainment carefully. Even a silly bird act can backfire. Here the paid staff planning the event set the president up to be the nitwit in a bird act. Talk about a formula for disaster . . . sure, it should work out just fine, but what if it doesn't?

That night the president felt that he looked stupid as he fumbled around with an upset bird on his shoulder in front of several thousand members of his organization. He also felt even sillier because he knew, and he assumed everyone in the audience knew, that the organization paid good money to have this prima donna bird as an entertainer at the fundraising event.

An old rule of thumb is to never follow an animal act, because you don't want to be one-upped by an animal.

That may be a good rule to follow, but perhaps a better rule is to never be part of an animal act, particularly if you are to be the animal's tricked partner. Onstage that night, it wasn't the next person onstage who was made to look like a fool. But perhaps the most important of all rules to follow for staff or other event planners is to take precautions to make sure entertainment is appropriate for the audience and infallible—and doesn't make the president of the organization (or anyone else) feel uncomfortable.

THE SILLY "talking-bird-on-the-shoulder" was no amateur act. This bird was a trained professional entertainer—a bird for hire—doing a performance. The bird (actually the bird's owner-trainer) was getting paid for the appearance. Professional entertainers are readily available for hire to perform at events. Many have special acts intended for conferences and events, such as fundraisers. Experienced event entertainers may know how to stage their acts to best support fundraising. In particular, event entertainers should know that their act is not the main attraction; the fundraiser is. Such entertainers can help ensure attendees keep focus on the host's real purpose by emphasizing the fundraising and mission of the nonprofit host during the show.

Entertainment and Entertainers

Given the foregoing discussion, it might appear entertainment is an important part of a fundraising event. After all, it is unusual to attend a fundraiser that does not have some kind of entertainment. Event planners enjoy meeting to decide which band, musician, politician, or sports figure to invite. In the course of making such decisions, members of the planning team often have an opportunity to interact with the musicians or celebrities. Discussion of entertainment options can be among the most exciting parts of event planning.

However, if I were to ask a sampling of event planners why they have entertainment at their

events, I doubt I would hear much about quantified analysis and increased fundraising success. Instead, I would expect to hear something like "because people come to be entertained" or "because every other organization's fundraiser has entertainment." So entertainment must be important to fundraising success. Right? Maybe not. In fact, many organizations hold successful major auction-event fundraisers that do not feature entertainment. I am familiar with one such organization whose members host thousands of events a year, but the recommendation to event planners is to avoid featuring entertainment.

What is the correct approach to entertainment and entertainers? Like so many other options in the course of planning a major fundraising event, the answer depends on the host's objectives and skills at planning and conducting events. In general, event planners who perceive entertainment to be a necessary part of an event often fail to honor the underlying premise of the fundraiser—to raise net revenue. I have no data as proof, but I believe entertainment is rarely used in a strategic fashion to boost fundraising success. However, it is possible. How to do so will be explained in this chapter.

Strategic Concepts to Consider

Event planners should evaluate how entertainment will affect fundraising success by objectively answering the following questions: (1) Will entertainment attract additional attendees who will participate in fundraising and increase net revenue? (2) Will entertainment promote greater involvement of attendees in fundraising activities and increase net revenue? If the answer to either question is objectively determined to be "yes," then entertainment should be pursued as an acceptable addition to the event. If the answer is "no" to both, then entertainment should be avoided.

There are potential costs when entertainment does not aid in reaching fundraising goals. These costs can be considerable, some measurable. Costs include the direct cost of paying entertainers fees for performing. Depending on the popularity of the act, this can be a considerable expense or minimal.

Entertainers may be willing to perform at reduced rates or for free for a charitable cause. But "free" entertainment can result in added indirect expense, as there can be costs for stage rental, publicity, extra sound systems, extra space, and so on. These costs can be measured.

Of more concern are costs that are much harder to measure. The greatest cost of entertainment, if entertainment is not integrally tied somehow to increasing revenue, is the cost of lost time for fundraising that results when entertainment distracts attendees from participating in fundraising activities. This can have a serious financial impact on fundraising success. This potential cost is the most important to take into account if considering entertainment.

The cost of lost fundraising opportunity is also the most misunderstood and thus commonly ignored aspect of event planning. There is only so much time during an event when fundraising is offered to attendees. Anything that reduces this time can adversely affect net revenue. Entertainers performing during active fundraising periods give attendees a ready host-supported escape from the fundraiser. Instead of moving about the silent auction area or milling among the tables offering games of skill and chance, attendees can comfortably sit or stand watching the entertainment, providing a ready alternative to participating in the nearby fundraising. Why give attendees a choice? Wouldn't the host prefer that attendees at a fundraiser participate in the fundraising, as opposed to taking in free entertainment—free at the host's expense and loss! What purpose does that serve?

I have attended many fundraising events, but I am rarely an active participant in fundraising. My attendance is more for professional reasons, so I spend my time talking to people and watching what is going on. When there is entertainment, I will often hang out near the performers, because invariably anyone not interested in taking part in the fundraising winds up there. It is a good place to talk and wait out the time silent auction tables are open and games are under way. It is also a good place to go to avoid raffle ticket sellers. The sellers learn quickly that people being entertained by a performance are the least likely to be interested in buying raffle tickets. The propensity of entertainers to distract event attendee's attention away from fundraising activities explains why the organization mentioned previously eschews entertainment. That organization has a time-tested formula for fundraising that focuses its fundraising subunit's events on fundraising, no more, no less.

Practical Use of Entertainment

To effectively use entertainment during fundraising events, ensure that performances do not conflict with fundraising activities and insist that performers take direct steps to support or enhance the host's objective to raise money. For example, entertainment can be confined to periods when there is no active fundraising under way. Do not carve out time for entertainment from the time allotted to fundraising by shortening the duration of fundraising activities, such as silent auctions or games. Instead, entertainment should take place when fundraising activities are not possible or are inappropriate. Such times may be during a banquet or meal, before or after the fundraising portion of the event, or during periods of transition, for example, if event-room space must be reset.

Sometimes the size or configuration of an event room will allow entertainers to perform entirely in the background. Entertainers may be interspersed throughout the room. The result is that attendees have no apparent spot to escape to during the performance—the entertainer's stage and fundraising activity space are one and the same. Roving clowns at a children's event and a wandering mariachi band are examples of interspersed entertainment. A lone piano player whose music is piped throughout the event's sound system is an example of entertainment taking place in the background.

Entertainment that does not conflict with fundraising can be provided when event attendees are divided into distinct groups and fundraising is not directed at all groups at once. Family-oriented events can fit in this category, for example, when children are present and a portion of the event caters to children but other portions of the event are more appropriate for adults. During more adult-oriented portions of the event, children may be entertained while adults move on to activities more to their tastes. And here I am referring to adults participating in activities that would be of little interest to children, not offensive to them. The entertainment reduces conflict with fundraising by providing entertainment to one group while the other is engaged in fundraising opportunities directed to them.

Entertainers Acting in Support of Fundraising

Here are a few suggestions on how to ensure performers support and enhance fundraising. Require performers to promote fundraising activities under way by having them make an emotional appeal to attendees. The host organization can help script this if necessary. At a minimum the entertainers must be somewhat knowledgeable about the organization, its mission, and the good cause money raised at the event will be used to address. The performer can point to the organization's activities under way and encourage onlookers to actively take part in the fundraising. If a performer is unwilling to work with event planners in this fashion, find a performer who is.

Roving entertainers dispersed in the event room can be particularly effective at encouraging people to participate, because these entertainers are in close proximity to attendees and are constantly moving about. It is even possible to integrate performance with fundraising. A magician working the floor can both entertain and sell raffle tickets. The same goes for a clown and a cheerleading squad. Any performer can help the host raise money, and some can be incredibly effective. Consider the huge positive effect of an endorsement by a true celebrity entertainer.

Entertainment as Moneymaker

There are two ways entertainment can provide an extra boost to fundraising success and can be included in an event with confidence. In the first, attendance at an event is integrally linked to the presence of entertainment. Entertainment is made one of the major themes and attractions of the event. As an example, an event may be well attended because a dance is held after the main live auction, where music is provided by a live band. Or a well-known figure relevant to the host organization's mission speaks during the banquet, drawing in many members of the organization who attend the fundraiser primarily to hear the speaker. A celebrity appearance or a performance can be leveraged in many ways to persuade additional people to attend an event. Regardless of what draws attendees, once there, they are likely to participate in fundraising, or at least they are likely to consider doing so. If people attend a fundraiser primarily for reasons other than participating in fundraising activities, event planners have both opportunity and challenge to present those attendees with fundraising attractions that are irresistible and fun. True success is realized when these people succumb to the allure of the event and attend subsequent fundraisers with the intent of engaging in fundraising activities.

The second circumstance occurs when the entertainment is so spectacular or the celebrity so well appreciated that people regularly pay significant prices to attend their shows and watch them perform. These are the acts usually seen in theaters, casinos, comedy clubs, movies, sports arenas, fairs, and so on. The performances are by well-known musicians and bands, comedians, authors, sports and political figures, magicians, self-help gurus, children's theater groups, and even talented animals doing tricks. Celebrated performers draw attendees, and event planners can use the appearance as a major draw to the event in its advertising. But there is something else about the addition of a celebrity entertainer that should be equally as compelling to an astute event planner seeking additional revenue: the event host can charge a hefty premium to attendees for the privilege of attending the performance of a celebrity or celebrated entertainer. As a consequence, the event entrance fee plays a major role in driving overall event revenue. The performance becomes a major feature of the event along with the fundraising. The performance and fundraising opportunities should be staged to complement each other, not conflict. Each must be allotted sufficient time to satisfy attendees.

The stature of the celebrity determines the upper limit that can be charged. Setting event admission price involves considering a number of factors, including recovering actual costs. If big-name entertainment is free to the host organization, there may be more latitude in setting price than when the host pays full price. Nonetheless, a true celebrity appearance offers considerable added fundraising potential. The event planning group should make every effort to capitalize on that opportunity, as there are additional ways to do so, along with charging a high price of admission.

Unusual Acts and Audience Participation

The talking bird in the earlier example could have cared less who it sat on. It could have been the president of the United States for all it cared. Acts at events frequently involve an organization's officers, "randomly" selected members of the audience, or celebrity figures. Use caution. Attendees are not there to become performers, and the host organization's officers are not actors. The host's officers may be excited about additional face time before members and supporters, but acting like an actor may not work out as they expect. With reality shows and so much exposure to media today, people forget not everyone is an actor. If all goes as planned, it can work well, but if something goes wrong, an officer's routine can fail. Although a trained performer may be able to recover from a mistake, and even do so without the audience noticing the mistake, an officer or friend of the host organization onstage left to deal with an acting job gone bad is placed in an uncomfortable position. Even the most gracious person can be made to feel awkward or embarrassed and become upset when hundreds or thousands of people watch as he or she flounders about. And it is so easy to forget a few lines. It is natural to get confused in the harsh glare of spotlights.

I can recall numerous times when I have spoken to someone not familiar with being on a major stage as he or she stepped away from the stage after the first experience. The first thing the individual usually says is, "I couldn't see the audience because the lights were so bright and in my eyes." It is hard to connect with an audience that cannot be seen. Blinding light can be unnerving. It is easy to make a mistake and then have difficulty recovering. Otherwise competent people can freeze up, or worse, they start talking without control—almost babbling. For whatever reason, when some people are onstage before an audience, they feel they have to do something, so they begin to talk, seemingly about whatever comes to mind. It can be embarrassing, because of what may be said and how inept that makes the person appear. Sometimes they actually need help to stop, because they simply cannot seem to stop on their own. Event planners who allow unskilled speakers to get onstage need to be prepared to step in if something goes wrong. Have someone standing by to assist a speaker recover. Such assistance may involve taking action to cut the speaker off in as polite a fashion as possible and escort the speaker offstage.

Entertainment Contracts and Agreements

Speakers, entertainers, and celebrities who are regularly paid for appearances will usually have contracts that require evaluation and negotiation by event planners. For the purposes of discussion in this section of the book, all of these performers are combined into a single category: "entertainers." Also included would be politicians who give speeches, poets, musicians, clowns, authors, self-help gurus, and any others whose main role at an event is to entertain.

Although events differ and contract provisions may differ among types of entertainers, it is important for event planners to know and understand the terms of an entertainment contract. Planners must negotiate contract terms to protect the host organization's interests. For example, what obligation will the host organization have toward the entertainer if the event is canceled? The contract will surely spell out the consequences of event cancellation. Many times dealing with contract provisions is not the only thing event planners find taxing. Many entertainers are represented by agents or booking agencies. In these cases, the planner does not deal directly with the performer. If the performer is known to members of the organization, this connection may be passed on to the agent or agency staff, but contractual obligations between the performer and agent/agency generally preempt the performer's negotiating directly with event planners.

Sometimes performers are not even allowed to do "free" performances. Some entertainers make specific provisions for donated performances. In other instances, performers may evade the letter of contracts by doing performances for nonmonetary incentives, such as oral side agreements for free merchandise. Such complications and many provisions may be included in a standard entertainment contract. In addition to contract provisions, host organizations can purchase insurance to reduce risk of loss should an entertainer fail to perform (see chapter 20).

Negotiations over entertainment-related services are best done by people with experience in the entertainment industry or by those who thoroughly understand the provisions of such contracts and can provide relevant counsel to protect the interests of the host organization. However, since there may be no person with such experience immediately available to event planners, this book provides various guidelines. But please observe the following disclaimer.

DISCLAIMER: *The material on negotiations is for informational purposes only and is not for the purpose of providing legal advice, including the application of law to any particular set of facts and circumstances. Readers are urged to confer with counsel and consultants about their particular facts and to address any particular legal questions.*

Agreements for entertainment should cover the host organization's responsibilities and address matters of mutual risk and liability. Two such risks to properly address in a contract are (1) the performer's responsibilities to the host organization should the performer cancel the performance, and (2) the host's responsibilities to the performer should the host cancel the performance. Sidebar 10.1 lists 12 recommendations and a number of provisions that may be

contained in an agreement for entertainment. Also see chapter 7 for other provisions to include in contracts, general negotiation suggestions, and options to insure against nonappearance of entertainers.

Required Entertainment: The Master of Ceremonies (MC)

As a testament to his own high opinion of himself, the master of ceremonies rambled on about nothing in particular. Reveling in his own wit, laughing at his own jokes, and butting in to the rhythmic sales mantra of the auctioneer, he droned on, oblivious to the souring mood of his audience. How much money the MC's inept performance cost the organization that night in lost auction revenue is anyone's guess. As I sat at the head table trying to appear interested, one of the organization's officers responsible for this growing mess was as clueless as the MC. The officer leaned over and whispered to me, "The MC was a great deal; he's doing this for nothing."

ONE OF THE MOST visible jobs at an event is that of master of ceremonies. In large part entertainer, the MC is announcer, timekeeper, attention getter, problem solver, and onstage personality. For better or worse, the MC becomes the overall face and voice of the event. The MC can have a huge influence over attendees, so it makes sense to choose one who has the ability to inspire attendees to participate actively in fundraising. The MC is the person who most directly works in concert with the auctioneer to help boost fundraising success. The potential power of the MC to influence success of the event is second only to the influence the auctioneer wields over bidders. A skilled MC helps the host raise money.

Choosing a skilled MC is important, but event planners often do not take the task seriously. They may turn to friends, officers of the organization, or themselves to serve as MC. That can work if the person selected is skilled and knows the job of MC, but

Sidebar 10.1. **Twelve Suggestions for Entertainment Agreements (Contract)**

Not all of the following may be relevant in all agreements.

1. Have a written agreement, signed by both parties, that covers all matters of the agreement discussed by the parties.

2. Establish the permissions and rights of the host organization to use images, passages, video, text, or other materials to which the entertainer has copyright or intellectual property rights. This should include detail of any transfer of rights to use materials or images, including any time or other limitations on transferred rights, whether rights are exclusive to the host or nonexclusive, rebroadcast of a performance, and whether the host can distribute materials for use by another party or sell rights to use materials to another party.

3. Detail compensation, including allowable expenses for reimbursement.

4. Detail nonmonetary compensation. Some entertainers may take certain benefits in lieu of cash payment. This could include special advertising on a Web site, an article in a magazine, a trip, merchandise or other product, service, or benefit.

5. Make it clear in the agreement that there will be no compensation if the entertainer is doing the event as a charitable donation.

6. Detail special consideration. Some entertainers have unusual or unpredictable requests, such as being presented flowers onstage or served a specific brand of beverage. The entertainer should list these special requests, and the host organization may approve those that are acceptable during negotiations.

7. Detail the exact nature of the entertainment to be provided, including, for example, length of performance, what the performer will do, and what the performer will do or say to promote the host organization or the organization's cause.

8. Include a provision in which entertainers guarantee that they own their act and any materials used in their act. If the performance is a tribute or "knock-off" act, the contract should include verification that the entertainer has permission to use materials and the performance will not infringe upon ownership rights of others.

9. Include liability protection for the host organization against any harm caused by the performer to anyone, including defaming or disparaging anyone or a product or service owned by another party.

10. Include a provision for the entertainer to indemnify the organization from any damages resulting from a breach of the contract.

11. Include provisions to address the circumstance of the entertainer canceling or otherwise failing to perform at the event or if the entertainment is materially different from that described by the contract.

12. Include provisions to address the circumstance of the host organization canceling the event or performance or materially breaching any provisions of the contract that affect the performer or performance.

it can also turn into a disaster. A poorly chosen MC simply muddles along, neither helping nor seemingly harming fundraising efforts. The damage done by an ineffective MC is the lost opportunity wasted during face time and talk with attendees. A skilled MC spends face and talk time effectively motivating attendees to participate in fundraising activities.

Roles and Responsibilities of MC

The job of MC entails specific roles and responsibilities that any MC must take seriously. The 10 most important of these are listed in sidebar 10.2. A skilled MC knows these roles and responsibilities and knows how to juggle them onstage. But sometimes the MC uses the event stage for something entirely different. The stage is not a soap box for

anything but fundraising and spotlighting the event host's mission. If the host organization has a social or political agenda as its mission, then that agenda is fair game for the MC's unbounded eloquence and sharp wit. Everything else of a controversial nature is out of bounds. The MC must be gracious and inclusive, at least for the few hours served as MC. Many MCs are well-known personalities, and as such they are visible in the community or beyond. They may have well-known, often-stated opinions. Of all people, they should know what one person finds likable in someone may be exactly what offends another. With visibility comes the likelihood of some controversy no matter how likable the person. The good MC keeps personal opinions to himself or herself in the course of helping the host organization raise money.

Sidebar 10.2. **Ten Most Important Roles and Responsibilities of the Skilled MC**

1. Act as key announcer
2. Act as auctioneer's key assistant
3. Entertain attendees
4. Introduce people who need to be recognized
5. Keep the event on schedule, and help the host maintain strict timing of activities
6. Promote the host organization and its mission, and explain why funds being raised are so important to the host's work
7. Help the host identify problems
8. Help reduce tension if problems arise in any area of event activities noticeable to attendees
9. Motivate attendees to participate in fundraising activities
10. Look for and act on opportunities to help the host achieve spectacular results

Where do organizations find good MCs? Sometimes the MC is a member of the organization or staff who is well known to attendees, liked, and a good public speaker. Sometimes the individual is not a member but a supporter of the organization who is well known to attendees, liked, and a good public speaker. Other times it is a person who is just well known to attendees, liked, and a good public speaker. The person could be a political figure, TV or radio personality, a famous author, and so on.

Does this mean anyone well known to attendees, liked, and a good public speaker will make a good MC? No. In fact, many MCs who clearly have all three of these characteristics make lousy MCs. They can be so bad that they may offend people, be the cause of delay and costly confusion during the event, and drive auction prices down. However, in some situations the need for skills may be outweighed by a host organization's need for a well-known and respected MC who can lend credibility to the event. After all, if the most reverend archbishop has agreed to serve as MC for a charity auction held by the local chapter of the Association of Reformed Mobsters, the fundraiser must be legitimate. Right?

The job of MC is often performed by one of the key staff or volunteer organizers of the event. This can work well if the person understands the job and has the skills to pull it off. Many times this is

simply not the case. Key staff and event volunteers should seriously question their own ability to serve in this role. Sometimes an objective third party can help provide advice. But proper advice may be hard to come by. Also consider that key staff and volunteers usually have other important duties at events. Someone will have to attend to those other duties, but should something go wrong, a key person tied up with MC duties will be hard pressed to do a credible job as MC and solve problems elsewhere. In addition, even if a key staff member or volunteer could do a credible job as MC, bringing on an additional person to serve as MC provides a safety net should the MC fail to show up or perform poorly. The staff or volunteer can fill in should the need arise. Since the MC is such a key position, having a backup plan is a good idea.

Time Keeping and Keeping on Time

One of the keys to a successful event is timing and keeping on time. It is the job of the MC to help event hosts keep activities moving and on time. Here is where the MC with dictatorial tendencies or a childhood desire to be a conductor on a train can become expressive. The MC must demand the event stay on time. This job is more than just fitting all activities into the time allotted. Perfect timing of event activities and keeping time start with planning each activity. Good planning ensures the duration of the activity is adequate to meet fundraising goals, and no longer. Set the time for an activity to start and stop. This timing needs to be listed in writing on a schedule of events that is the MC's reference book. Dragging activities beyond a reasonable duration wastes volunteer or staff worker time and bores attendees. The MC may need to depart from the schedule based on what is happening on the event floor, but varying the schedule should be done only for good cause.

Meals that go on too long due to poor service, dragging auctions, ill-timed silent raffles, and raffle tickets drawn too slowly will take time away from something else and result in lost fundraising time where it counts most. This time cannot be made up by dragging the event out later and later. In many cases event rooms are rented for a set period, or the room must be vacated by a set time. Besides, attendees can be held only so long before attention wanes, nerves fray, and people leave. A quick pace is essential to keeping attendee interest up. The MC is in charge of keeping an eye on progress of the event and maintaining a proper pace.

The MC Who Can't Be Taught

TV personalities, radio hosts, and others who MC or otherwise talk for a living may sound like great choices to MC an event. Some are, but being a good talker or talking for a living doesn't mean a person knows how to effectively MC an auction event. This could prove to be a problem if the person is not ready to be taught how it's done. Those who rely on the gift of gab for a living may be more prone than most people to think they know everything they need to serve as MC. Elected officials may fit into this category as well, because for many officials about the only thing they really have going for them is an amazing ability to say the right things at the right time. Getting a person who talks for a living to do a proper job as MC may be the greatest "personnel" challenge faced by the host planning team.

Politicians as MCs

Politicians often appreciate the opportunity to MC charity events because it gives them a platform for visibility and associates them with a (presumably) worthy charitable cause. Assuming an elected official has the skills and experience to do a good job as MC, the host benefits from the attraction a well-liked elected official can be to potential attendees. There are also strategic reasons to ask an elected official to be MC that has nothing to do with his or her ability to do a good job. Many organizations depend on some level of public funding that is under the control of elected officials. Providing an elected official visibility and association with a good cause that would benefit from public funding can be mutually advantageous.

The elected official has to know or be told the job does not include making political announcements or any form of electioneering. But even when on best behavior, many politicians are controversial. This can be a draw or drawback to the host. If attendees will all be of like mind about politics, a carefully selected politician might prove to be a hit. If attendees will be a political mixed bag, there may be no safe choice of politician to have at an event, as MC or speaker.

Finally, nonprofit organizations recognized under IRS Code Section 501(c)(3) are prohibited from engaging in certain political activities. Such organizations should carefully consider the advisability of choosing as MC any elected official who will be actively engaged in running for office at the time of the event. There is some chance the organization's selection may be used to allege the organization was helping or endorsing the candidate. It is also possible for an official of the organization to accidentally make a statement during the course of the event that could be interpreted as endorsing the candidate. A close connection between the candidate as MC and organization would be hard to deny. This could cause undesirable scrutiny by the IRS of the organization's charitable status.

11

The Mission and Strategic Speech Making

One of my favorite volunteers used speech opportunities at fundraising events to extraordinary advantage. He was so good at boosting event fundraising through his speech making that he had become a regular speaker during the evening fundraising. By the time I met him and watched his performance, he was no longer an officer of the organization, although that's what started him down this path and where he gained his experience. His time for ranking within the organization had passed, but his time at the podium had as much currency then as when he had been president.

His speech was always an emotional one. He worked with physically challenged youth, and the organization raised money for this work. He always had one or two of the young men or women he had worked with at the event. They would appear onstage with him. They would talk, or attendees would be shown a video. As this was taking place, past or current officers who had personally donated money to this work would arrive onstage, seemingly drawn by the unfolding emotion. As this was taking place, the speech making would continue growing in emotional appeal. This was not a dirge, nor was it happening by chance. It was a quick-paced, well-orchestrated drama.

When all was in place, seemingly from out of nowhere, a person would be heard from the floor of the event room. He or she would ask, "May I speak?" The individual would then say, "I want to make a contribution. May I do so?" The person would be told "yes." Then another would stand and ask the same. All attendees heard the exchanges.

What the attendees did not hear were the conversations that had taken place in advance of the speech. These occurred when the supporters who came to the stage and the donors who stood and pledged funds discussed the sequence of this carefully crafted strate-gic speech and stage play. Invariably, others would stand and make pledges. These were attendees following the lead of the first two, but all orchestration had ended by this point. The new people who stood and contributed had been compelled by the speech and appeal of others. Considerable funds would be raised.

As a final option to the orchestrated speech, an item in the auction to follow was sometimes linked to the moti-vational speech. Attendees would be told that proceeds from the auction of the particular item would be dedi-cated to fund the program that was the subject of the speech. The speech maker would join the MC and auc-tioneer when bidding started on that item.

This is strategic speech making at its best, and there is nothing deceitful about it. The speech maker was effec-tive because he was personally compelled by the work and the work was in line with the mission of the host organization. He meant everything he said. He person-ally contributed time and money to the work, and all the people who stood in support contributed as well. This was an honest display of support and an honest depiction of the work done and need for funds. The fact the appeal was well orchestrated and rehearsed did not make it any less sincere. It made it more powerful.

ATTENDEES AT A fundraising event need to hear about the host organization and the important mis-sion and work to be funded by the proceeds of the event. All speech making to this end needs to be brief, orchestrated, and scripted to ensure it is well presented. It should not be so detailed that listeners become bored or so long that attention wanes. But these are speeches just the same. This advice con-trasts with the belief among some event planners that no speeches whatsoever be allowed at events. Speeches, they say, may distract attention of atten-dees away from fundraising.

I say baloney to any advice that discounts the fundraising power of pitching the host's cause. Ban-

ning speeches about what the organization does discounts the organization's mission as a cause to celebrate. It ignores the idea that an impassioned emotional appeal can increase fundraising success. The MC should remind attendees throughout the course of an event about the host, the charitable cause, and why funds raised are so important in ac-complishing good works. The host has an obligation to speak to attendees, if for no other reason than to inform them of the work that justifies the organiza-tion's nonprofit status. This information need not be presented like a memo to the board of directors. Instead, it should be presented in a personal, well-scripted, emotional, and orchestrated way. It should draw attendees to the host's mission and tug at their hearts to be part of the host's work through spend-ing money at the event.

The Event Host's Greatest Fundraising Asset

The mission is the heart and soul of a nonprofit charitable or social advocacy organization. This mission is often also called its "cause." The orga-nization's work is presumably to accomplish this mission and further the cause. And presumably, the proceeds from an organization's fundraising event will mostly or entirely be used to fund the work, further the cause, and over enough time and with enough funding eventually accomplish the mission. Presumably this is so. Savvy host organizations want attendees to get the message that money from the event will fund and eventually accomplish the mis-sion. This message is a powerful potion used to af-fect attendees' attitude toward fundraising opportu-nities offered at an event. It can also boost overall attendance.

Leaders of nonprofit organizations should wel-come recent research that confirms the primary motivation for charity supporters to attend fundrais-ing events is a personal connection to the cause.[1] For many years I have leaned toward the notion that attendees come because they were asked by a friend or business associate. I have never discounted the

1. Research and the following statistics are from *The 2010 Charity Event Market Research Report*. CharityHappenings.org.

motivation of cause, but I have seen far too many instances in which attendees have no understanding of the host's mission, nor did they care. I put myself partially in that category many times, as I have attended events where I had no personal affinity for the cause. I was there only because I was asked. For business or personal reasons, I accepted.

But there is one aspect of an organization's fundraising that most donors or event attendees also want to know about—that the host actually spends money raised at the event on the cause. We want to know the money gets spent on the real cause, not on funding an organization's bloated operations because of failure to be efficient. In this I join with 87% of eventgoers: We hope over half of the revenue of an event goes to the beneficiary cause of the host. Over half of us want to see at least 75% go to the cause. That said, one would expect event attendees to hunger to hear about the mission and work of the organization. They don't. Again the research: long-winded speeches are the greatest turnoff to eventgoers.

Taking the research into account, we see that a connection to the cause motivates attendees' support; however, attendees don't want to hear long, grand speeches. The challenge to event hosts, and key factor in the success of an event and future fundraising, is to somehow get attendees to understand what the organization does and connect them to the mission. So how does a host organization show off its greatest fundraising asset—the mission and good work—during the event? Everyone on the host's event team must talk about the mission and talk about the work. Show pictures when the talking stops. Everyone is a communicator, in particular those members of the event team assigned duties that include speaking directly to all attendees, such as the MC and auctioneer. All this has to be done strategically. Here's how.

Keep the mission talk short. Keep it very short. Get 1,000 words across by using pictures, and pepper everything said or done during the course of the evening with mission- and work-related sound and sight bites. Use display posters. Project images of the host's work in conspicuous places, but do it in a way that allows attendees to look or not. This should not conflict with fundraising activities but should complement or be neutral with the money raising. Aim for the subconscious. Subtly or overtly, and juxtaposed with all the exciting fundraising opportunities, explain the organization's mission wherever an attendee may turn. Even games of skill and chance can be adapted to exhibit the host's work. Projected visual information should not require audio for watchers to get the message. Forget lots of text; just use pictures. If there is entertainment, require performers to deliver sound bites about the work of the organization. The same goes for the MC and auctioneer. Here and there have them say a few (very few) words about mission and work accomplished or under way, but have then do it over and over during the course of the event. Personalities at the event help, too. There is power in their endorsement of mission and work. Advise them about being brief but persistent.

Introductions and Praise

Several categories of people need to be introduced and praised during a fundraising event.

Volunteers

Event volunteers need to be openly recognized and praised during an event. This can be done in many ways, but preparing the MC with information about volunteers and having announcements made from the event stage is one of the easiest. Volunteers should be called by name to stand or come to the stage and be thanked. A good MC can think of ways to lavish praise on volunteers. At large events this may be difficult to do on an individual basis because of the large numbers of volunteers involved. Besides, volunteers are usually very busy during the event, so it may be best to point them out from the stage, as opposed to having them stop what they are doing and come onto the stage. Nonetheless, volunteers must be recognized in some way. Names listed onscreen and pointed out by the MC is another way. With a little thought, visual aids can be used to acknowledge volunteer efforts en masse.

Why bother to acknowledge volunteers' free help?

Because at many events volunteers do all the work, and when attendees hear none of their dollars given at the event will go to pay for event workers, they know the host organization is serious about raising as much money for their mission as possible. In addition, praise to volunteers just makes common sense. It is expected. For many volunteers, satisfaction over doing a good job is a form of compensation, but putting on an event can be challenging. Sometimes there are conflicts among volunteers, or between volunteers, staff, and officers. Sometimes things go wrong, and volunteers get blamed. It is a lot of work—for nothing, or at least not for money.

The positive feelings that originally drive a volunteer to agree to work on an event may be affected greatly by emotions felt after an event is over. Event work is exhausting. For many people exhaustion creates a heightened level of sensitivity. What is said during the course of an event and immediately afterward can have an inordinate and lasting effect on volunteers (and staff). Statements made to volunteers that are perceived as positive will have a building effect and help pump up their ego and sense of personal satisfaction. Making positive statements about volunteers is a critical element of the MC's job. Praise to volunteers can also be delivered by leadership of the host organization. Whoever does it needs to do it well. Negative statements, even slight criticism, can have a lasting negative effect. Volunteers may feel unappreciated and possibly resentful. They may feel they "wasted" their time.

Treat volunteers well no matter what happens or who is to blame for problems. Volunteers who are pumped up with praise become emotionally charged and are probably going to want to help again. If they are really energized by the experience, next time they may encourage a few of their friends to volunteer. On the other hand, volunteers who feel unappreciated will most likely not want to return and may discourage others from volunteering.

VIPs

People who attend an event define the event's credibility and character. An event attended by society's upper crust raising money for a new play-

ground for a low-income housing project will have a different character than an event attended by residents of a low-income housing project raising funds for a new playground. Pointing out attendees whom the host wants everyone to know are associated with the event is one way event planners shape the character of an event.

How does the host decide who is a VIP? It's entirely up to the host. In general, a VIP is anyone having sufficient stature in an area of importance to the host that the host sees benefit in providing recognition. An event hosted by an organization supporting cancer research might recognize the director of a local cancer center and several doctors working there but may ignore many other well-known local figures such as the president of a large business, principal of the high school, or a novelist. Some VIPs will be VIPs regardless of any consideration by the host, such as the town mayor. Hosts ignore truly well-known figures at their peril, particularly ones who may have influence over funding, permits, or anything else the organization may have need of in the future. Once VIPs are identified at the event, the MC should be informed of their presence and given instructions to point out and recognize them.

An event is enhanced when well-known, credible people attend. Well-known figures draw press and may draw others to attend. VIP attendance and its the effects on fundraising are factors that build over time. An event that is always attended by local VIPs will become known for that, and many people will consider it when making a decision to attend.

Sponsors

Event sponsors need to be recognized. Sponsors are often businesses that donate for the exposure and "advertising" value of being at the event and associated with the host's cause or host organization's members. Sponsoring businesses generally appreciate, and expect, recognition at the event. The MC needs to have a list of sponsors in hand and make acknowledgment as the event progresses. Given adequate time, the MC can be provided a few sentences of "advertising script" for each sponsor. How much time is spent on such activities depends on time available, value of sponsorships, and the number of sponsors and others who need to be recognized. During the course of an event, sponsor recognition needs to be done equitably.

Staff

Where the host organization has paid staff, those staff working at the event should be recognized for their efforts. This will also identify staff to attendees in the event an attendee has a question about the organization or the event.

Fundraising as Entertainment

Sometimes an auction-based fundraising event is combined with an organization's annual convention, the members' business meeting, or a special conference on a topic of importance to the host organization. Such meetings always involve the organization's officers and often attract important friends. These are important people for an organization's members to hear from, and business meetings typically provide them an opportunity to speak. However, when a fundraising event is associated with an organization's major business meeting, the event provides potentially profitable "entertainment" as well as an attractive added opportunity for high-level speech making by officers or celebrities. Fundraising typically starts after the business sessions end, but speeches by the highest-level officers and high-power guests can continue to take place during the fundraising event. Usually speeches follow dining but precede the main live auction.

Some speech making can be mixed in with fundraising activities. Done strategically, mixing speech making with fundraising can work to increase fundraising success. Unfortunately, most event planners give no thought to a strategy for such speech making. Speeches can drone on. Timing of speeches can disrupt the tempo of the auction. And even when speech making is well scripted and timings are maintained, speeches that are not synchronized with the fundraising at hand either do nothing for fundraising or serve to distract attendees' attention away from fundraising activities. Neither scenario is productive to an organization dependent on the success of fundraising.

There is a productive alternative, assuming the speech makers are as interested in the success of fundraising as the event planners are. Since event planners and the host organization's officers are often one and the same, designing a strategy for motivational speech making should be easy. The motivational intent here is to get attendees to dig a little deeper into their pockets. Given a little thought and maybe some help at orchestration, speech makers can take almost any topic and turn it to fundraising advantage. All it takes is an emotional appeal and a connection to the host organization's mission and work.

Awards and Business Sessions

Auction events are often combined with an organization's annual convention or members' business meeting. This can sometimes also include presentations of awards to members, supporters, and friends of the organization. Accommodating those activities amid the various fundraising options can be challenging. Many organizations will hold more than one day of meetings, staging the fundraising activities on the last day. When all activities and the fundraiser are held on a single day, organizations will typically hold business meetings in the morning or early afternoon, followed by a break when the fundraising event is set up by member volunteers or staff. Fundraising activities take place in the evening. Awards can be presented at business sessions earlier in the day or onstage in the evening in front of all attendees during the main event immediately prior to the live auction. An awards ceremony and speeches can be accommodated within a fundraiser, but they require planning, orchestration, and strict adherence to scripts and timing.

12 Publicity

Occasionally I hear about an annual event that has truly found a place in the hearts and minds of attendees, one that "everyone" knows about and attends without fail, and without need of reminder each year. Officers and staff of the host organization take for granted that people will attend without having to be prompted. They proudly say, "Everyone in town comes" or "All our members will be there." For some events it is not even necessary to let people know when and where the event will be held. "Everyone" knows the day of the month, the time, and the location where the event will be held, because it is held on the same date, at the same time, and in the same place each year rain or shine.

When an event achieves this stature, a funny thing happens. The event becomes possessed. No, not a supernatural haunting kind of possession, although given how amazing this may sound, many readers might assume that is exactly what I mean. Instead, I mean possessed in the sense that it is possessed by the people who come every year. Regular attendees come to believe they "own" the event. It occupies the top spot on their annual social calendar. They consider it their event, and short of insurrection, attendees will continue to come each year. Although hard to believe, it can and does happen.

Planners of such events may skip this chapter on event publicity. May we all reach the point where this chapter is irrelevant, because the event we plan requires no advertising. But for now, for all the rest of us, getting the word out about an event can make the difference between resounding success or budget-busting failure. We must read on.

PUBLICITY PROVIDES several benefits. As a form of advertisement, publicity announcing an event can entice people to attend. The type of media carrying publicity and where it is placed will affect who will be influenced and potentially attend. Publicity can be internal to the host organization, with notices placed in media, such as newsletters, or e-mail received only by members. Or publicity can be placed in media not controlled by the organization, making it visible to the general public. It can be cast widely or narrowly. It can be carried electronically through "green" technology-based social media or printed on a visually polluting highway billboard that gets the message across to tens or hundreds of thousands of passersby. An article carried in a major daily newspaper will reach a wider audience than an article in an alternative weekly. An announcement by a classical radio station will reach a different audience than an announcement by a station that plays only rap music.

Even if an event is for its members only, publicity in media beyond the host's own can provide the organization considerable benefit, because publicity surrounding an event may also help the host advertise its cause. Every little bit of publicity promoting an organization is beneficial. An event provides the occasion to further educate the public about an organization and its work. Promotion of an organization can also help increase membership through increased local recognition of the value of the work the organization carries out. This can come from publicity in advance of and after an event. Finally, positive press carried in credible media proffers an air of credibility to the organization and its cause.

Techniques, hints, and advice on how to generate publicity for an event and simultaneously deliver added benefits to the host organization are discussed in the following sections.

Enlist Volunteers to Get the Word Out

The ready, willing, and able advertising force of any organization is (or should be) its members. Perhaps the best means of advertising an event is to arm members with information and enlist them to act as public relations agents and event advertising executives on the street and through use of their social-media alternatives. If every member asked 10 other people to attend an event, and if 50% of those asked came (including half of the members), the number of attendees would equal five times the number of members. If the same members use social media and reach out to 100 "friends," the outreach increases by tenfold. The number may be large or small, depending on an organization's overall membership, but this means of soliciting attendance can provide meeting planners a solid base for planning.

For this method to be most effective, members need to be asked to help, provided instructions on what and how to promote attendance at the event, and provided brief background materials about the event and organization. Don't assume that just because a person is already a member of an organization that he or she is truly knowledgeable about the organization. Sidebar 12.1 provides a template for providing information to members who agree to assist in promoting an event and asking people to attend.

Throughout this chapter, publicity-seeking event planners and volunteers are directed to make contact with reporters, newspaper publishers, radio and TV station managers, and other people in the media. Approaching such people can be intimidating; after all, these are very busy people. It need not be intimidating, because it is no bother at all for members of the media to receive information from people unknown to them and to establish relationships. Through such relationships members of the media get the leads they need to do their job reporting on the news and stories important in the community. Once contact is made, send notes, e-mail, social-media messages, or call on the phone—whatever seems to work best. All of these ways are how the media stays in touch. It's really no bother at all.

Sidebar 12.1. **Information to Provide Volunteers to Assist in Promoting an Event**

About the Event

Provide general information about the event, including date, time, location, price of attendance, and any special features that might influence a person's decision to attend. For example, hearing that the event is a children-friendly, family-oriented event might be the deciding factor for a single mom to attend, whereas that same information might save a grumpy old man from becoming even grumpier and the event host from dealing with a dissatisfied attendee.

Provide copies of the event registration or admission ticket, showing payment options. It may be necessary to make provision for accepting payment, although reference to online registration options provides a better way to address handling cash, checks, and credit cards.

Include a separate sheet listing event information if desired. More detailed information can be included here, such as donor and sponsor information and how to contribute even if a person does not want, or is unable, to attend the event. Further information can include a list of fundraising activities that will be held, a description of entertainment, and mention of food and refreshment.

Organization Overview

Provide a statement about the organization, such as when it was founded, how many members it has, where members live, how it is organized, and what its tax status is. For example, if the organization is recognized by the IRS as a charitable organization, then that information should be provided along with a statement that contributions to the organization may receive tax advantages and that donors should confer with tax advisers to determine how that might affect their personal taxes.

Mission

Provide the mission statement.

Membership

Provide a succinct statement describing the typical member. For example, some organizations have set criteria for membership, whereas others allow anyone who has an interest to become a member. Respectively, examples of these would be an organization of licensed pilots who fly wilderness-rescue missions and an organization of people who have interest in supporting schools that teach wilderness survival skills to young adults.

Organization Programs and Benefits

List what the organization does and any benefits to members. This should be short and easily understood. It can include, for example, a list of education programs, lobbying, social services, publications available, insurance, member support, and help centers run.

Social Media

Members who volunteer as event promoters can also turn to technology-based social media to advertise the event. This can be a powerful yet inexpensive medium for passing on a message that resonates well among those who receive it. People receiving the message who connect positively with the host organization and the purpose of the event may pass on the invitation to others. Under the best circumstances, this forwarding occurs spontaneously. People inspired by the work of the host and the prospect of the event may open up their address books and forward to all their friends. Some organizations and some missions may not sustain this kind of response through social media, but others will. For those, use of social media should be among the first options that event planners and promoters discuss when forming a promotional plan for an event.

Internal Publicity

Internal publicity can be generated by using the organization's various media and member contact outlets. What these are and how best to use them should be readily apparent to any organization ready to step up to major event fundraising. The following options are listed without a great amount of detail.

The most fundamental use of internal media is as a vehicle to carry event advertisements and notices directly to members. Advertisements for an event can be placed on the organization's Web site, in print or electronic newsletters, and in newspapers and magazines. Advertisements or invitations, including event registration materials and tickets, can also be sent directly to members by mail and e-mail. Some organizations have established "phone trees" that are used to communicate rapidly among members, for example, when there is urgent need for members to contact elected representatives about a pending vote. Phone or e-mail communication trees can be used to issue invitations to an event.

Another way to use internal media to advertise an event is to place stories in internal media that connect to the event. A story about a well-known entertainer who will be entertaining or speaking at an event carried in the organization's newspaper is an example. Or the organization can hold a contest or conduct a survey that invites members to apply or participate in an activity that features the event in the course of the activity. As an example, members could be invited to take a quiz in which they rate the games of skill available at the previous year's event. The quiz could even include a prize for anyone who comes up with a new game to play, as voted on by readers. There are many possibilities, but in every case, the idea is to gain visibility and publicity for the upcoming event.

Maintain an Event Web Site and Web Presence

Web sites can be designed to carry all the information anyone needs to know about an event. Major annual or recurring events should have an established, year-round event Web site maintained as a constant reminder of the event and a means to keep the host organization's members and event attendees informed of evolving features of the next event as it is being planned. The Web site can also serve as an online information exchange and virtual "meeting site" for volunteers and staff involved in event planning, as well as a means for prospective attendees to communicate with representatives of the host organization. Sidebar 12.2 provides an anatomy of well-thought-out event Web site.

Even if a full-feature event Web site is too expensive, technically challenging, or an excessive luxury for planners of small local events, any event host can establish a Web presence with little or no skills

or expense. This is done through setting up free or low-cost online profiles on networking sites, such as Facebook, LinkedIn, Twitter, and other constantly evolving opportunities. The first thing many people do when hearing of an event in the community is conduct a quick Internet search. Credibility is often established in seconds if an explanation of the event and mission funded is readily found in association with a trustworthy organization's Web site or networking profile.

Focus for Efficiency and Effectiveness

Organizations promoting events beyond their own membership that have sufficient resources can purchase advertisements in local newspapers and magazines, rent space on billboards, and run commercials on TV and radio stations. Such broad advertising along with a notice in the organization's own publications and Web sites may be sufficient to generate interest in an event. But many (probably most) nonprofit organizations lack funds for advertising and do not have staff to do promotional work. Although limited capacity is clearly not an advantage, lack of resources for advertising does not need to be a detriment to effectively promoting an event. Limited resources make it reasonable, or necessary, for promotion to be conducted in the most efficient and effective way possible. In this case, access to social media helps address cost limitations and offers a means for powerful messaging.

For event planners, efficiency and effectiveness in promotion are gained by targeting services or products only to those people who need or want the service or product. Even though that may sound obvious, promoters of nonprofit organizations often spend time designing and distributing mass-media materials that reach more people than necessary, such as by issuing news releases, seeking TV news stories, and producing radio public service announcements (PSAs) that reach out to everyone. They do so because they believe strongly in their cause and feel everyone needs to hear about the organization and its good works, and that everyone will want to come to the event. That may be appro-

Sidebar 12.2. **Anatomy of an Event Web Site**

- Information that establishes the identity of the host organization and its mission to be funded by event proceeds
- Information that establishes the authenticity and professional nature of the event
- Invitation to the event
  - General information, such as date, time, place, parking, access to public transportation, and link to a map
  - General information on nature of event and guidance about who should attend (some events are oriented to families; some are not)
  - Lodging and accommodations (with a link to hotel Web site and instructions to book rooms)
  - Information on attire (formal, casual, theme)
- Event activities
  - Fundraising activities (auctions, raffles, games)
  - Event program
  - Speakers and celebrities who will attend
  - Awards to be presented
  - Entertainers and entertainment
  - Field trips
  - Receptions
  - Exhibitions or trade shows
  - Extra activities, such as special tours for spouse or guests
- Online registration
  - Registration form, including options for individual, couples, or group registration, and online registration deadline
  - Registration information, such as what is included with an event ticket and registration for extra activities
  - Early-registration incentives and early-registration deadline
  - Online secure payment form and method-of-payment instruction
  - Statement about security and use of information acquired from Web site users
- Online confirmation and e-receipt, including required information for tax purposes (see chapter 21)
- Online contact form and comment page
- Frequently Asked Question (FAQ) section
- "Updates" section
- Link to "Bring-a-Friend" form
- If the event will feature auctions, include the following:
  - Descriptions of auction items and values
  - Photos or video of auction items
  - Auction and bidding rules and policies
  - Bidding instructions for people who are new to auctions
- If the event will feature raffles, include the following:
  - Description of the raffles, including photos and video of raffle items
  - Raffle rules and any required legal notices
- Request for underwriting and sponsorships, including description of incentives for sponsors and contact person for further information
- Donation solicitation section, including donor information, a donation form, and contact person
- Donor, sponsor, and underwriter acknowledgment and links to sponsoring businesses
- Description of special features of the event
- Event policies, procedures, and legal notices
- Mission and programs page providing information and photos/video of how event revenue is or will be used to further the host organization's mission (this can be a link to other sections of the host's Web site)
- Past-events page showing fun activities and happy attendees at the host's past events, including acknowledgment of past donors, sponsors, and underwriters

priate if the target audience really is "everyone," but if the target audience (e.g., for our purpose, people who would want to attend a fundraiser) is narrower than "everyone," why spend time and money marketing to everyone else?

The key to efficient, effective promotion is to first define the ideal attendee for the event in terms of marketing. Define this person by specific demographic profile, where he or she lives, what he or she reads or listens to for news, and so on. The pur-

pose here is to objectively match the organization with people most likely to relate to the organization's mission or the fundraising objective of the event. An organization serving the homeless may want all event attendees to be millionaires, but defining the ideal attendee as a millionaire and then directing all marketing to millionaires will just waste marketing effort. On the other hand, if the charity event will raise money to replace the stables at The Club's aging polo grounds, it is probably a waste of resources to advertise the event to people who don't have a membership to The Club and have never even seen a polo match.

Once the ideal event attendee is defined, then promotional efforts can be directed to the corresponding specific geographical areas and to the media the ideal person relies upon for information. Use specific language or text in promotional materials that the ideal attendee will appreciate. This language should help the person relate to the work of the host organization. A decision to attend an event is a decision on how to spend a period of time and presumes future purchase of fundraising "products" at the event. Some added social considerations that influence a decision to attend a fundraiser may not come into play when purchasing a hard-goods product. However, marketing an event by directing promotional efforts to the people most likely to want to attend results in the same high efficiency as targeting marketing of hard-goods products to the people most likely to need or want to buy that product.

Get Broad Publicity

There are numerous means to gain broad publicity for an event by working with members of the media or through advertising. The level of publicity desired by a host organization will vary greatly. Planners of many events are satisfied when an event draws a nice cross section of their own members, whereas planners of other events strive to turn out large numbers of the most influential, wealthiest, and most elusive members of a community, or of a nation if that's the scope of coverage of the organization. Need and desire for publicity vary.

An organization's members, officers, and staff spread the good word about an organization by keeping its work and fundraising efforts in front of the media and public. They seek to have the work shown in a good light. But organization representatives will be disappointed if they believe their event and mission are so newsworthy that media representatives will flock to the organization and beg to hear the story. It's not easy to get noticed. News releases just don't generate stories like they did in the

past. Budget cutting has left fewer news staff to deal with releases, and the ease of Internet distribution of releases has flooded the media. News has become more contrived and standardized. Serious reporting on soft news has become a luxury many newspapers simply no longer support. Nonetheless, there are ways to increase and even ensure success in getting placement of news items and announcements, such as discussions with editors and reporters.

What follows is a brief guide for event planners who want to take an aggressive, proactive approach to promoting an event and gaining publicity for the host organization. It provides essential information needed to get started, but it is not intended to be a complete guide. Gaining publicity can be as simple as mentioning an upcoming event at a civic club meeting. Or it can be more complex, such as contacting news directors or reporters in the local area and establishing a working relationship, and then drafting news releases and public service announcements that are sent to the news directors or reporters. Opportunities will become apparent given a little thought. Here are some ideas.

Build a Media Kit

Organizations that want to put their best foot forward in providing the press an opportunity to report on an upcoming event prepare a media kit. The kit should contain information about the event, the organization, its mission, and the uses of funds to be raised. Include an invitation to members of the press to attend and cover the event.

When developing a media kit, consider the importance of a good first impression. Make sure the kit conveys a strong positive image of the host organization and its work. Provide solid, substantial information, including accurate facts and figures. Be sure to include the name and contact information of a knowledgeable person to contact for more information. If the event will draw attendees from the local community, which is most often the case, it may be helpful to establish a connection between local members of the host organization and the press, so include a list of officers or event planners (ask their permission before providing their names to the press, so they can be prepared to answer questions).

Make it easy for members of the press to learn about the event and the host organization by providing a one-page overview as a quick reference. Also, include any public service announcements produced, directions to the organization's Web site, a copy of any newsletters, brochures, fliers, and previous news articles that describe the event or the organization and its activities. However, don't overload the kit.

Put it all together with style and polish by taking time to proofread everything, use proper grammar and syntax, and if possible, use an eye-catching folder and sequence the information so it makes sense as the reader looks through it. Finally, if possible, put all information in an electronic format as part of the organization's Web site or provided as electronic files in addition to the package. This is the most efficient and effective way to do it, but getting it noticed still requires contacting and establishing a relationship with members of the media.

Write a News Release

A news release (also called "press" or "media" release) contains written information prepared and positioned to present a message to the media in the clearest, most favorable fashion possible. A well-devised release presents media representatives with a recognizable, well-accepted source of news and information. It also offers the writer a means to convey that information with the least chance for media misinterpretation or error. This can be an effective tool to issue information about an event because the release "spells it out" for the media. Subsequent reporting should be accurate. The release also allows control over timing of information release, because a news release can be quickly prepared and distributed when desired. The release also allows for total control over the message and the designated contact for media questions. Sidebar 12.3 provides 10 key points for crafting a news release. Figure 12.1 shows an example news release template.

Media outlets typically receive dozens of news releases every day. Any one release may be over-

shadowed, neglected, or bumped aside. Impact increases when a release is sent directly to an individual who knows the sender of the release or to an individual who has already expressed an interest in the event or the host organization. This requires that members of the host organization or its staff get to know members of the press.

As the release is being prepared, try to picture the ideal attendee and provide information in the release that will appeal to this person. What is it about the organization, mission, or event that will be of interest to and motivate this person to attend? Make the information newsworthy to the media. The release may wind up as nothing more than a one-line announcement on a Web site, listed along with similar announcements for events and activities, or in the weekly list of events and activities carried in the Sunday edition of the local newspaper. As a result, how the release is written will determine how the announcement reads. If it includes just time, place, date, and Web site address for more information, not much will be delivered to the reader, but at least best effort was put forth and an announcement is published. The objective of the release is to generate a short article published in print or on a Web site, or a feature article, radio announcement, or TV story including interviews.

Contact the Press: Newspapers and Magazines

There may be more than one logical recipient at a large newspaper for a news item or event announcement. It is acceptable to send new releases to several media people at each outlet to enhance chances of receiving coverage, but there is no substitute for sending a release to a friend or acquaintance at the newspaper. In lieu of having a friend in the business, here is some general information about who does what at a typical newspaper, with smaller papers combining many of these roles into single positions.

Owners and publishers run the newspaper and greatly influence what gets published. News executives, such as the editor, managing editor, and editorial page editor, are the managers who oversee coverage of news: what gets printed, how it is covered, and who covers it. For example, a person having

Sidebar 12.3. **Ten Key Points for Drafting a News Release**

1. Provide the name(s), phone number, and e-mail information of one or two representatives of the host organization the media can contact for more information.

2. Designate the time of the release (e.g., "For Release Friday, August 23, 2012" or "For Immediate Release").

3. If applicable, attach a photo to the release, such as a photo of a celebrity who will appear at the event (requires permission as part of the celebrity appearance agreement to release images).

4. Emphasize a key element of the event in your headline. Grab the reader's attention. Answer the question "What's in it for me (the reader)?"

5. Use a subheading after the title of the release when a little more information would increase reader interest.

6. In the body of the release, place the most important points first; then work down the text from most important to least important. Thus, if editors cut the story at any point, the most critical facts will have been covered first. Try to include the "who, what, where, when, why, and how" of the event.

7. Use the body of the release to include details. Err on the side of brevity. Once a first draft is written, edit out superfluous words and extraneous information. Avoid the use of jargon and acronyms. Assume the reader will not know anything about the event, the host organization, or its mission.

8. Put people in the body of the release to provide an active voice. For example, include quotes from well-known individuals, officials, or celebrities endorsing the event, the organization, and work to be funded through the event. Identify how people quoted are related to the event.

9. Close the release with a paragraph summarizing the basic facts about the organization hosting the event.

10. Distribute the release by e-mail. If the release is sent to media representatives known to the sender or the sending organization, precede the mailing or follow-up with a call or separate e-mail to that media contact.

one of these titles will decide if a letter to the editor about an organization holding a fundraising event gets published.

The newspaper may have a separate section for covering activities in the community. Newspapers use various names for this section, but it here that fundraising events, such as society galas and walk-a-thons, are covered. The editor of this section assigns reporters and decides on the extent to which an event is covered. Reporters and staff working in this area also maintain the paper's community bulletin board, social media, and Web site coverage of events. It is relatively easy to have an event listed, and some Web sites even allow event promoters to post their own notices.

A news release or request for coverage sent to a newspaper will probably be routed to the community events section if the release or request focuses only on the event. However, if the release focuses on work of the host organization and mentions the event only as a means to fund that work, the story may be routed to an editor in the news or features section of a newspaper. Here the editor decides if the story gets covered and, if so, makes the assignment to reporters.

Contact the Press: TV and Radio

Who's who in TV and radio starts with the real decision makers. Owners or their representatives set editorial policy, and station managers oversee news and entertainment programming. A news director decides what gets covered and who covers it. At radio stations, the news director may be the only newsperson on staff. Assignment editors are the staff members at TV stations and radio stations in large markets who assign reporters to cover stories.

Producers work with the news director to decide whom to invite to appear on programs, which stories to carry, and how much time each receives. Reporters are the people actually reporting the news; they typically research their own stories and conduct interviews. Unlike newspaper reporters, TV and radio reporters tend to be recognizable personalities, as they are usually the stars of their own broadcasts. They work fast. Time between assignment and broadcast may be only a few hours or even minutes, in the case of "live" reporting.

When requesting a TV or radio station to air a report or announcement about an event, it is necessary to designate a spokesperson for an "on-mike" or "on-camera" interview. This person should be comfortable speaking into a microphone and be able to summarize an announcement or main points of the story in 15- to 30-second "sound bites."

News from

<Name of Host Organization>

Address   Phone Number   www.website.org

For Immediate Release

Contact name at telephone; e-mail

HEADLINE—GRAB INTEREST!

Subheading—Tells a Little Bit More

City, State (Date)—**Lead paragraph. Most important information comes first. Who, what, where, when, why, how.**

Body of release. Provides details, quotes, facts, and figures. Use short paragraphs. Place a quotation near the beginning. Most important information goes first, followed by less important information.

Final paragraph provides only information on the organization hosting the event and its mission.

FIGURE 12.1. Example news-release template.

Work the Media: Opinion-Editorial

The opinion-editorial, or "op-ed," presents an opportunity for event promoters to write their own story about the work of the organization and how an upcoming event will help fund that work. To be published, an op-ed must tell a compelling story. A simple event announcement probably will not be published, but mention of the event in the context of an interesting persuasive story is acceptable. The op-ed presents a powerful format for getting out a message. If skillfully written, it is likely to be published, particularly by small newspapers. Here are some tips for writing an op-ed.

Submit the op-ed far enough in advance of the event to allow time for review and publication. Particularly in large communities and large newspapers, op-ed writers compete for limited publication space. The more compelling and interesting the op-ed, the more likely it is to win out over other submissions. Stay focused on one issue. Begin by briefly telling the reader how the host organization's work affects them or others. Use facts if available. Introduce the reader to the upcoming event and how funds raised will help people or otherwise benefit the cause. Be provocative if applicable. This is the place to provoke an emotional response. The ideal reader response is to support the host organization's quest for funds and attend the event. There are usually instructions available for writing op-eds. Locate these instructions in the newspaper or on its Web site, and follow instructions exactly. Include the writer's name and contact information to verify authorship. Follow the directions to submit the op-ed.

If the op-ed has not appeared after about one week, call the editor and ask if the op-ed is under consideration for publication. Use this conversation as an opportunity to let the editor know of the importance of the fundraiser and ask if there is a way for the paper to help—even if the op-ed isn't going to be published. If rapport is established, suggest a meeting or ask if there is a reporter who should receive information as background. Establishing a positive relationship with the editor may not get the op-ed published, but it could be helpful in the future.

Work the Media: Letter to the Editor

A letter to the editor is written and submitted in a fashion similar to the op-ed and can have the same effect to promote an event. Letters are reviewed by editorial page editors, published in the opinion section of the newspaper, and provide the writer full control over what is written. Although op-eds often (but not always) initiate discussion on a topic, the letter to the editor is often (but not always) written in response to a topic of discussion already raised. Letters to the editor are usually shorter than the op-ed. Letters are written subject to instructions found in the newspaper or on its Web site.

Since letters to the editor are most often written in response to a story carried by the newspaper or an earlier op-ed or letter, following this format of responding to something just published may enhance the chance of getting a letter published. This is where the media-savvy event promoter can shine. Search the news for a story or comment article that can be used as a springboard for a letter to the editor. Here the connection can be to the host organization's mission, an entertainer who will appear at the event, or something in the political world. Consider how natural it would be for an organization that holds events to raise money for cancer research to write a letter to the editor in advance of a key vote in Congress on a federal appropriation for research on a new cure-all cancer drug. Letters written in response to a current event or in reaction to a story should be sent to the editor as soon as possible, and the letter should make specific reference to the previous story or event.

Work the Media: Public Service Announcement

Public service announcements are aired by TV and radio stations as a public service to the community. The PSA announces details of the event, explains what money raised will be used for, and maybe covers a few points about the host organization. This must be done very concisely, because PSAs are very brief announcements, generally produced in several lengths to fit into tight time slots: PSAs are aired in several lengths: 10, 15, 30, 45, and

60 seconds. Airing may be confined to times when there are relatively few listeners or viewers (when paid advertising rates are lowest).

Video PSAs of broadcast quality can be expensive to produce, but radio PSAs can be done quickly and inexpensively. It is sometimes possible to get volunteer assistance from a radio or TV station and have a video or radio PSA produced for free. Organizations hosting local events need only concern themselves with local TV and radio stations. These stations are likely to employ staff known by members of the host organization. Station staff can be asked about helping the host organization with a PSA. The procedure can start with any member of the station's staff, but it will probably officially begin by talking with the station manager or a producer and making a direct request for assistance.

If the host organization produces its own PSA, getting it aired may still require the assistance of station staff known to members or a direct request to the station manager. Stations receive numerous PSAs for airing; thus, personal contact with station staff is more effective than simply sending the PSA along with a written request. However, if all else fails, write a letter or make a call requesting airing of the PSA. The more compelling the request, the more critical the issue to be addressed by the funds to be raised, the more likely the PSA will get aired.

Work the Media: Media Event

A media event may be beyond the scope of many event promoter's plans, but for organizations raising money for particularly newsworthy causes or for which celebrities are helping promote the fundraising event, news conferences, press events, or photo opportunities are all workable possibilities. Media events are staged opportunities for the press to meet with the celebrity or representatives of the organization who will provide information or allow the press to ask questions and take photographs.

Consider the response of reporters to an invitation to a press conference being held by an organization hosting an event that will feature an appearance by a recently divorced A-list movie star. The

advisory to the press announcing the conference guarantees a photo opportunity with the celebrity. The star's bad luck in marriage will probably be good luck for the host seeking publicity for its event. The press will probably flock to the press conference and to the event. The host controls the agenda at the press conference, but questions from members of the press can make for interesting and unplanned interchange. Such conferences can be restricted to print press or broadcast press, but for the purpose of promoting an event, all press should be invited.

Nuance is involved in holding an effective press conference. Sidebar 12.4 lists 15 key suggestions, but the best advice for an organization planning a press conference is to have a professional helping or at least standing by to help if needed. There are no excuses for a failed press conference, although it is very common for a carefully planned press conference to be upstaged by a major breaking news story. In such a case, the only option may be to reschedule the press conference. Notwithstanding a catastrophe on the day of the press conference, the initiator of the conference sets the time and place and controls who comes, who speaks, what the speakers say, and when the conference ends. The initiator controls success or failure. What the initiator can't control is what the press will ask or do in follow-up to the conference, and therein lies great risk.

Seek Out Special Media

Getting press to the fundraising event itself may be a challenge in large cities or anywhere large numbers of organizations are all fundraising at the same time. But some media seek information about events, including fundraisers. These outlets can publish announcements and full-feature articles. Included in this category of media are Web sites or pages dedicated to announcements about community events and charitable activities. Civic-oriented businesses, such as banks and coffee shops, often have newsletters or bulletin boards providing space to announce events. Newspapers, community magazines, and TV and radio stations may have special sections and programs to announce events, and their

Sidebar 12.4. **Fifteen Hints for Holding a Successful Press Conference**

1. Write a short script. Short quotable phrases can be prepared and rehearsed in advance. A good "sound bite" well delivered is an effective communication technique to use during a press conference.

2. Choose well who will represent the host organization and moderate the press conference. Does the spokesperson understand the possible repercussions of his or her answers, possess the depth of knowledge and public speaking ability to field questions, maintain a poised presence, and realize when silence is the best answer? Sure, the purpose of the press conference is to promote a fundraising event, but invited members of the press may ask any question they wish. Some organizations or members of organizations do things that are controversial and may be of interest to the press. Anything can come up at a press conference, no matter what conference organizers may do to orchestrate the actions of reporters. Be prepared. The best defense is using a cool, level-headed approach ensuring that only designated spokespersons speak to the media, and ensuring that these spokespersons have a thorough knowledge of the topic, have anticipated likely questions, and have formed their responses ahead of time.

3. Issue a written invitation to the press one month before the date, and send a follow-up invitation one week before. Call by phone or e-mail to confirm attendance as follow-ups to the two invitations. The written invitation should include this information:

• The purpose of the press conference and availability of celebrities if applicable
• Date and time
• Location
• Spokespersons' names
• A clear statement describing the significant news value of the fundraising event

4. Entice the press to attend and create a center of attention by featuring the appearance of a celebrity or by doing or presenting something at the conference that is unmistakably newsworthy.

5. Enhance media appeal by offering one-on-one interviews with spokespersons, and let the media know about this opportunity in advance. Include a local, state, or national personality as one of the spokespersons.

6. Hold the conference between midmorning and midafternoon. Avoid Fridays and days before holidays. Be sure to check media deadlines for scheduling to ensure availability of press.

7. Hold it at a convenient, easy-to-reach location for media.

8. Write a statement for the spokesperson(s) to give at the conference, and have copies of the statement available for distribution at the conference.

9. Have the host organization's representative speak first to describe the work of the organization and announce the fundraising event. Follow with other speakers, and end with the statement or appearance of the celebrity, if one is involved in the event.

10. Rehearse the entire conference, including introductions and presentation of the prepared statement, and hold a mock question-and-answer period.

11. Prepare printed written and visual materials for distribution at the conference. Include materials about the fundraising event, the organization, and the work of the organization. Include photos or video of the host organization's work if available. Television reporters particularly need something visual.

12. Plan the room, and make sure everything in the room is properly arranged. Make sure there are a sufficient number of chairs and a lectern if needed. The room must be large enough to accommodate TV crews and all their equipment. Plan for unobstructed filming or 6- to 12-inch risers behind the last row of chairs so camera crews can shoot over those sitting in front.

13. Arrive 30 to 60 minutes early to double-check arrangements. Test the microphones, arrange name tags for invited guests, and distribute media kits.

14. Provide a written agenda, including any restrictions, and have the principal spokesperson or a moderator control the conference.

15. Keep a record of reporters and producers who attend, and follow up. Send thank-you notes, and let them know the organization's members saw the coverage. Keep the press informed about future events.

Web sites may provide a space for listing. Finally, many newspapers and community magazines have special sections that cover society events. Getting an announcement on the society page can be a critical endorsement in some communities. An even grander mark of distinction is having an event covered by a society section reporter and photographer, and a story and photos are run after the event. Event planners work hard to ensure such coverage takes place.

Turn the Quest for Event Publicity Inside Out

Up to this point the chapter focus has been on seeking publicity for an event by putting facts about the event first in solicitations to media. In the course of succeeding in that quest, good press can flow to the host organization, the cause, and how money raised at the event will help accomplish the organization's mission.

There is another way to get to the same place. Turn the emphasis of the solicitation inside out. Instead of focusing on the event first, focus on seeking press for a problem the host organization hopes to fix by using money raised at the event. Now the emphasis will be on pitching a story about a problem. Media kits, press releases, and contact with reporters will spotlight work that the host organization has under way to fix the problem.

For example, if the host organization is going to hold the event to raise money to help feed families displaced by a flood, then the subject of the pitch to media would be the flood and the effect on families. The story would naturally turn attention to the host organization and its efforts to raise money for food by holding the event. Another example is to describe the loss of species expected to occur if global warming continues. Species are the feature of the story, but the organization's role in discovering the connection between species loss and climate is also mentioned. Of course, this story would not be complete without mentioning the upcoming fundraiser to pay for species research funded by the organization.

In places where the media are constantly being asked to run PSAs or stories about events, there might be some reluctance to provide free advertising. In this case it is probably best to seek a story about the problems to be solved, such as the food needed for families and the research needed on global warming. After all, newspapers, magazines, and TV and radio stations all sell advertising. They may be as likely to say "buy an add" as run a story about a fundraising event, but the media are always looking for a good tale to tell.

Follow Up

After the event, stay in touch with editors, reporters, and others contacted during promotion of the event. Do this even with those who failed to cover the story. Assign this responsibility to a person on the planning group who will continue helping with the event in the following year. It need not be a difficult or time-consuming task. An occasional handwritten note or an e-mail or two are all that is needed.

If the event itself was covered by the media, thank the people responsible. Also write to thank TV and radio station managers and publishers of magazines and newspapers that ran stories. Let members of the host organization know about the coverage by acknowledging the media coverage in newsletters, on the Web site, or by mention in the host organization's magazine or newspaper. A note of appreciation to a community magazine publisher or editor is particularly warranted if a story about the event was carried on the society pages of the magazine.

13

Donation Acquisition

My family accompanied me to an auction event being held by a chapter of the national organization I was working for at the time. It was at a beach resort, so there were other families at the event. My children were present during the early fundraising activities, among which was a raffle with a series of prizes. I bought a few tickets and split the stubs among my three daughters.

Sure enough, my lucky daughter who was about six years old at the time held a winning ticket. She was soon engulfed in a police-style jacket, with all the labels cut out. What I mean by "cut out" is that all of the labels normally sewn into the fabric of the jacket had been sliced out, leaving holes where the labels had been. It was obvious this was a "clearance" or "surplus" item from a uniform supply house.

The host organization had obtained this and many other items by soliciting local businesses. This prize was out of character for my daughter, but the real issue was that the prize was also out of character for virtually all the other attendees. So were many other prizes. Old cheap fishing rods, out-of-style items of clothing, and wind-up merchandise in a digital age stocked the raffles. The auctions fared no better, with old prints, faded merchandise, and useless services among offerings. I have attended events where auction and raffle tables stacked full of useless goods gave me the impression the event was a garage sale.

There is plenty of "stuff" for attendees, but is it the right stuff? I suspect it would be for attendees with a passion for unsalable and out-of-date merchandise, but that is a rare demographic characteristic and not one typically targeted by event planners. Why offer a sophisticated crowd unsophisticated auction items and raffle prizes? The host organization's volunteers had collected all that stuff in a door-to-door canvass of local merchants. They got exactly what they asked for, which was probably "a donation of merchandise or a service." The volunteers obviously took whatever the merchants had handy to give. The result was an event full of odds and ends, some new, some old, some good, some not.

For some events, a hodge-podge of out-of-date, surplus, and bargain-basement items might be acceptable, but for most events it is definitely not. Events that are full of items unattractive to attendees and that have values poorly matched to attendee spending potential produce lower revenue than those where attendees are presented more appropriate items. But not just net auction revenue suffers. Year-to-year attendance at an event is often influenced by memorable experiences of attendees of past events. People talk to each other, and friends bring friends to events. If an event becomes known for its auctions and raffles being "full of junk," that becomes the talk among potential attendees for next year's event. Who wants to attend an event full of junk? Not me! How about you?

AUCTIONS UNDERPIN effective fundraisers because people are given an opportunity to purchase something that they would like to have *and* make a donation to their favorite charity at the same time. Auction items should be affordable and match the interests of the people who will attend the event. It does no good to offer a fabulous trip on the Yangtze River in China, which everyone at the auction might find absolutely irresistible, if none of the people who attend can afford to offer a minimum bid. On the other hand, significant revenue is lost when bidders are offered items such as a weekend stay at a local resort when they would prefer a trip on the Yangtze River and can afford to bid on such a trip to full fair market value and beyond. The success of an event rests on the attractiveness and affordability of items that will be offered to attendees. This includes all auction items as well as any raffle items or game prizes.

Know the Attendees and Bidders

The look and feel of an auction event is largely determined by the kinds of items offered to auction bidders and raffle ticket buyers. This interplay between "feel" and "fundraising offerings" plays a large role in the success or failure of an auction event—and in meeting net fundraising goals. Auction and raffle items need to "match" the buyers' interest and willingness (ability) to spend. Items too fancy or expensive will not sell to a blue-collar crowd who cannot afford the items or have no use for them. Items too cheap or tacky will not sell to a highbrow crowd seeking unique and flashy new toys for their homes and offices.

Whom the event planners wish to attract and who will actually come to the auction and bid determine the kinds of auction items to acquire. Realistic planning requires catering to the interests of those who will actually actively participate in bidding and other fundraising activities. The success of any live or silent auction depends on matching auction items with actual bidders. This is a subtle point that event planners often miss. Yes, it matters who attends an event, but the only ones who matter during fundraising activities are those who bid, buy raffle tickets, and otherwise pay to play.

Some knowledge of the demographics of the host organization's membership is helpful, provided it is the organization's members who will make up the bulk of bidders. Perhaps a different group is being targeted for attendance at the fundraising event. If so, auction items should be acquired with the demographic makeup of the bidders in mind. Demographic information of value in planning an event includes economic information, such as household income, and other factors such as recreational interests, buying patterns, family status, home ownership, travel patterns, and type of employment.

In most instances event planners will already have a general idea of the interests and economic status of members and probably many potential bidders. Many events are attended mainly by friends and neighbors or members of the host organization. As a result, event planners may have a very good idea what kinds of auction items will receive an enthusiastic response. A case of fine wine might work well at an auction held in a neighborhood where many of the attendees enjoy neighborhood progressive dinners. This may have nothing to do with the mission of the charitable organization hosting the event, but many of the attendees at the event will be known as participants in the neighborhood dinners who will compete with each other bidding on the case of wine. That same case of wine, however, might not be appropriate if the host organization is raising funds to fight drunk driving. In a similar fashion, a Labrador puppy might be the hit of an auction where there will be many duck hunters attending, but the same cute puppy might be out of place if funds are being raised to end human oppression of animals.

If events are focused on reaching out beyond the organization's membership into the local community or farther, planners may have to depend on research and evaluation for determining items and services to offer. With a little research, planners should at least find obvious answers. For example, if the majority of prospective attendees have household incomes of less than $40,000, the host organization is unlikely to receive acceptable bids on $10,000 wilderness vacations in Alaska or $2,000 binoculars. Equally obvious should be the wasted revenue potential if many of the expected attendees have household incomes greater than $100,000 and the most attractive auction items offered to bidders are a $100 makeover at the local spa and dinner for two at the best restaurant in town.

Another obvious way to match attendee interests with auction items and raffle prizes is to focus event fundraising offerings on the special interests of the host organization. Specialty-item auctions can match well with an organization's specialized membership who have unique interests in common or are working on a common cause. Similar demographics or unifying characteristics are often the basis for membership in charitable organizations. Offering items too general in nature at events attended largely by such an organization's membership does not take advantage of serving that special interest.

Here are some examples of how to match auction and raffle items with the desires and spending capacity of attendees:

- At the event of an organization supporting exploration of the last wild places on earth, attendees are offered a wide range of adventure vacation trips, from pole to pole.
- At the event of an organization raising funds to preserve old films of national parks in the West, attendees are offered an assortment of old movie posters where national parks were featured, apparel worn by film stars in old western movies, and various props used in famous western movies.
- At the event of an organization advocating water conservation, attendees are offered a wide range of green products for home and garden.

Also see chapter 18 for additional details on determining the perfect mix of fundraising items for use at different types of events and groups of attendees.

Develop a Plan for Item Acquisition

Through group discussion involving the event chairperson and all members of the fundraising or donation-acquisition team, develop a plan to guide acquisition of all items to be used in auctions, raffles, and games. The objective is to set goals about what types of items to obtain, how many items of what type to obtain, and if appropriate, exactly what item to obtain, right down to model number, size, color, and so on. This planning should take into account an assessment of what kinds of items will be most attractive to the people who will attend the auction event, how many people will attend, and what their spending capacity is.

Details of the plan should include goals for acquisition of items for each of the live and silent auctions, the various raffles and games, table and door prizes, and giveaways that go to all attendees. Included in this planning should be a realistic assessment of which items can be obtained for free through donation and which may have to be purchased and at what price. Game prizes may be very specific in nature (relating to the game) and often need to be purchased in bulk quantities, especially for children's games where all players receive a prize. Establish a budget to cover any items that must be purchased. Item-acquisition budget planning can be done within the context of developing the event business plan or as an add-on to that planning (see chapter 5).

Although auction items or raffle items are referred to in sections of the book covering acquisition of donations, the same principles of acquisition apply for all solicited donations, whether cash, merchandise, or services or whether the donations will be used for auctions, games, raffles, underwriting, prizes, door and table prizes, or giveaways. Items for auction are obtained in various ways. Because there are so many types of nonprofit organizations, and because the memberships of organizations vary greatly, it is difficult to provide a single rule of thumb to follow in setting out to acquire event merchandise and services. Following are the four major categories of items:

1. *Full donation.* Full donations are items or services given to the host organization at no cost and with no obligation.

2. *Partial donation.* Partial donations are items or services for which the host organization must pay some portion of the value of the auction item to the donor should the item sell at auction. There is often a minimum bid set for such items, and if the item gets no bidders, the item is not sold and is returned to the donor. This partial payment can be a set fee, a percentage of the bid price (called a split), or an in-kind payment such as special ad space in the host organization's magazine.

3. *Quid pro quo donations.* Partial donations for which a donor expects compensation, goods, or services that are not insubstantial in return for a donation to the charity event are also called quid pro quo contributions. The host organization has specific legal requirements to advise the donor of the value of the goods or services to be received in return for this donation if it is valued at more than $75. Quid pro quo donations and what constitutes an insubstantial contribution are defined by IRS rules (see chapter 21).

4. *Full purchase.* Items can be purchased at the usual retail price, at wholesale, or at a special discount given by service providers, retail merchants, manufacturers, or artists.

Don't Ask for Junk

This chapter started with a story about the unfavorable effect of presenting attendees with auctions and raffles full of useless excess inventory obtained from merchants. When merchants donate such inventory to a charitable organization, they may receive tax benefits, generally equal to whatever the merchant originally paid for the item. That may sound like a pretty good deal to a merchant. The donation is a way to get a little publicity and perhaps the only way the merchant will ever break even on an item that has been collecting dust for the past several years. But the good businesspeople in town may not be the only people seeing a charity fundraiser as an opportunity to unload unwanted junk and at the same time receive a tax benefit. For detailed information about tax deductibility and benefits, see chapter 21.

Individuals often donate items, such as works of art or antiques. These may be items considered valuable, or maybe the item is just junk the donor no longer needs. A donation can provide a little recognition and maybe a little tax break. However, the tax advantage of donating merchandise and services to charity events for individuals is less attractive than many donors realize (as will be further explained in chapter 21), yet some charity events are filled with other people's old stuff.

Without policies governing acceptance of event donations, item-acquisition team members can quickly fill an event with junk from merchants, friends, and neighbors. In the end, the fundraiser is like a white elephant gift exchange—everyone leaves with something useless. Given the propensity of donors to donate junk and perceived tax benefits of doing so, how do event planners obtain the desirable merchandise and services needed to pull off a financially successful event? The answer is simple. There is a saying in fundraising that "people give only when asked to give."

How and what donors are asked to give is the

key to what they give. If the request to a donor is an open request for any kind of donation, that will be the result. That includes any junk lying around that may come to the attention of the donor at the time of the request. It could be anything—donations become strictly a matter of chance. Even a provider of a specific service may surprise the person soliciting donations by offering something completely unexpected—something just lying around. For example, the operator of a bike-tour company may donate a case of water bottles featuring the company's name and logo instead of a bike tour as was expected by the person making the request. If the request is for a specific item, then the donor's response focuses on the item requested and that's where the discussion starts between the donor and the person making the request.

The key to effectively asking for a donation is to know ahead of time what to ask for and then ask for that specific item. If the donor is willing to make a donation, but not of the item requested, then a discussion begins. It may be possible to come up with an excellent alternative to the original request or fill another need. Continuing with the example of the bike-tour operator and water bottles, let's say the person asking for the donation was well prepared and initially asked for donation of a bike tour, but the operator said no and offered a dozen water bottles instead. The member of the acquisition team might see value in using the bottles as prizes for one of the children's games, but needs at least 100 bottles. At that point the discussion can turn to donation of more bottles.

Get the Right Stuff

Event planners need to use their best judgment when planning their first auction event. For subsequent auctions, planners will have the benefit of experience, and in particular when setting goals for auction-item acquisition. When in doubt, the best option is to seek out and enlist a person with fundraising experience with the prospective attendees. If an auction event was held in previous years, people with experience may be available to help. Help

could range from someone who gives simple advice, to an adviser who participates on the event planning committee. If such a person is not available or this is the first auction fundraiser, the event planner should try to consult with others who do have experience.

As has been detailed previously, the kind of auction and raffle items offered should match the interests of attendees and their ability to pay and generate excitement. Particularly during periods of economic downturn, it is critical to offer attendees items they truly want or need. Otherwise, spending beyond token amounts may be hard for attendees to justify. A charitable organization strikes gold when attendees are presented a menu of merchandise or services they are already poised to buy on the open market. For example, an event held a few weeks before Valentine's Day could feature affordable romantic gift items for men and women. Attendees may see the auction as a chance to get a gift they need to buy anyway and have fun doing so while they also make a contribution to the host.

A majority of nonprofit organizations are special-interest organizations by nature, if not by name. In many cases, members share a common interest, and it is this interest that planners need to take into account when setting goals for acquisition of auction and raffle items. This can be an interest in religion, education, wildlife, pets, sports, personal wellness, or certain goods or services (such as a love of wine or a craving to visit state parks to bird-watch). Many of these interests have obvious ties to products and services that can be used as the basis of auctions and raffles.

Items relating to an organization's specialized interests should generally make up the largest category of auction and raffle items. An example is an organization dedicated to protecting access rights to streams for paddle sports whose fundraising auction is filled with canoeing, kayaking, and rafting items. Another example is an organization that raises funds to protect African elephants whose annual auction and raffle is filled with sightseeing tours of wildlife parks in Africa, paintings of African wildlife, and various items for the home depicting elephants.

However, there is a balance to be considered,

and this balance point is hard to describe in a generalized fashion. If there are too few highly desirable items that yield high net revenue, then the host organization loses some level of potential revenue. However, if there are too many items of one kind and level, it is possible to reach a point of diminishing return, as prices for all these items may become depressed. It is possible for an auction to offer "too much of a good thing." Planners need to use judgment and, if available, experience in finding the balance point.

As an example of finding a balance point, consider the past craze over wildlife art prints at auctions held by wildlife conservation organizations to benefit species habitat protection. During this period nicely framed wildlife art prints sold well. Some events featured dozens of prints as auction and raffle prizes, even in small towns. Soon values dropped because too many prints were being offered at auctions and people began to realize that just a few art prints at home and in the office were nice enough. Once walls were filled with wildlife art prints, there was no need or desire for more such prints. Art is still a popular and effective item in the auctions and raffles of wildlife organizations today, but only when offered in moderation. Find the balance, and then use experience to monitor and adjust over time.

Planning for a Different Crowd

Event planners for special-interest organizations should know what will entice their members to an auction and have them bidding like crazy. But sometimes members come from a true cross section of society, or an organization's members are not the target of fundraising efforts. Sometimes an organization would rather nonmembers be the major contributors to an event. Some charitable organizations have no individual members. In these cases two good options are available to the host organization: (1) general merchandise and services events and (2) theme merchandise and services events. These can offer something for everyone, which is exactly what is needed if there is no special unifying interest or demo-

graphic factor among attendees. However, it will still be necessary to do sufficient homework to match merchandise and services with prospective attendee general interest and financial capacity to pay.

OPTION 1: GENERAL MERCHANDISE AND SERVICES EVENTS

Sometimes the best item selection for an event is just a good assortment of new high-quality general household, outdoor, and personal items and services. This kind of general assortment can be most effective in small communities where attendees will have medium-level incomes and no uniform special interest—it provides something for everyone. Even though not all people will be looking for the same things, they will still be excited to find something in an auction or raffle that they want or need. Provide a general assortment of useful and quality items, and attendees are likely to find something. This is particularly an effective option if attendees may be reluctant to bid on items just for the sake of bidding or making a contribution to the organization. Here, people bid on what they need, either to replace something that is worn out or to get something new that they want.

However, just because auction items are general in nature does not mean that the items can be acquired in a hodge-podge fashion. In fact, choosing items needs to be done just as carefully for an event featuring a general selection of items as an event featuring specialty items or a specific theme. That is, auctions and raffles that give the appearance of a garage sale will do no better than a garage sale. In addition, over time such auctions and raffles ultimately will attract only those people who normally go to garage sales, the pattern of buying will become similar to that at garage sales, and the proceeds from the event will likely reflect this.

General merchandise needs to be carefully selected to provide just the right assortment of quality merchandise and services that will appeal to the widest variety of local interests at a price level consistent with the attendees' willingness and ability to pay. Sidebar 13.1 provides a list of example items for a general merchandise raffle.

Sidebar 13.1. **General Prize Assortment for Mid-Level-Value Auctions and Raffles**

Top Live-Auction and Grand-Raffle Items	Gift certificate to the local mall
Lawn tractor	Wheelbarrow
Patio furniture	Camping equipment
Spa/hot tub	Plumbing fixtures
Showroom auto detailing with free car washes for a year	Round of golf with lessons from the pro
Set of golf clubs and bag	Dog-obedience training classes
Weekend getaway to a nearby city or vacation resort	Plants from a local nursery
Laptop computer	Case of wine
New kitchen cabinets and countertops	Wall paint
Playground set	Fence materials
Quality tool chest or power tools	Family photo session
Cooler containing 100 pounds of beef	Party-room fixtures
Set of quality car tires	Day at a spa
	Telescope or binoculars
Second-Tier Live Auction, Silent Auction, and Raffle Items	Sports bag
Garden tools	Six-month membership to a fitness club
Restaurant gift certificates	Youth sports equipment
Fishing trip with a local guide	Oil and filter change
Moderately priced jewelry	Designer mailbox
Art print	Vacuum cleaner
Lamp set	Fireplace screen and tools
Electric fan	

OPTION 2: THEME MERCHANDISE
AND SERVICES EVENTS

Auction items can be acquired and an auction event designed in a fashion that is somewhat general in nature but creates extra excitement by forming fundraising activities around a theme for the event. A specialty-theme event can result in spectacular success for the host, even if the specialty products or services offered have nothing to do with the goals of the host organization or its members' interests.

For example, an organization supporting preservation of a historic fish hatchery could host an "Exotic Fishing Vacation Gala" by offering an auction with the central theme of fishing vacations in faraway places. To do this successfully, the host would have to be reasonably certain that a sufficient number of attendees would have the financial ability to buy exotic-vacation getaways at the auction. The theme could be carried through with a selection of other moderately valued auction and raffle items. Old

fishing creels, fly-fishing vests, art prints of fishing scenes in remote locations, and other kinds of fishing accessories could be offered. To maintain value, the host would limit actual vacation getaways to a reasonable number, based on the number of attendees anticipated and their ability to pay.

An example of a theme event for attendees of more limited finances is a "Dining Out" event with items focused on local or regional restaurants, bed-and-breakfast lodges, and associated services, such as babysitting, limousine service, or tickets for "dinner and a movie."

Increasing Value by Adding Auction Features

Matching auction items to the interests and giving potential of bidders makes perfect sense to maximize both net revenue and revenue to value of items auctioned. But there is another twist to add to this formula for success. Certain auction items may be offered that do not meet these usual criteria. They are selected for the explicit purpose of adding fun, creating a tradition, making a point, or introducing a person, company, or product to attendees. Sometimes these "added features" can provide unpredictably huge net revenue as well, for example:

- The ugly necktie being worn by the MC, who is also a local TV news anchor
- Tickets to the Super Bowl to watch the local professional football team play—the tickets good only *if* the team makes it to the Super Bowl
- The keys to the city auctioned off by the mayor
- A family dinner cooked in the winning bidder's home by the sponsoring organization's executive director and served by the sponsoring organization's president
- The pieces of the bat most recently broken by the local minor league baseball team's star slugger, signed by him in person onstage

At one auction a "traveling" outhouse—full-sized—was auctioned off. This "high-value" auction item apparently is auctioned off each year and relocated annually to the backyard of the successful bidder. One truly high-value item, on which the winning bid was double its value, was a white two-seater sports car with the hood signed by numerous pro ballplayers. The imagination is among the best tools available for selecting or creating featured items for auction. However, such items should be limited to one or two in any single live auction.

Deciding on what to auction off can be fun, but the decision shouldn't be taken lightly, because the right item can deliver serious revenue at virtually no expense. A poorly selected item that brings low bids just wastes time, because these items often have little or no real value. Sometimes auction of a fun item just happens. For example, at the end of an auction a prominent member may simply stand up and offer an extra auction item, and there it is, an outhouse is placed on the auction block. Amazingly and unexpectedly, a tradition is born, and the host organization gets a revenue-producing outhouse that is passed on from bidder to bidder, event to event.

Understand That Price Matters

A key factor in generating high auction revenue is providing high-quality merchandise and services that match the interests and demographic profile of attendees. But an equally critical factor is understanding the financial capacity of attendees to buy what is being auctioned. It's simple: The range of values of auction items must generally match the range of attendees' disposable income. This may seem obvious, and it may be repetitive to state the obvious, but failure to understand what it means to make this match is one of the most common errors of event planners.

If auction items are fully donated to the host organization, event planners may perceive no harm if bidders pay far less for auction items than the items are worth. They may not even see the more obvious harm when bidders would pay more if presented with opportunities to do so. After all, the host organization has no more or less expense if bids are low or high if auction items are 100% donated, so any bid is a good bid in the opinion of unsavvy event planners. But they are wrong. There can be harm because not all bids are good. Host organizations have an obligation to seek a fair price for each donation. Fair market values are always listed for each item in an auction, but that is not the "fair price" referred to here. Bidding doesn't have to reach beyond fair market value to be a fair bid. A bid is fair if it is high enough to satisfy both host organization and donor that the item was properly featured and received a sufficient bid.

If attendees do not have the capacity to bid appropriate amounts for items solicited, the host breaks faith with the donor and may even be accused of misrepresenting intentions at the time donations were solicited. For example, how can an organization ask an artist to donate an original work of art valued at $3,000 or a sporting goods store manager to donate a $4,000 all-terrain vehicle (ATV) for an auction event where attendees will be retirees on fixed incomes who cannot afford to spend more than a few hundred dollars? Sure, the art and ATV will be auctioned off and the host will receive some net revenue, but if these items are bought for only a fraction of value, the host loses considerable potential net revenue and the excess or added value of the donation is wasted.

Long-term revenue potential of an event can be compromised when donors of items see them go for far less than value, diminishing the worth of the donations. This can embarrass or upset the donor. A likely consequence is that the donor will not make donations in the future or donations in subsequent years are of lesser value. The only winner in this situation is the bidder who gets a bargain.

The alternative situation is no less a problem—bidders are presented with items of a value far less than they are willing to pay. Here the host organization loses potential revenue and in a sense wastes the time of attendees. Attendees presented with low-value items in auctions and raffles may quickly lose interest in the event and may not attend in subsequent years. The host organization ultimately loses even more as potential bidders with a high capacity for giving fail to return.

Gather Event Merchandise and Services

All the merchandise and services must be acquired and assembled for the fundraising event. A number of techniques and options are available.

Matching People to the Task of the Ask

Someone has to ask potential donors to donate items for use at an event. That job goes to members of the fundraising or item-acquisition team. This team of volunteers and staff is designated and delegated responsibility to solicit and acquire donations. Members of the team should be outgoing, have good relationships with potential donors, and be willing to ask for donations. The team also needs the flexibility to enlist other volunteers on a case-by-case basis who may have access to certain potential donors. Team members should be able to represent the organization when speaking to potential donors about making gifts and be able to clearly describe the purposes of the organization, as well as provide details about the event and any benefits donors will receive for making donations.

The nature of the event and the kinds of items the host is seeking will influence who should be selected to be a member of the acquisition team. For example, members of the team may need to have a strong local base of contacts if items are to come from local merchants. If the host is an international organization and will be seeking donations from service providers in many different countries, then acquisition team members need to have global contacts who can provide items such as a photo safari in Kenya or a riverboat trip on the Amazon River. If the host organization is focused on a special interest and bidders will come from the membership, then acquisition team members should have contacts among providers of the specialized products and services of interest to the organization's members.

Getting to the Asking Point

There are numerous ways acquisition team members can locate auction items. It may be easy if the team members already have relationships with potential donors and thus already know where to look. But when team members do not know where to locate desired items, they can conduct research on the Internet, search catalogs, and contact trade associations or experts if necessary to locate specialty or one-of-a-kind items. The objective is to obtain current contact information for retailers, manufacturers, artists, and other producers and service providers who can furnish the items sought. Several sources for a particular item should be obtained, because several potential donors may have to be contacted before one is found willing to make a donation. This becomes more difficult when seeking one-of-a-kind donations for which there may be a single source or just a few sources worldwide.

Large corporations generally have a contact person who deals with requests from charitable organizations. This person can be identified by calling the corporate offices and talking to one of the top administrative assistants. In smaller companies the principal contact is invariably the owner. When team members are seeking art and one-of-a-kind productions, the contact is usually the artist.

Once sources for items are located and contact

information is available, there are several ways to initiate contact and ask for donations. In all instances a direct request—an ask—must be made. The more specific and compelling the ask, the more effectively appropriate items will be acquired.

Soliciting

The best way for team members to acquire auction items is to personally ask service providers, retail merchants, manufacturers, artists, craftspersons, private collectors, and so on to make a donation. This works well when team members already have a personal relationship with people who have something to give. The ideal acquisition team is one in which each member has close personal relationships with people who can donate items perfectly matched with prospective bidders' most cherished wishes. Such "dream teams" and cooperative bidders are a rarity.

More typical are acquisition teams in which each member has a few good contacts, but nowhere near the number needed. This is particularly the case when very specific or one-of-a-kind auction items are sought. Acquisition team members quickly find that not all of their prospects are willing to donate the items solicited. For the typical acquisition team, that means team members need to take solicitation beyond their acquaintances, which requires a willingness to do research to locate prospective donors and ask these complete strangers for gifts. Sidebar 13.2 provides rules for starting down this path.

The Art of Asking

Be specific with requests. Donors may agree to make a donation, but if the request is not specific, the donor may donate an item that has little or no value to prospective attendees and bidders. Even worse, a winning bidder may receive a defective product or find that some additional payment is required to make a donated service meaningful. As an example of winning bidders being confronted with unexpected added costs, consider the dilemma presented by a dream vacation to the world-famous sand dunes of Sossusvlei in Namibia. Upon arrival,

the winning bidders—a couple looking for adventure and romance in a faraway land—find that to truly enjoy the magnificent red dunes, they will need to rent a four-wheel-drive vehicle. In addition, they soon learn they will have to pay extra for the once-in-a-lifetime sunrise balloon flight and the romantic camel trek under the stars. After making a trip halfway around the world, they will likely purchase these extras, but the surprised couple will be much more wary next time they come to the host organization's auction—if they ever come back. The host and winning bidder need to know the quality and specific details of donated items.

MAKING COLD CALLS

The best way to make a cold call is to warm it up by having someone make an introduction first. Through the introduction, an acquaintance of the donor vouches for the acquisition team member or the host organization. If an introduction is not possible, a truly cold call may be the only way to make an ask for an item.

If the donor is located nearby, call on the telephone and ask for an appointment to visit. Explain the reason for wanting to meet, and state that the conversation will take no more than 10 minutes. If it becomes clear during the phone call that a personal meeting is not going to work out, change the request and ask for a few minutes of the potential donor's time on the telephone. Otherwise, make an appointment to meet the potential donor. Whether done by telephone or in person, make the request to the donor brief and explain the following:

- The nature of the call—to request a donation for a charity event
- The organization hosting the event
- The cause for which money is being raised
- The event where the donation will be featured
- Any benefits or advertising value to donors
- The specific item requested for donation
- The reason that the requested item is so special to the people who will attend the event

This is a lot to cover briefly, so acquisition team members need to have their thoughts and state-

Sidebar 13.2. **Five Essential Rules for Obtaining Auction and Raffle Items**

1. *Obtain each item at the lowest "price" possible.* Preferably items will be donated at zero cost to the host organization. Such items are called 100% "full" donations and offer the host organization an opportunity to receive an almost 100% net return on the item. Why almost 100%? Because there are often costs associated with auction items, even when the item itself has been donated, free and clear. These can be costs such as shipping, materials and labor to construct special display stands (or rental costs), production of marketing materials such as auction catalogs, frames for artwork, or security guards hired to watch particularly valuable items.

2. *Obtain items of the right type, quality, value, and profile.* Bidders bid on what bidders want. Know the bidders, what they want, and what they can spend, and then give it to them at auction. Perfect auction items drive bidders wild, because the items are exactly what the bidders want or need.

3. *Obtain donations with the intent of establishing a long-term relationship with the donor.* It is easier to retain a donor from year to year than to find new donors each year. How a host organization's representatives treat donors and donated items plays a critical role in whether or not a donor will donate again in the future. During the solicitation process, be polite, explain the organization's goals, describe the event, invite the donor to attend, describe the benefits to the donor of making a donation, invite the donor to become a member or offer a free trial membership if appropriate, and follow through on all promises or statements made to the donor. During the event and afterward, thank the donor in a warm and sincere fashion. Follow up immediately after the event with a letter or other means to extend thanks, and do so at least once again maybe six months after the event, but at least prior to soliciting the donor for the following year's event.

4. *Follow the rules.* The host organization should develop and follow a written acquisition plan and policies. The acquisition

plan details the acquisition objectives, specific items, number of items, and so on. Acquisition policies govern the rules by which the organization will acquire and use the items. From the acquisition team members' perspectives, policies help take the guesswork out of acquisition and lower the risk of liability. Any concerns and questions team members or potential donors have should be covered by a well-prepared set of policies. Policies also help ensure consistency in working from one donor to the next. No donors should be given preferential treatment over others. If that happens, particularly in small towns, talk among donors will eventually raise questions about differential treatment. Since the host organization sets policy, when acquisition team members follow the acquisition policy, they are assured of faithfully and consistently representing the organization. Donors also gain assurance that acquisition team members will treat them in a fashion approved by the host organization. Donors also gain added confidence that any deals offered by acquisition team members are approved by the host organization.

5. *Get it in writing—period.* Items and services donated for an event should be clearly described, in detail and in writing, on specifically designed forms that are signed by the donor (see figure 13.1). Getting the donation described in writing is particularly important for service items, items being made or modified for use at the event, or any merchandise that may come in different models, colors, sizes, pieces, and so on. It is important to establish the exact donation. Also important to put in writing are conditions of the donation, particularly if the item will be auctioned on consignment or if the donor will receive any payment, partial payment, goods, or services in return for the donation. If possible, also have the donor provide an estimated fair market value for the item. If the item is merchandise, a list price will suffice. The donor's estimate of value provides a starting point for fulfilling the host organization's obligation to use good faith in listing fair market value for all auction items worth more than $75.

ments well organized in advance of talking to prospective donors. Address all the initial questions. If the potential donor is able and willing to make a donation, the initial solicitation will extend into a discussion in which more details can be covered.

A potential donor may be familiar with the host organization and event. This will most likely be the case in small cities and towns. This familiarity may be good or bad, depending on the perception the perspective donor has of the organization or event. A

bad impression may be difficult to overcome, but the request for a donation presents an opportunity to address what may be a misunderstanding about the organization or event. Possibly a small donation can be used as a means for the organization to redeem itself in the eyes of the donor. Ultimately, it may not be possible to get a donation, but perhaps some headway will be made and the prospective donor may agree to pay closer attention to the organization in the future or to reevaluate the bad impression.

If the potential donor is a local retail store owner or manager who is usually present in the store during business hours, it is acceptable to simply go into the store unannounced and make a request in person on the spot. Provided the prospective donor is not obviously busy, just approach the person and make the request in the same fashion detailed previously. For prospective donors located some distance away, make the request by telephone. Simply call and either ask immediately or arrange a time when a call would be convenient to the prospective donor.

If large numbers of auction items are needed, cold calls can be made en masse by the acquisition team by setting up a telemarketing operation. To do this, create a list of prospective donors and assemble a group of team members at a location where several telephone lines are available. Split the list of prospects among team members and make solicitation calls. By doing this as a group, synergy can be achieved, and it helps make the work more enjoyable.

SOLICITING DOOR-TO-DOOR

In small to medium-sized communities and in cities where neighborhood merchants may be familiar with the host organization, perhaps the best way to acquire auction and raffle items is to solicit merchants in business districts, shopping centers, and malls in a door-to-door fashion. If this solicitation is not done by an acquaintance of the merchant, this is a cold call and, as such, requires use of the same quick presentation and request described previously. The blanket coverage of going door-to-door makes this a more community-based form of solicitation than any other technique described in this section.

Because door-to-door solicitation is so effective in achieving a positive response from so many merchants, it is important to have a specific item in mind to request from each merchant visited. Otherwise, it is easy to end up with a large selection of items that may be useless. It is acceptable to ask for specific items. Because it is likely a merchant will be unable or unwilling to provide the exact item requested, it is a good idea to be prepared with a response. This can be a conversation focused on finding an acceptable substitute or a graceful apology about why a substitute offered by the donor is unacceptable. If a substitute is offered, it may be a good substitute, so acquisition team members must be able to make decisions and use good judgment. Negotiating a substitute requires authority to act on behalf of the host organization. But if all tactics fail, it does no good to accept donation of items that are of no use to the organization. Acquisition team members must be able to tactfully relate to prospective donors the particular needs of the host organization.

In the event of having to reject a donation, explain to the jilted donor the specific needs of the host organization and the requirement that each donation be used fully on the organization's mission. Say that at this time a particular type of donation is needed to fit into the event as planned. In the future, other types of events may be planned and new needs may be met by donation of other items. Regardless of the outcome, thank potential donors and keep them informed about the host organization, perhaps by sending occasional notes or newsletters.

In addition to requesting donation of auction and raffle items during door-to-door solicitations, team members may ask retail merchants if they wish to underwrite or become sponsors of the event in addition to (or in lieu of) donating an item. Finally, should a merchant decide not to make a donation or become a sponsor, or in the event a donor's offering is simply unusable, then it is always an acceptable last resort to ask for a cash donation.

SOLICITING BY MAIL

In addition to making personal contact, team members can solicit potential donors by letter or e-mail if addresses are available. Although this can be a very efficient way to reach a large number of potential donors, mass mailing is a "shotgun" approach that provides the acquisition team little control over the outcome. The results may be extraordinarily disappointing. It is just too easy for a recipient to ignore a letter. It is even easier to disregard e-mail, as it is common practice to automatically filter what appear to be solicitations or to manually delete e-mail without opening.

Even a positive response to a mass solicitation

may not result in a serviceable donation. A retail firm solicited by letter or e-mail for a particular item may decide to donate something entirely different. Often this can be an item of excess inventory or something unsalable. Instead of a three-speed ceiling fan and light, a lighting company may decide to donate an old plastic radio alarm clock that has been sitting along with several dozen just like it in the warehouse for a decade or more. If the item is accepted, the donor must be afforded all manner of appropriate recognition and extended benefits commensurate with the value of the donation. This needs to be done no matter how marginal the value of the donation and even if it adds nothing to achieving the acquisition goals of the host organization. Sidebar 13.3 relates a story about donations received through mass solicitation.

In making direct-mail solicitations, the team can assemble lengthy lists of potential donors. The lists can focus on manufacturers, retailers, other non-profit organizations, and so on. Such lists can even be purchased, usually at a price per 1,000 labels. Through use of computers, each letter can be "personalized" to the donor and mailed by a mailing service. Although this may seem to be an easy way around the more personal forms of soliciting donations, it is no substitute for the more targeted approaches described elsewhere.

CULTIVATING POTENTIAL DONORS

Multiple contacts with merchants or providers of a specific service may be necessary to obtain a single donation. Success should improve over several years for events that are held annually, because merchants and service providers will become familiar with the organization and the event. In particular, when the acquisition team is seeking unique or specialized items, success may require establishing a relationship with a potential donor before receiving the first donation.

Keep track of who was contacted and the reception the acquisition team member received. Do not assume that simply because a request was rejected one year that a request for a donation in subsequent years will receive the same treatment. As an investment with minor cost, consider sending a let-

Sidebar 13.3. **Why I Love Being Solicited by Mail and E-mail for a Donation**

When I was heading organizations, I would get numerous requests for donations from people I knew or organizations we worked with, and usually we would select an appropriate donation representing our organization. I also received many mass-mailed letters and e-mail requesting donation of items for use as auction, raffle, or door prizes. In most cases, I had never heard of the person making the request or the organization holding the event. Sometimes the event was to be held thousands of miles from where my office was located. I suspect the good folks responsible for acquisition of donations for these far-flung events found my organization's name on a list in a directory. There was nothing personal about these requests, although they were generally well written and polite. Despite not really knowing much about the organization making the request, I usually would respond with a donation, but I suspect most who received them did not. Why would I bother to make a donation? Because it was so easy and maybe the donation would help.

I kept an assortment of old merchandise for just such occasions. The only real expense to my organization was the cost of mailing and handling. My donations were items no longer of any use, yet they were serviceable as a donation. I remember a time when I received a few cartons of excess-inventory shirts. The shirts were made of high-quality materials. It was clear why these particular items had become excess inventory. All were extra colorful and covered with interesting designs of the sort that would appeal to some people, but certainly not everyone. In addition, most of the cartons contained men's shirts sized XXL and XXXL.

It was hard to imagine what to do with so many shirts so large in the colors and patterns I saw before me when I first opened those cartons. But it didn't take long to figure that out. I used the shirts as donations in response to mass letters and e-mail requests. I would often send several shirts in response, and as long as I had shirts remaining, all who asked for a donation would receive at least one shirt. In return for my donation, I usually received a nice letter of thanks, a copy of the program where my organization was listed among donating sponsors, and sometimes a nice framed certificate or small plaque of appreciation.

Even though the requesting organization did receive a donation as a result of their mass-mailed request, the usefulness of items I sent was probably limited. The shirts were what I had available at the time of the request; however, while extra-large shirts might serve as door prizes or table gifts, they are of little value as quality raffle or auction prizes.

ter to prospective donors who do not make a donation to thank them for listening to the request. Be sure to invite potential donors to the event, even if they do not make a donation. It is also a reasonable long-term investment to provide the potential donor occasional information about the organization and the fundraising done by its members.

In subsequent years when contacted by representatives of the host organization, the potential donor may be willing to make a donation. Invest time in cultivating potential donors. Successful cultivation may take several years, but it takes no more effort than seeking out entirely new potential donors, who also may need such cultivation over time.

Purchase Auction Items

With all the emphasis in this chapter on acquiring items free as donations, why buy anything for an event? Although getting everything free as full donations is the ideal situation, it is unlikely that absolutely everything needed for an auction event can be obtained completely free of charge. Sometimes the ideal auction item or raffle grand prize simply cannot be acquired as a full or even partial donation. Small prizes used in arcade games may be needed in bulk, so the only way to get them may be to purchase them at full retail price. Any items purchased should be bought at the lowest price possible, perhaps by seeking the item as a partial donation by the merchant.

Ask for Money

No luck acquiring that special item from your friend the manufacturer? Then buy it, but use money donated for just that purpose. Paying cash for items can be made much less onerous to the host organization if the money used to do so is donated for that very purpose. For example, not everyone asked to donate that perfect item will be willing to do so, but he or she may still agree to support the event. The best option in such instances is to ask the potential donor to underwrite the event by donating cash.

Underwriting helps defray expenses and is a di-rect donation to the charitable organization. Such donations can be directed at covering specific expenses, such as purchase of a specific auction item. The donor would then be acknowledged as paying for those expenses. Or the donation can be used for general purposes, in which case the donor would be acknowledged as underwriting the event itself. For businesses or prominent members of the organization or community, underwriting provides the option of being recognized during the event as supporters of the event, organization, and cause without the added complexity of handling merchandise or making sure a winning bidder is satisfied with a donated service.

Offer Incentives

People give donations if and when asked. To get items for an auction, someone has to ask potential donors to give, and what they say in the course of asking will have a large bearing on whether or not a gift is donated. Getting enough items of just the right kind to conduct a successful auction event can be difficult and may take more than simple requests. Sometimes special negotiating techniques or offers of benefits in return for a gift are necessary to obtain desired items.

Solicitation of specific auction items may take more incentive than a donor's good feelings in helping a good cause. In fact, the donor's first thought when asked for a gift may be directed toward what he or she may get from the deal rather than any notion of charitable giving. Particularly when the item solicited has a high-dollar cost to the donor (high donor investment), some deal making may be necessary. Here are some special deal-making techniques that may help.

Benefits for Donors

Donors may deserve or even demand benefits when they donate items for auctions or raffles. If benefits are offered, donors need to hear about them as part of the solicitation. These become negotiating points and are incentives acquisition team members can use to entice donors to make a gift. The more

---

Sidebar 13.4. **Example Benefits to Offer Donors**
- Publicity
- Listing in event marketing materials and on-site programs
- Free tickets to the event and/or special "donor table" seating at the event
- Invitation to a donor's reception
- Visibility onstage during auction of the donated item
- Mention in newspaper and TV advertisements thanking donors
- Free membership in the organization
- Special donor gifts
- Free ad space in the host organization's newsletter or newspaper

benefits available, the more options the acquisition team has to use in negotiating a gift.

The host organization should determine what benefits donors may receive and develop a policy to ensure all donors are treated equitably. Benefits can even be provided to donors as a written list, somewhat in the form of a contract once a donation is secured. Benefits can increase with an increase in the value of donation to the organization, but any benefits to donors of merchandise and services must also be considered in the context of benefits provided to others, such as sponsors. Donors must be informed of the value of any benefits, goods, or services that are insubstantial, according to IRS regulations (see chapter 21). Sidebar 13.4 lists typical benefits available to donors.

Regardless of benefits offered, all donors should be treated in a consistent, but not necessarily equal, fashion. Benefits can be designed to vary for donors according to the value of donation. Differing levels of benefits should be made known to all donors. Donors will generally accept differential treatment based on the level of donation, but any arbitrary differential treatment is likely to be discovered quickly and create hard feelings toward the organization. Donation policies should be written with a list of benefits included. Once established, the policy needs to be followed by everyone representing the host organization.

"Free" Advertising

A commonly described benefit to the donor of items to a charity event is the advertising the donor gets during the event. If the item donated is used in the main live auction, the donor gets the added benefit of prominent display of the merchandise or service. There is considerable advertising value when an item from a local merchant appears on center stage at an event attended by a large number of members of the local community, especially if the event is attended by people who may personally be interested in the product. The merchant may even wish to participate in the auction by appearing onstage as the item is auctioned.

Donors should be encouraged to view the event as an effective and economical way to obtain very targeted marketing, the nature of which may be impossible to achieve or very costly to attain any other way. This is particularly the case if the host organization's membership is specialized in a particular area of interest and the donated item is one that caters to that interest. As an example, donors to events held by wildlife conservation organizations usually provide items of interest to people interested in wildlife. Thus, if a famous wildlife artist donates an original piece of art to a national wildlife conservation organization, that art, the artist, and the artist's support of the organization and mission of conservation are prominently displayed before the entire membership of the organization. Members of such organizations are the artist's primary customers. There is no better way to reach these customers than through their own organization's efforts to thank the artist.

Negotiating Splits, Consignments, Contingencies, and Other Payments

Some donors agree to donate an item only under the condition that they receive some percentage of the bid amount or a set fee in return. Such partial donations are often negotiated with potential donors of unique or high-value items, such as cars, antiques, or original artwork.

A potential donor is understandably hesitant or

perhaps unable to donate expensive or one-of-a-kind items in full. In this special case of negotiating for donations, services or products are specifically made available on a more commercial basis for event fundraising purposes, and a partial payment or a split of the winning bid is returned to the donor. The donor expects to make a profit, and the host organization receives net revenue. The split amount is often subject to negotiation, but auction of these items requires setting a reserve that satisfies the agreement with the donor to return some portion of receipts from sale of the item. The donor and host organization both win.

NOTE: *Use splits with caution.* The host organization may actually not win if split arrangements are used indiscriminately. Improperly used, splits harm net revenue. There is only so much money to be had in an auction room where attendees' capacity and willingness to spend is limited. A high-value auction item, whether presented on a split basis or not, takes a great deal of money out of an auction room. If spending is limited, purchase of a high-value item most likely completely taps out the attendee who wins. The bidder is finished bidding for the remainder of the event.

Equally priced auction items carrying no split will yield a higher net revenue for the host organization than will items carrying the cost of the split arrangement. Because fully donated items provide higher net revenue, auction the fully donated items of similar value first. Leave the auction items carrying splits until near the end of the auction. This ensures bidding will take place first on those high-value items providing the highest net revenue to the host. Splits should be used only for items that can be obtained in only that way and are highly desirable to attendees. If the item is truly desired by one or more attendees, they will wait for the item's turn at auction. If a sufficient number of attendees have the capacity and willingness to bid on all the items at auction, these considerations are irrelevant. In this case, offer the most desired items a bit after the midpoint in the auction to generate and maintain auction excitement and momentum.

Because of the nature of some donated services, in addition to any percentage split, the donor may receive additional money or opportunity to make additional money. Donated vacation tour packages are sometimes constructed in this manner, where organizations seeking vacation packages for events may find a selection available for "donation" through various booking agents and resorts that require nothing more of the host organization than a minimum bid and a set percentage split between the host and donor. When the winning bidder takes the vacation trip, a variety of additional tour opportunities are offered, each for an additional fee. The donor receives additional money if the winning bidder purchases any of these "added attractions." As long as the basic vacation tour package provides the advertised value, there is nothing inappropriate about a vacationer having the opportunity to do additional things, for a price. This is no different from the availability of activities in a resort location, in addition to the packaged activities that come with a resort hotel's vacation package.

NOTE: *Acquisition team members need to be certain that any items or services obtained through negotiation of a split are accurately detailed and properly valued. This information needs to be clearly communicated to potential bidders in advance of bidding. Winning bidders should not be surprised by items or services received. Winning bidders should never receive less value than advertised and expected.*

Under some circumstances, relatively low-value items may warrant a partial payment or reimbursement from the host organization. An example is a case in which the host organization believes a particular item or service will receive a high bid, but to get the item or service, the host must make some special arrangement or payment. Let's say the acquisition team wants to acquire an auction item that offers a popular local chef preparing a meal for eight in the home of the successful bidder. The preferred chef may be more than willing to donate her time to prepare the meal, but she says that she simply cannot afford to personally pay for the food and wine for such a meal. Through discussion the chef agrees to the donation on the condition that the host organization pay the direct cost of any food and alcohol.

In particular, whenever a specific item is sought, it may be necessary to negotiate some partial payment or benefit arrangement. This is not much different from accepting an original artwork from an artist who provides the art without a frame. To make the art salable at auction, the host organization must "contribute" the cost of the frame.

Determine Tax Deductibility and Acknowledge Donations

Promises of tax deduction by acquisition team members and misperceptions among potential donors over tax deductibility of charitable giving can create misunderstandings. In general, tax deductions are allowed for various kinds of gifts to qualified charitable organizations for use (sale) at charity events, but the amount of deduction allowed for many kinds of donations is probably less than most prospective donors may assume (see chapter 21 for detailed discussion of tax matters). Deduction for gifts of services may be completely disallowed. In addition, some organizations that hold events are not qualified to receive tax-deductible gifts. Although a donor is free to donate items to such organizations for use at events, the donor cannot claim the donation as tax deductible.

Donors may receive a tax advantage for their donation if the host organization is a qualified charity, and donors must be told of any benefits that may affect tax deductibility for any donations more than $75 in value. Donors may be eligible for tax advantages whether the item is donated 100% free to the host organization or whether the donor specifies a set fee for the item, a percentage of the final bid price, or some other contingency or in-kind payment in return for the donation. The various ways tax deductions for event merchandise and services are calculated must follow IRS rules explained in partial detail in chapter 21. For additional information, readers should refer to IRS rules governing charitable donations. However, apart from the host responsibility to provide donors certain information

as written verification of donations, any tax matters are strictly the responsibility of the donors and their tax advisers. Figure 13.1 provides an example donor-acknowledgment letter (see chapter 21 for discussion of additional information and requirements).

Request Donations Exactly One Year in Advance

Soliciting donors for event items should begin exactly one year in advance of the auction. Solicit donations for next year's auction during the current year's auction event. Consider this example. A donor's item was bid up to a high price, and the donor is excited about how well the auction went, featuring his donation. He is talking to everyone around his table, and everyone is excited. This exact point, while the donor is excited about the event and his donation, is the best time possible to solicit a donation for the following year's event. This doesn't mean asking the donor to send next year's donation immediately. The donor should be asked to make a commitment to donate again next year. It might even be a good time to ask for an upgrade. Here is a way to ask: Move up to the donor's table as the item he donated is auctioned off. His item fetches a good price. He is excited. Just after he settles back in his seat, it's time to say to the donor,

"Gee Dan, that set of golf clubs you donated fetched a phenomenal bid tonight. That money will go a long way toward helping get Mary through her first year at the university. It's too bad about her parents passing away in that car accident—it was so sudden. But giving people a helping hand after accidents and disasters is what this charity is all about. This went so well tonight; why don't we sign you up for another set of clubs for next year's fundraiser? And next time we add a personal golf lesson by you, and we get you up onstage to help the bidding along. What do you say, Dan?"

Numerous other opportunities will be available during the event to request support and donations for next year. Watch the reactions of donors. If they are excited about the event and their dona-

<Name of Fundraising Event>
A charitable fundraising event to benefit <Name of Host Organization>
<Location of auction>
<Date of auction>

Acknowledgment and receipt of cash or items donated for auction or charity prizes

Donor's name: _____

Donor's address: _____
_____
_____

Donor's e-mail: _____

Date of receipt of donation: _____
Amount of cash donation: _____

Name and/or description of item(s) donated for auction or prizes:

_____
_____
_____

Goods or services having a fair market value of $_____ were provided in exchange for this gift. If an amount of $0 is entered above, then no goods or services were provided in return for this gift and the entire gift may be tax deductible. Donors should consult with financial or tax advisers to determine eligibility of this gift for a tax deduction. For gifts valued above $250, this acknowledgment and receipt is required to substantiate the charitable donation. Please keep this receipt with your records for tax purposes.

Receipt issued by: _____<Signature>_____ Date: _____

<Host Organization> is incorporated in the State of <State> and is recognized by the Internal Revenue Service as a 501(c)3 charitable organization. Donations may be tax deductible.

Print on host organization's letterhead, including address. If the organization has no official letterhead, place the name of the organization and address clearly at either the top or bottom of the page.

FIGURE 13.1. Example donor-acknowledgment letter.

tion, ask them to make a commitment for next year. If they look displeased, talk with them and find out if there is a problem. It may not be a good time to ask them for a donation, but it is a good time to find out if something is wrong and try to make corrections. This is also an especially good time to speak to attendees who were asked to make a donation but did not do so. Talk to them about making a commitment to donate at the next event.

Solicit Early Donations

Although it's never too early to solicit a donation, it can be too late. Last-minute solicitations make event committee members appear unorganized and may leave the impression the organization is poorly managed. Potential donors don't like being rushed into a decision. Donors want assurance that any event to which they donate will be conducted in a well-organized manner. A potential donor's impression of an event or host organization may start with the initial solicitation for a gift. Let it be a positive impression.

Of course, once a donor becomes a participant in an event, the event itself—all aspects of the event—will drive future decisions to donate. If an event is well run and the donor receives the benefits he or she expects, there is a high likelihood the donor will donate to subsequent events and the job of the acquisition team is made a little bit easier.

PART 3

Conducting the Fundraising

14

Tickets and Other Advance "Sales"

The year our local area was in the grip of a disastrous downturn in the economy, our largest employer, the state government, cut salaries an effective 20% through Friday furloughs. Statewide, public works spending of $17 billion had been suspended indefinitely. These and other cuts had collapsed the local economy like a house of cards. My office staff hosted an auction event every year where we usually had about 120 attendees, with year-to-year differences of only about 10% to 15%. So it was with some concern that staff set about to plan an event in these troubled times.

Just a few weeks before the event date advance ticket sales began to indicate attendance was not going to be low. It appeared we might have solid attendance. Within a week of the event, estimates started indicating we would have an extraordinarily high attendance. A day or two before the event attendance was projected at 250. This was based on advance ticket sales and the fact we always had quite a few walk-ins who bought tickets at the door.

We had planned an event for fewer attendees; instead, we had to accommodate more than double the usual number. Was that a good thing? Yes, and maybe. We weren't sure we had room to fit that many people into the space available to hold the event. This event was held outside in a fenced, gated parking lot, under a very large tent. We had a six-game arcade, a jazz band and stage, a large silent auction, a large bar, and the live auction area. We squeezed dinner tables and the live auction under the tent.

In the end we were lucky, because attendance was actually a bit lower than we had projected in the last days before the event. The usual walk-ins arrived, but a few of the advance ticket buyers did not show up. Our event was jammed with about 225 people. Were we surprised? Yes, but it was a good surprise. We were able to make adjustments in catering, table and chair rental, and number of prizes and auction items. The event and all attendees just fit. It was tight. It was a surprise, but successfully so.

We would have been even more surprised if we had not been monitoring advance ticket sales and not able to make accurate attendance projections based on detailed records of past attendance numbers, walk-in rates, and ticket-buying patterns from past years' events. We would have been surprised in a more precarious way had we continued planning for reduced attendance, of say 80 to 100 people based on the poor economy, and had to deal with 225 people the day of the event.

EFFECTIVE MANAGEMENT of an event is facilitated by having an accurate count of attendees in advance. The more accurate the count and farther in advance an accurate count is achieved, the more effectively the host can control expense and plan fundraising activities. Failure to have an accurate count is the Achilles' heel of event planning and cost management. Unless an event is a known or planned sellout (limited seating), the number of attendees is generally estimated. As the date for the event nears, planners work hard to improve attendance estimates, but as the previous story shows, even seasoned event planners can be surprised.

Tickets and Attendance

Successful events are those events attended by an adequate number of people who actively participate in fundraising activities to meet the host organization's net revenue goal for the event. Without an adequate number of people who actually participate, no event can be successful. Without a reasonably sound idea of how many people will attend an event, planners cannot plan effectively and event budgets cannot be developed accurately. An event unrealis-

tically planned for 1,000 people will carry huge excess expense when 150 people show up. An event planned for 150 will perform well below its potential if 1,000 people show up. In both cases the host organization is exposed to the community as clueless in regard to event fundraising.

Attendance needs to be estimated as accurately as possible, using realistic assessments. For an organization hosting an annual event, initial estimates can be based on past experience. For an organization hosting its first event, planners need to think carefully about attendance, talk with others in the organization, and possibly investigate attendance at similar events held by similar organizations in the local community.

Seasoned and novice event planners should use whatever means they can find to provide a reasonable initial estimate of attendance and then be prepared to make continual adjustments to the estimate, the event budget, and all aspects of planning that are based on number of attendees. Done properly, these adjustments will continually bring the attendance estimate in line with actual attendance as the event date nears. The sooner planners become confident the estimate and actual attendance number are as close to each other as possible, the sooner and thus more effectively event costs can be controlled to provide just the right services for the number of attendees.

Accurate estimates of attendance are most effectively based on two factors: advance ticket sales and past experience. For the planner of first-time events, advance ticket sales may be the only solid information available. For the planner of annual events who has some experience, records should be reviewed to determine past patterns of ticket sales and walk-in rates (provided walk-in admission is allowed). Why look at records? Because ticket-buying patterns of the past are the best predictors of future buying patterns, but these rates also vary. They vary based on how tickets are sold, who is being asked to buy tickets, the use of premiums to promote ticket sales, and the buying patterns of people asked to buy tickets. These present quite a few variables, but over time and with records kept, event planners can use this information to their advantage.

In general, people will wait until as late as possible to buy tickets. One recent study showed three out of four eventgoers buy tickets no earlier than two weeks before an event, with more buying less than one week before the event than three or more weeks before.[1] The savvy event planner takes steps to sell tickets as early as possible. This helps with planning, because the sooner accurate estimates of attendance can be made, the sooner planners can gain control of costs. Early ticket purchasing also provides early event revenue that can be used for deposits and for offsetting other advance expenses.

Ticket Sales

A person or team is generally assigned volunteer responsibility to sell tickets. These are the people who develop the strategies to market tickets and implement those strategies, and they sell tickets directly to potential attendees. The ticket sales force can be instantly expanded by enlisting all of the host organization's members to sell tickets. Although this may not apply to all organizations, because the nature of nonprofit organizations' membership varies, it does apply well to organizations holding events in local communities where the organization's membership can be readily contacted. Members can form the largest possible ticket sales force for the event. Soliciting members to sell tickets also serves as an invitation to those same members to buy tickets. Of course, not all members will buy tickets, and maybe fewer will sell any tickets, but this sales technique provides an effective initial marketing effort. Such members' solicitation can be enhanced by adding a premium for sales by members or other incentives. For example, members who sell a certain number of tickets (this can be as few as one ticket in addition to the one they buy for themselves) can be entered into a special drawing.

INSTANTLY DOUBLE ATTENDANCE

Encourage members of the organization and regular event attendees to bring a friend. If all do, event

---

1. *The 2010 Charity Event Market Research Report*, CharityHappenings.org.

> **Sidebar 14.1. "Bring-a-Friend" Marketing Ideas and Promotions**
>
> - Provide a special reception for regular attendees and their first-time attendee friends, during which they meet officers of the organization and any special guests or celebrities who will be at the event.
> - Give a premium to people who sell one or more extra tickets and "bring a friend." Premiums could be offered on a sliding scale with more costly ones offered for more extra tickets sold. Example premiums include logo coffee mugs, logowear, and a nice book. It may be possible to receive sponsorship funding for "bring-a-friend" incentives.
> - Offer a discount for a group table. For example, if tables seat eight and tickets are usually $100 each, market a "bring-a-friend" group table discount for $700. At least four members of the group must be first-time attendees.
> - Provide special seating placement (closer to the stage) for regular attendees and their first-time attendee friends.
> - Offer two-for-one event admission tickets for regular attendees and their first-time attendee friends. This can be effective when there are no hard costs to the host offset by ticket revenue; for example, if ticket price covers a meal, this option may not be cost effective.
> - Award the regular attendee a quantity of tickets for the general raffle for each friend he or she brings, if there are no legal complications in doing so.
>   - Hold a special "bring-a-friend" raffle during the event for all regular attendees and their first-time attendee friends, if there are no legal complications in doing so.

attendance is instantly doubled. If they bring two friends, attendance is tripled. Couples can be asked to bring another couple. Of course, this need not be limited to a friend bringing a friend or couples inviting only one additional couple. It is even better when one person invites many friends or a couple invites many couples. In this fashion, groups are formed. If a dinner or other meal is included in the event, entire group tables can be marketed and sold in conjunction with friends and couples bringing others. Sidebar 14.1 lists several marketing ideas that can encourage members or regular attendees to bring a friend.

Even without encouragement, a host organization's members or regular attendees inviting others is one of the primary reasons first-time attendees decide to go to an event. Because this method of recruiting attendees works so well, and people tend to do it anyway, savvy event planners remind members to bring a friend and market or reinforce this idea through various promotions.

Publicity prepares people to buy tickets, but few tickets are sold to first-time attendees or to first-time events by publicity alone. Most tickets are sold face-to-face, through personal contact and friendships. Social networks can also be used to "mass-market" personal invitations to friends.

EARLY-BIRD INCENTIVES

A key advantage in event planning is knowing attendance ahead of time. The savvy event planner devises ways to lock attendance numbers in place as early as possible. Ways to do so include setting a deadline for reservations and limiting number of attendees. Let invitees know reservations will no longer be accepted once attendance reaches a certain level or after a certain date. Although these may be effective ways to aid planners, limiting attendance or cutting off reservations by a certain date may unnecessarily limit the number of people who attend and the potential amount of net revenue the organization raises.

A better means to lock in estimates of attendance early is to provide incentives for early ticket purchase. Typical methods of encouraging early purchase of tickets is to offer a premium for tickets purchased before a certain date. For example, if allowed by law, early registrants can be given an entry to a special "early registration" drawing. Other incentives include invitation to a special "early" event reception for early registrants, where they meet officers of the organization and any special guests or celebrities who will be at the event; special items, such as logo coffee mugs, a logo umbrella, and so on; first choice at dinner seating; and a discount on ticket price.

The key to selecting just the right incentive is to find one that works, which may require some experimentation over a few years, and that impacts net revenue as little as possible. For example, raffle tickets, a few extra people at a reception, discontinued logo products, and special dinner seating carry little added cost to the host. But discounting ticket price

and premium items specifically purchased for an event are hard costs that will have to be offset by increased revenue.

Ticket Pricing

Ticket price may be the first thing someone considers after being asked to attend an organization's fundraising event. Even the wealthy will question a ticket priced too high, as any event on the philanthropist's social calendar carries a market price based on a number of factors that will be discussed later. People with limited finances will just say no if price is too high, regardless of market price for the event. Tickets priced too low will cause a prospective attendee as much consternation about the true nature of an event as a ticket priced too high.

There is a market price for events, with pricing based on various cost factors, but also including pricing of other similar events being held in the local area. People who frequent fundraisers become accustomed to events of a certain nature being priced within a certain range. Eventgoers naturally gravitate to those events where they feel comfortable, and pricing is a factor people use to decide whether or not to attend an event. Price may not outweigh the urging of a friend to attend a particular event, but it can have a deciding effect on a person reading a public announcement about an event. If the price of admission to a fundraiser is "within market range" given the nature of the event, ticket price is given only a moment's notice. The prospective attendee then goes on to consider other factors in making the decision to attend, such as "Who else will be attending the event?" and "Am I available that evening?"

If this sounds complicated, it is. Following are other factors that need to be considered in setting ticket price, all of which contribute added complexity to what would seem to be a pretty simple decision. Setting the ticket price is not just a matter of adding up the costs per expected attendee of food service, drinks, and event-facility rental and then adding in a little extra for good luck. The savvy event planner also takes into account other factors described in sidebar 14.2 and in the following paragraphs. However, if ticket price doesn't cover the

Sidebar 14.2. **Factors to Consider When Setting Ticket Price**

- Basic expense of services per attendee, such as cost of food and beverage and facilities rental
- Nature of the event, including special entertainment or features (e.g., formal versus casual, hotel versus outdoor park, gourmet catering versus home cooking)
- Economic status of attendees
- Age of attendees
- Current IRS rules governing the amount above which charitable organizations must provide a written disclosure statement to donors of any quid pro quo contributions (in 2011 this was set at $75)
- Extent to which underwriting, sponsorships, and fundraising revenue are expected to offset overall event expenses
- Event planner's strategic evaluation of the effect of price on attendance and subsequent fundraising revenue from attendees
- Whether to include in the ticket price the cost of a membership in the host organization
- The host organization's mission and objective of the event

basic costs, there needs to be solid assurance those expenses will be covered in some other way. Once ticket price is set and a few tickets are sold, there is no turning back no matter what happens as the event nears. The host organization needs to make do with the revenue raised.

The nature of the event has a large bearing on an attendee's willingness to pay. A black-tie dinner-auction, featuring celebrity entertainment and an open super-brand bar held in an upscale hotel ballroom, will allow the event host to charge a much higher admission price than a fish fry and auction event featuring all the beer you can drink that is held on the picnic grounds of a volunteer fire company. Prospective attendees understand the need to charge higher prices for fancy ballroom events. After all, a highbrow ballroom event is going to cost the host a whole lot more than a fish fry, and ticket revenue will be needed to help pay for it all. Right? Maybe not, but savvy planners of the ballroom event will want attendees to believe it's an expensive affair. Planners will want people who come to the ballroom event to pay a high price for the tickets. Event planners for the fish fry may also want people to

pay a high price for tickets, maybe as much as those going to the ballroom, but they won't be able to get it. But in truth, the amount of cost covered by ticket revenue may be the same for both events. It could even be less for the ballroom event.

For example, if the planners for the fish fry receive no underwriting, sell no sponsorships, and are paying full price for rental of the fire company's grounds, a tent, tables, chairs, auctioneer, public address system, security, and so on, there may be a great deal of expense the fish-fry host is seeking to cover with the ticket price. On the other hand, planners of the ballroom event may already have all expenses covered through underwriting, sponsorships, and donations of services. Those planners may be projecting no expenses to cover with tickets, and they can set the price of the ticket solely on the basis of getting as much extra revenue as possible. Given the highbrow nature of the ballroom event, they can charge a high amount with all of it contributing to the event's net revenue.

The bottom line on ticket price is don't go too low. Consider the potential consequences of setting ticket price too low, even below the cost of the meal and beverages. Planners probably assume attendee spending on fundraising during the event will cover the additional cost of the meal and more. Some event planners set ticket price low to attract more attendees, for example, to allow people of limited financial means to attend. Unfortunately, people attracted to an event by low-priced tickets may not participate in fundraising if there are few fundraising activities for people of limited income. In such a situation, these attendees may enjoy a good meal and an entertaining evening at the host organization's expense. If the planner succeeds in attracting large numbers of additional people based on setting low ticket prices and the event is packed with people who do not contribute beyond the ticket price, the host organization is financially harmed even further when it orders all those extra meals to accommodate all the extra diners.

The auction event is a fundraising event. Every aspect of planning and holding an event must focus on raising net revenue. The ticket is just one among many revenue-producing features of an event. Attendees expect to pay for admission. Do not disappoint them. If they get food and drink, they expect to pay for that as part of the ticket price. Do not disappoint them. They are accustomed to paying a price equivalent to the level of event and consistent with other locally held events. Do not disappoint them. They will even pay a little extra if they can be convinced the event will be extra exciting, fun, and filled with people they want to be with and will offer items they want or need. Do not disappoint them.

Some event planners think by lowering ticket prices, they are doing a favor to prospective attendees and that the attendance of bargain-hunting eventgoers will enhance an event. They won't enhance revenue, and bargain ticket prices may even drive away affluent attendees. Event planners who "cheapen" an event and forgo opportunities to enhance net revenue do the host organization no favor. Consider all the factors, and then charge as much for the ticket as the market will bear. Period. No more, and for the sake of the host organization's mission, not a penny less!

Marketing to Those Who Market to You

Sometimes event planners focus only on marketing event tickets to the host organization's members and to people in desirable social circles (these may not be elite social circles; they are ones event planners believe are compatible with members). In the excitement to sell tickets, service providers to the host organization or compatible businesses may be forgotten.

Consider what motivated the unexpected large attendance in the event depicted in the story opening this chapter. The response was without precedent, so there was no prior experience on which to base a prediction. All employers had been hard hit by cuts in funding. Construction and engineering services were among the hardest hit of all industries in the local economy. Some $12 million in environmental-enhancement construction and engineering work my office had under way to restore wetlands came to an immediate halt. Most employers released staff and just stopped working. We used aggressive and innovative fundraising to replace those funds

with other funding, so my office had become one of the only employers still working, employing our own staff and continuing subcontracting with outside engineering and construction services. We were still buying supplies and replacing equipment. We had become one of only a few shining stars during a very dark time. In response to staff's solicitation to buy tickets and attend the event, it was in large part grateful service providers buying tickets and tables that added the extra attendees. As an example, a limousine pulled up to the event entrance with the owner and a half-dozen salesmen from a local car dealership. We had purchased several vehicles from the dealer in the preceding year.

Owners and managers of businesses that do business with the organization are usually easily sold on making donations, buying tickets, sponsoring, and buying entire tables. Turn to them early, because they are likely to make quick decisions on attending.

Ticket Requirements

Tickets should contain specific information. Even in this age of Internet purchasing and electronic messaging, old-fashioned paper tickets and the electronic equivalent must be provided to attendees and must contain certain information if the host organization is qualified to accept tax-deductible donations and the ticket price is greater than $75. If not, tickets and what they may contain are optional. The remainder of this section assumes the event host organization is a qualified charity charging more than $75 for admission to a fundraising event.

Event tickets should contain the name of the organization hosting the event, date, location, and time of the event. Tickets should provide information about qualification of the organization to receive tax-deductible donations. If price of event admission is more than $75, the event host must inform the ticket buyer the extent to which admission price is tax deductible. Payment for a ticket to a charitable fundraising event is tax deductible only to the extent the ticket price exceeds the fair market value of the goods and services received in return for purchasing the ticket. For example, if the ticket costs $80 and admission to the event includes a $25 dinner, then only $55 of the ticket price is deductible. This information must be given to the ticket buyer by placing it directly on the ticket or admission receipt. See chapter 21 for detailed information on admission tickets and tax deductibility, including specific language to use on tickets that will address IRS requirements.

Making Event Attendees Members

The most precious commodity for sale when an organization has an open and paid membership is a membership in the organization. To advance prospective members along the path to membership, many organizations include a "free" or trial membership along with the event admission ticket. Membership purchase can also be offered to attendees as an option. Sale of memberships is critical to future growth of the organization, to success of future fundraising, and to the organization's visibility in the community. An auction event provides a good opportunity to sell memberships, for example, at a membership booth located near the entrance to the event. An auction event also creates an opportunity to introduce large numbers of prospective members to an organization, provided the event is not restricted to existing members only.

If the cost of membership is added to registration, attendees may or may not be informed the cost of membership is included in the registration fee. Some organizations that include membership in registration fees may advise attendees they will receive a "free" membership by attending the event. The savvy attendee may question such a statement because he or she may understand there is always a cost to membership. It is not really free. Even if a benefactor underwrites the cost of memberships, the host organization loses funds for mission work, as the benefactor diverts money from its mission to provide attendees with membership benefits. Do not state memberships are free if added to the price of event admission. Do use the opportunity presented by an event to aggressively recruit new members both in advance of and during the event.

At a minimum, providing a trial or reduced-benefit membership to people who attend an auction event will allow the organization to keep in touch with these people throughout the year by sending newsletters or other information, because along with membership come mail and e-mail addresses. The host organization can let them know of upcoming events, member opportunities, and activities of the organization. This is particularly useful if there are restrictions on use of certain means to contact people, such as telephone solicitations. Organizations may be exempt from such restrictions if contacting its own members. Regardless of how it is done, keeping in touch with people who have contributed to the organization is a sound investment in future fundraising.

Memberships can also be offered through a low-key sales pitch, with membership applications made available to attendees at the registration desk, or recruiting new members can be an overt objective of the host with the event featuring a well-promoted sales booth or a roving membership sales force. Since the host organization is doing great work, the attendee who is a new member will see proof of that good work and clamor to attend future fundraising events and pay for full memberships in subsequent years.

Members recruited through an event carry little or no recruiting costs and offer high immediate revenue potential. This is a considerable advantage and is one of the reasons why memberships "included" in registration fees make sense. However, members recruited through events often have relatively low renewal rates if attendees do not have strong personal affinity to the organization's mission. This is generally the case if attendees come to an event mainly for social reasons, for example, when accompanying friends or neighbors who are active in the host organization. In other words, just because a person attends a charity event does not mean he or she has strong personal feelings toward the charity and wants to become involved beyond the event.

Some organizations charge a membership fee as part of event registration even if the ticket buyer is already a member. If attendees then begin receiving duplicate benefits, such as multiple copies of the organization's newspaper, magazine, and fundraising solicitations, long-standing members may lose confidence in management of the host organization. Dues-paying members understand there is a cost to service each membership. Magazines obviously cost money, so providing duplicate benefits to members cuts into funds available for mission-related work. Organizations often have difficulty merging membership information if names and addresses are slightly different in their membership data records. As attendees register for an event, they often take shortcuts in filling out forms with their name and address. Even minor differences in how names and addresses are listed can result in computer applications registering the slight differences on records as separate people. There are ways to merge such lists, but it can be a challenge.

If memberships are linked to event registration, the host organization should design a means to reduce the potential for duplicate memberships. One way is to request a unique identifier on event tickets and registration forms, such as some item of personal information. However, many people are reluctant to supply such information. Even a request to supply the last four digits of a Social Security number may not be well received. Small organizations can go through records manually, but organizations with many thousands of members will have more difficulty.

Event Underwriting and Sponsorships

The key to hosting a cost-efficient event is to have all costs paid before the event begins. Among advantages, this greatly reduces the effect of unexpectedly low attendance or other unanticipated adverse impacts on revenue. Here are a few ideas for using underwriting and sponsorships.

NOTE: *Event planners sometimes use the terms "underwriting" and "sponsorship" interchangeably.* Sponsors get recognition by the host and often receive benefits in exchange for their contributions to the event. Underwriters generally get no benefits except recognition by the host. Underwriting and sponsorships can come from individuals, businesses, public agencies, and even other nonprofit organizations.

Underwriting provides general financial support to the host organization and can be used to offset a variety of costs, including purchase of items for use in auctions, raffles, and games and for door prizes. The ideal situation is for all such items to come to the organization as full donations, but sometimes that doesn't happen. Sometimes items are available only at a discount, and sometimes certain items desirable for auction cannot be obtained through donation. Underwriting can also be used for deposits, rentals, printing, and many other basic costs of an event.

Sponsorships fund specific activities or costs of the event, with sponsors receiving explicit credit for hosting the activity or covering the cost. For example, sponsorships can be offered for hosting a reception. Here the sponsor would pay for all costs of the reception. A sponsor can fund a specific item sold in an auction. Sponsorships can also be designed as "purchase of a table"; in this case the sponsor "buys a table" for an amount exceeding the cost of individual tickets to fill a table and can invite guests to sit there.

Offering Sponsors Value for Sponsorships

Sponsorships can be particularly effective when the host offers something of real value to the sponsor—so much value in fact that potential sponsors compete with each other for the privilege of sponsorship. Let's look at "selling" host opportunities as part of sponsorship perks.

What is of value to a potential sponsor? The answer is somewhat different for (1) business and commercial sponsors, (2) government and nonprofit sponsors, and (3) individual donors, such as members of the organization or philanthropists. The nature of the event will expand opportunity or limit it, as will be evident when reviewing the following examples. Consider that some major events are part of a larger meeting of an organization, such as its annual members' convention lasting a day or two. Events of this nature offer substantially greater sponsoring opportunities than a quick event limited to a single auction held with minimal food service. The key incentive to attract sponsors is to offer them substantial and exclusive hosting opportunities.

The host organization can promote and "sell" opportunities to host the following services:

1. *Specific meals (breakfast, lunch, or dinner), with the cost to the sponsoring host based on the full (best) or partial cost of the meal.* Besides recognition in the program, on posters, and during on-stage acknowledgments, the sponsoring hosts must be allowed to have a few minutes during the meal to speak, make a video presentation, or whatever else they want to do. Let them say whatever they want in front of the group during the meal, but encourage sponsors to promote giving during the event. This speech should last just a few minutes. But if it is a commercial enterprise, let them pitch what they sell. If a nonprofit organization or public agency, let them tell about their mission and work they do. Give them time to speak. Options for sponsorship contributions in this situation are (1) charge a set amount, based on a specific menu described up front to the potential sponsor; (2) allow the sponsor to work directly with the event facility's food-service provider to set the menu, negotiate price, and pay the provider directly; or (3) a combination of 1 and 2, where the event host works with the sponsor and food-service provider to establish a menu acceptable to the sponsor and then receive payment directly from the sponsor.

NOTE: *Although not necessary, allowing sponsors an opportunity to set the menu engages them and allows them to determine the level of service, as some sponsors might pay for a spaghetti dinner but would prefer to make a bigger splash and would spend a little extra to have steak and lobster instead, which attendees will probably like better.*

2. *Coffee, dessert, or snack service, with the cost to host based on the full (best) or partial cost of the snack.* In this case the sponsoring host needs to be provided an opportunity to set up some extra display, a banner, or materials at the service station. The sponsor needs to be recognized in some way.

At a big event lasting one or more days, a dozen or more exclusive hosting opportunities may be available in this category.

3. *Transportation (if needed).* This sponsorship would cover all or partial transportation, depending on needs. The sponsor gets a banner at the airport (if airport transport is needed). Transport to event locations could include banners in the buses or some other recognition.

4. *Added field trips and excursions.* Each trip or activity planned can be hosted, reducing costs to registrants. Sponsors can be provided a menu of hosting opportunities.

5. *Host shirts or jackets.* This sponsorship allows the sponsor to buy the host shirts, vests, or jackets worn by host staff and event workers during the event. The sponsor gets the business logo on the shirt and advertising during the event.

6. *Takeaways.* Sponsors purchase the event takeaways, plus pay an added premium for the sponsorship. The sponsor can put a message on the takeaway along with the event host's name and logo. Takeaways include carry bags, mugs, shirts, umbrellas, and so on. Make advertising on the takeaway an exclusive sponsorship, and charge an extra premium. Decide what is desirable as a takeaway, and keep it limited to maintain exclusivity. A carry bag is often appreciated and provides a lot of room for advertising, so it is attractive to sponsors. It is also appreciated by attendees at events where they may collect items to carry, such as at an event that includes exhibits and exhibitors. A very nice shirt with the host's logo discreetly applied is also good, but only if it is apparel that someone will actually wear after the event. Quality mugs are good. For logo opportunities on takeaways to be attractive to sponsors, the takeaway needs to be an item that will be used and seen on a regular basis. Things like goofy hats and goofier T-shirts are not good sponsorship options—and not good for anything else.

Marketing Sponsorships

Sponsorships should be marketed selectively. Solicit potential major sponsors individually for specific hosting opportunities that allow the sponsor to make a splash, and for this opportunity the host organization receives added funds. Opportunities that have the highest profile, thus probably the greatest attraction to a potential sponsor, should be marketed first. These can be sold for the greatest net difference between actual cost and price of the sponsorship and are probably also the most costly to the host.

The highest-profile sponsorship opportunity is generally the meal during the most-attended portion of the event (usually held immediately before the main live auction); next highest are lunches, then the carry bag takeaway, and then breakfasts. These are usually the most sought-after sponsorships. Tours and field trips are also highly sought-after hosting opportunities, but availability of these and many other types of sponsorships is dependent on the kinds of opportunities afforded by the nature of the event.

When soliciting sponsors, treat them as the individuals they are. Visit with them, and describe specific sponsoring opportunities that make most sense for them. Call them on the telephone if a personal visit is not possible, or at the absolute minimum, send a personal e-mail. Have an acquaintance help make the ask or arrange an introduction so whoever is assigned to make the ask is not making a cold call. Contact sponsors with the greatest potential to sponsor the biggest-ticket items first, and ask them to sponsor those big-ticket items.

Mass solicitations by mail or e-mail are among the least effective ways to sell sponsorships, or raise any funds for that matter. Mass solicitations such as sending all potential sponsors the same letter of request in the course of soliciting significant sponsorships could even negatively affect revenue received. For example, it would not create a problem if a tiny company decides to sponsor a big-ticket item, but revenue could be affected if the largest sponsors all chose minimal sponsorship opportunities, leaving the big-ticket items unfunded. This could happen simply because all potential sponsors got the same mass mailing at the same time and none received the courtesy of a discussion with the host. Potential sponsors with fewer resources may not have the ca-

pacity to sponsor the larger items, so the large items are unsponsored. This is usually not a problem, however, because response to mass mailing is so poor that the lack of any response usually overwhelms any other issues with such solicitation.

Why provide specific sponsorship opportunities instead of just asking potential sponsors to underwrite the event in general? Underwriting is generally more advantageous to the host organization than sponsorships due to the flexibility in use of funds. But underwriting is more difficult to get. Sponsorships provide potential contributors an attractive menu of exclusive opportunities and the prospect of valuable advertising or exposure at the event. Thus, sponsorships offer more value and exclusivity than underwriting. When the host organization is asking for large amounts of money, the techniques of packaging sponsorships and a personal contact will result in efficient and effective fundraising.

Nonexclusive sponsorships or underwriting leaves contributors with little to differentiate them from any other contributor. They never get a chance to shine. There's really not much in it for them except to support the event, which is fine, but the host organization can give "added value" to a sponsor to make the sponsorship an easier sell. The host then has more opportunity to obtain more funding (ask for more money than it otherwise could) with a greater likelihood of success.

With either underwriting or sponsorship monies the event host is able to more effectively budget costs and revenues, because the host can put a much better-defined event business financing plan in place. With costs such as meals, transport, and takeaways covered by dedicated sources of funding, should attendance falter or uninsured disaster strike, the liability for payment lies elsewhere for many of the key expenses.

Follow up discussions, calls, or mailings (e-mail) with tactful reminders for those who have yet to commit to a sponsorship. For those who have made a commitment to sponsor, update them on progress in planning the event, and in particular let them know about that part of the event relevant to their sponsorship.

15

The Live Auction

I had just started my first full-time professional job and was in no position to advise the organization holding the auction. As a representative of the national parent organization of the affiliate holding the fundraiser, I was there to give a short speech about lobbying for environmental conservation.

I had looked at the live auction items and liked several. None of them were items I could afford. As the auction went on, bidding proceeded well beyond my budget until one medium-sized piece of art was brought onstage. To that point a mix of art prints had been auctioned off. All had been reproductions, and all were well presented in mats and frames. This was the first item of art that was not immediately recognizable for what it was—this was an original painting.

The painting was presented in a poorly matched, low-quality frame. The bidding started slowly and stalled at around $20. I was pretty sure it was an original but began having doubts. After all, how could the organization hosting the auction allow an original work of art to go for $20? I placed a bid at $25 and waited.

I might have succeeded in winning a bargain if the auctioneer hadn't taken a quick look and said, "Hey, this is an original piece of art; I'll bid on this myself, put it in a decent frame, and hang it on my wall if you people won't do better than twenty-five dollars." The next bid came quickly, knocking me aside. The final bid was around $200, which was quite a lot of money for that event.

THE AUCTION ITEM in the story might have fetched an even higher final bid had event organizers been more careful evaluating donated items and developing corresponding promotional material for display in advance of bidding. They also could have increased net revenue had they spent a few dollars to put the painting in a better frame. Added excitement over the item could have been generated, prospective bidders could have more carefully examined the piece, and comments from auction hosts and the MC could have increased bidding considerably. The artwork was very nice, despite the poor trappings provided by the ugly cheap frame. As a print, it would have been just another low-cost piece of colored paper without the benefit of a value-adding frame. But as an original piece of art, it represented many hours of work by the artist. Savvy bidders will overlook an ugly cheap frame if the artwork within has true value.

But most people who go to charity auctions are not savvy enough about art and other items that appear on an auction block to recognize true value without help. Prospective bidders need to be properly informed and provided an opportunity to carefully inspect items that catch their interest. They also need to be told the true fair market value for each item in an auction. Through advance advertising, marketing materials, information in the program, floor display, video presentations, notice on the event Web site, value assessments, social-media profiles, and other means, prospective bidders need to be informed, enticed, reminded, and invited to bid with confidence that they know exactly what they will get if successful on the auction floor.

There is an additional lesson to be learned. The host organization would have "lost" at least $175 that evening if auction planners had failed to employ the services of a skilled and experienced auctioneer who was able to quickly see the mistakes made by the host and take decisive action in the host's favor. Having a skilled, experienced, and professional auction team can greatly enhance net revenue, quickly outdistancing added costs of employing such help.

The Auction Defined

An auction is the event where items are offered for sale in either a "silent" or "live" fashion, and people are given an opportunity to offer to pay whatever amount they choose for the item. This offer is called a "bid." The person offering to pay the greatest amount of money—the highest bidder—receives the item for the amount bid. The bid becomes an oral contract and, at well-run auctions, a runner presents the winning bidder a written contract for purchase of the item immediately after the winning bidder is declared.

Live auctions are interactive with all bidders, either present at the event or in some other fashion communicating with an auctioneer on a real-time basis. They may bid over a telephone or by using an Internet connection. Each item in the auction is displayed and described to bidders; then the auctioneer opens bidding. Bidders hear each other as the bidding proceeds and bid amounts increase. Auctioneers may set a starting bid, or bidders may open with any amount they choose. Auctioneers generally try to move bidding along quickly by advising bidders that each subsequent bid be at or above a certain level. The auction of an item proceeds until there are no bidders willing to bid higher. The last and highest bidder is awarded the auction item.

Live auctions are fun and generate excitement for the bidders and audience. Unlike raffles and games of chance, items in auctions are absolutely attainable to those who choose to participate—and who bid to the end. In addition, live auctions offer the bidder a spectacular forum in which to make his or her contribution to the charitable cause of the organization. By the same token, the donor of the auctioned item gets credit and may even be involved by going onstage and promoting the item as it is auctioned. For those seeking "credit" for their contribution to a charitable event either by buying an auction item or donating one for use in an auction, the live auction provides maximum exposure.

Another form of auction is the silent auction. In silent auctions people write their bids on bidding lists at their leisure during a set period of time.

Items in the auction are usually displayed on tables or in a well-marked, demarcated location. During the time the silent auction is open to bidding, bidders can bid as many times as they wish, as long as the bids continue to increase. When the time period for the auction closes, the person who offered the last highest bid wins (buys) the item. Silent auctions are described more fully in chapter 16.

The Auction as Stage Play

The live auction is the main fundraising event. All other fundraising activities are just side acts; all prior attractions are mere trappings. The auction takes place on center stage—it is center stage. All seats have a view of the auctioneer. The auctioneer "owns" the room and the audience during the live auction. No others may compete for attention with the auctioneer during the live auction. The auction is in large measure a stage play, and treating it as such is one avenue to success.

Before the live auction begins, all activities, motions, sights, and sounds serve to titillate the attendee and heighten interest in the upcoming auction. Every effort, no matter how large or small, complements the live auction, and nothing ever competes with it. All other activities stop as the live auction begins. Nothing interferes with the progress and timely completion of the auction. The live auction itself must proceed at a rapid pace, building and maintaining excitement and momentum.

The more money at stake, the higher the drama. More drama can be generated through more action. Sometimes the more outrageous or loud, the better. Other times a more sophisticated form of action is warranted to appeal to the sensitivities of a conservative crowd. Comedy can sometimes be a good form of action. Whatever the proclivity of the audience or subject of attention, action, drama, and spectacle increase the number and interest of bidders. It is about putting on a show—a fundraising show. The auction event is a stage play to raise funds for a cause, and it works.

When the live auction ends, only a few minor details are left before the entire event ends—remaining door prizes are awarded, and final raffle prizes are announced. This takes place quickly. The live auction has ended, and the event is now extending beyond its grand finale.

The Auction Players

Auctioneers, spotters, runners, and models work together to present exciting visual imagery of the auction items. They tantalize all with descriptions and testimonials. And most important, the "actors" in this stage play involve the bidders and onlookers in the intense drama of rapid-fire bidding and determined competition. Side conversations are held with bidders and then repeated for all to hear. Runners or models carry wearable fashion items or jewelry to bidders to "try on." A rideable "green" electric lawn mower up for bidding zooms between tables. A big motorcycle onstage is started up with a roar. Bidders are pitted against each other, but always in a fun way.

Live auctions can provide a phenomenal source of net revenue for an organization, but poor execution of any aspect can result in frustration for all concerned, as well as potential financial ruin for the host organization. It was a pure stroke of luck that the auctioneer in the story at the beginning of this chapter noticed that the art piece was an original. It is not the auctioneer's job to be an art expert, but the auctioneer does want to get the best bid possible for each item. That organization was lucky; it is much better to prepare and be prepared than to hope to get lucky.

Assembling just the right cast of characters is one of the keys to a successful live auction. Here are the members of that cast revealed.

The Master of Ceremonies

Until the main live auction begins, the MC is the center of attention, the ring leader, orchestra director, and main character in the play unfolding onstage. But when the auction begins, attention immediately shifts to the auctioneer. From this point until the auction ends, the auctioneer, not the MC, commands the full attention of the audience. The role of the MC remains important but secondary. Knowing how to play that role is a mark of an outstanding MC.

During the auction, the MC supports the auctioneer by serving as the auctioneer's primary onstage assistant. The auctioneer and MC work together to determine the exact role to be played by the MC. The MC is often assigned the jobs of announcing and describing auction items, introducing donors or members of the audience who give testimonials about auction items, and helping the auctioneer keep order in the room by making announcements and giving notice to unruly attendees. All of the MC's activity is at the direction of the auctioneer while the auction is under way.

The MC's being oblivious to the respective roles and responsibilities of the MC and auctioneer creates disaster. That can happen when the MC continues to lord over the event, butts in to the auctioneer's dialogue with bidders, makes decisions about bidding, and undercuts the auctioneer. In the "spirit" of getting into the act, sometimes MCs even take over the job of auctioneer either partially or wholly. They may do so either because they are so full of ego they just can't stand anyone else playing the top role onstage or feel they can do a better job than the auctioneer in auctioning off items. A professional auctioneer may have the skills and courage to deal effectively with such MCs, but if the auctioneer is also an amateur or lacks experience with event fundraising, the event goes downhill fast. Even a skilled auctioneer may bow out when an MC oversteps the role, considering MCs are often celebrities, significant personalities, or officers of the organization. An auctioneer may be unwilling to step on such authority figures no matter how badly an egomaniacal MC affects bidding. After all, it is the charitable organization's event, and if the organization wants to allow some bozo MC to mess it up, that is its problem, especially if final bids do not affect payment to the auctioneer.

The MC needs to be informed of and agree to a certain role during the auction. The MC can work out the details with the auctioneer just before the auction begins, but if the host organization has doubts about an MC's ability to play the role of "humble" assistant to the auctioneer, the host's financial future is best served by finding a different MC.

The Auctioneer

The auctioneer is the person who conducts and manages the bidding process. These are the only duties assigned to the auctioneer in a well-managed, well-staffed auction event. However, skilled auctioneers also know it is part of their job to learn about the items to be offered to bidders and take time to learn about the bidders themselves. They also may have expertise useful if problems arise during an event. A good auctioneer is critical to the success of an auction event. The entire event leads up to and hinges on the success of the main-event live auction. Auctioneers are in the keystone role. They can single-handedly make or break the event's financial success, as well as the more intangible success that comes from hosting and being part of an enjoyable well-organized and well-managed event.

CHOOSING A PROFESSIONAL OR AMATEUR AUCTIONEER

Because the success of a major live auction hinges on the skill and experience of the auctioneer, it is critical to engage a competent one. Check reliable references, or attend charity auctions to find a skilled auctioneer. Select an auctioneer who demonstrates competency. One way to increase the likelihood that an auctioneer has sufficient skills and experience is to engage a professional auctioneer, who usually knows how to help manage complicated situations that may arise on the bidding floor, control a crowd, and maintain a fast and effective pace that increases final bid amounts.

In an attempt to save costs or to accommodate volunteer enthusiasm, event planners may take on the role of auctioneer themselves or have an acquaintance serve in that role. Sometimes the person chosen as auctioneer has done it before, but strictly as a volunteer with no training, certification, or long-term experience. Some amateur auctioneers do a credible job managing bidding, and some have gained considerable experience. If available, such an amateur auctioneer may be a good choice, especially for small, low-value auctions. However, many, perhaps most, amateur auctioneers do not have the experience needed to effectively manage the bidding process on a large auction floor, increase bidding to the highest point possible, manage unforeseen situations, and control an unruly crowd if necessary.

Many amateur auctioneers (and some professional ones) do not do a good job at charity events. They do not know how, or maybe they just don't bother to make an effort, to maintain proper pace or deal with bidders mixed into a crowd that may be more intent on socializing than following an auction. The auctioneer may not know what to do in situations where professionalism and experience come into play in increasing bidding amounts or solving a crisis. Using a poorly skilled auctioneer can result in a poorly run, confusing, boring, and excessively lengthy auction that brings only very low bids.

EMPLOYING A PROFESSIONAL AUCTIONEER

Professional auctioneers are available for hire. Find them like any other service provider through Internet searches and trade-association lists, or contact event planners for other organizations that hold auctions. Ask for referrals. Charitable organizations can often obtain professional auctioneer services for free, at a reduced cost, or for simple reimbursement of expenses. Always check and verify their references. Auctioneers do their job in a visible fashion. Any auctioneer who claims to be experienced can refer to hundreds or thousands of eye-witnesses. Ask to speak to event planners and others who have worked with the auctioneer. Ask the references about the auctioneer's competency, professionalism, demeanor, ability to increase bidding, and willingness to pitch in to solve problems on the auction floor. Also ask if the auctioneer created an atmosphere of fun, enjoyment, and trust during the auction.

Look locally for an auctioneer with whom it may be possible to build a lasting relationship between the auctioneer and host organization. It helps if the auctioneer relates well to the host's mission. Make the auctioneer a member of the organization. An auctioneer who relates well to attendees and knows the event is a very valuable asset in event fundrais-

ing. It may take several events, or several auctioneers, to find this match, but once such a relationship is established, it should be safeguarded and treasured.

PREPARING THE AUCTIONEER FOR SUCCESS

Auctioneers should arrive at least an hour or two before the auction so they have time to prepare and deal with any unforeseen circumstances. Since auctioneers participate in many events, they can usually tell within a few minutes if the event is being well managed. It will be hard to hide anything from an experienced auctioneer. The auctioneer should have received information about the event, especially information about the auction items, well in advance of arriving at the event. Event planners should have everything in place before the auctioneer arrives.

Once the auctioneer arrives, at least one member of the event planning team should discuss each auction item with the auctioneer. A good auctioneer will already have reviewed the advance auction program and will have questions. Key areas for discussion include minimum opening bid price desired for each item and minimum acceptable final bid.

The auctioneer will also want to know how much discretion he or she will have to close off bidding, in lieu of a reserve or minimum acceptable bid. Sometimes an auctioneer will purposefully close off bidding quickly, before the apparent high bid is reached. This is usually done in an effort to speed up bidding, where a slow pace and small bid increments are boring the audience and killing bid momentum. With this "warning," bidders know to get on with it or risk loss of the item to the whim of an impatient auctioneer. This is also the kind of move that can cause a misunderstanding between an event host and auctioneer if not discussed in advance. Inexperienced event planners may not recognize this tactic, seeing only an item sold for a lower price than what might have been received had bidding been allowed to proceed. Usually an auctioneer will do this with relatively low-value items and only after some level of bidding has taken place. It is also generally accompanied with a warning to bidders that if they really want to win an item, they had better wake up and bid early and often.

The auctioneer will also want to know a few other things. Will testimonials be offered? If so, on which items? Who will introduce people making testimonials, and who will control their time onstage? Will donors be acknowledged onstage? Who will do that? Should the auctioneer help promote the donor's contribution? How much time do event planners intend to spend on the auction? The auctioneer may offer advice on timing and will want to know who will control time management in the event of unforeseen circumstances, such as a failed audio system or a testimonial that goes on too long.

The auctioneer will want to meet the MC and make sure the actions of the MC and auctioneer are orchestrated onstage. Although managing bidding is the sole responsibility of the auctioneer, the MC or a member of the event planning team works in concert with the auctioneer to introduce the item onstage with a viewing of the item and description. This can also be done by the auctioneer, if necessary, but it is best if the auctioneer is supported onstage by having someone else present or describe the item. The auctioneer can always add to the presentation in advance of, or during, the bidding process. The onstage description or presentation is in addition to descriptions in the program. This is the last chance at marketing an item before bidding starts.

The Spotters

Spotters are the auctioneer's eyes and ears on the auction floor. Spotters spot bidders and bring bids to the attention of the auctioneer. They confirm and mark the current highest bidder. There is generally one spotter for every 50 to 75 bidders. Spotters also help bidders understand the sequence of bidding and answer questions they may have about items or bidding procedure. For this reason, spotters must be well versed in the rules of live auctions.

Spotters are also visible players in generating and maintaining auction momentum. Skilled spotters often get into the act by joking with bidders and creating excitement on the bidding floor by playing back and forth among each other or with bidders as bids are exchanged. They are an integral part of the live auction act, and their role in generating higher bids and keeping order on the bidding floor should not be underestimated.

The Runners

Runners deliver paperwork to the bidder. Bid-confirmation runners help ensure that auction paperwork is completed fast and flawlessly. This paperwork is called a "buyer's agreement" and contains a description of the item, the item's fair market value, the name of the host organization, the winning bid amount, any additional fees or taxes that must be paid, and any disclaimers or warranty information (see figure 15.1 for an example buyer's agreement; see chapter 21 for more detailed information on fair market values and the buyer's agreement).

The bidder is asked to sign the buyer's agreement to confirm the winning bid amount and that any information about the item matches what the bidder understood as correct during bidding. This is essentially a purchase contract for the item. The runner can explain the buyer's agreement, point out the final bid amount, and make sure the bidder signs the form properly. The runner can also help the bidder get back into bidding action as soon as possible.

Runners start with partially prepared paperwork. There is a separate buyer's agreement prepared for each item well in advance of the auction. The runner stands by as each item is auctioned. Once the final bid is received, the runner or a cashier fills in the winning bid amount on the paperwork, and the runner carries the form to the bidder.

All paperwork should be completed at tableside with the bidder's full attention. The runner leaves a duplicate signed copy of the buyer's agreement with the winning bidder and takes the other copy to the cashier's booth (payment center). The runner makes sure the paperwork is handled properly, removing that responsibility from the bidder. Where bidders may be consuming alcohol, it is best to have procedures in place and followed to ensure financial matters and agreements are handled properly and professionally. This helps avoid disputes and maintains good relationships with donors, bidders, and attendees at the event and afterward.

<Name of Fundraising Event>
A charitable fundraising event to benefit <Name of Host Organization>
<Location of auction>
<Date of auction>

Buyer's Agreement

I acknowledge acceptance of the following auction item(s) for the winning bid amount
listed below and according to the auction rules and regulations published by <Host
Organization>. My signature below represents an agreement to purchase the item
described.

Name and/or description and specific characteristics of auction item(s) purchased:

_____

_____

_____

Value: $_____

Winning bid amount: $_____

Buyer's name (print): _____

Buyer's signature: _____ Date:_____

<Host Organization> representative's signature: _____ Date: _____

*<Host Organization> is incorporated in the state of <State> and is recognized by the Internal Revenue
Service as a 501(c)3 charitable organization. Donations may be tax deductible.*

Print on host organization's letterhead, including address. If the organization has no official letterhead, place the name of the organization and address clearly at either the top or bottom of the page.

FIGURE 15.1. Example buyer's-agreement form.

Cashiering is done at the convenience of the bidder but before the winning bidder leaves the auction room. Require payment by the end of the event, and require the payment be made prior to removal of items from the event area. Winning bidders pick up the item at the cashier's booth or a special pickup location. Some organizations may provide winning bidders an extended period for payment. If so, such extensions must be handled consistently among all bidders, and a written policy should be in place to govern such "credit." If winning bidders are provided an option for extended payment, the item should not be transferred to the buyer until payment is complete. After all, charitable organizations may have virtuous missions, but they are not loan offices.

The Auction-Item Sales Team

Once the auction begins, it's nonstop showtime. Each item is promoted in turn. An item is brought to the stage and held up before bidders. Depending on what it is and its size and weight, it is either displayed onstage or is walked around the room so bidders can make a close inspection.

Use of a projection system and big screens enables a quick description of the item to be displayed followed by an illustration of the item for all to see. The item continues to be projected on-screen during bidding. In the case of a service, such as a spa treatment or a vacation tour, a short video or slide show may be available that can be set to loop continuously during bidding on the item. The item number should be prominently displayed to enable prospective bidders to follow progress of the auction.

A new cast of characters whose role is to market the auction items may now come into the play. Models, spokespersons, shills, and even the audience can become part of the marketing action.

THE MODELS

Models take the show to bidders and, in the course of doing so, literally may be that little voice whispering in the ear of a bidder that generates the next bid. Models model the auction merchandise or otherwise assist in its display. This includes taking auction items tableside, directly to a bidder as the bidder decides on the next bid. For example, an experienced event model will quickly spot a person who appears on the verge of, yet indecisive about, making a bid. The model will move to the indecisive person to better display the item and may suggest a bid. Even a service, such as a vacation cruise, can be marketed tableside by an experienced, well-informed event model. Event models work closely with the auctioneer to ensure each item is displayed and properly marketed to bidders.

When I refer to event models, some readers may assume I refer to scantily clad women models who are the calling card of some (fewer today than yesterday) events catering to leering, drunk men. For inappropriate events like that, such models are exactly what I do refer to, but for the kinds of events discussed in this book, scantily clad women models are simply not appropriate. Instead, I refer to women or men in dress appropriate for the event who work to display event merchandise.

Many events feature the children of the host organization's members or other completely inexperienced people as event models. This is perfectly fine if the event is a small neighborhood affair where bids will be made and budgets spent regardless of the effectiveness of sales pitches during the auction. There is little to be gained or lost by using sophisticated marketing techniques at such events—it doesn't matter. However, if an event is a critical fundraiser, where tens or hundreds of thousands of dollars in auction revenue is at stake and event planners are seeking to create an environment for maximum net revenue, use of amateur models is one of the most common, most misunderstood mistakes made in event fundraising. Failure to market live auction items effectively and strategically during the auction can undermine all the work and expense in advance of an auction and result in reduced net revenue.

Models have assisted in raising funds at auction events since the inception of the auction event for nonprofit organizations, but only recently have event models turned this work into a profession, with skills and techniques that help sell auction merchandise. This refers to effective sales techniques. Attractive, poised, and professional men and women skilled and experienced at supporting event fundraising grace the floors of many of today's most successful major charity auctions. They serve to display event merchandise, sell raffle tickets, and otherwise help boost net proceeds. They can be very effective. They can also range from very sexy to conservatively elegant; these are among options available to event planners.

As professionals, event models adapt to the requirements of each job. They can be hired as independent service providers or through agencies specializing in event models. Some services are better than others, and it can be easy to confuse service providers advertising modeling because different kinds of services are available that may be called modeling in directories and advertisements. Thus, it is important to make needs clear when contacting modeling agencies.

References and interviews are important in making sure models are well matched to the event and host organization. Such service providers are generally most readily available in areas where there are a large number of events, but the proliferation of auction events in rural areas held throughout America now means that well-skilled professional event models can be found almost anywhere, although selection of service may be limited. For example, an agency may have models that understand modeling as practiced at trade show events, but have no experience promoting auction merchandise to bidders. The key to making a proper selection of service provider is to make sure the models know auction events and how to sell event merchandise, including working with auctioneers to sell auction items.

As it is with employing a professional auctioneer, employing experienced professional event models can easily make a significant difference in bid amounts (and sale of raffle tickets and other marketable items). At many events children, sometimes teenagers and older, and spouses of host organization volunteers are the raffle salespersons and event models. In very few instances do these very attractive, hardworking, and dedicated event models employ effective sales techniques in displaying auction items or selling raffle tickets. Sure, they hold an item up in the air as bidders bid on it, but that much could be done by anyone randomly picked from a crowd. Amateur event models are generally clueless about sales, how to read and approach potential buyers or bidders, and how to close a sale. Shame on event planners who entrust a portion of the organization's financial future to a bunch of inexperienced kids—or inexperienced adults. (This recommendation is not relevant to the many small youth or family organizations that hold small "backyard" events where sales pitch is largely irrelevant to funds raised. At such an event, by all means allow the kids to be event models, ticket sellers, or whatever else they can do to help out.)

THE TRUSTWORTHY SPOKESPERSON

One of the most effective ways to market a service item, such as a vacation trip or golf lessons, is by use of a "testimonial" by a reliable person familiar with the service or trip who comes before the bidders and provides positive comments. Sometimes this testimonial can include video or photographs projected for all to see. Hearing from someone known to attendees about how great an auction item is can be a powerful motivator in the midst of bidding.

THE DONOR AS HAWKER

Another potential participant in the onstage marketing of an item is the donor. If the donor is well known in the community, participating directly in the auction by standing onstage and making a pitch for the donated auction item can have a big influence on bidding. When the donor comes onstage, bidders see the person tied to the donation and know that he or she will be watching who bids and for how much. This can be a very compelling means of marketing items at events in communities where people are likely to know each other.

Having a donor comment on the item donated is particularly helpful if the donor is personally involved in a service or activity up for bid and if there may be questions about the service. For example, the donor may be a famous personality, and the auction item may be a gourmet meal cooked in the winning bidder's own home by the famous donor. Hearing the donor talk about the meal and about how much fun the dinner will be will be tempting to bidders. But bidders may want to ask questions about possible menus.

As another example, a fisherman renowned for knowing where to catch the big ones donates a guided fishing trip. During the auction the donor can talk about the trip and show pictures of big fish caught where fishing will take place, as well as make additions or clarifications to the trip while onstage. It is not unusual for a donor to change what a donation includes while onstage. For example, a two-person trip can be modified to include two additional people if the donor decides to do so. This often happens after a bit of dialogue with bidders reveals that a slight increase or change in the donation might increase the final bid amount appreciably. This is the kind of revenue-increasing dialogue generated by an experienced auctioneer, spotter, or model.

THE BIDDERS

Bidders come in all shapes, sizes, and dispositions and, of course, have different-sized pocketbooks. Keeping donors happy, excited, and engaged during the auction is what this stage play is all about. The bidders themselves also play a role. Some bidders love to get involved; for example, during bidding the auctioneer may engage with the bidder in a joke, and the bidder loves it and eggs other bidders on for more as bidding continues upward. This creates added motivation for some people to bid but can get tricky. Some bidders do not react well when another bidder becomes part of the stage play, and some do not appreciate being made part of the stage play. While it is common for an auctioneer or a spotter to try to engage a bidder in a side play, the bidder may simply not want to play along. It comes down to the simple fact that some people like attention and some do not. The host's team putting on the auction needs to remain sensitive to bidders' feelings about being drawn too far into the fun and playacting that go along with many charity auctions.

THE SHILLS

Do not let an item fall out of the auction for lack of a minimum bid. Minimum opening bid amounts

are a necessary evil. A donor of an item should not be allowed to suffer the embarrassment of having a high-value item "stolen" for nothing. By the same token, the host organization should receive a reasonable price for items commensurate with value.

All auction items, even items fully donated for auction at the event, should be assigned a "reserve" price. This is the price below which the item will not be sold. Sometimes this reserve price is stated up front, in the program, and in other descriptions of the item. At a minimum, the reserve price may be announced at the beginning of bidding. Reserves need not be advertised or announced. Sometimes a more strategic approach to dealing with reserve prices is to keep the reserve hidden from bidders. This is called a "silent reserve." The reason for keeping the reserve hidden is to avoid tipping bidders off to the minimum price. Bidders may equate this reserve price with the base price and bid not much beyond, considering the reserve more an asking price than a minimum.

If the reserve is hidden, the auctioneer simply doesn't accept a bid for any less than the reserve. If the reserve is not met, the auctioneer may say something like, "I can't take less than one hundred dollars for this, can I?" The auctioneer then turns to the MC or representative of the host organization for a confirmation or advice. That advice may very well be to pull the item from the auction. But there is another alternative. When opening bids are too low or too slow in coming, sometimes all it takes to open up bidding is for someone to break the ice with a bid. Sometimes that may be an assigned duty. The "job" of opening bidder may fall to one or more persons designated by the event committee to purposefully get bidding started at a reasonable set amount decided on beforehand. This person is referred to as a "safety-net bidder" or "shill."

For whatever reason, some people just don't want to be first, so bidders may be reluctant to start. In addition, there may be some skepticism about whether an item is really worth what the donor or MC states it is. Bidders may be waiting for the auctioneer to call for a lower bid, but they are reluctant to suggest a very low bid themselves. If someone bids the opening amount or at least makes a reasonable opening bid, skeptics are more likely to join in the bidding, because now others have endorsed the item by believing the item is worth at least the opening bid. Sometimes that's the only way bidding gets started.

If after the opening bid, no one else bids, then the item goes to the safety-net bidder, who then "resells" the item back to the host organization after the auction is over. Is this deceptive? A little, maybe. It may not be an appropriate technique for some organizations, and it may be considered unethical by some event planners. Then again, when a person opens with a minimum bid, that bid does not force the next and subsequent bidders to bid. Additional bidding is entirely spontaneous and voluntary. Also, with the safety-net bidder in place to bid an opening appropriate amount, donors will perceive their donation was used and helped the organization raise money. The alternative for the donor of the item, should it fail to receive any bids, is likely to be embarrassment or frustration with the event or organization.

Either way, if no bids are received at all or if a safety-net bidder opens bidding and no other bids are received, the host organization will have to determine how to dispose of the item. The organization could keep it for future use or return the item to the donor. If the organization has a cost or a split with the donor and no minimal bid is received, the item will be returned.

THE AUDIENCE

Members of the audience can become potential marketers in their own unique fashion. They don't just have to sit there like bumps on a log waiting their turn to bid. With bids climbing, action usually comes down to battle between two, or maybe three, finalists. At this point members of the audience can help urge bidders on and upward. This kind of encouragement and endorsement can be infectious and quickly engulf an entire auction audience. As it grows, it is one of the few things that can happen on an event floor to catch the attention of chronic socializers. Even they will be turned into involved participants as the entire audience becomes engaged in urging on bidders. The whole auction floor comes alive with excitement and vocal participation in the bidding. These are the moments talked about for years afterward. Full engagement of attendees is what makes one event fabulous and separates it from all the others. Everyone is engaged and having memorable fun.

For the event host, these moments when the audience and auction become one are the times bidding goes to unanticipated heights. These moments do not usually happen by accident. Total engagement of the audience generally starts with the skilled encouragement of an experienced auctioneer working in concert with skilled spotters and models who see an opportunity to get the audience involved in bidding. They manipulate willing members of the audience to engage, who, in turn, encourage others to follow. What erupts is carefully orchestrated enthusiasm to help bidders bid higher. Done well, involving an entire audience in increasing bid amounts is the most potent marketing tactic a skilled auction team can employ.

Bids and Payment

Auction bids are not pledges or proposals. They are decisions to purchase, with payment to be collected on-site no later than after completion of all bidding. Immediately upon end of bidding on an item, a runner should present the winning bidder with a buyer's agreement, as described earlier. This form is produced in duplicate, and the bidder signs each copy. The bidder keeps one, and the other is retained by the host organization. Items are rebid if agreements are not signed, so it is important to clear the paperwork immediately upon completion of bidding. If bidders are allowed to wait until the auction ends, there will be no means to rebid an item if the bidder refuses to make payment or claims a misunderstanding.

The form must be signed and returned to the payment center before auction end. It is best to do this immediately after bidding on the item is completed with well-prepared forms that do not tie up bidders in lengthy paperwork, because the bidder may be interested in bidding on other items. Forms must be preprinted with information about the auction item already on the form. The bid price is added before presenting the form to the winning bidder. All the bidder should have to do is confirm the bid amount and sign the form.

Auction-Item Sequence

Because each auction varies in the kinds of items available, it is impossible to give anything but general guidance on the sequence in which auction items should be offered to bidders. In general, start with two or three items of moderate value (relative to items offered at the auction) that will be popular to bidders. This helps generate early excitement. The moderate values and popularity should generate quick interest by bidders. Throughout the auction, mix up the kinds of items offered. In other words, if there are four art prints available for auction, spread them out. Don't offer them one after the other. Build toward the middle of the auction with the highest-value and featured items coming at or just after the midpoint. Once the featured items have all been auctioned off, wind down to the end.

The basis for this sequence is to (1) generate excitement early, (2) build to the middle of the auction, and (3) give unsuccessful bidders for the most featured items an opportunity to bid on some very nice items after the most highly featured items are all gone. Consider that not all bidders will be able to take home the most desired items. If the most desirable items are offered at the end of the auction, anyone who has held off bidding in anticipation of winning a featured item will have nothing to bid on if he or she doesn't win the desired item. On the other hand, if most featured items are auctioned off first, the highest drama and excitement of the auction are over almost as the auction begins.

Special Situations and Advanced Techniques: Good, Bad, and Ugly

Auctions offer seemingly endless opportunities to market items to a captive crowd who have assembled themselves for the openly declared purpose of contributing their money to the host organization

and its mission. Many innovative and sometimes quite elaborate means to raise these funds have been devised. Yet, as in any situation where a number of people assemble to exchange money, and maybe to have a few or many alcoholic drinks, situations will arise that need to be handled. Here are solutions and advice on situation handling.

Absentee Bidders

It is acceptable to make provision for absentee bidders. An absentee bidder is a person unable to attend silent or live auction(s) in person who wishes to place bids on auction items through a representative of the host organization. To do so, the person gives the host organization's representative absentee bid instructions. Bids are then entered on the absentee bidder's behalf. The host organization's representative attempts to purchase the item at the lowest price possible but never for more than the maximum amount the absentee bidder specifies.

Such bidders can ensure a base-level bid for an auction item. This may be valuable for getting bidding started on an item. If the host organization allows absentee bidding, there needs to be a policy drafted or a disclaimer that the host organization's representative will not be held liable for failure to bid properly or for any errors in making bids. Absentee bidders should be required to provide a pre-approved credit card or other guaranteed method of payment in advance, with clearance to charge the maximum bidding price approved by the absentee bidder. The host organization may wish to add other restrictions to absentee bidding, such as a limited number of items per absentee bidder, or require the absentee bidder to be a current member of the host organization.

Keeping Order in the House

There is no doubt that a well-run center-stage auction provides many spectacles for bidders and onlookers. Despite the best efforts of the auctioneer and helpers to maintain an interesting show and orderly bidding process, side acts may divert attendee and bidder attention. Where possible, obvious disturbances need to be hushed, but often attention is diverted in ways not easily identified or circumvented.

If attendees are at large tables, which is often the case if the auction is preceded by dinner, side conversations may get started that never seem to end. Some attendees simply have no interest in bidding and are there for purely social reasons, and the result is constant and noisy socializing. Some attendees may not even realize their conversations are disturbing attendees who may want to follow the bidding action and bid themselves. Attendees who have had too much alcohol can sometimes cause a commotion, and alcohol often causes potential bidders to drift in and out of the bidding, as their attention comes and goes. Although there is no easy way to maintain strict control of all that is happening on an auction floor, it is reasonably certain that some or many people are not paying strict attention to what is going on.

When people who lose track want to reengage with an auction under way, it is critically important to make it easy for them to do so. There must be an obvious, quick, easy way for an attendee to figure out what is happening in the auction without disturbing others. Ways to allow for reengagement include having a well-designed program in every attendee's hand or a ready supply on each table and at strategic locations around the room, such as near drink bars.

There should also be displays on screens or on big signs showing what is up for bid and the current point in the bidding processes. These displays should be readily obvious, easily seen, and understandable, with information displayed large enough to be easily read in low light and by people who may have less than perfect eyesight. Maintaining such information is facilitated by auctioning items in sequence, and in the sequence shown in the written program. That sequence is displayed along with presentations of the items themselves, and the position of the item currently up for bidding is shown and obvious for all to see. This allows distracted potential bidders to quickly reorient to the auction and participate.

Auctioneer as Crisis Manager

Sometimes auctioneers must take on other roles, beyond just managing bidding. In such situations the value of a truly competent auctioneer becomes apparent. Circumstances requiring auctioneers to help in other ways include the all-too-common situation in which a professional auctioneer arrives at an event and finds event workers in a state of chaos. Event planners, officers, volunteers, and staff may be inexperienced and panicked over one or many things that have not gone according to plan. Or maybe they have no plan. In some instances too few workers are available to fully staff the event, and some necessary work is not getting done. Audio equipment is notorious for breaking down and being mismatched with requirements of the auction room. Auctioneers must be heard clearly throughout the auction room and become adept at working around audio problems. Event workers may not know how to work display equipment. It is not unusual for unforeseen circumstances to stump even experienced event hosts. All of these circumstances and more challenge the auctioneer and the host's efforts to hold an effective auction.

If event planners had the foresight to hire or otherwise acquire the services of a professional auctioneer, it is likely the auctioneer has the skills and experience to provide guidance to the event hosts in various areas of botched event planning. The auctioneer may be able to help organize the auction and possibly even rescue parts of the failing event. In such an instance the auctioneer would attempt to help where possible by providing advice or personally taking charge. This may involve seeing to work that should have been done well in advance of the auction, for example, by explaining proper display and handling of auction items during the bidding process. It could also include taking over the role of MC, last-minute marketing of auction items, and managing volunteer and staff workers, including providing a briefing on their roles during the auction and providing onstage, live coaching from the podium. The auctioneer can also help see to the tasks of identifying high bidders and making sure event workers properly handle bidders.

All this is added burden on an auctioneer, and some will not offer to help. It is really not their job. But whether they do or do not help, the event will be less effective and efficient than if the event had been properly planned and managed in the first place. One of the marks of proper event planning is having everything in place for the auctioneer in advance so the auctioneer can fully concentrate on the bidding process, learn about the items up for auction, and gain an understanding of the bidders. An auctioneer doing extra work in an attempt to remedy problems diverts his or her attention from the bidding process. While not an ideal situation for either party, the alternative of doing nothing and allowing the event to fail is worse. If event planners fail to obtain the services of a professional auctioneer, problems in advance of the live auction may simply be a prelude to continued disaster when the amateur arrives on the scene.

Bargain Hunters

Some people just can't resist a bargain. Others buy only when they find a bargain. Do not assume that just because a person attends a charity auction that the individual is willing to pay more than the retail price for an auction item. Some attendees are looking only for bargains, and some auctions may attract a large number of bargain shoppers. Maybe this happens because general commercial auctions are places people go to find bargains. Or maybe the reason is that so many people have been exposed to auctions through Internet auction sites that entice bidders on the basis of finding bargains.

There is nothing wrong with bargain hunters attending charity auction events. After all, part of the fun for bidders is getting a good deal. However, when virtually all attendees are looking for bargains, the host organization may find the return on items relative to retail value lower than expected. If most or all auction items are acquired as full donations, the host still earns net revenue per item auctioned. Although this may simply be the fate of some organizations that host auctions, setting a stage for bargains is the objective of others.

Managing the Manipulative and Monopolizing Bidder

In small communities and where event attendees are members of the same small organization, it is likely many or most of the attendees know each other. This usually includes knowing information about each other's economic status, including how willing individuals are to spend money at charity events. Having such intimate knowledge about fellow bidders can put a damper on bidding at live auctions. This occurs when attendees know the person bidding can and may make the decision to outbid them, and challenging the bidder will just result in an item more expensive than the budget allows. It can also affect silent auctions, but not as directly.

I have seen it too many times to consider it accidental. When the wealthy couple in the room decides to bid on an auction item, others simply do not challenge the bid. Occasionally a person will bid up a little. Some people take on the task of always trying to bid up the rich folks. That works well if the challenger is also rich, but if not, having one or two bids go unchallenged ends that game abruptly. Other bidders believe they don't have a chance, so they simply stop bidding. This is a common situation that can affect overall auction momentum and success. It is not unusual for two or three bidders to monopolize or manipulate an entire auction, unintentionally or not. This can happen relatively easily if there are not a large number of bidders and all but a few bidders are of limited financial means. Sometimes the aggressive bidders believe they are helping the organization by bidding items up to a very high price, because the organization wins and only they can afford to make such high contributions. Often these bidders will bid up relatively modestly valued items, taking them beyond the reach of all but one or two attendees.

Managing auctions of this nature is challenging. In this case an organization's officers and, if one exists, the chief paid officer, need to evaluate the situation and decide on a course of action. Action may be to have a discussion with one or all of the several wealthy bidders about ways for them to contribute most effectively to the organization. For example, instead of having people contribute only through auction bidding, ask them to underwrite the event with a high-level event sponsorship but, of course, bid on a few items. This would give the contributors a high profile at the event and allow for some, more limited bidding so others can participate as well. Maybe the best course of action will be to do nothing at all. If this is to be the nature of the event, fundraising activities can be modified to account for it. For example, more mid-value raffles and mid- to high-value silent auction items can be added with fewer but higher-value live auction items used.

Payment Center

Every auction event has a place where event workers and attendees make financial transactions. This is usually called the "cashier's booth," "payment center," or "bank." This is the location where credit card transactions are processed, ticket sellers deposit cash received or receive cash to make change, auction-item winners come to make payment, and all other financial transactions take place. It is the only location financial transactions take place at an event. The host organization's chief financial officer or event treasurer and workers on the finance team manage and staff the booth. It functions throughout an event but may become very busy at the conclusion of an event if all the winning silent and live auction winners try to pay and take possession of their items at the same time.

Set Up the Cashier's Booth

Treasurers usually have a professional background in finance or accounting and, if there are no paid financial staff, are relied upon by the host organization to set controls in place to handle cash and credit cards and manage and secure financial transactions at the event. The treasurer or the host organization's paid financial or accounting staff set up the cashier's booth. Policies and procedures are set in place to manage all financial transactions, tax requirements, and record keeping during the event.

This includes responsibility for controlling access to auction items and other security matters (see chapter 22 for detailed information about event security).

Setting up a cashier's booth and financial controls must be done by the staff or volunteers who will be personally liable for the effectiveness of those controls. These staff or volunteers must be comfortable with and confident in the rules and procedures set into place.

Follow these guidelines for setting up the booth. Even at small events, at least two workers should always be present at the cashier's booth when transactions are taking place. As long as cash or financial materials are present in the booth, it should be occupied by members of the finance team. These two precautions help reduce the risk of problems. Having two people present and the booth occupied at all times reduces the risk of someone removing something from the booth. Having two people in the booth when money is being handled reduces the opportunity for a single individual to take advantage of the host organization and also reduces the likelihood of claims an individual event worker purposefully mishandled money (one person provides witness for the other).

Count cash and count it again. Do the same with checks. Have two different people count. Look for checks that are made out improperly. Make sure there are telephone numbers on checks. Have policies and procedures in place for payment and handling transactions, and publish these in the advance and auction programs. See chapter 6 for example payment and other event-related policies and procedures.

Meet Requirements

The treasurer has responsibility to ensure receipts the cashiers give to winning bidders and other materials available to bidders at or before the event contain information that will help prove tax deductibility of payments if the host organization is a qualified charity. The following information pertains to events held by qualified charities. See chapter 21 for detailed information about tax deductibility, determination of fair market value, example materials, and forms discussed later in this chapter.

PURCHASE RECEIPT

The IRS allows donors who purchase items at a charity auction to claim a charitable tax deduction for the amount of the purchase price paid for an item over its fair market value. The fair market value of any auction item won must be listed on a receipt that the organization is required to provide to successful bidders at the time they pay for the item. In addition to fair market value, this receipt must include the amount actually paid for the item, a description of the item (goods or services purchased), the name of the organization, and a statement that the organization did not provide additional goods or services in return for the charitable portion (if any) of the contribution. See figure 15.2 for an example auction-item purchase receipt.

DURING THE AUCTION

A good-faith estimate of the fair market value of each item should be provided to or displayed to bidders. Receiving a tax deduction requires the bidder at an auction to somehow demonstrate that he or she knew in advance of bidding that the value of the item was less than the amount paid. It is important for host organizations to help attendees meet this requirement by complying with IRS rules requiring display of fair market values to bidders in advance of and/or during silent and live auctions. For live auction items, list the fair market values for each item in the printed auction program given to all bidders or display and announce the fair market value as the item is auctioned off. For silent auction items, a good-faith estimate of the fair market value of each item should be listed directly on the bid sheet.

Maintain Records

The greatest asset to event planners is detailed information about attendees' spending patterns at events. Although there is no easy way for planners of first-time events to have such information about anticipated attendees, a base of such information can be assembled over time by keeping careful records of auction purchases. These records should be kept in detail, but attendees' privacy must be maintained. Records are most useful if kept consistently over time and used in future event planning. The treasurer or paid financial staff of the host organization should be responsible for developing an appropriate record-keeping system for attendee buying and spending patterns and for seeing to its effective use in future event planning.

Deal with the Paying Crowd

The key to managing a crowd of auction-item buyers awaiting their turn to make payment is to design and use a method of processing payment that is fast. If people waiting in a payment line see the line moving quickly, they won't be as upset about the wait as if there appear to be problems and the line just creeps along. The best way to process payments quickly is to be well prepared and have procedures in place that facilitate fast processing. Workers in the cashier's booth should carefully look through silent auction bid sheets and the results of the live auction for names of bidders who have won more than one item. Processing for all items from a single bidder can be combined ahead of time, so when it is that bidder's turn to pay, the cashier is not burdened with finding multiple bid sheets or dealing with a bidder who can't even remember everything purchased. Winners can pay for all items at once, and single receipts issued listing all items, values, and other required information. This will greatly speed payment processing for these most-valued attendees.

Other means to speed payment processing include using a computer-based accounting and processing system. Have bid sheets in order and keyed into a computer application by the time bidders begin to crowd the payment center. Which application to use is up to the treasurer, who should be comfortable with the methods employed in the cashier's booth. With a little organization and advance preparation, payment processing can be done quickly and efficiently. Winning bidders, and especially those very important bidders who in the past have stood for hours in payment lines at poorly managed events, will be very appreciative.

<Name of Fundraising Event>

A charitable fundraising event to benefit <Name of Host Organization>
<Location of auction>
<Date of auction>

Acknowledgment and receipt for payment for auction item

Buyer's name: _____

Buyer's address: _____
                  _____
                  _____

Name and/or description of item purchased at auction: _____
_____
_____

Amount paid for auction item (excluding sales tax): $ _____
Sales tax (if any): $ _____
Fair market value: $ _____

No goods or services were provided for any amount paid over the fair market value of the
item purchased. Any amount paid over fair market value may be tax deductible for
federal and state income tax purposes.

Receipt issued by: _____<Signature>_____   Date: _____

Print on host organization's letterhead, including address. If the organization has no official letterhead, place the name of the organization and address clearly at either the top or bottom of the acknowledgment letter.

FIGURE 15.2. Example auction-item receipt.

Sometimes a large crowd forms when the live auction is over. When (if) it becomes necessary, create a means to manage buyers waiting to make payment. Crowding is a consequence of all winning bidders coming to the cashier's booth at the same time to make payment. Workers at the cashier's booth must take action or risk making the event's most important attendees—those who bought something—very upset. Effective action can include creating a lineup or orderly waiting area using ropes and post stanchions, or by some other means to organize people waiting to make payment. The key objective is to keep people from crowding around the payment booth or table to maintain security where large amounts of cash are being openly handled and held and where financial papers are being exposed to others' line of sight.

No matter how diligent finance team members may be, the cashier's station at many events is anything but a secure area. Cash is being handled in the open, and financial documents are often within arms' reach of anyone who comes up to the cashier's table or booth. If a cashier's attention is diverted for a moment, money or documents could quickly be taken. In addition, transactions at events generally take place in an unsecure fashion. It is usually easy for any onlookers to see documents such as credit card receipts. If several or dozens of people are crowding around the cashier's booth or table, there will be no security. Visual security is important, because receipts, credit card materials, and other records that may be placed into plain view can contain confidential information from donors and buyers. People making payments may feel uncomfortable, and anyone who might be looking for an opportunity to steal an identity or take cash may find an easy mark. In fact, because so many events have lax security and unsecure payment-processing areas, they are known to present easy targets for crime and attract criminals. See chapter 22 for detailed information about security risks and preventive measures to take, and chapter 21 for ways to reduce risk of liability to the host organization and volunteer event workers.

An alternative is to take measures to prevent the crowd from forming in the first place. This can be done by encouraging or facilitating payment for items throughout the course of the event. For example, once a silent auction is over and winning bidders' names are announced, these winners can be encouraged to make immediate payment. Once payment is complete, all the buyer has to do is show a receipt for each item purchased at the auction-item pickup location and take possession of items won. However, immediate processing has two disadvantages: (1) processing payment diverts the attendee's attention away from ongoing event fundraising activities, and (2) payments made on an item-by-item basis preclude processing payment for all items purchased by the bidder in a single transaction.

Arrange Pickup of Auction Items

Winning bidders should be allowed to take possession of items won only after payment has been received. Immediately after bidding is completed on each auction item, take the items to a secure area for temporary storage. The winning bidder may make immediate payment and pick up the item. The cashier gives winning bidders a receipt or pickup claim check after payment. They take the receipt or claim check to the pickup area to receive possession of the item or arrange for its transport. An alternative is to have runners go to the pickup area to retrieve items on behalf of winning bidders who make payment.

If there is space available, the pickup area can be located immediately adjacent to the cashier's booth. If this is possible, overall processing can be enhanced by having winning bidders' items retrieved for pickup as payment is being processed. Upon successful processing of payment, the bidder is handed the item purchased. This requires close coordination between finance team members in the cashier's booth and workers handling auction items. Regardless of location, the pickup area must be secure. It can be located in a closed room, situated behind a counter, placed in a roped-off area, or guarded in place. An event worker or security guard must provide constant surveillance of the pickup area.

Establish Shipping Policies

Winning bidders may not wish or be able to transport auction items themselves. Some items are too large to transport in a personal vehicle. If a portion of attendees travel by air to an event, it is appropriate for the host organization to supply a shipping option. For these and other reasons the host organization should establish a procedure and fee schedule for shipping auction items on behalf of winning bidders and a policy to cover the risk of liability in providing such service. For large events where many items may be shipped, an independent shipper may be used to provide shipping services. See chapter 9 for example shipping and other event-related policies and procedures.

Expect Slackers

Sometimes people bid on silent auction items and fail to check to see if they won. These winners will not show up at the cashier's booth to make payment. Sometimes live auction winners fail to show up and make payment. As a first step in seeking payment, make an announcement while there are still people present at the event to see if the winners can be found. If they have left the event site, use the information on the bidder's registration materials (phone number or address) to make contact with them as soon as possible, preferably the day following the event. Some events provide an option for bidders to leave an open credit card for auction purchases. This option provides a solution but creates its own set of complications. At this point there are

many reasonable explanations for a person failing to pay. A simple telephone call to the winning bidder is usually all it takes to arrange for payment and pickup or delivery of the auction item.

In the end, event hosts may have to deal with a few truly derelict bidders. Some people make bids they can't afford or sometimes even remember. The reasons vary and are driven by the very nature of the event. Some bidders are driven to bid in excess by the overwhelming excitement of an event. Others see an opportunity, often lubricated by alcohol, to make themselves appear to be a big spender in the community or a bigger-than-life supporter of the host organization. The host organization can attempt to enforce the agreement for payment or just let it go.

Winning bidders are often members of the organization or known in the community. In light of the close relationship of many attendees to the host organization, generally the host organization just lets it go. However, an option that allows the host organization to sell these silent auction items is to contact the next person on the bid sheet to see if the individual still wants the item. For live auction items, the runner-up bidder can be contacted if known. However, it is likely the losing bidder will say no.

The excitement and lure of items offered at an auction come from winning the item at the event, and doing so as part of the event. Being offered the opportunity to buy something outside an event is like receiving a call from any business in town and being asked to buy something. It's just not the same as winning it at auction.

16

The Silent Auction

The silent auction is among the most common fund-raising techniques used at charity events. Just set up a table. Lay out a few auction items. Then place a bid sheet in front of each. As attendees wander about the event, they are attracted to the silent auction table, sometimes for lack of anything else to do, and if they see something they like, they write their name on the bid sheet next to an amount. Event planners come back an hour or so later, pick up bid sheets, and collect payment. Therein lies the secret to fundraising success! Or so many event planners believe, considering how indifferently they treat the silent auction.

I once attended a nice fundraiser at a popular event location. Not all who attended were affluent, but many were, and there had to be at least 250 of us there. At the table where I sat were two couples with "unlimited" giving potential. Both were multimillionaires with a history of charitable giving. There were others with such capacity for giving in the room. Keep in mind this was a fundraiser, not just an evening get-together.

When I arrived, I expected to be greeted by a few volunteers selling raffle tickets. There were no greeters or raffle ticket sellers as far as I could see, but there was a raffle. I suspect people could find someone to ask for tickets if they looked hard enough. The organization had paid staff. I guess I could have asked one of them. I didn't bother. Most people who attend events won't bother either.

As I walked around, I noticed a silent auction table tucked away in a corner of the large room. There were five, maybe six items up for auction. They were low- to mid-value items of a random nature. None were things anyone would need. I also doubt they were items people would have thought about wanting before arriving at the auction. Since the items had a low bid price,

I suspect some attendees thought them attractive enough to place a bid, as all were sold. There were no announcements about the auction. There were no advertisements or promotions for any of the items. Perhaps one or two of the items had been made by well-known artists or craftspersons. Potential bidders in the room would never know. The silent auction was just that—silent.

This scene is not an unusual one at events. Many host organizations just don't get it. Fundraising is an active, not passive, undertaking. For some reason the silent auction in particular seems to be mistaken as the most passive of all fundraising techniques. Just because it's called a "silent" auction doesn't mean event hosts have to be silent about it.

SILENT AUCTIONS treated passively by event hosts are passively treated by attendees. Like any fundraising opportunity, silent auctions need to be stocked with items people want or need, and the opportunity to bid and win those wanted or needed items must be promoted. Consider a raffle for which raffle ticket sellers passively sell tickets. That's a formula for disaster. Why passively hold a silent auction? Attendees mob aggressively promoted and well-stocked silent auctions. Particularly aggressive bidders will fight to get the last bid.

At the event I attended, the hosts were as silent as church mice about the silent auction. Given the poor selection of auction merchandise and too few items for a crowd of 250, that was probably a good thing. After all, for the savvy event attendees in that crowd, the silent auction was a glaring example of poor event fundraising. And why embarrass the volunteer officers of the host organization by purposefully pointing out a botched fundraising opportunity? Had the auction been properly promoted and appointed with appropriate items, event planners could have added a few thousand dollars to the organization's net revenue for the year. This was not a large organization, but no organization can afford to ignore easy money.

What Is a Silent Auction?

During a silent auction, bidders "silently" write bids on bid sheets for auction items. Auction items are generally the same kinds used for live auctions, consisting of merchandise, services, and trips. The items up for bid are generally placed on display in a defined area, such as on a row of tables, and bid sheets are located with the displayed items. Bidders place their bids on the bid sheets that contain all other bids, so bidders have full knowledge of the highest current bid by just looking at the bid sheet. Bidders may bid as many times as they want on as many items as they want, as long as their bid is higher than the most previous bid or is equal to or greater than the next bid increment. Bidding generally takes place over a period of 60 to 120 minutes, but bidding can be as short as 30 minutes or can occur over much longer time periods. The ending time for each silent auction is posted in the silent auction area and announced over the public address system prior to close of bidding. Some silent auctions are opened as soon as an event begins and not closed (bidding called to a halt) until the main live auction is about to begin. Silent auctions are usually held only for fundraising purposes, whereas live auctions can be held for commercial purposes as well as for fundraising.

The advance program and auction program list the time silent auction items will go on display and when bidding will start and end for each silent auction. Bidder numbers are generally provided to attendees as they register to facilitate bidding, but assigning numbers is optional. Registration of bidders is important as it ensures each bidder is legitimately registered for the event. Registration also provides contact information about bidders. At a minimum, bidders must be registered and may use their names and signatures in bidding.

Silent auctions are versatile fundraising activities. They offer a great deal of flexibility to event hosts and are attractive to donors and attendees for these reasons:

- For donors, the silent auction provides great advertising value provided the host organiza-

Sidebar 16.1. **Eight Helpful Hints for a Successful Silent Auction**

1. *Print bid sheets in advance.* Use a large font for printing the name of the item and all major descriptive information on the sheet. Provide ample space between lines for people to write their bid and signature.

2. *Bring plenty of pens, markers, and tape.* Make sure there are lots of pens available near bid sheets. Use pens, not pencils, for writing down bids. Pens don't need to be sharpened, and ink can't be erased by an overly aggressive bidder.

3. *Tape down bid sheets as close to the corresponding item as possible.* It is easy for bid sheets not attached to the table to fall on the floor, be moved, or otherwise become misplaced.

4. *Set up silent auctions well in advance, and plan to be challenged by perfecting the display of all auction items in the space available.* Arrangement may be particularly difficult where there is not enough space for the number and size of items or where there are too few auction items to comfortably fill an overly large space. All items should be plainly visible, and bid sheets easily accessible and plainly corresponding to the auction items.

5. *Have a person monitoring each silent auction all the time.* This person should know the rules for the auction and be ready to answer questions, ensure bidders are following the rules for bidding, direct people to the silent auction, promote bidding, reset auction items that may fall off the table or otherwise be displaced, and keep the silent auction area clean of trash. The monitor will also be the person who enforces the end of the auction and picks up bid sheets as the auction closes. At the close of the auction this person needs to mark the winning bid and draw a line through any empty spaces of the bid sheets, so no new bids can be added after the auction closes.

6. *Get bidding started on a silent auction item if necessary.* Do not let an item fail to sell for lack of a minimum bid. Sometimes all it takes to open up bidding is for someone to break the ice with a bid. Have an auction worker or staff member ready to write in a minimum bid if an item seems to be stuck at the start. There could be skepticism about whether or not an item is really worth the value listed on a bid sheet. If someone bids the opening amount, skeptics are more likely to join in the bidding. Sometimes such help from the host's auction workers is the only way bidding gets started. If after the opening bid, no one else bids, then the item goes to the bidder, who "resells" the item back to the host organization. The alternative is the item fails to sell and goes back to the host organization anyway.

7. *Give attendees plenty of warning as the time to close a silent auction approaches.* Better yet, make regular promotional announcements of progress of the silent auction. A good MC well briefed on the silent auction and any featured items in the auction will know how to effectively promote bidding through regular announcements.

8. *Scan silent auction bid sheets for names of bidders who have won more than one item.* Winners can pay for all items at once, and receipts can be issued listing all items, values, and other required information. Workers should also scan bid sheets to make sure the winning bidder followed the rules for minimum bid and minimum bid increments. If the final bidder did not meet the minimum bid increment, the most recent high bidder who did follow the rules and was above the minimum bid increment wins.

tion understands the value of promotion and provides promotional opportunities to donors. Also, donors may receive tax advantages if the event is held by a qualified charity.

• Attendees like silent auctions because such auctions are simple. There is no risk because bidders choose how much to bid and pick and choose among items. Auctions can be enormous fun when bidding becomes competitive. And if the host organization is a qualified charity, winning bid amounts above fair market value may be tax deductible.

• For event hosts, silent auctions may be the most time- and cost-efficient fundraising option for use in a full-feature event. Silent auctions can be very general, catering to a diversity of tastes and budgets, or very narrowly designed, offering a specific type of service or merchandise in a very narrow price range. Multiple silent auctions can be held simultaneously or consecutively. They can take up a huge expanse of floor space or be designed to take up only a few square feet of space.

Sidebar 16.1 provides helpful hints for holding successful silent auctions.

Bid Sheets

In its most basic form, the bid sheet provides space for bidders to write down bids. A valid bid will consist of the bidder's name or bidder number, and signature. A well-run silent auction will provide additional information on bid sheets to assist bidders and meet added requirements. Bid sheets should contain at least the following information:

- Name and description of the silent auction item
- Name or business name of the donor
- A good-faith estimate of the fair market value of the item
- The minimum starting bid
- The minimum incremental bid amount
- Instructions and special notes
- A series of lines for bidders to bid in ascending increments

See figure 16.1 for an example silent auction bid sheet.

Additional pages with added lines can be taped to the bottom of bid sheets if necessary. Also, instead of leaving bid increments blank, where a minimum bid increment has been set, the auction form can list printed bid amounts so that bidders need not write in the amount of the bid. All they need to do is add their name or bid number to the space next to the bid amount. IRS rules require charitable organizations to provide bidders with a good-faith estimate of the fair market value of goods or services to be auctioned prior to, or at the time of, bidding. Fair market value is defined as the amount of money a person would pay for the goods or services on the open market. By listing the value directly on the bid sheet, the host organization meets this IRS requirement (see chapter 21).

In addition, the IRS allows donors who purchase items at a charity auction to claim a charitable tax deduction for the amount of the purchase price paid for an item over its fair market value. But qualifying for that deduction requires the donor to demonstrate he or she knew in advance of bidding that the value of the item was less than the amount paid. The IRS rules place a burden on the auction-item buyer to prove there was intent to make a charitable contribution if a tax deduction is claimed for the payment. By listing the value directly on the bid sheet, the

host organization allows buyers to meet this burden (see chapter 21).

Silent Auction Options

Event planners can set up silent auctions in several different ways. These options are discussed in the following sections.

Buy-It-Now Option

Although silent auction bidding usually is done in suggested increments, a bidder can exceed the suggested minimum at any time. A "buy-it-now" option can also be offered. This is a bid amount marked on the bid sheet purposefully set very high that a bidder can choose to instantly win the auction item. By choosing this option, the bidder closes the auction for that item and instantly wins. This option has become popular due to the success of its use in online auctions. If used, the "buy-it-now" price needs to be set high. It is an option. It can be used on all or just some items in an auction. This option adds still more versatility to the silent auction. To add "buy it now" to a bid sheet. Just add the words "Buy It Now" on the last line on the bid sheet, and place the price to buy it now in the adjacent space provided for writing down the bid amount. The bidder selects "Buy It Now," and bidding is over on that item.

Sealed-Bid Silent Auctions

A sealed-bid silent auction is a variation in which bidders are unable to see what others are bidding for the same item. Bids are placed on bid cards, and each bidder can bid only once for any one item. Bidders submit bids in sealed envelopes or place bid cards in closed containers. Generally, silent bids are "logged in" or deposited in sequence to address tie bids. In the event of a tie, the first bidder wins. Bidders can bid on as many items as they choose. Just as in silent auctions where bidding is open, sealed-bid auctions run for a fixed period of time, from as little as 30 minutes to as long as several days. Auction items can be displayed with bid boxes placed in front of each item, or auction workers can staff a central bid

\<Name of Fundraising Event\>

A charitable fundraising event to benefit the \<Name of Host Organization\>

Silent Auction Bid Sheet

Item Description: River raft trip for six (6)

Details: Renowned river guide Patty Anne Rose will take 6 people on a leisurely raft trip down Diablo Canyon. The trip must be taken between June 1 and September 30. The trip will take 5 hours and start at 10 a.m. All equipment and lunch will be provided. Rafters must be aged 8 or older. Winning bidder will be responsible for arranging a date that is mutually acceptable.

Donated by: Patty Anne Rose, owner of Water Dog Raft Tours

Fair market value: $350

Minimum bid: $150   **Minimum bid increment:** $25

Name/Bid number	Bid amount
_____	$_____150_____
_____	$_____
_____	$_____
_____	$_____
_____	$_____
_____	$_____
_____	$_____
_____	$_____
_____	$_____
_____	$_____
_____	$_____
_____	$_____
_____	$_____
_____	$_____
_____	$_____
_____	$_____
_____	$_____

FIGURE 16.1. Example silent auction bid sheet.

deposit booth. Sealed-bid auctions can also be run using a bid board on which all items are described in an auction program or at a poster display area. At the conclusion of the bidding period, the outright winner or the declared winner of a tied bid will be determined. Because bidders bid only once, this type of silent auction can be run more quickly than a silent auction in which bidding is open and bidders take turns increasing bids.

Silent Auctions on a Board

It may be difficult or impractical to hold a silent auction with items on display. An example is an auction featuring bulky items, the event room is small, and there is too little floor space for a large silent auction area. Even small items may be difficult to display in silent auction format in a very small event room. Silent auctions containing the usual 20 to 25 items can take up a lot of room. But there is a solution.

In such situations, conserve floor space by building an auction "bid board." In this space-saving auction, bidding is conducted on large bid boards where bidders post bids on bid sheets attached to the board for each item up for auction. Bidders refer to the auction program for detailed descriptions of auction items or look at posters describing the items located on or near the bid board. Bidding proceeds as in any silent auction. The highest bid from the bid board will be highlighted and a winner declared.

Holding a silent auction on a bid board also makes sense if auction items cannot actually be displayed, such as a series of services or vacation trips. Usually such items are described on a sheet of paper or poster placed on a table along with a bid sheet. In the case of service and trip descriptions, there is no reason such descriptions or posters need be displayed on a table or even displayed at all. For example, bidders can readily read detailed descriptions of vacation trips or professional services in a well-designed silent auction program. Everything that would be displayed on a table can be reproduced in the program, along with photographs and maps or other enticing material descriptions.

Because of the compact and rather self-contained nature of silent auctions run on bid boards, several such auctions can be conducted efficiently simultaneously or one after another in a small space. When one auction is over, just carry the entire auction away and replace it with the next. Bid boards can be prepared well ahead of time, making setup at the event very simple. Auction bid boards can be a ready solution for event planners faced with time or space restrictions or a large number of trips and services for which display at the auction requires no complicated handling.

Silent Auction with Sealed Final Bid

In another silent auction option the first round of bidding is open, with bidders placing bids on bid sheets located with the items or on bid boards. Open bidding continues for a set time, during which period all bidders can see all bids. Bidding can remain open for 60 minutes or much longer. To this point the auction proceeds like a typical silent auction. At about 30 minutes before the end of the auction, open bidding ends and closed bidding using sealed bids begins. Anyone who wishes to submit a sealed bid may do so. A clearly marked drop-box for sealed bids is usually placed near the silent auction. Bidders can submit one sealed bid per auction item. Bidders have 30 minutes to submit the sealed bids, after which any sealed bids are opened and a winner declared.

The winning bidder is the person submitting the highest bid, whether submitted by sealed bid or on the open bid sheet. As with a regular sealed-bid auction, if the winning bid is a tie, the winner is determined by the time the bid was received. Earliest bid received wins. To determine which bid was received earliest, sealed bids are accepted and kept in order of receipt or an auction worker can write time of receipt on bids. In the case of a tie and the host organization can obtain or has two of the auction items, both bidders can be awarded the item.

Display of Silent Auction Winners

An efficient way to announce silent auction winners is to display winners using a projector or placing the list of winners on a large display board. This kind of announcement circumvents the need to announce each winner orally from the stage. Displaying winning bidders saves stage time for fundraising activities. Using stage time to make such announcements earns no new money for the host organization. Projecting winners also lets everyone see who the winners are.

Payment for Silent Auction Items Won

Payment for silent auction merchandise takes place in the same fashion as for live auction merchandise won. There is no difference in payment options and the form of receipt required for tax purposes. See chapters 6, 15 and 21 for more detailed information.

Promote Silent Auctions

The host organization need not remain silent about silent auctions. The advance program should describe each silent auction and the auction item. These auctions can be highlights of an event, especially if promoted as such. In addition to receiving advance promotion of silent auctions, attendees at an event need to be told of all the excitement available at the silent auction tables or boards. Posters can feature the auctions and items. During the event regular announcements should be made about silent auctions. This is in addition to announcing the beginning and end of the auction. The MC should be briefed about the silent auctions and any unique characteristics or items and should be told to make regular pitches to promote bidding. A good MC will know how to weave promotion of silent auctions into whatever other announcements are being made or in the course of onstage activities. Promotion helps boost bidding, which increases final bid amounts and net revenue. It's a pretty simple formula for success, but one many host organizations fail to consider, even after going to all the trouble to set up a silent auction—unfortunately, they set up a truly silent silent auction.

17

Raffles and Other Moneymakers

One of my friends is an expert at supplying organizations with just the right auction and raffle merchandise. He may be the only person I know who can create the perfect "auction in a box" for an organization seeking a low-cost alternative to soliciting auction and raffle items.

He had just attended an event where attendees paid a high fee for admission, which included dinner and a single raffle ticket that would be drawn at the event. The grand prize was a well-appointed sport utility vehicle (SUV). Attendees were limited to 600. There was only one fundraising activity, which was a "reverse raffle" for the fancy SUV. In a reverse raffle, all tickets are drawn, one by one, until the last ticket drawn wins the grand prize.

He was aghast at seeing 600 people assembled in one place who would not be presented with a single additional fundraising opportunity on which to spend money. After all, these 600 people had already paid $350 per person for admission, some making that payment months in advance. They knew the price of admission included a chance on the SUV and a few other prizes that would come at points in the reverse raffle. Surely, he said, some of the people just might have had a few extra dollars they could have donated through a bucket raffle, roving raffle, rubber-duck game, or any one of hundreds of other possible fundraising activities.

Why would he care? Because like most people who go to fundraising events, he goes to support what he believes to be a worthy cause. Unlike many others, however, he sees fundraising through the eyes of a professional. Consider what happened as the reverse raffle wound down. There were 600 tickets to be drawn—and that's a lot of drawing. This can be boring, and it was. Sure, there were a few prizes given out along the way, such as for the first, fiftieth, one hundredth, and *two hundredth ticket drawn, and so on, but most tickets drawn resulted in no prize for the bearer. Once a person's ticket was drawn, there was little reason to remain at the event; thus, the room began to clear out early in the evening. Since ticket drawings began as soon as people start arriving—after all, there were 600 tickets to be drawn— many people left very early, not even waiting for dinner.*

Not only did the host organization miss an opportunity to create some added excitement that could have delivered additional net revenue around the reverse raffle; they also missed an opportunity to give people a reason to stay for the duration of the event. The way in which the event was conducted gave many people a reason to leave before the event had hardly begun. It didn't have to be that way.

USED IN AN EFFECTIVE fashion, a reverse raffle or any one of dozens of other raffles and fundraising games can be excellent money-raising additions to any fundraising event. This chapter provides information on how to creatively use dozens of fundraising activities to add excitement and increase net revenue. These are intended to be fun activities, many of which can provide added value for families. Some may have the potential to deliver high net revenue, whereas others have relatively limited revenue potential but still add value to an event. As with any fundraising activity, revenue potential is dependent on the spending potential of attendees. A raffle featuring an SUV can and should deliver more revenue than a raffle featuring a guided bird-watching tour at a local wildlife refuge. However, many of the million or so charitable organizations cannot support an SUV raffle and would be thrilled to receive the revenue from a well-run raffle featuring a guided bird-watching tour. Raffles can also feature very low-value items, such as a set of lawn darts or a candy basket. The price of raffle tickets varies with the value of the prize and the number of tickets expected to be sold.

Raffles

Raffles are games of chance played with tickets, markers, or some other means to identify a winner who is chosen when the person's ticket is drawn at random. Basic requirements of a raffle are that the winning tickets be drawn in a fashion that is reasonably acknowledged as random and that every ticket in a raffle have an equal chance of being drawn.

Potential for High Net Revenue

Raffle tickets are priced at a fraction of the perceived value of the prize or prizes. When setting the price of tickets, planners should estimate (or set) the total number of tickets to be sold and adjust the ticket price accordingly given the actual cost to the organization of the prize(s) and the perceived value of the prize(s). Thus, the actual cost of the prize(s) and number of tickets that will be sold are the prime considerations in setting ticket price and estimating net revenue.

In some instances, it may work best to offer tickets for a very low price to encourage sale of large numbers of tickets and ease of purchase by people regardless of income levels. In other instances, a smaller number of tickets can be sold but at a higher price each. Both options, and everything in between, have a place. To some extent the demographics of attendees may dictate which option to choose. If demographics of attendees are unknown or highly varied, it may be best to hold several raffles and vary the raffle options available.

Of all fundraising activities that can be added to an auction event, raffles offer the potential for the greatest percentage net return on investment in prizes. In addition, raffles can be conducted quickly or "in the background." If prizes have been donated at zero cost to the organization, raffles also may offer the highest differential between the perceived value and total revenue received. The reason for such a high net return on raffles is that the potential number of tickets that can be sold on any raffle item is limited only by the number of tickets made available, the prowess of ticket sellers, and the willingness of people to buy tickets. Generally, people can buy as many raffle tickets as they wish, and raffle ticket sellers try to sell as many tickets as possible. Some specialized raffles have rules that restrict the number of tickets a person can buy. Such raffles can be effective, but revenue potential is set.

Restricted Raffles

If the number of raffle tickets a person may purchase is limited, the raffle is called "restricted." Such raffles can be used, for example, if there is a desire to ensure that each person who enters the raffle has exactly the same chance of winning as anyone else who enters. In such instances, purchase of tickets is restricted to one ticket per person.

Another example is restriction of the total number of tickets available. This offers people who enter the drawing an exactly known probability of winning. For example, in a raffle restricted to 100 tickets where all tickets are sold, each ticket carries a 1 in 100 probability of being drawn. Buyers know the odds, so they feel they have a better understanding of the value or potential return on investment of ticket(s) purchase. Sometimes high-value items, such as cars or expensive trips, are raffled off using a set number of tickets, often limited to 100 or fewer, which are sold for high-dollar amounts. People can usually buy as many tickets as they wish, with ticket price set to yield revenue in excess of expense, assuming all or a set minimum number of tickets are sold.

Seven Lucky Moneymaking Raffles

The follow sections describe seven types of raffles as options to raise revenue at a fundraising event.

1. GRAND RAFFLE

The grand raffle is the most common type of raffle at events. It is also a very simple raffle to hold and can provide significant revenue if well managed. Players buy raffle tickets singly or in "books" of tickets. Buyers tear off a portion of the ticket and place it into a large mixing canister or tub. They retain the ticket stub. Both the stub and ticket bear identical numbers. Winning tickets are drawn from

the large container for one or more raffle prizes. Prizes are usually displayed prominently on a table at the event, sometimes directly in front of the auction stage. There can be large numbers of tickets sold and large numbers of prizes that may vary in value. Single-ticket price is usually kept low, so anyone who attends the event can afford to buy at least a few grand raffle tickets, although ticket price can be varied to suit attendees' willingness to pay. The grand raffle tends to be among the most-played fundraising opportunity at fundraising events. The low price of play, simplicity to conduct, and (usually) large number of prizes make it an attractive fundraising option for the host as well as attendees.

The tiered grand raffle, a variation on the simple grand raffle, involves offering prizes at different value levels, or tiers. Ticket buyers receive tickets for higher-level tier (value) prizes based on the total number of grand raffle tickets they buy. For example, individual grand raffle ticket price may be $1. Sellers may offer a book of 25 tickets for $25 dollars, and in addition, the buyer receives a single ticket for a higher-tier prize. Maybe the lowest-level tier prizes ($1 ticket) have an average value of $20, but the next-tier prizes have an average value of $100. This can be extended through three tiers very simply. For example, a $100 book of tickets could include 100 tickets at $1 each for the lowest-level tier, 5 tickets for the mid-level tier, and 1 ticket for the highest-level tier where prizes have an average value of $500.

2. BUCKET RAFFLE

Bucket raffles are among the most exciting and fun filled of all the raffles because there is an interaction between the ticket buyer and the raffle itself. Prizes are placed on a table or in a demarcated area and spaced to allow raffle players to look closely at each prize item. In front of or near each prize item is placed a container or bucket. Raffle players place raffle tickets into the bucket corresponding to the prize(s) they wish to win. Each item with its corresponding bucket becomes a separate raffle. Players can buy as many raffle tickets as they wish and place as many tickets as they wish into any of the buckets. Bucket raffles are, in effect, a series of single-item raffles in which players select which items they seek to win and then place their raffle tickets on those specific items. As a result, bucket raffles require numerous prizes. Space used by bucket raffles is about the same as used by silent auctions, so the number of items offered as prizes in a bucket raffle can be a consideration where space is limited.

Because of the generally low cost of tickets and variety in prizes, virtually everyone participates in this raffle. Players feel they have more control over bucket raffles than most other raffles and games because they can control the relative odds of winning one prize over others, creating the highest probability of winning the prize(s) they desire most. And they have no chance of winning something they don't want. The buckets can be open to view so that people can see how many tickets are in each bucket, or buckets can be "closed" with only a slit at the top through which tickets are deposited. Either way has advantages, but the open bucket allows people to see the "odds." This can generate excitement when a bucket with few tickets in it is found by a person looking for "good odds" or when a bucket matched to a coveted item begins to overflow.

Bucket-raffle tickets are generally sold in bulk. Cost is usually between about $0.25 and $2.00 for each ticket. Discounts can be offered for higher quantities of tickets purchased to promote ticket sales. The idea is to encourage the purchase of a large number of tickets, because the ticket buyer is offered plenty of opportunity to use many tickets. The buckets can be large, if the idea is to encourage using many tickets. Price of tickets can be higher than $2, for example, $5 to $10 tickets can be used for high-value items. Cost of individual tickets versus how many tickets eventually go into buckets does not affect revenue as much as the atmosphere created around the bucket raffle itself. The key is setting the price per ticket at the point where attendees find the game fun. Ticket price should also be keyed generally to value of items in the raffle.

Having lots of tickets to place in buckets tends to enhance fun, but there is a limit. Setting the price per ticket so low that an average player will buy several hundred tickets is excessive. Besides, receiving several hundred tickets that have to be torn and deposited in buckets creates a lot of work for the player and wastes time the attendee could use to play other games. Set the price at a point at which attendees will buy between 50 and 100 tickets. An event drawing attendees who have high wealth may be excited to pay $2.00 per ticket and many may buy 100 of them, whereas attendees having limited wealth may be motivated more by $0.25 tickets and buy 100. Price per ticket also depends on the value of bucket-raffle items. A vacation trip bucket raffle will bear much higher ticket prices than a bucket raffle featuring small stuffed animals.

The result of bucket-raffle play should be monitored closely. Planners should vary conditions of play from event to event to determine just the right price per ticket, number of buckets (items), and level of prizes for the event's attendees. Whatever the situation, event planners using bucket raffles should seek a standard for the game that encourages the highest level of total spending on tickets possible, regardless of individual ticket price.

Prize items need to be prominently displayed near each corresponding bucket. If the raffle prizes are large or heavy, they can be placed on the floor, but the bucket must be nearby. For items such as trips, gift certificates, or services, a card or poster displaying a description of the prize is placed on a table beside the bucket to allow people to identify and learn about the prize.

Generally, between 10 and 20 items, up to 30 for very large events, are needed to create an exciting raffle and entice people to buy many tickets. Items can vary in value. Gauge how many prizes to offer, what kinds of items to select, the value of items, and the number of tickets likely to be sold. Consideration needs to be given to the number of people expected to participate in the auction event, their interests, and the amount of money participants will have to spend overall on fundraising activities. It may work better to hold two bucket raffles of 15 prizes each instead of a single large one of 30 items. In this way the two raffles can be varied to meet different objectives, or they may be configured to more strategically use floor space than a single large raffle.

Bucket raffles are an especially good fundraising attraction at events where games of chance and skill are being offered simultaneously. In this situation, bucket-raffle tickets can be offered among prizes in the games of chance and skill. What makes the tickets such great prizes is that they can be given out at no cost to the host organization, but to the winner, each ticket has a perceived value set by the price per ticket. This is a win-win for the host organization and prize winner.

3. ROVING RAFFLE

Roving raffles, self-contained raffles that "rove" among attendees who are potential raffle ticket buyers, offer the greatest level of versatility of all fundraising options at the auction event. Roving-raffle ticket sellers rove the room looking for buyers. Items in the raffle can be displayed in a central location for all to see. However, the most successful roving raffles truly are roving raffles. All parts of the raffle are roving together as a self-contained unit: the raffle ticket seller and the raffle prize.

Roving-raffle ticket sellers can work alone or may have to work in teams of two, depending on the item being raffled. Several self-contained roving raffles can be offered at the same time at a large event. For example, three teams of two could sell raffle tickets for three dream vacations. One of the teams could be raffling a resort vacation in Hawaii. One member of this team holds a large display board showing pictures of the resort and people enjoying themselves on a beach in Hawaii. Large text on the display board gives the particulars about the prize, "Win a Dream Vacation to Beautiful Honolulu." The other member of the team sells tickets and handles the money. The team with the Hawaii vacation and teams raffling vacations elsewhere rove about the event room selling tickets. Sales stop before the live auction begins. At some point during the event, possibly immediately after the live auction, the drawings for the roving-raffle dream vacations are held.

This raffle method works particularly well if the member of the team displaying the item encourages people to view or touch the item. For example, a sculpture can be held up and turned in front of potential buyers, a designer coat can be modeled and stroked by potential ticket buyers, and a set of skis can be held high and examined by buyers. Individual roving-raffle ticket sellers can sell tickets for

raffles on items they hold or wear. In this situation the person selling tickets must be able to sell tickets, handle money, and effectively display the raffle prize. Items that can be raffled off this way include backpacks, jewelry, fine handbags, and jackets.

All things considered, the roving raffle is most effective when teams of two work the crowd. Some of the most effective items in this raffle are those that provoke close inspection or that can be touched. Raffle prizes are brought into direct, close personal contact with ticket buyers, and the ticket sellers hustle buyers to buy tickets. Nonetheless, a centrally displayed large item, such as a set of patio furniture or travel trailer, can also be an enticing prize in a roving raffle.

4. REVERSE RAFFLE

The reverse raffle (like the raffle in the story at the beginning of this chapter) has the potential to create a great stage show, but such raffles can take a long time to conduct. The idea of a reverse raffle is to sell a limited number of raffle tickets, with a high value item as grand prize, and then draw all tickets one at a time. The last ticket drawn receives the grand prize. Other prizes are usually awarded at various points during the drawdown.

The number of tickets sold can vary from just a few to several hundred. It doesn't take too long to conduct a reverse raffle of 25 tickets sold at $500 each for a chance to win two tickets to the Super Bowl. But consider the time involved in drawing down 500 raffle tickets sold for $100 each for a chance to win a new hybrid automobile. Because reverse raffles can deliver relatively high levels of revenue, they are sometimes used as the central focus of a fundraising event. Unfortunately, they are also among the most misused raffles. This is particularly so when the reverse raffle is the primary or only fundraising activity at an event.

When I first began learning about event fundraising, I was taught the techniques involved in holding a successful "Cadillac Banquet." At this type of banquet a reverse raffle is held with a Cadillac as grand prize. Today there are plenty of other vehicles that fit the high-recognition marquee of a Cadillac, but the name still sticks in my mind. For the Cadillac reverse raffle 100 tickets were available. Each ticket was priced at a level that allowed the host organization to receive net revenue at least equal to the total perceived value of the prizes. This provides for a perceived 100% "markup." Most people who buy such raffle tickets know the odds and compute the return to the host organization—it's human nature to do so. People often overlook the added value of all the secondary prizes, so the value of these prizes should also be made apparent to buyers.

Pricing is critically important. Too high a price can hamper sales. A price too low means the host organization can expend a lot of effort for very little net return. For example, consider a reverse raffle of 200 tickets and a grand prize of a sports sedan having a perceived value of about $35,000. It should be available from a willing dealer for no more than $28,000. For the car alone, tickets should be priced at between $200 and $400 each, but the organization would meet its investment if tickets were priced at $140 each if the only expense were the car. Now add in taxes and all the other secondary prizes, such as an LCD TV for the first ticket drawn, $100 gift certificates for dining at the best restaurants in town for the tenth, twenty-fifth, and fiftieth tickets drawn. And don't forget the runner-up prize for the next-to-last ticket drawn, a weekend stay at a fabulous resort in Tucson, Arizona. All these prizes will cost money as well.

For people to wait around as 200 raffle tickets are drawn, the grand prize had better be good and valuable, and reasonably valuable prizes must be awarded as the countdown progresses. The reverse raffle can be made even more exciting by allowing for a little extra drama as described in Sidebar 17.1.

5. RAFFLE BOARD

The raffle board is a variation of the raffle concept in which prize items are prominently displayed on a large board, wall, or table or in a booth. The objective is to offer an assortment of desirable prizes, all of roughly similar value and generally of a similar nature, and sell as many raffle tickets as possible (although the number of tickets available in this type of raffle could be limited). Usually, between about 5 and 15 prize items are available and on prominent

---

Sidebar 17.1. **Reverse-Raffle Extras**

An additional feature of the reverse raffle is the opportunity it affords for the final ticket holders to negotiate among themselves to buy and sell remaining tickets. This takes place in the open and onstage in full view of the audience as the final draws of the raffle take place. This buying and selling generally become most intense when only two or three ticket holders remain. With the finalists onstage, this drama is played out before the entire crowd.

The host organization may or may not wish to allow this buying and selling to take place. The rules of the reverse raffle can specify how such buying and selling will proceed. For example, the organization sponsoring the raffle may make these "side deals" subject to a percentage surcharge. If one of the remaining ticket holders offers to buy another finalist's ticket for $1,000 and the person is willing to sell, the transaction would be subject to a surcharge by the sponsor; thus, the sponsoring organization would receive a percentage of the $1,000 sales price.

The basis of this rather odd aspect of the reverse raffle stems from the unusually high value of the grand prize. With the finalists onstage, this side action is highly visible and injects considerable drama into the final stages of the raffle. This provides a level of drama that keeps event attendees riveted to their seats.

Note: The side deals may be considered distasteful by some, so any organization holding a reverse raffle should carefully consider whether or not to allow side deals among ticket holders and address this issue by providing information to ticket buyers in advance.

---

display. The price of tickets is generally set relatively high and keyed to the cost of the raffle prizes, the number of total tickets expected to be sold, and the spending capacity of attendees. Tickets are drawn at random. The holder of the first ticket drawn gets first choice of all the prizes on the board. The holder of the second ticket drawn chooses among the remaining prizes, and so on, until the holder of the final ticket drawn receives the final remaining prize. Ticket holders must be present to win, because winners actually select their prize.

A twist to this kind of raffle is to add more prizes to the board as more tickets are sold. This is a particularly effective twist if individual ticket price is set high. For example, if the value of prizes is an average $250 and ticket prices are set at $100, one additional prize can be added for every five additional tickets sold. Players need to be informed that the number of prizes can increase and how that will happen. The price should be set high enough so that most players will buy only a single ticket, with only a few players buying at most two or three. Number of tickets sold and number of prizes added can be tracked on a progress board displayed for all to see. This encourages additional ticket buying.

In most raffles the odds of winning are reduced as the number of tickets sold increases, but when the number of prizes increases with increasing raffle ticket sales, players will understand that the odds of winning one or multiple prizes potentially increases. This creates considerable incentive to play this high-net-revenue raffle. Sidebar 17.2 lists raffle-board ideas.

6. DIRECT-MAIL RAFFLE

Raffles can be advertised and started in advance of an event. In this type of raffle, tickets are sold either by volunteers in a one-on-one fashion, or direct-mail-raffle tickets are sent through the mail to members or others for purchase. One or more prizes are listed on the raffle ticket or on accompanying information, and the raffle ticket stubs are returned with payment. Virtually anything can be the subject of this kind of raffle. Tickets are sold before the event. That can be the end of it, and winning tickets are drawn at some point during the event. Generally, ticket purchasers need not be present to win. Moreover, a variation on this raffle is to also sell tickets at the event where the actual prize items can be displayed.

LEGAL CAUTION: *If tickets are distributed and sold directly through the mail, certain local, state, and federal restrictions may apply. In addition, because raffle tickets may be sold apart from the event itself, there may be additional requirements to consider. Seek counsel if planning direct sale of raffle tickets in advance, especially if sales will be solicited through the mail or e-mail.*

7. SPEED RAFFLE

A speed raffle is designed to take place very quickly. It is generally used where a large number of people are gathered together and seated. Speed raffles are often played during lulls in the live auction, in particular if there is a temporary delay. The speed raffle helps keep fundraising momentum going. It is an exciting activity with high net return when done well. Although anything can be the subject of a speed raffle, cash seems to generate the speed needed to conduct a successful one. Here is how it is conducted from the live auction floor.

The MC announces there will be a speed raffle and explains the rules. In this example a framed fan of five $100 bills will be the prize, and individual raffle tickets will be priced at $20. The MC announces a $500 speed raffle will be held and says,

"In the next several minutes fifty raffle tickets will be sold for twenty dollars each for a chance to win five hundred dollars. When the fiftieth ticket is sold, the tickets will immediately be placed into a container and mixed, and one will be drawn at random. The holder of that ticket will receive the five hundred dollars. Please take out your twenty-dollar bills and hold them in the air so ticket sellers can see you want to buy a ticket. A ticket seller will come by your table, take your money, and give you a ticket. Buy as many tickets as you want. Go!"

Spotters, runners, and models who have been briefed on the rules become raffle ticket sellers on the auction floor. They have 50 tickets in hand among the group and are ready to go. When the MC announces "Go!" the ticket sellers begin to sell as many tickets as they can as fast as they can. They try to generate excitement during the buying, and the MC joins in promoting speed of buying. As soon as the fiftieth ticket is sold, the raffle stops and the drawing is held. The winner immediately receives the $500.

The speed raffle can be repeated immediately until play slows or until the auction delay is over. Instead of 50 tickets, 100 tickets can be sold. The raffle can be repeated during additional lulls in the auction. However, attendee willingness to play this raffle needs to be very carefully watched and assessed after each play. Nothing falls as flat as a speed raffle that does not sell the full number of tickets available. Failure to sell out creates two problems for the host: (1) everyone on the auction floor sees a failed fundraising effort, and (2) the prize must be awarded regardless of how many tickets are sold. If the speed raffle results in a net loss to the host, it will be obvious to all. Ordinarily, the audience may not know what the host organization's investment is in any one item, but they know the investment in the speed raffle because the raffle is totally based on using cash in open play.

For this to work well, everything must be ready to go, a common denomination of money must be used ($1, $5, $10, or $20) as the individual ticket price, and players must be told to have their money ready and waving in the air. Ticket sellers race around the floor exchanging raffle tickets for bills. It's as simple as that. An experienced auction-floor team and an enthusiastic group of attendees can conduct a speed raffle in less than five minutes.

Special Attractions and Raffle Twists

Although most raffles involve selling paper tickets from a large roll or package of tickets, raffle "tickets" can take many forms. The only requirement is that there be a positive way to identify the winners of the raffle drawing. Sidebar 17.3 describes seven ticketless raffle ideas.

Sidebar 17.3. **Seven Lucky "Ticketless" Raffles**

1. *Art raffle.* Signed numbered art prints are sold. The raffle prize is the original artwork from which the prints were struck. The numbers on raffle tickets correspond to the numbers on the art prints. Everyone who enters "buys" and may keep a signed numbered print, and one print buyer wins the original work of art.

2. *Coin raffle.* Numbered coins are designed and struck for the event, commemorating the event or displaying the host organization's logo. The raffle players purchase individually numbered coins. Tickets having corresponding numbers are drawn for the raffle prize. Everyone who enters gets to keep the commemorative coin.

3. *T-shirt raffle.* Specially designed and individually numbered T-shirts are sold. The T-shirts carry a design unique to the event or host organization. Raffle ticket numbers correspond to the numbers on the numbered T-shirts. Everyone who enters the raffle by buying a T-shirt gets to keep the shirt.

4. *Hat raffle.* Commemorative caps are designed for the event and individually numbered. Numbers are drawn, and winners get to keep the cap.

5. *Mug or tumbler raffle.* Specially designed commemorative mugs or tumblers are designed for the event, which serve a dual purpose. First, each is individually numbered, and the number is the ticket holder's entry number in a raffle. Second, the cup can be used during the event for a free drink(s). This can be free coffee, hot chocolate, spiced cider, and so on for the mug, and a free cocktail or similar drink for the tumbler. Other glassware can be used, for example, "Coke" glasses or beer steins, with the free drinks fitting the theme of the item. Everyone who enters keeps the mug or glassware.

6. *Duck raffle.* Rubber ducks are individually numbered and sold from a tub or small pond. Ticket numbers correspond to numbers on the ducks. Everyone who enters gets to keep the duck.

7. *Balloon-pop raffle.* Individually numbered slips of paper are placed inside helium balloons. Ticket numbers correspond to the numbers on the slips of paper inside the balloons. People buy the balloons, carry them around or tie them to their chair until the drawing, and then immediately before the drawing everyone breaks his or her balloon to get the slip of paper. To prevent the numbered slip of paper from flying off, balloon buyers are asked to pinch and hold the balloon bottom where the paper slip is located when the balloon is popped.

Raffle Hogs and Ticket-Buying Psychology

Some people become well known for buying large numbers of raffle tickets. They do it every year and may even flaunt their hoard of tickets in front of everyone at the event. This can happen at any event where there are raffles, but it can create a particularly counterproductive situation if the event features a single raffle offering multiple prizes. This format can entice one person or a few people to purchase huge numbers of raffle tickets. Large piles of raffle tickets held by these mass buyers can become highly visible to others who may be considering purchase of tickets. Some people may choose not to purchase tickets if they perceive a few people have already bought, or will buy, so many tickets that the chances of anyone else winning are seriously reduced. This may be a form of logic that defies the laws of statistical probability, but perceptions can be powerful influences on how people choose to spend their money at fundraising events.

This may be troublesome and affect overall net revenue at small fundraisers or where there is considerable variation in income levels of the members. Consider that the revenue-to-cost ratio from raffles can be very high, often much higher than from auctions, although overall revenue may be lower than from auctions. Auction hosts want people to buy raffle tickets—lots of tickets. So it is counterintuitive to interfere with or otherwise restrict purchase of raffle tickets. Besides, buying large numbers of raffle tickets may be how some event attendees choose to make their contribution to the host organization. Some people may not be comfortable bidding on auction items, as they may feel intimidated by competing with others, even if that competition is only at a silent auction table. Given a choice between buying raffle tickets or bidding to win an auction item, they spend all the money they budgeted for an event on raffle tickets. The result is that at every event they attend, they are seen holding on to piles of tickets.

Despite perceptions of attendees, if the total number of tickets in a raffle is limited and all are sold, each ticket carries an identical probability of being drawn. If the number of raffle tickets in a drawing is "unlimited," the statistical probability of any single ticket being the one drawn is reduced as each new ticket purchased enters the drawing. For this reason, people who buy lots of tickets have a better chance of winning an unlimited raffle than a person who buys only one ticket.

Preempt raffle misperceptions by having several kinds of fundraising activities, including several raffles and different kinds of raffles. This helps even out the perceptual playing field by introducing considerably greater complexity in raffle ticket buyers' chances at winning raffles and ensures that attendees can find a way to participate in fundraising activities in a fashion comfortable to them.

Arcade Games

The arcade is exactly what it sounds like—a collection of booths or an area where people pay to play games of chance or skill. Most people have visited arcades at carnivals, amusement parks, and circuses. The only difference between the carnival arcade and a fundraising arcade is that net revenue from the fundraising arcade goes to a charitable cause. Fundraising arcade games are completely fair, unrigged, and designed to create maximum fun. Arcades can be solid contributors to net revenue at an event, but their main purpose is to create excitement and fun for attendees. If an event is geared toward families, arcade games can be designed to provide a way for the entire family to participate in fundraising, especially if the cost of play is reasonable.

The revenue potential from most arcades is generally not as great as some of the other fundraising activities described in this chapter. However, with a little forethought, arcade games can be designed to deliver an attractive return on investment. The potential for a high net return on investment can be increased by offering high-dollar prizes and charging high-dollar amounts for each play. The arcade is a risky proposition if too many people get lucky or if the level of skill required to win is less than planners anticipated, but there are ways to minimize risks.

Winning: Prizes and Risks

Arcades involve game-oriented activities. People pay to take a chance, such as the spin of a wheel, or they pay to engage in an activity requiring some skill, such as throwing a dart at a balloon. When arcade games of chance or skill are oriented to children, everyone who plays should receive a prize regardless of the outcome of play. Some prizes may be better than others, with the prize won based on the results of the play. When adults play, all may receive a prize or prizes may be limited to specific play results.

A key attraction to arcade games is that everyone can win with every play, because every play of a game of chance or skill provides the player with an opportunity to win. The stipulation that everyone can be a winner creates some level of risk to the host organization. This is also what differentiates arcade games based on chance from raffles. Not only can everyone who plays an arcade game be a winner every play but everyone who plays can also win a top prize. For example, if the arcade game is a card draw with the top prize going to anyone who draws an ace of spades, if all who play were to draw the ace of spades, all would receive the top prize. Given the low probability of pulling an ace of spades from a shuffled, full deck of cards, it is unlikely such an event would occur repeatedly, but that is the risk in games of chance.

Generally for games of chance, a series of prizes are available and displayed. Prizes range in value, with the top prize being the most valuable and presumably the most difficult to win. In the fifty-two-card deck-draw example where the deck is shuffled after each draw, the top prize could go to a person who draws the ace of spades. A lesser-value prize could go to a person drawing any one of the other three aces. A lesser-value prize might then be awarded to anyone who draws any one of the 12 face cards in the deck. No (or a very low-value) prize would be awarded for drawing any of the remaining 36 cards in the deck. The risk is obvious, and the price per play needs to be commensurate with the value (particularly any cost to the host organization) of the prizes and the probability of winning

a particular prize on each draw. The probability of winning the top prize (ace of spades) is 1 in 52, while the probability of drawing any other ace is 1 in 17.3; drawing a face card, 1 in 4.3; and drawing any winning card, 1 in 3.3.

A few ways to reduce costs and lessen risk include acquiring the grand prizes on consignment, buying only the minimum number of prizes needed, keeping an example of each prize displayed where a finite number of prizes exist, and ending the game when the prizes run out. A variation that limits the level of potential costs to the host organization is to set the number of prizes. Using the deck-draw game again as an example, in this instance the deck may be shuffled after each draw, or it may not be shuffled. There are 16 prizes displayed, one for each of the 16 winning cards (aces and face cards, where different cards receive different-value prizes). As the winning cards are drawn, the prizes are awarded and winning drawn cards are discarded from the deck. When the prizes are all gone, the game is over, or the game can be reset with another round of 16 prizes and played again.

The problem with this variation is that once the top tier of prizes is gone, there is little incentive for people to continue play. If top prizes are awarded early in the game, revenue will be adversely affected because few or no people will want to play the game. Even when all prizes are contributed 100% free to the sponsoring organization, there is a loss of potential added net revenue. As a result, do not use this variation except where the game delivers a prize to everyone who participates and prize values are low, such as in children's games. If the number of prizes is restricted, risk of the host losing money on a game is reduced. There is no risk that there will be several winners of the top prize if only one top prize is offered per game. There are two ways to reduce risks and achieve fundraising goals using games offering a set number of prizes: games in which all players receive a prize and games in which the prizes awarded during previous plays of the game are not obvious to subsequent players.

1. ALL PLAYERS RECEIVE A PRIZE

Games can be set so all players win. This is often done in games for children. Prize values and cost of play must be kept low, and the game should be simple and interactive with the players. The "duck pond," described under "Arcade Games of Chance," is a game that fits this category. Such games can deliver a modest level of net revenue if the price per play is set appropriately. It is probably best to determine the price per play and then carefully purchase prizes, taking into consideration how many people are expected to play the game. Net revenue will depend on the number and cost of prizes purchased, cost of setup, the price of each play, and the number of plays.

Hedge a bit while gaining experience with this kind of game by being conservative about the number of people who will play. Buy prizes accordingly, and end the game when the prizes are all gone. If you are able to obtain prizes on consignment, there will be more room for error. Prizes should be appropriate for the players and will determine the players. Expand the age groups the game will attract by offering winners a choice of similarly valued prizes that would appeal to varied age groups.

2. PRIZES AWARDED EARLIER NOT OBVIOUS TO SUBSEQUENT PLAYERS

In this variation, prizes are matched to a number of exactly known winning plays. For example, certain cards from a shuffled card deck win prizes, such as the 16 aces and face cards, with 16 prizes ranging in value associated with these 16 cards. Players pay for each draw of a card, with each card either a losing card or a winner. If it is a winning card, the lucky player receives a prize, but the prize comes from "under the table," whereas the prize on display associated with that card remains on the display board. Winning cards are removed from the deck in play. Subsequent players are not told about previous winners, so they may not know if the grand prize (awarded if the ace of spades is drawn) has been won.

This method is a bit hard to manage; some people demand to know about previous winners. However, there is a twist that can be added to help remove any perception of deception. All players, regardless of what card they may have drawn, winner or loser, are automatically entered into a raffle for a displayed grand prize. For example, each card drawn can be

cut in half, with one half going into the raffle and the other half retained by the player as proof of entry into the grand-prize drawing. That makes removing cards from play more acceptable to players.

Arcade Games of Skill

Net return from arcade games may not be as much as from some of the other kinds of fundraising activities, but these games provide excitement and fun. Games of skill are at the top of the fun list. In fact, games of skill can be so much fun that planners need to be careful that these games do not interfere with the silent auction and any raffles that are under way before the main live auction begins. If necessary, encourage movement of people among all the fundraising activities by appropriately pricing these games and limiting their duration. The arcade could be open for a limited period of time, perhaps opening early, then closing before the silent auctions and raffles close.

Games of skill are those that might be seen at a block party, carnival, amusement park, or circus (bean-bag toss, darts, quarter toss, basketball swoosh, baseball throw, and ring toss). Building an arcade is a time when a planner's imagination can run wild. Make up fun and exciting games, or copy the old favorites. Put the host organization's mark on the games by featuring mission-related play ideas and prizes. Sidebar 17.4 describes five example games of skill.

Gather the game parts, assemble the games, and build the booths. In some metropolitan areas, it may even be possible to rent arcade games at party-supply businesses, booths and all. Games and game pricing should be appropriate to the age level of expected players. Generally, three levels of games cover most situations: approximately ages 3 to 6, 7 to 12, and 13 to adult. An exception to this is any game of strength, which could require more levels of play to make it fair.

Age level also needs to be considered in selecting the types of prizes to offer. The value of prizes needs to be considered in pricing play. If the game may be attractive to most age groups, such as a dart game, it may be best to offer two levels of play: a youth play

Sidebar 17.4. Five Fun Games of Skill

1. *Dart throw.* Darts are thrown at small balloons, playing cards, circles, or some other kind of target. Prizes are awarded for hitting the target. It is common to give three darts per play.

2. *Bean-bag toss.* Players toss bean bags at boards tilted at an angle with holes in the board for targets. If the bean bag passes through the hole, the player wins. To make the game fun and competitive for all ages, have three targets, each with a different-sized hole ranging from large to small. The more valuable prizes are won for getting the bean bag through the smaller holes. Here, the lowest-level prize should cost the host organization considerably less than the price of entry. This should be something like a pencil with a charitable message, a logo-embossed key chain, or an item of similarly low value.

3. *Softball throw.* A softball is thrown at an object, such as a bowling pin, in an attempt to knock it over. To make the game fun and competitive for players of all ages, have the objects to be knocked down close for the kids and farther away for adults.

4. *Basketball swoosh.* Players try to throw a basketball through a basketball hoop. This game can be made more fun and competitive for players of all ages by placing the basket for adults farther away and higher than for the kids.

5. *Ring toss.* Small rings are tossed onto pegs. To make the game fun and competitive for both children and adults, have rings of two different diameters, the larger diameter for kids and the smaller for adults.

at a low price and an adult play at a higher price, where prizes differ and winning top prizes requires different levels of skill. Typical prizes for games of skill can include coffee mugs, stuffed animals, umbrellas, hats, stadium seats, key rings, raffle tickets, CDs of inspirational songs, and so on. Prize items can be affixed with the organization's name and logo.

When the value of the prize increases with the number of winning plays, the different levels of prizes should be displayed. In the dart game, for example, the outcome of breaking three balloons on one play could result in the award of a key ring. If a player is skillful enough to win five key rings, these could then be "traded up" for a large stuffed bear.

Rules of Play

What if a professional dart player decides to play the dart game? Because games of skill at charitable events are for fun and charity, unrigged, and (usually) built by amateurs, it is often the case that the skill level required to win is less than expected by the planners. It is perfectly acceptable to place a limit on the number of top prizes that may be awarded to any one player. Few players seem to mind this sort of limitation, because the game is for fun and charity. Such limitation is just part of the rules of play that should be established, displayed in a fashion that is visible to players, and enforced to ensure everyone who plays is treated equally.

Here's what can happen if rules of play are not established or if rules are ignored. During a family outing when my three daughters ranged in age from four to nine, we visited a large amusement park. While the older two rode with their mother on a rather high-flying and wild ride, my four-year-old and I stayed below. I noticed a nearby arcade and walked to the dart booth. Play was three dart throws for a dollar, and the targets were tiny hearts on cards about 10 feet away. There was only one prize level. A dart in the heart won a large stuffed cow. My daughter watched as I stuck the first dart in a heart. The attendant handed me a cow. I gave it to my daughter. I stuck the next heart for a cow, and then much to my amazement, my last dart stuck a heart for a third cow. It all happened in less than a minute, and my daughter toddled away hugging three large cows.

I was udderly lucky, but if it can happen to me, it can happen to anyone. Don't allow three cows for a dollar. There is no reason on earth to "lose the farm" by giving away that many cows for a buck. Limit grand prizes to one per play, or one per person. Rules of play also reduce the likelihood of disputes between booth attendants and players. One of the main rules of play should be, "In the course of any dispute over whether a player wins or loses, the decision of the booth attendant shall be final."

Arcade Games of Chance

Games of chance are won or lost strictly according to statistical probability, as is the case with the wheel spin or pulling any particular card from a shuffled deck. Other games of chance are won by simple luck, as is the case with the jelly-bean-jar guess. These are simple games that can be made fun for the entire family. In most cases they can be constructed in a very simple fashion out of ordinary materials. They can also provide a reasonable return on investment in the cost of game materials and prizes. Following are descriptions of four fun games of chance.

I. DUCK POND

Small rubber ducks are floated in a tub, trough, hot tub, old-time bath tub, or some other large watertight container. Players pay to pick a duck from the water—some ducks are winners, and some are losers. Here is how to set up the game. Purchase about 50 small rubber ducks. With an indelible marker, write a number on the bottom of each duck. The numbers correspond to a list of prizes. On a board behind the duck pond is a list of winning numbers and what prize is associated with each number. Many numbers are "losers," and no prize is won. Vary this game by writing the name of a prize on the bottom of some ducks. Ducks are returned to the water after each play and mixed into the "flock." A pump in the tub can be used to circulate the water to help move and mix the ducks. Turn on the "bubbles" if using a hot tub.

Another variation of this game, which is especially effective for young children, is to assign a prize to each duck. Each duck then becomes a winner. A few ducks can be assigned a higher-level prize to offer additional enticement to players. Display the prizes. In choosing prizes and the number of prizes to purchase, consider that the price of play needs to cover the cost of the prizes and that top prizes may be won over and over. Once a particular prize runs out, all ducks awarding that prize must be removed from the pond.

Sidebar 17.5 describes another variation on the duck-pond game. This variant spotlights high-revenue fundraising and should be considered a serious means to raise revenue.

2. PIG-IN-A-POKE GAMES: FISHING POND GRAB BAG

Bag up various odds and ends of donated or purchased items, leaving a lip at the top of the bag that

---

Sidebar 17.5. High-Revenue Duck Pond

The duck pond provides considerable opportunity for innovation, including using it as the fundraising platform for a featured high-value grand prize. For example, the hot tub in which the ducks float can be the grand prize in a duck-pond raffle. Players buy a chance to pick a duck. The cost of picking a duck is set to more than cover the cost to the organization of the grand prize.

Players buy a duck, and pick that duck from the water. All players win a number of raffle tickets for the prize when they select a duck, but different ducks award different numbers of raffle tickets. Each duck is marked on the bottom with a number that corresponds to the number of raffle tickets for the grand prize the player receives by selecting that duck. For example, with 50 ducks in the pond there can be 30 ducks marked for 1 raffle ticket, 15 ducks marked for 5 raffle tickets, 4 ducks for 10 tickets, and 1 duck for 20 tickets. Ducks are replaced in the pond after each pick.

Because the ducks are replaced after each pick, the odds for picking the various levels of winning ducks remain constant throughout the duration of the game. The odds of any individual raffle ticket winning the grand prize, however, decrease as people play, because each duck picked results in at least one new raffle ticket in the drawing. The number of raffle tickets awarded with each winning duck does not influence revenue, so the host organization can be generous in how many tickets are made available to each winner. Revenue is determined solely by the number of plays or the total number of ducks that people pick.

---

a player can catch with a hook. Players are given fishing poles with a large (unsharpened) hook on the end with which they snag or hook bags stacked in a "fishing pond." Bags should be opaque so players cannot see prizes in advance. The "pond" can be made of a child's plastic swimming pool. Players pay to catch one bag (fish).

A display should be placed behind the pond that gives players an idea of what items may be placed in the bags. Players should know the general kinds and value of prizes possible. This is especially critical if high-value items are placed into some of the bags and the cost of play is more than a few dollars. Some bags contain better items than others, but everyone wins something. Pricing of game play needs to be set based on (1) the total cost of prizes and (2) the total revenue potential, both of which are known exactly in this game. The only unknown is whether or not grab bags will sell out. Risk of loss is minimized if all items are obtained free or at very low cost.

This game can be very effective for children, because they win every time, but prizes must match the age group. Accommodate children of various ages by having bags of different colors correspond to different age groups. For the very youngest children, it may be necessary for the game attendant to help hook the bags.

3. WHEEL SPIN

A player spins a wheel of chance and wins whatever prize the wheel indicates when it comes to a stop. Prizes can be written directly onto the wheel of chance, or numbers can be written on the wheel that correspond to prizes or prize levels. Prizes should be prominently displayed behind or near the wheel.

Divide the number of stops on the wheel by the number of winning stops to determine the probability of winning any single prize, assuming the wheel revolves freely and each stop peg in the wheel has an equal resistance on the catch and is equidistant from any other. If the number of stops is 52, which is the number of cards in a typical poker deck, then the computation of probability is the same as in the example of drawing any particular card from a shuffled deck. For example, if a single stop is assigned the top prize, there is a 1 in 52 chance of a top winner on every spin of the wheel. Because there is a probability, although perhaps small, that top prizes can be won multiple times, planners need to consider the odds in setting price per play and determining how many prizes at different levels need to be available. The game can also be adapted for very young children by assigning a small prize to every stop on the wheel.

4. JELLY-BEAN-JAR GUESS

Set a very large clear jar containing a large number of jelly beans on the counter of a booth, and have players pay to take guesses on the number of beans in the jar. Players pay for each guess and can buy as many guesses as they wish. Each guess is recorded on a large board or sheet displayed immediately behind the jar. No two people are allowed to guess the

same number, so the display serves to let people know which numbers have been taken by earlier players. One way to organize the guesses is to produce a long sheet on which numbers are listed in sequence. When people guess a number, their name (or bidder number) is written directly beside the number on the sheet of numbers. This sheet may contain many thousands of numbers, depending on how many jelly beans are actually in the jar.

The grand prize for guessing the number of jelly beans in the jar should be displayed near the jar. The prize can be anything, but since this is a fun and somewhat wild event, the prize should reflect that character. Play continues for a set period. The guess closest to the real number of jelly beans in the jar is announced onstage during the event. Bring the jar up onstage during the announcement, along with the prize.

Combined Games: Skill and Chance

Games are fun to play and fun to design. Try a variation where the fun of skill is combined with the excitement of chance. Here is an example of poker darts, a game that does just that. Shuffle a full deck of poker playing cards. Pin each card to a board, face against the board and spaced apart. The board must be of a material to which darts will stick. Skill is necessary to hit a card with a dart. Chance comes into play because dart throwers cannot see the face of the cards so can't see which card is which. Arrange the cards randomly on the board, as long as each is separated from any other. Once a card is hit by a dart, remove it from the board. Prizes are awarded for hitting certain cards.

Prizes associated with certain cards can be handed to winning players immediately, but to keep excitement about the game rolling through the entire deck, try this. Assign a set number of raffle tickets to each card, and when players hit a card, they get the associated number of raffle tickets as their prize and the card is removed from the "deck" (backboard). Display a desirable raffle item with a perceived value, for example, of $150. Players could get 1 raffle ticket for hitting a number card, 5 raffle tickets for a face card, and 10 raffle tickets for hitting an ace. In assessing the potential net revenue and pricing for this game, it does not matter how many raffle tickets are awarded for any card. Players must perceive that hitting any card, even if the result is only a single raffle ticket, is a good deal for play.

The odds are clear to players, because the maximum number of total raffle tickets to be awarded is exactly known. For pricing in this example, at $5 for one dart and $10 for three, even if everyone who plays at $10 hits three cards, which is highly unlikely, the game will produce $170 ($17 \times $10) on a raffle item of a perceived value of $150. Adjust pricing as desired. Once the cards are all gone, or the period allotted for playing arcade games is over, the drawing is held and the winner is announced. Or hold the raffle drawing at the conclusion of the main live auction. Holding such raffle drawings after the conclusion of the auction helps hold the audience through the event.

Theme Arcades

Arcades offer the host organization an opportunity to feature its mission through game play. A charity serving underprivileged children in an African country can feature games played in that country and prizes made by the children who are the subjects of the organization's work. Another example is a host organization that works to protect ducks and wetlands habitat offering games such as the rubber-duck pull and "pluck-a-duck," a game in which play is conducted by pulling "feathers" carrying a chance at a prize from a wooden duck decoy.

Legal Issues with Raffles and Arcade Games

Raffles and many arcade games are games of chance. As such they may be regulated by local, state, and federal authorities. Laws, rules, and ordinances governing raffles, games of chance, lotteries, bingo, and other fundraising activities vary by state and sometimes by county and by city within a state. There may be restrictions on the sale of raffle tickets if sent through the mail or sold outside the event itself. Raffles where cash is the prize may be prohibited in some locations. Restrictions may apply if

raffle tickets are sold in a state other than where the drawing will be held or in another country. Some localities prohibit giving out certain types of raffle tickets for free. Sometimes, a specific statement needs to be added to raffle tickets or a specific registration needs to be completed prior to conducting a raffle or holding a game of chance.

Since games of chance and raffles are considered gambling, they are regulated under state and/or local gaming laws. Although special exemptions to gaming laws are generally available to nonprofit organizations that wish to conduct raffles and hold games of chance, the conditions under which exemption is granted can be extraordinarily detailed and complex. This often requires substantial attention to detail and reporting by the sponsoring organization. Here are some of the more common requirements that may apply to nonprofit organizations that sponsor raffles:

- Detailed application forms must be filled out well in advance.
- Raffle tickets must contain certain language and be printed in a certain way.
- Raffle drawings may be required to be held in a certain fashion.
- Raffle proceeds may be taxed.
- Permits must be displayed at the time of drawings.
- Minors may not be permitted to purchase tickets.
- The sponsoring organization must own prizes and pay all normal sales taxes prior to the drawing.
- Prizes may not exceed certain values.
- Drawings must be held and prizes awarded even if too few tickets are sold to cover cost of prizes.

There may be different requirements for different types of games, so event planners need to know well in advance the specific nature of all fundraising activities planned for an event. For example, a city ordinance may place different requirements on holding a straight ticket raffle than on holding a bingo game. It is important to make sure activities planned are compatible with local requirements and proper permits are acquired.

Required reports are often lengthy, with records required to be kept for varying periods. Records often include name and address of winners, beginning and ending ticket numbers, total number of tickets sold and unsold, description of each prize and value, records of transfer of prizes to winners, records of efforts to distribute prizes not claimed, and more. There may also be restrictions on how raffle proceeds are used. In Alaska, any funds raised through raffles must be spent within a year of receipt in the state of Alaska on the host organization's stated goals and purposes as set by the organization's bylaws.

Chapter 20 provides additional details on legal issues or requirements that may need to be addressed in the course of event fundraising. However, the purpose of this book is not to give legal advice. Because laws and regulations vary by state and local area, consult with legal counsel to ensure that any raffles or other games of chance comply with all legal requirements.

Special Category: Casino Games

Casino games are exactly that—games ordinarily played in a casino. Included in this category are blackjack, roulette, five-card stud, and craps. These can be popular additions to a fundraising event, but they tend to be rather complicated to conduct and more time consuming than the other games described in this chapter. Remember that the main live auction is the focus of the auction event; everything leads up to the auction, and everything else moves quickly, providing added fun, excitement, and net revenue along the way.

"Casino-night" events can be quite successful with virtually all fundraising revenue coming from the casino games. The stand-alone casino-night format works very well, but for it to be effective, players need time to get oriented to the games, move among the gaming tables, and spend considerable time at the tables. It is a time-intensive format for fundraising, much better conducted as a stand-alone activity than trying to combine it with

a major live auction event. Also, casino-type activities often are somewhat more regulated than other types of games, and local regulations may need to be addressed. However, if planners want to add casino-type activities to an auction, or if they want to conduct a stand-alone casino event, there are service companies that specialize in staging casino events. They provide all the equipment, dealers, and support materials. Such companies also should be aware of any local rules and deliver their services in a fashion consistent with prevailing laws.

Merchandise Sales

Whenever a nonprofit organization in search of funding has gathered a large group, the organization should offer its merchandise for sale. Your organization has no products to sell? Nonsense; every organization has something to sell—or could have if members or staff gave the idea a little thought. Memberships, cookbooks, T-shirts, hats, coffee mugs, cookies, and so on are regularly sold by nonprofit organizations. Sidebar 17.6 lists 20 top items commonly sold by nonprofit organizations.

Although a nonprofit organization cannot operate as if it is a for-profit organization, rules for nonprofits allow sale of mission-related items and logo-identified merchandise. It is perfectly acceptable for a charitable nonprofit organization to market a line of logowear that helps advertise the organization and its work. Examples are wearables such as shirts, hats, and jackets. These can feature the name of the organization and its logo, name, or other identifying mark. As an example, a species-conservation organization might sell a T-shirt featuring an image of a blue whale, the organization's logo, and the phrase "Save the Whales!" printed across the front. This provides great advertising for the organization and one of its causes. The sale of such items is perfectly allowable under state rules of incorporation and is acceptable to the IRS.

Merchandise sales should not interfere with event fundraising, but offering products where potential buyers are gathered makes sense. People will see merchandise displayed and learn what the organization has for sale. The host organization's prod-

Sidebar 17.6. **Twenty Top Items for Sale at a Fundraiser**

1. Windbreaker jacket
2. Tote bag
3. Sweatshirt
4. Rain jacket (stuffable)
5. Hat
6. Umbrella
7. Cookbook
8. Car windshield shade
9. Coffee mug
10. "Polo" shirt
11. Eyeglass carry case
12. Whiskey glass tumblers
13. Welcome mat
14. Stadium seat
15. Good-quality pen
16. T-shirt
17. Dog and cat collars
18. Comfort blanket
19. Wine and beer pint glasses
20. Hummingbird feeder

uct catalogs can be distributed. If the products of an organization are part of a critical education mission, it is important that those products be offered during the auction event. Essential items would be products like the educational books of a conservation organization, the motivational CDs of a self-help organization, and the safety videos of an organization promoting safe driving habits.

Sales and merchandise delivery can be conducted at the event. But if on-site sales are a logistical challenge, available products can be displayed, with orders taken for later delivery. Order forms and catalogs can be distributed to people who look at the product display. Regardless of how it is done, the organization's products, membership materials, and mission-related products should be prominently displayed at the event. Where it is appropriate, items should be made available for purchase to prospective buyers.

When an organization sells merchandise containing its name and logo, all such items should be reasonably priced. After all, when such items are worn or used, it is just like advertising for the organization. Wearables or other items prominently displayed serve to remind the user and any onlookers about the organization and its charitable cause. Take advantage of people willing to carry the message by making it easy for them to do so. While not as obvious as a sandwich board, it is no less effective to have an organization's logo paraded around town on jackets, hats, shirts, tote bags, and umbrellas.

If possible, at an auction event, make at least one logo item available at a ridiculously low price or give something away for free. The key is selling (or giving away) something that people will wear or use. Match the item with the personal tastes of the target audience. Stay away from the goofy stuff, in sales and in gifts. Sure, a hat with wings or rabbit ears is an attention getter. It may have a place as a stupid auction item or gag prize, but let's face it, no one will wear it after the event is over. Any recognition an organization might receive by a person wearing something is lost if it never gets worn because it looks ridiculous. Choose items in style that people really wear or use.

18 Putting It All Together

Two organizations had been holding events in the same communities for years. One was a statewide organization and the other a national organization, both with local committees doing the fundraising. The statewide organization was a splinter organization of the national one, the result of a long past dispute between leadership in the national organization and members in the state. So it evolved that these organizations went head to head in competition with events in the same communities. Event organizers and attendees were cut from the same cloth. The organizations' cause was the same. One event appeared the same as any other. Funds raised were used to accomplish the same mission, and the kinds of raffle and auction items available at the events were the same.

Volunteers and event workers would float between the two organizations, sometimes a result of continued inabilities to get along. Many people contributing to the cause supported both organizations, which was the real strength of both organizations. Getting people to attend the events was relatively easy, as both organizations knew exactly what prospective attendees wanted, and the events were stocked full of irresistible raffle and auction goodies. The fiercest competition was not for attendees and the dollars they brought to the events but for the much harder-to-get event volunteer workers, the folks who do the hard work of hosting an event. Asking for donations, making arrangements, getting publicity, selling tickets, and so much more are chores. Getting people who have busy lives to volunteer to put on an event is not easy. And if something should go wrong with an event, event volunteers get all the grief. Who needs that? So the two organizations vied in small and large communities for the limited pool of people interested in the cause of the organizations, and the even smaller pool of volunteers who had not already had their fill of putting on events.

Both organizations paid for many of the items used in raffles and auctions. Event planners also sought underwriting to finance such purchases, meaning both organizations carried considerable overhead for purchased merchandise and services into their events. Despite this overhead, in competing with each other, the organizations' approach could not have been more different.

The national organization focused volunteers' attention on earning net revenue, efficiency ratios, and numerous other event-related measures. Event fundraising was subject to intense analysis. Events held in communities in this and other states were judged and ranked against numerous criteria and each other. The national organization awarded recognition in various categories of performance among events held within the state and throughout the nation. I don't mean to imply intense analysis of fundraising is a bad thing. Such analysis is exactly what all organizations should do in the aftermath of an event, but far too few actually do. The internal competition was motivational and valued by most participants.

However, the national organization's local event volunteers, who also had the statewide competitor to deal with, found themselves being held to an exceedingly high standard. The national organization's emphasis on earning net revenue, increasing net year to year, adding new volunteers, and many other statistics was pressure the statewide organization simply did not place on its volunteers. The national organization's event committees were tightly run; the events were highly efficient and very business-like. There was rarely an "excess" of prizes. A basic formula for fundraising was generally followed. Although volunteers could have considerable fun working at an event, some complained about being pushed too hard to raise money.

The statewide organization took a different and looser approach to fundraising. Volunteers had considerably more latitude on types and amount of merchandise used for auction at an event. Standard items were available, but the number of items volunteers could place into an event could be very high. People liked to attend the events, because there were so many prizes. Volunteers liked to work at the events. The result was the statewide organization appeared to gain a competitive edge on the basis of volunteers having more fun being volunteers.

When volunteer event workers were asked why they liked to work the statewide organization's events, they said working these events was more fun because they won more prizes. Volunteer workers can also be participants in the events held by both organizations. Attendees also said the statewide organization's events were more fun because they won more prizes.

The national organization's events were more efficient and, attendee for attendee, made more money for charitable mission-related work. In the world of charitable giving, the amount of money going to fund an organization's mission versus the amount it costs to put on an event is an important measure of event efficiency and fundraising success. I would have expected attendees and volunteers to take that into account in making choices between the two organizations. I know some people did, but not to the extent I expected. When presented a choice, many attendees and volunteers really just wanted to win prizes and have fun.

THE MIX OF fundraising activities, length of time for each, and the types, values, and number of prizes can have a significant effect on attendees' spending as well as enjoyment of an event. At some point in the process of planning an event, planners must make a series of important decisions about the number and types of fundraising activities to provide attendees, the exact mix and number of prizes to obtain for each of the specific fundraising activities, the length of time to make available for each fundraising activity, and the price to set for each activity (e.g., raffle ticket and game-play prices). This is the process of "putting it all together." It can be a daunting, complicated task.

Choices made at this point will make the difference between a cost-effective event returning significant net revenue and a cost-inefficient event that results in low revenue. Planners could perfectly set up the trappings for the event, get great publicity, sell an unprecedented number of event tickets, but fail to set an equally perfect menu of fundraising opportunity. Truly bad decisions on fundraising mix can result in a net financial loss for the host organization, even when all other aspects of an event are flawless. Many event planners ignore or never gather information readily available to help plan the fundraising mix for an event. It's a shame. All that hard work, a fun event, but in the end little or no net revenue to show for it.

This chapter takes the reader deep into the nuances of setting out the perfect mix of fundraising activities for any group of attendees and type of organization. Although it is impossible to anticipate every scenario, examples and adaptable planning tools should provide even the most inexperienced event planners a basic understanding of how to think through their own situation and get it right the first time, and even better the next.

Getting the Mix Just Right

There is only so much money to be contributed by any group of people that come together for an event. Some attendees will be there to participate in the fundraising and contribute to the organization. Others will be there only to socialize. Almost all who come will have decided, before they arrive, on an approximate upper limit to the amount of money they will spend. It may not be as much as their capacity to spend, but it will be their willingness to spend for the duration of the event. This becomes their "event budget." A few attendees may exceed their budget given the perfect auction item or game prize, but everyone will undoubtedly spend less if not given the opportunity and sufficient enticement to spend it all.

The key to success is to offer the right mix of fundraising time, value, price, and opportunity for all attendees to spend their entire event budget. Providing too much time, too many raffles, too many games, or too many auction items will produce no greater revenue than providing just the right amount of time and mix of fundraising opportunities. Overstocked events usually carry excess costs that will decrease net revenue. Understocked events where items are undervalued and too little time is provided

for fundraising result in leaving money in attendees' pockets and thus less net revenue.

How does an event planner determine the right mix, considering the characteristics and mind-set of attendees may be very different from one event to another? The following sections provide objective answers. But events vary, as does the mix of people who attend. As a result, there will always be some error and risk involved in arriving at the "perfect" fundraising mix.

It's Not a Guessing Game

Some planners may feel there is more art than science in making choices about fundraising mix. The "art" here means planners use feelings to make choices, like using "gut instinct" and "experience" to come up with the mix. The more I thought about the notion that there is an art to making fundraising choices, the more I realized this is really just guessing. No more, no less. "Science," on the other hand, refers to use of objective information, such as hard numbers, in coming to conclusions about what fundraising options, prize mix, number of auction items, and so on to offer. Savvy planners acquire information through research and record objective information from one event to the next. They keep track of number of attendees and attendee spending at events. They use science and simple formulas to plan.

The host organization that relies on planners (experienced or not) who guess places its financial future into the hands of people who fail to use readily available relevant information to strategically design the mix of fundraising activities. If event planners planning the same event year after year continue to guess, earlier bad decisions that go unchecked compound the inefficiency of fundraising in following years' events. In the end, if all critical decisions are based on guesses made in previous years, with no subsequent objective analysis of results from event to event, what good is experience? Basing fundraising on such experience is basing fundraising on ignorance. For each new event, the fundraising mix is based on either a new guess or an old one recycled. There is a better way. The end result of event fundraising is, after all, just an easily calculated number:

Net revenue = total revenue – total costs

It makes little sense to come to critical decisions about fundraising without analysis, statistics, evaluation, or numbers. Although effective experienced planners do not discount experience or gut instinct, they do effectively combine it with science (numbers and evaluation). This results in powerful planning, and that is definitely not guessing.

Bringing Science into the Planning Picture

Science is applied by using information and numbers as necessary for effective planning and by keeping records from event to event about attendees' spending. Information—not guessing—is then used to set fundraising into place:

- The estimated number of attendees and their spending capacity/willingness to spend
- The number, size, and kinds of fundraising activities
- The number and kinds of auction, raffle, game, and gift prizes to acquire
- The length of time to hold each fundraising activity

There are three important steps to offer opportunity for attendees to spend their entire event budget: (1) estimate as accurately as possible how many people will attend the event and how many of those people will be active in auction bidding, games, and raffles; (2) estimate how much money attendees will be willing to spend on fundraising at the event; and (3) relate this spending potential to the mix of fundraising activities and items that may be offered to attendees.

STEP 1: DETERMINE NUMBER OF ATTENDEES

Estimate the number of attendees expected. This estimate must be well reasoned, but no matter how hard event planners try, there will be uncertainty unless attendance is limited to a set number of people. Event planners often know with reasonable

certainty how many people will attend an event. This kind of information comes from having held events before or having information about similar events held by other organizations. For events that are held in a location with a maximum capacity that sell out each year, the number of attendees equals room capacity.

STEP 2: DETERMINE ATTENDEE SPENDING

Once the number of attendees is estimated, divide attendees into categories that correspond to their expected spending at the event. This is important additional information planners often lack or fail to consider in a meaningful objective fashion. Yet understating how much money attendees are willing to spend at an event is the key to setting the stage for efficient fundraising. The best way to estimate attendee spending is to evaluate spending patterns at past events. If records of attendee spending from past events have been kept, this information is known exactly. If not, or if planning is for a first-time event, attendee capacity to spend can often be estimated using a variety of research tools or by indirect means.

Research can provide information such as household income based on where people live that can be used to help in planning. Zip codes or school districts can often be used as a proxy for specific information on an individual. People living in an area defined by a zip code or school district often have similar household incomes. Particularly in urban areas and the suburbs of large cities, people tend to congregate in subdivisions or school districts roughly based on income level. Even where zip codes or schools are not useful, event planners who know where attendees will be coming from will probably know the approximate financial capacity of people living there. Planners can use this information to group attendees into "demographic profiles" or categories.

Indirect means to determine attendee spending will provide varying degrees of accuracy and usefulness. It is impossible to look up in a database a person's willingness to spend (event budget) at any particular auction. Too many personal factors come into play. However, a general capacity to spend can be estimated if people can be put into groups for which economic or spending data are available, as described previously. Even though a few attendees may exceed their event budget given the perfect auction item, very few will ever exceed their capacity to spend. Thus, capacity to spend provides a ready baseline to attendee spending.

Grouping attendees generally into a few categories of potential spending capacity is usually not difficult. Of course, there will be some error, but for planning purposes a little error is fine. Guessing is far more subject to error, so use of reasoned estimates is an improvement over complete guesses. The following two examples use grouped attendees' spending and demographic information based on zip codes to relate this to a real-life situation. Let's assume that planners in both examples expect 500 attendees.

1. About 50 attendees are expected to come from a suburban area where households have an average income between $80,000 and $125,000. The other 450 attendees are expected to come from an area where average household income ranges between $25,000 and $35,000. Given this information, planners will know to offer a substantial number of low-cost fundraising opportunities and silent auctions with values ranging between $25 and $100. The main live auction could offer at least several items valued at up to $500, with most items below $250.

2. Event planners know that in the past three years at the annual auction about 10 attendees bid heavily up to $1,500. But event planners also know the bidders live in multi-million-dollar homes and probably have the capacity to spend more than $1,500. Planners run a charitable-giving search on the bidders and find they contribute an average $25,000 per year to charity. In addition, about 90 attendees are expected to come from a suburban area where households have an average income between $125,000 and $200,000. Another 100 are expected to come from households having an average income between $100,000 and $125,000. The remaining 300 attendees are hard to assign exactly, because they will come from throughout the city's higher-income

neighborhoods, with an average household income of $50,000 to more than $200,000.

Given this information, planners know to offer medium- and high-value fundraising opportunities, such as a high-value raffle board, low- and high-value raffles, games of varied value, and silent auctions with values ranging between $50 and $250. In the live auction, the majority of items should not exceed $500, but as a trial, one or two items in the neighborhood of $3,000 to $5,000 with an appropriate reserve can be used in the live auction. If bidding is strong on these items, in the following year an item or two valued at more than $5,000 may be added as a new trial.

STEP 3: RELATE SPENDING POTENTIAL AND NUMBER OF ATTENDEES TO THE MIX OF FUNDRAISING ACTIVITIES TO OFFER

Generally, a large number of auction, raffle, game, and gift items will be needed for an event featuring a large number of auctions, raffles, games, door and table prizes, and giveaways, where a large number of people are expected to participate in fundraising over a lengthy period of time. This may seem to be common sense and is generally a correct statement, but it provides vague guidance. It sounds good but is of little value to the planner faced with making some very specific decisions. Following are details on how to make these decisions.

Many types of fundraising activities, described in this book as raffles, auctions, games, and so on, can be offered. The number of these fundraising activities per type, the number of items offered as prizes in raffles and games or for sale at auctions, the price or value of prizes, and the amount of time available for fundraising for each type of activity can be varied. Different types of fundraising activities are more or less effective or efficient for groups of attendees having varying demographic characteristics. Maximum event efficiency is attained when the highest net revenue is raised for the least number of prizes, activities, and time provided at the event. It may be impossible to even determine this point exactly, but coming as close as possible is the goal when deciding on the mix of fundraising activities for an event. As examples, consider these two scenarios:

1. If only three people are expected to attend an event who have the capacity to pay for a $500 auction item, then having a live auction with three $500 vacation getaways is risky. Even having one $500 item in an auction is risky unless event planners know through "inside information" that at least one of the three attendees capable of bidding on the item is likely to do so.

2. Event planners have specific spending information from past events on 30 attendees anticipated to be active in the live auction. These 30 bidders have all bid as much as $500 for auction items in the past. In general, there should be a minimum of three potential bidders for any specific item, but having five potential bidders reduces risk in circumstances of some uncertainty. Thus, planners can confidently plan on having between 6 and 10 items for auction valued at about $500. (If specific bidder information is lacking but general capacity to spend is known, 10 potential bidders per item reduces risk.)

Factors Affecting Decisions about Fundraising Mix

Attendees must match up comfortably with fundraising options. The following sections present detailed discussion and a planning tool to help planners sort through the many options. Everything described here delves deeply into the factors that influence specific decisions about fundraising mix but is approximate, can be subject to experimentation, and may relate to or be affected by still other factors. Sometimes these factors are subtle yet can be influential for some events and meaningless for others. Readers should pick and choose the sections and examples for information that relate best to their events or interests.

WHAT ABOUT COUPLES?
In making determinations about number of auction bidders and capacity to spend, treat couples as one. Even though members of a couple may bid

separately, they ultimately spend like an individual because they usually share a common budget. There are exceptions, and exceptions should be identified and accounted for in future events, but lacking any prior information, it is prudent to treat a couple as an individual attendee.

LIBERAL VERSUS CONSERVATIVE APPROACH?
An event can be designed with either a liberal or a conservative approach. In the liberal approach, events may offer many prizes or prizes having very high value for only a few attendees or attendees having a low capacity to spend. In the conservative approach, events may offer very few or low-value prizes for a large number of attendees or attendees having a high capacity to spend. For example, consider two events attended by the same number of people. The event using a liberal approach might provide 30 raffle prizes for a grand raffle, whereas an event using a conservative approach might provide only 5 grand-raffle prizes of similar quality. A typical event might provide between 10 and 20 prizes.

This more liberal or conservative approach may be carried throughout the event, at games, raffles, and the silent auction. As another example, one event may be more liberal than another by offering higher-value merchandise for the same price as another event. The more liberal event might provide 10 grand-raffle prizes of an average value of $250, whereas the less liberal event might provide 10 grand-raffle prizes having an average value of $50. Ticket price per chance for both raffles is the same. In another example, both quantity and value of items are higher for one event than the other, with all other attributes of the events roughly equal.

Event planners must determine how to "position" an auction, and the considerations presented here are just a few among many. The following sections assume an event with neither a liberal nor a conservative approach.

GAMES
Games can take up considerable space. In small event rooms the number of games that can be used may be constrained. There may be no space for any

games at many events, but if used, games can be made accessible to all attendees (price to play can be adjusted as desired). Use two to four games at events with fewer than 150 attendees, and up to six games at larger events. Game setup can be adjusted to match the number of attendees likely to play. For example, some games have a set number of plays available, some can be reset, and some provide an unlimited number of plays. Prizes may be given to all players and are usually inexpensive, with a few grand prizes available for certain winners. The number of prizes on hand and available for award at an event must be matched to anticipated level of play.

For children's games, the chance to win should be at or near 100% for minimal prizes, and at least 1 in 10 for nicer prizes. To make games a viable and exciting fundraising attraction for adults, provide about a 1 in 5–10 chance of players to receive a low-level prize. Grand prizes should be awarded at about a 1 in 50–100 chance.

RAFFLES

Raffles are highly versatile and offer a wide range of options, from low-cost tickets accessible to any attendee to ultra-high-value raffles having a limited number of tickets for a single high-value prize (e.g., a motor vehicle or boat). High-value raffles affect attendee budget for silent and live auction items. Raffles with minimal individual ticket prices have a negligible effect on other fundraising opportunities, unless merchandise in those other opportunities is mismatched with attendees' needs or wants.

- Low-price grand raffles are accessible to all attendees. The number and types of raffles can be adjusted to provide excitement. Attendees with limited financial means generally spend their event budget on raffles. In general there should be a sufficient number of prizes and opportunities to provide at least one low- to mid-level prize per 8 to 10 attendees, one high-value prize per every 25 to 50 attendees, and one very-high-value prize per 100 to 200 attendees in the grand raffle.
- High-price raffles are of different varieties, such as a multiprize raffle board and a single prize

reverse raffle. One high-dollar raffle per event up to 500 people is sufficient. However, one effective variant is to start a high-dollar raffle in advance of an event, with the drawing for that raffle held at the event. This allows for an additional high-dollar raffle to be started and held only at the event.

- Bucket raffles should include between about 15 and 20 items each. Because individual ticket price for bucket raffles can be set low, bucket raffles can be made accessible to all attendees, who can buy just one or as many tickets as they wish. As a result, bucket raffles do not strongly affect spending on silent auctions or the live auction, so they can be added without commensurate adjustment to the silent and live auctions. Bucket raffles are good additions to events where many attendees will have limited money to spend. As a general rule, there should be about one item per 10 to 15 attendees, up to about 150 attendees, and about one item per 20 attendees after that, up to about 25 items per raffle.

SILENT AUCTIONS

The number of silent auction items to offer is based on the number of anticipated attendees. A rule of thumb is to provide about one item per 10 to 15 attendees, but any one silent auction should contain no more than 25 to 30 items. A silent auction can run as long as two hours (or even longer for events lasting one or more days) or for as little as 30 minutes. A good length of time for a silent auction is 60 to 90 minutes. Short-duration silent auctions are "speed auctions." They must be closely monitored and heavily advertised with continuing announcements. Silent auctions can strongly affect attendee money available for other activities, because spending can be significant (value should match attendees' willingness to spend). The number of silent auctions and the value of items need to be assessed for the effect on attendees' funds left after the auctions to spend on the live auction.

Have multiple silent auctions. In general, it is better to hold two or more smaller silent auctions than one very large one. Multiple silent auctions can be run in stages, with one starting and ending 15 or 30 minutes before the next. For example, if there are only 60 minutes available for silent auctions, instead of holding one 40-item silent auction over the course of an hour, hold three 20-item silent auctions of 30 minutes each, starting (and ending) at 15-minute intervals over the course of an hour. The formats can vary. For example, the first could be a general auction, the second a specialty-item auction, and the third an auction featuring low-priced items. For many events it may be best that multiple silent auctions be roughly equivalent to provide maximum fundraising opportunity: multiple silent auctions provide attendees opportunity to buy more items per amount of time than a single large silent auction.

During the course of any silent auction an individual bidder may place bids on many items. Bidders who have an event budget that well exceeds the value level of the auction may place unbeatable bids on whatever items they want and walk away. More typical bidders seek items at the lowest price and keep watch over multiple bid sheets. They bid minimum amounts as the auction progresses. In the end, however, they must choose which among the items they will watch to the end so they can be sure to be the last bidder. They may win, but if they lose, a second or third silent auction having similar items provides these bidders second and third chances.

LIVE AUCTION

With a large number of attendees, there should be a sufficient number of silent and live auction items combined to satisfy attendees' desire to participate in bidding, with a reasonable chance to bid and win. The main live auction should feature the most valuable and exciting items and services at the event. It is the onstage finale of the event. The focus should be on quality of items, with value matched to attendees' capacity to spend.

Time is limited for the main live auction. One and one-half hours is a good maximum length. This time limit sets the maximum number of items that can be auctioned, but number of attendees and capacity to spend also must be considered in making downward adjustments to time. There should be no

more than 25 to 30 live auction items. This equates to one item auctioned off about every three minutes. Have fewer items if the auctioneer is inexperienced or an amateur.

The number of auction items and length of the auction may be reduced if there will be fewer than 100 attendees. If no other fundraising opportunities are made available before the live auction, a general rule is that there should be no more than 20 to 25 items for 100 attendees. If games, bucket raffles, and other fundraising activities are under way during a silent auction, reduce the number of items to no more than 15 to 20 for 100 attendees. Maintain a higher number if there is reason to believe all items are highly desirable, attendees' event budgets can cover the number of items offered, and all will be sold. If most items up for auction have a high-dollar value, then it is possible to have a successful event with fewer items than just recommended. Net proceeds of events with high-dollar values should be higher than with low-value items, and high-dollar items warrant more time for bidding, interaction with bidders, and spectacle in promotion.

If there are a small number of bidders who have specialized and expensive interests, it is possible to hold a very successful event with as few as 8 or 10 very exclusive and expensive auction items. Even if the auction speeds along and is over in 30 minutes, having a quick, profitable event with only a few items is a very good event. Bidders become frustrated, and there is no value added, if bidding is purposefully slowed without an obvious need to do so. In fact, the faster the bidding, the better, as long as bids increase and true maximum bids are received.

Adding Up the Numbers

The preceding sections described the fundraising mix in relation to the number of attendees and their anticipated capacity to spend. Notions such as a more or less liberal approach to number of items or value of items lend to the complexity of creating the perfect mix of fundraising options. Planning aids are provided to help compile, manage, and use such information. These involve using a simple matrix by

Attendees' capacity to spend ($)	Door prizes	Raffles and games	Low-value silent auctions	High-value raffles, high-value silent auctions, low-value live auctions	Low-value sponsorships, mid-value live auctions	High-value sponsorships, high-value live auctions	Ultra-high-value auctions, one-of-a-kind items
$0	X						
$1–$25	X	X					
$26–$100	X	X	X				
$101–$250	X	X	X	X			
$251–$1,000	X	X	X	X	X		
$1,001–$5,000	X	X	X	X	X	X	
Unlimited	X	X	X	X	X	X	X

FIGURE 18.1. Attendees' capacity to spend on event fundraising opportunities (approximate).

which planners can organize information on paper or a computer spreadsheet. If a spreadsheet is used, when one number is changed, other numbers can be set to adjust automatically. This will be helpful when using the aids to "test" different fundraising options.

In the following examples attendees' willingness to spend (event budget) is ranked by categories. These categories can be adjusted however a planner wishes to fit information available for attendees. It is likely attendees can be more readily divided among a few categories than many. Instead of using the categories in the examples, an event planner may decide to place attendees into three spending categories: high, medium, and low. The planner would then break the number of attendees down into those three groups for planning purposes.

Figure 18.1 provides a very generalized overview matrix of fundraising activities and attendee event budget. Fundraising activities can be varied in price to play, so an activity can be made to fit any event budget.

Tables 18.1, 18.2, and 18.3 provide sample evaluations of three events that will each have 300 attendees. Each event draws a different mix of attendees. As a result, the fundraising options and prize mix available at each event are different based on anticipated attendees' capacity to spend. Various factors that vary from event to event are considered and listed as "planning assumptions" for the evaluations. For example, table 18.1 considers attendees will mostly be of limited means, whereas table 18.2

looks at attendees of moderate to high financial means. Table 18.3 shows an evaluation for a family event to be attended by 300 people, 50% of which will be young children. The approach for planning a family event is different from that for events attended by adults only. In addition to factors mentioned earlier, planning for family events requires additional evaluation of what constitutes a "family" at the event.

The example in table 18.3 assumes an average of two children per family. An additional factor to consider is the nature of child participation. If children will be of markedly different ages, the mix of game play and prizes will have to be adjusted to be appropriate. Planners should work to determine the mix of ages. Let's assume for the example in table 18.3 that all children will be very young, children will receive a prize for each game play (prizes can be minimal), and each child will want to play all six games at least once. The next step is to determine the makeup of families. A percentage of families will usually consist of a single parent (for the purpose of event planning, this just pertains to the number of adults accompanying children, not the status of child custody). Assume 50% of families will be single parent. Also for our example, some attendees will have no children accompanying them.

Based on information gathered so far, if all 300 people come, 50% (150) will be children. Those children will be from 75 families. Half of those families will consist of one adult and two children (on average). The other half will consist of two adults and

Table 18.1. **Event 1: Fundraising activity and prize-planning evaluation for 300 attendees.**

Number of attendees expected	Attendees' capacity to spend	Door and table prizes	Low-cost grand-raffle prizes ($1–$5 ticket)	Game prizes	Low-price bucket-raffle prizes ($0.50–$5 ticket)	Specialty high-value bucket-raffle prizes ($5–$20 ticket)	High-value raffle-board prizes ($25–$100 ticket)	High-value raffle prizes ($100–$500 ticket)	Silent auction			Live auction				
									Low-value items ($10–$50)	Mid-value items ($50–$200)	High-value items ($200–$500)	Low-value items ($10–$50)	Mid-value items ($50–$200)	High-value items ($200–$500)	Very-high-value items ($500–$10,000)	Ultra-high-value items (over $10,000 one-of-a-kind items)
0	$0	0	0	0	0	0	0	0	0	0	0	0	0	0	0	0
50	$1–$25	5	5	0	5	0	0	0	0	0	0	0	0	0	0	0
200	$26–$100	20	20	0	20	0	0	0	20	0	0	10	0	0	0	0
40	$101–$250	4	4	0	0	0	0	0	0	8	0	0	10	0	0	0
10	$251–$1,000	1	1	0	0	0	0	0	0	1	0	0	0	3	0	0
0	$1,001–$5,000	0	0	0	0	0	0	0	0	0	0	0	0	0	0	0
0	Unlimited	0	0	0	0	0	0	0	0	0	0	0	0	0	0	0
Totals																
300		30	30	0	25	0	0	0	20	9	0	10	10	3	0	0

Note: Planning assumptions: Most attendees are of limited financial means. Capacity to spend is very low, but a few attendees have the capacity to purchase mid-value auction items or buy high-value raffle tickets. Emphasis is on low-cost fundraising opportunities: low-cost raffles, no high-value raffles, and silent auctions emphasizing low-value items with a few mid-value items; the live auction is limited to a mix of low- to mid-value items. Door prizes at 1 per 10 attendees. Not a children's event. No room for games.

Table 18.2. **Event 2: Fundraising activity and prize-planning evaluation for 300 attendees.**

Number of attendees expected	Attendees' capacity to spend	Door and table prizes	Low-cost grand-raffle prizes ($1–$5 ticket)	Game prizes	Low-price bucket-raffle prizes ($0.50–$5 ticket)	Specialty high-value bucket-raffle prizes ($5–$20 ticket)	High-value raffle-board prizes ($25–$100 ticket)	High-value raffle prizes ($100–$500 ticket)	Silent auction			Live auction				
									Low-value items ($10–$50)	Mid-value items ($50–$200)	High-value items ($200–$500)	Low-value items ($10–$50)	Mid-value items ($50–$200)	High-value items ($200–$500)	Very-high-value items ($500–$10,000)	Ultra-high-value items (over $10,000 one-of-a-kind items)
0	$0	0	0	0	0	0	0	0	0	0	0	0	0	0	0	0
0	$1–$25	0	0	0	0	0	0	0	0	0	0	0	0	0	0	0
10	$26–$100	2	1	0	0	0	0	0	0	0	0	0	0	0	0	0
30	$101–$250	6	3	0	0	3	0	0	0	6	0	0	2	0	0	0
100	$251–$1,000	20	10	0	0	5	0	0	0	0	10	0	0	8	0	0
150	$1,001–$5,000	30	15	0	0	15	0	0	0	0	15	0	0	0	15	0
10	Unlimited	2	1	0	0	2	0	0	0	0	2	0	0	0	0	2
Totals																
300		60	30	0	0	25	0	0	0	6	27	0	2	8	15	2

Note: Planning assumptions: Most attendees are of moderate to high financial means. Capacity to spend is relatively high. Emphasis is on mid- to high-value, high-price fundraising opportunities: high-value and specialty raffles and mid- to high-value auctions. Door and table prizes at 1 per 5 attendees. Not a children's event.

Table 18.3. **Event 3: Fundraising activity and prize-planning evaluation of a family event to be attended by 150 children (from 75 families) and 150 adults**

Number expected											Silent auction			Live auction				
Families	Unaccompanied adults	Attendees' capacity to spend	Door and table prizes	Low-cost grand-raffle prizes ($1–$5 ticket)	Game prizes	Low-price bucket-raffle prizes ($0.50–$5 ticket)	Specialty high-value bucket-raffle prizes ($5–$20 ticket)	High-value raffle-board prizes ($25–$100 ticket)	High-value raffle prizes ($100–$500 ticket)	Low-value items ($10–$50)	Mid-value items ($50–$200)	High-value items ($200–$500)	Low-value items ($10–$50)	Mid-value items ($50–200)	High-value items ($200–$500)	Very-high-value items ($500–$10,000)	Ultra-high-value items (over $10,000 one-of-a-kind items)
10	2	$1–$25	0	1	120	0	0	0	0	1	0	0	1	0	0	0	0
25	15	$26–$100	0	8	300	4	0	0	0	3	0	0	3	3	0	0	0
20	12	$101–$250	0	6	240	3	0	0	0	2	3	0	2	4	0	0	0
15	8	$251–$1,000	0	5	180	2	0	0	0	1	3	0	1	4	0	0	0
5	1	$1,001–$5,000	0	1	60	1	0	0	0	0	1	0	0	1	0	0	0
0	0	Unlimited	0	0	0	0	0	0	0	0	0	0	0	0	0	0	0
Totals																	
75	38		0	21	900	10	0	0	0	7	7	0	7	12	0	0	0

Note: Planning assumptions: Attendees are a mix reflective of the demographics of the entire city. This is a family event with 300 attendees: 150 children from 75 families, and 38 unaccompanied adults. Capacity to spend is mixed. Emphasis is on a variety of fun fundraising opportunities: low-cost raffles; games (six games will be available to children and adults); and auctions emphasizing a mix of low- to mid-value items. Door prizes at 1 per 20 attendees.

two children. That makes a total of 112 adults, but families spend like couples at an event: they spend as one. Thus, the number of family units is 75 regardless of number of adults in each. There are an additional 38 unaccompanied adults. Use the planning tool to take all this into account and set the prizes and values on the basis of family units and unaccompanied adults, not on the simple number of attendees as is done in non-family-oriented events.

The example evaluations display use of a planning aid. In the end, the number of prizes and choice of fundraising options are a matter of the planner's choice. There is nothing exact about using a planning aid. It is simply a means to help order thoughts and provide a way to lay out available options in an organized way. The numbers of prizes and choices of fundraising options in the examples presented could be argued, but choices made using the aid are based on a rational framework. This is more defensible than the guessing game played by most planners in organizing fundraising activities and deciding on how many of what value auction item to use. It also helps in pricing raffle and game play.

Planning for an Event without Limits

Some events have an "unlimited" number of attendees. There are so many people in attendance for the set duration of the event that even having a large number of auction items will not exhaust the capacity of attendees to bid and win them, as long as the cost of fundraising opportunity is not beyond their individual willingness to spend. An adequate number of appropriately sized and priced fundraising opportunities need to be provided to attendees to realize the potential for giving amassed at the event. Fortunately, many exciting fundraising activities can be added to an event to cater to all attendees, regardless of their economic situation or how many people attend.

Record Keeping

As an event unfolds, it is important to keep track of spending for use in future event planning as well as for evaluating the success of forecasts used for the event under way. The planning tools described in this chapter become more and more useful to event planners as the information filling them increases in quantity and quality. Attendee spending needs to be tracked to determine if attendees in the various categories of anticipated spending are spending as anticipated. This may be difficult to track for all attendees, but it is possible to identify a sample of people within each spending category and keep track of their spending. Consider that many event planners already do this in regard to event attendees expected to bid on high-dollar items—event planners watch known high-level bidders like hawks. Such attendees are generally known from past events or are known in the community.

Although event planners watch high bidder spending, few do anything with that information after the event. Even fewer track such information for the full spectrum of event attendees. Doing so is not as difficult as it may seem. The level of accuracy need not be very great. The idea is to gain a general understanding of spending patterns of attendees so that future years' events can be better structured to meet attendees' needs and spending.

There will always be a great deal of variation in attendee spending information, so it is also important not to establish false expectations of accuracy in use of data collected. Economic conditions vary from year to year. People have varying demands on their finances. But in the end, tracked information on past spending patterns of attendees will be much more reliable than guessing for use in planning an event. For event planners just starting out, the techniques described here will produce far better results than guessing without the benefit of any experience at all. For veteran planners, the techniques can be used to help make the most of experience gained at previous events.

19

The Big Event

The staff and everyone else backstage heard the loud voice. Many in the audience heard it, too, faintly carried over loudspeakers as sound was picked up by a distant microphone. The voice was a familiar one. It was the president of the organization's board. Demeaning comments were followed by the president shouting, "I'm taking over!" The reason for the president's outburst was a missed detail. Backstage staff were being blamed, as many in the audience were now embarrassingly aware. In truth, the president had ignored his stage rehearsal earlier in the day, and the mistake that was the object of his outburst had become larger than life to him due to his poor understanding of what was happening onstage.

Paid staff were directing the event stage show from backstage. These staff were professionals in event management and had orchestrated the stage show in minute detail. It was directly at these staff the president aimed his frustration as he took over. Staff were told to leave, and there stood the president alone and now in charge. Stagehands waited to be told by someone, anyone, what to do next. By now the president was in trouble because he didn't know what to do next.

At this point, on the one hand, one hoped the president would fail in some embarrassing way, maybe to teach him a lesson; on the other hand, no one wants to see an otherwise successful event, raising money for a worthy cause, fail because of a ham-fisted officer. As it turned out, the staff had been very good at their jobs. So good that every move onstage had been scripted well in advance, put in writing in minute detail, and rehearsed.

All that needed to be done was for everyone who was left to follow the written script. It also didn't hurt that other volunteer officers of the organization came *to the rescue. These were volunteers who had attended rehearsal and knew what was going on. The stage show continued. Maybe not as flawlessly as it might have had staff been present directing backstage activities, but the show went on.*

IF AN EVENT is well organized, planned, and managed up to the final day, don't blow it all when the event-room doors open.

Plan What to Do, and Do What You Plan

Hundreds of details need to be addressed during an event. Everyone who has a role needs to take the responsibility seriously and do what is necessary to make the event successful financially and ensure attendees have an enjoyable experience. During the course of an event, team leaders and the event chair may find themselves in the uncomfortable position of seeing something go wrong. Instead of being good coaches and helping their team members solve the problem, they may succumb to the urge to push people aside and take over in an attempt to do it themselves. Although that may get the job done, the effect on workers pushed aside can result in a cascade of other problems not easily managed.

As bad as a problem may seem, it can get worse if team leaders fail to remain calm. An event chair or team leader faced with a problem may panic and behave erratically, possibly lashing out at whoever is perceived as causing the problem. It could be an event worker, staff member, or even a group of attendees. Given the nature of events and the assortment of people who may attend, there are many possible targets for a frustrated person.

The nature of an event joins people who have never worked together before to do a complicated job. They come from varied backgrounds, have varied experiences, and handle stress in varied and unpredictable ways. Until the event itself, stress-

related behaviors may never be expressed. But in the caldron of an event, problems can come up that challenge even veteran event managers. Inexperienced people who don't usually deal with such stress can react in unpredictable and problematic ways.

All of the recommendations to this point have focused on planning and managing an event effectively. That includes anticipating problems and minimizing inefficiency to maximize financial success and increase effectiveness. The end point is an event that runs flawlessly. If the advice in this book is followed, there should never be a problem at an event. Unfortunately, no book can provide instruction that anticipates all the things that can go wrong at an event, particularly those involving the effect of stress on human behavior.

An event is a place where a wide range of personalities are likely to be confronted with challenging situations. Problems arise even at the best-planned and best-managed events. Anticipating problems, even problems of an unknown nature, and planning appropriate action in response is just another step in creating the "flawless" event. One means to do so is to hold a rehearsal.

The Rehearsal

There may be no easy way to control how some people react to stress or to foresee all event problems, but there is a way to anticipate problems and plan an appropriate response in advance. Hold at least one rehearsal. Several rehearsals can be held to cover different aspects of the event or can be held by different event work teams. Make the rehearsals as realistic as possible. The idea is to work out problems before the event. In particular, the work teams assigned registration and collections should rehearse. Those rehearsals are in addition to any training or instruction given to workers, such as briefings for the MC, merchandise models, spotters, and auctioneer.

Although it may not be possible to conduct a full dress rehearsal in advance of the event, because of the complexity of setting up a full-event room, it may be possible to hold a dress rehearsal the day of the event if the room is set up in advance. This can even take place immediately before opening the doors. For example, if there will be speakers and a considerable amount of onstage activity, it is possible to do a run-through involving all the onstage participants before the doors open.

Rehearsals should include staging a series of mock problems and emergencies. The event chair, team leaders, and the host organization's leadership should engage in these mock exercises. Various problems and emergencies should be listed and run through a rehearsal to make sure everyone knows the procedure for dealing with them. Problems are matters that impact the flow and effectiveness of the event, such as malfunction of the public address system, a traffic jam that delays arrival of half the attendees, or an attendee who screams that there was cheating going on during the silent auction. Emergencies are situations in which there is a threat to attendees or a person is harmed, such as a bomb threat, a complete loss of lighting that leaves the event room pitch black, or a person receiving a severe electrical shock from stepping on a frayed extension cord.

Event leaders should go over the technical procedures for dealing with emergencies and problems, but how they react and act in the course of dealing with an emergency or problem is important and should be among discussion items during rehearsals and mock response simulations. Leaders should be seen to remain calm and competent to address whatever situation arises. Situations involving a worker's mistake should be handled through calm, knowledgeable coaching. Problems involving removal of a worker because of a serious behavior or performance problem should be handled professionally and involve security if necessary.

Emergencies should be handled in a fashion that puts everyone's safety first, and if appropriate, security, medical, or other professional responders should be called in. In no instance should event leaders be seen to lose control, make threatening moves or statements, or act beyond their authority. They should also respect the job assignments of event staff and workers and, as appropriate, remain focused on conducting the event according to plan.

However, if it is necessary to compensate for the results of a problem or emergency, then the event should be modified as quickly and expertly as possible in consultation with appropriate event leaders.

Motivation and Harmony

Although many people may believe the event chair fills the most important job, the truth is that accomplishing the tasks in each functional area of work is important to the success of an event. Everyone who contributes to that end is therefore important to overall success. All functions are important. Work differs and people do different things. Team leaders should work to ensure that all team members feel that their work and tasks are important. This is critical to the success of the immediate event, but it is even more critical to future events when it is again time to recruit volunteers. An empowered, valued, motivated, high-energy workforce will overcome obstacles and work hard for success. Workers who feel unappreciated, undervalued, exploited, and overworked are unlikely to make their best effort—success will be more a matter of luck than planning and hard work.

Importance of Staff-Volunteer Relationships

Many events are totally dependent on volunteer efforts. Some are run by a combination of staff and volunteers. Others are run entirely by staff. Of course, staff generally get paid for the work, although there can be some staff volunteer time in the mix as well. Volunteers may grumble about how much work they do for free while staff working right alongside them are getting paid. By the same token, it is common to hear staff complain about volunteers who are pushy, may not be competent at the job, and cause problems.

Volunteering doesn't mean there are no benefits. "Payment" comes as enjoyment, responsibility outside the normal course of work, an opportunity to meet people, and so on. Staff who work at events usually do so well outside the usual nine-to-five schedule, and it can be challenging work. Staff may be committed to the cause or just working a job. This is an area of great variability, so staff motivation varies.

It is the job of event team leaders—staff and volunteer—to stay in touch with staff and volunteers and address any serious griping that puts staff and volunteers into conflict. It is counterproductive and can affect bottom-line net revenue. There is no one cure for such conflict, as it tends to be a result of only a very few individual conflicts between people who simply do not know how to act in a responsible, respectful manner toward each other. This is not a matter unique to event management and team building, but that does not make it any easier to deal with. My advice is look out for it, and if it emerges, deal with it immediately, decisively, and with finality.

PART 4

Applying the Rules and Covering All the Angles

20

Laws, Risks, and Liabilities

A complaint was registered with the state's attorney general that our organization was engaging in un-licensed gambling during its annual fundraising conven-tion. The complaint was passed on to the agency having jurisdiction. Shortly after an inquiry, we received a cease-and-desist order. We learned of this a few weeks before the day the convention was to begin. The date and location of the convention had been set for at least three years.

The subject of the order was a series of raffles we ran at the event. Raffles had been run for years in the state with no problem. We had retained the services of counsel and thought we had been diligent in complying with all laws. No one suspected problems, but there it was: an order to halt all raffles until we applied for and received a proper permit.

We quickly learned it was a simple matter to receive a permit, which was required by the locality in which the event was being held. All we had to do was submit a proper application and pay a required fee, but given the length of time it would take to process the applica-tion, we had no choice but to cancel all raffles planned for the event.

Fortunately, the cease-and-desist order covered only raffles, and these were not a major contributor to over-all event income. We still lost more than $100,000 in net revenue that year, all because we could not stage raffles. We did not have the required local permit, be-cause we did not know all the rules.

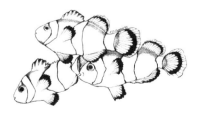

LAWS, RULES, AND ordinances governing raffles, games of chance, lotteries, bingo, and other fundraising activities can vary by state, county, and city. Games of chance and raffles are considered gaming and are usually regulated under state or local gambling laws. These activities are generally allowed for nonprofit charitable organizations but are subject to rules that must be met. There can be different requirements for different types of games, so event planners need to know well in advance the specific nature of all fundraising activities planned for an event. For example, a city ordinance may place different requirements on holding a simple ticket raffle than on a bingo game. It is important to make sure planned activities are consistent with local requirements and proper permits are acquired.

It is not just gaming permits and regulations that can be complex; rules governing public gatherings vary greatly by location and require the attention of event planners. Additional requirements may need to be met and permits obtained for various aspects of an event. This may be particularly so for events held outside regular event and meeting facilities. These are a few common permits (in addition to gaming permits) that may be required to hold an event: food service, noise, street occupancy, fire code, parking large numbers of vehicles, large gatherings, alcohol service, gatherings before or after certain hours, tents or temporary structures, open flames, use of compressed gases, temporary electrical wiring, park use, and temporary vendor and merchandise sales.

In some cases inspections or special certification may be required to receive permits. For example, temporary structures such as tents may have to be inspected and meet safety and fire codes. Food handlers may have to acquire training and certification. Parking may require a public safety officer to direct traffic. These types of permits or certifications are generally required where large numbers of people will be involved and there is a public safety concern. In these examples, the concerns would be injury from a tent collapse or fire, illness from mishandled food, and traffic congestion.

There also may be unusual requirements from state to state regarding what kind of fundraising is allowed or special regulations covering some auction items. For instance, vehicles that are auctioned may be subject to special requirements. Use of alcoholic beverages as auction items may be subject to special requirements in some states; for example, in Texas, their use in auctions requires a special charitable auction permit and adherence to a number of other rather arcane requirements.

The following sections provide advice on meeting requirements and reducing risk of liability when hosting fundraising events.

WARNING AND DISCLAIMER: *This book is not a legal text, does not provide legal advice, and is not a substitute for legal advice or professional counsel on matters of law, legal liability, insurance, contract matters, or other subject areas covered where professional counsel may be obtained. Event planners should seek legal or other professional advice when appropriate. Discussion of risk-related topics in this book is intended to help event planners understand and identify legal risks and aid planners in recognizing when to seek professional counsel. Although efforts have been made to ensure the accuracy of information presented, laws change over time, and the multitude of state and local regulations governing nonprofit organizations and fundraising makes it impossible to address all of them or the potential effects of all of them in this book. In particular, legal requirements from one locality to another may vary, even within the same state. For this reason it is especially important to seek competent assistance for advice on complying with local regulations and obtaining all required permits. The author assumes no responsibility for any errors or outdated materials or for any actions by anyone as a consequence of reading this book, including the actions of anyone who takes action in disregard of this warning and disclaimer.*

Risk Management

Although there is always some risk involved in holding a fundraising event, most people probably assume that the greatest risk is that attendance will be low or people will fail to spend as much money as expected. There is always a chance that an event will lose money, but there are far greater risks and liability to the organization holding an event, including cancellation of the entire event at the last minute, a service provider failing to perform and causing damage to an event site that the host has to pay for, or injury to attendees resulting in a suit against the host organization, staff, officers, or volunteers. All of these can have catastrophic consequences, but all can be minimized, more or less.

Consider that whenever large numbers of people come together and engage in an activity hosted by a responsible party, such as a nonprofit organization, potential exists for something bad to happen to someone, and the host may be found liable. An improperly assembled stage could collapse, injuring people and damaging expensive equipment. Someone could get food poisoning or hepatitis from improperly handled food. Some outside events are held in temporary structures. What if a tent collapses on people? Audio speakers are often set atop elevated stands or poles. What if one falls over on a child, who just happens to be trying to climb up the speaker pole? What if an excited bidder has a heart attack and the host organization neglected to have on-site medical emergency-response equipment required under the organization's special-events permit? What if a child is discovered missing from a fundraiser attended by large numbers of children and one of the event volunteers, also missing, is identified as a convicted child molester? The possibilities are endless. Situations like these are rare but can happen. The consequences for the host organization are dire if required permits and inspections are not obtained and conditions adhered to, or appropriate steps not taken to reduce risk and insure against claims (including making sure that contracts with service providers also address risk and liability).

As the number of attendees increases, and the complexity and length of an event increase, the potential risk of liability increases. Holding an event outside in temporary structures can increase risk, as temporary structures are more likely to collapse than a meeting facility built to modern construction standards. Service of alcohol can greatly increase

risk. Several of the situations described earlier might be considered the result of negligence by the organization's employees, volunteers, or service providers. It is not unusual for people to get sick from food served by caterers at events, for example. But if a service provider has no insurance to cover injury, if required food safety inspections are not made, or if the event host organization's representative signed a contract indemnifying the service provider for any and all consequences of its actions, including negligent actions, then the host organization will be stuck paying for or dealing with the consequences— maybe even paying for defense of the service provider for the provider's injurious actions.

Some event service providers may be nothing other than paid "volunteers" who are providing a "professional" service, but without insurance and licenses typically carried by real professionals. This is a common situation that can take the host into a gray area. Is the service provider an actual paid employee of the host organization? It really won't matter if nothing goes wrong, but who will be held liable if another person is hurt by the actions of the unlicensed, uncertified, amateur service provider?

Following are ways host organizations can help reduce the risk of liability for staff, officers, and volunteers who plan and manage events.

Conduct Education and Training

One of the most important ways to reduce risk is to educate staff, officers, and volunteers about their roles and responsibilities in reducing risk and the appropriate response to situations involving liability. Incidents creating liability can result from simple misunderstandings or lack of knowledge of what is required or how to react to a situation. It is important that staff and volunteers be educated about risks and responsive measures relevant to their specific duties as assigned by the organization.

One way is for the organization to provide an orientation program or workshop for new staff, officers, and volunteers who will be working on an event. Focus training on the kinds of emergencies that are likely to occur at the event. This can be extended beyond the event where relevant, as risk of liability is encountered in the course of any activity of a non-profit organization. Some liability insurance carriers may even require education, training, or orientation programs as a condition of issuing an insurance policy.

Have an Emergency-Response Plan

One of the best means to facilitate comprehensive training is to do so in the context of an emergency-response plan that details basic steps to handle potential emergencies at an event. It makes clear the role and responsibility of each staff member, each officer, and each volunteer. Developing such a plan for an event may seem like overkill, but it is one of the best ways for an organization to demonstrate due diligence, which helps reduce risk of liability. The presence and implementation of such a plan prove the host took reasonable action to protect attendees, staff, and volunteers. And where harm or an emergency occurs anyway, having and employing such a plan in a competent way can help in forming the organization's defense against liability claims.

An emergency-response plan should be developed with the assistance of local emergency responders. If an event is held in a meeting facility that has its own emergency-response plan, the event host's plan for the event should be written to complement the facility's plan. Although the purpose of this section is not to provide instructions on how to develop an emergency-response plan, sidebar 20.1 displays some kinds of situations that should be covered and types of information that should be included in a typical plan.

Emergencies are of varied consequence; less threatening emergencies that may be covered in a response plan include minor traffic accidents, keys locked in a car, and a fallen tree across the road (road obstruction).

Verify Education and Training

Education and training should be verified and evaluated to reduce risk of liability even further. In this way an organization proves that steps taken to

Sidebar 20.1. Typical Items Covered in an Emergency-Response Plan for a Major Fundraising Event

- Emergency contact information for various emergency responders, including police, ambulance, and fire, but also responders should electricity be lost, a road washed out, a hazardous chemical spilled, or a key locked in a car
- A clear statement of who is in charge so there is no confusion about who is responsible for what
- Medical emergency plan designed to stabilize a victim of illness or injury until emergency medical personnel arrive
- Death
- Missing or lost child
- Hazardous-substance release
- Gas leak
- Loss of electricity or other mechanical failure
- Evacuation procedures
- Person suspected of having consumed considerable alcohol about to drive a vehicle
- Physical altercations and assault
- Unlawful presence of firearms or threatening weapons
- Verbal threats, intimidation, gang behavior, or threatening behaviors
- Vandalism
- Theft
- Bomb threat
- Explosion
- Fire
- Natural disasters, such as flooding, tornado, wind, and earthquake
- Suicide threat
- Demonstrations
- Staff, officer, and volunteer training procedures and schedule covering use of the emergency-response plan
- Verification of training and procedures to keep the plan up to date

educate and train staff and volunteers were effective. One way to conduct verification, for example, of an organization's efforts to ensure its staff and volunteers are prepared to respond to a medical emergency at an event, is to have a local medical emergency-service provider meet with staff and volunteers and run a mock emergency drill. This shows the host organization was serious in its efforts to reduce risk to event attendees and its own staff and volunteers.

Provide Written Work Descriptions and Work Assignments

Workers should be provided written work assignments, but this is particularly important for volunteer workers to help ensure coverage under the Volunteer Protection Act of 1997 (discussed later in the chapter), which requires volunteers be "acting within the scope of the volunteer's responsibilities in the nonprofit organization."

Complete Licensing, Certifications, Registrations, Inspections, and Permitting Requirements

Staff and volunteers may have duties at events that require a special license, permit, registration, inspection, or certification. An example is a certificate for safe food handling often required for people who handle food served to large numbers of people. Sometimes event food-preparation areas must be inspected. Temporary outdoor electrical or housing structures, such as tents, must be inspected and permitted. There are many other areas where such licensing or inspection requirements must be met. These requirements are there to reduce risk of harm to people. If an organization ignores acquiring applicable permits and someone is injured in an area where an inspection, permit, or other type of certification was required, the staff member, volunteer, and/or organization may be subject to increased liability for failure to take reasonable or legally required risk-reducing measures. In particular for volunteers, any indemnification under the Volunteer Protection Act of 1997 requires the volunteer to be "properly licensed, certified, or authorized by the appropriate authorities for the activities or practice in the State in which the harm occurred."

Provide a Safe Workplace

Employers are required to ensure a safe workplace for employees. By the same token, the host organization has an obligation to ensure its volunteers have a safe place to work in the course of planning and managing an event, as well as to ensure event attendees are not placed into an unsafe environment.

Document Efforts to Address Risk

It is important to document risk-reducing decisions in writing. Such documentation can be used years afterward as proof that the organization, staff, and volunteers took reasonable actions to reduce risks. For instance, if a volunteer molests a child, the level of liability to the organization may be reduced somewhat if it can prove the organization took reasonable precautions through screening to make sure no one with a history of child molestation was allowed to work at an event. Documentation that the host organization directed a volunteer to take a certification exam for food handling, and the volunteer's reply that the certification course was taken, can be used to prove the organization took reasonable precautions to ensure that food handlers were trained properly.

Select Volunteers

Employers usually carefully select employees and are required to maintain employee records. Likewise, volunteers should be subject to some level of scrutiny, and, if unsuitable for a particular job or for other reasons, they should not be accepted as volunteers. Of course, volunteers are generally "self-selected." But there is no requirement for an organization to accept a volunteer. An organization's acceptance or "selection" of a volunteer carries liability. In the case of accepting volunteers who will work to plan and manage an event, the host organization takes on as much risk of liability for accepting a volunteer as its selection of employees. Staff and volunteers generally work side by side during events, with the difference between volunteer and employee blurred in terms of responsibility and risk of liability to the organization.

Conduct Special Screenings for Youth-Oriented Events

Staff and volunteers involved with youth-oriented events should be screened for a record of incidents involving children. Some youth-oriented events may be of a nature that such screening is not applicable. But where there is any chance of risk, screening should be conducted with the consent of the volunteers. Yes, this creates an awkward situation in which volunteers may feel they are being treated like a suspect, screened for horrible acts, and (hopefully) cleared. Many organizations fail to take precautions, believing such problems cannot happen in their organizations. Taking such a simple precaution is more critical to the well-being of the children and the organization and its members than any indignation suffered by the staff and volunteers screened. If a volunteer refuses screening, consider that an acceptable loss of a volunteer, and possibly a successful preventive measure.

Supervise

The host organization could be found liable for a failure of a staff person or a volunteer to supervise others or pay attention while providing services. For example, if a volunteer is conducting a game of skill where several children are throwing darts at balloons and a child throws a dart at another child and causes injury, the volunteer and the host organization could be held liable. They might not be liable for the actions of the child who threw the dart, but they could be held liable because the volunteer did not adequately supervise the wrongdoing child.

Be Overly Cautious

As an example of being overly cautious, even if there are no requirements to have trained responders or emergency medical-response equipment on-site at an event, to reduce risk of liability from a medical emergency, the host organization can have emergency personnel on-site or can alert emergency responders about the event. Staff or volunteers can be trained in emergency procedures to stabilize vic-

tims of illness or injury. Emergency equipment, such as a portable defibrillator, can be stationed on-site.

Volunteer Protection Act of 1997

Volunteers plan and manage many, maybe a majority of all, fundraising events held each year. Many organizations have paid staff, but usually only the largest nonprofit organizations use no volunteer help at fundraising events. A person who does a job, even as a volunteer, is legally responsible for what and how he or she does it. As a result, volunteers assume risk just as a staff person paid to do the same job assumes risk. If lunch at an event is self-catered and volunteers working to serve food fail to maintain proper food temperature and someone dies from food poisoning, the volunteers who failed to maintain proper temperature may be held liable. If a volunteer fails to properly assemble a sales booth and it collapses and destroys several thousand dollars' worth of merchandise, the volunteer assembler may be found liable.

The bottom line is that a person who volunteers risks having a claim filed against him or her by anyone who believes he or she has been harmed by the action or inaction of the volunteer. If this involves physical injury to a person, claims can be substantial, both for medical recovery and added claims for pain and suffering. Moreover, when a volunteer is acting on behalf of a nonprofit organization, the organization itself may also be liable for the reason that the volunteer was acting as the organization's agent under the organization's direction.

The Volunteer Protection Act of 1997 is often pointed to as providing indemnification of volunteers acting in the course of volunteerism. Although the act provides certain protections to volunteers, a volunteer is not completely indemnified. To receive protection against claims, the act requires that the volunteer be acting within the scope of duties as assigned by the nonprofit organization at the time of the incident. The volunteer must truly be working in an uncompensated capacity. There are other limitations. For example, the act does not cover a volunteer who causes harm to another person while driving a car or any other mode of transportation requiring a license or insurance to operate. In the same fashion, if the volunteer was doing a job requiring a legal license, certification, or authorization by authorities of the state in which harm took place, the volunteer would have to possess a valid license or certification at the time of the incident to receive coverage under the act. In addition, individual states may opt out of providing coverage under certain conditions, may require additional conditions of the organization for the act to apply, or may provide enhanced coverage. Conditions by states for coverage of volunteers may require nonprofit organizations to conduct certain volunteer training and carry certain insurance. But an organization may neglect to do so.

The act also covers only volunteers working for charitable and certain other nonprofit organizations recognized by the IRS under Sections 501(c)(3) and 501(c)(4) of the Tax Code. Organizations qualified as social clubs, sports clubs, or professional associations may also hold fundraisers where volunteers do work, but the act may not cover them. The act does not cover willful or criminal misconduct, gross negligence, crimes of violence, harm caused when the volunteer is under the influence of alcohol or drugs, reckless misconduct, situations in which the volunteer has violated federal or state law, or flagrant indifference to the rights or safety of others. These exceptions are important to consider, because a claim for liability may still be brought against a volunteer by alleging the volunteer's harmful actions were "gross" negligence or "flagrant" indifference, or that causing harm was not part of the volunteer's assigned duties. Finally, the act does not disqualify a nonprofit organization from making a legal claim for liability against one of its own volunteers for causing harm to the organization. The act provides no immunity to the organization for the actions of volunteers working on its behalf.

Protecting the Organization as a Whole

The nonprofit organization protects itself against the acts of volunteers, as well as its own staff and officers, by carrying comprehensive general liability insurance. Among other coverage, this should protect the organization against bodily injury, death,

and property damage claims. Coverage should extend to the organization's employees, officers, and volunteers.

Although the Volunteer Protection Act of 1997 provides some immunity to volunteers, there are so many qualifying conditions and exemptions that the most prudent way an organization can help protect itself and its volunteers against liability is to secure adequate insurance. But general policies may not normally cover liability of volunteers, so organizations that depend on volunteer help should always purchase additional coverage that extends to volunteers. This will also protect the organization in the circumstance of a volunteer acting in the course and scope of duties who is injured by someone else, such as an event attendee.

Auto liability insurance should be maintained that extends liability coverage to the nonprofit organization's own vehicles and vehicles of others while acting on behalf of the organization. Purchase host liquor liability coverage to protect against risk of liability from alcohol-related accidents. Directors' and officers' insurance should be part of any nonprofit organization's insurance portfolio, regardless of liability concerns related to fundraising events. Finally, make certain any insurance policies include in their coverage payment of the costs of legal defense.

Event Cancellation and Nonappearance Insurance

Severe weather, power outages at an event facility, celebrity entertainers or an auctioneer stranded on an airport runway, and many other catastrophes can turn what would have been a spectacular event into a dismal failure. In such circumstances, the financial health of an entire organization may be jeopardized. And it can happen in an instant. There is always a point in time when the host organization has incurred considerable expense but has yet to raise any revenue. It is the point at which the host organization is most vulnerable, most at risk. All host organizations arrive at this most frightening point, where the deficit spread between expense and revenue is greatest.

How does an organization reduce vulnerability and risk from such disastrous yet familiar circumstances? For organizations truly at risk of insolvency or where the financial consequences are truly significant, insurance is available to reduce risk of such incidents. This is generally called "event-cancellation insurance" or "nonappearance insurance." Cancellation insurance reimburses the host organization for quantifiable net loss if an event or an integral part of an event must be canceled or postponed due to causes generally beyond anyone's control. This provides coverage for lost revenue.

Policies include a list of covered causes and a list of exceptions, with coverage varying in price based on specific inclusions and exclusions. Example inclusions of event-cancellation policies are fire, earthquake, flood, hurricane, tornado, blizzard, lightning, and other natural and weather disasters that prevent a majority of attendees from reaching the event site or using it once they arrive. Also generally included are travel delays, equipment breakdown, power failure, and causes beyond anyone's control (where not excluded).

Generally excluded are financial failure that would include too few event tickets sold or lack of donations, war, civil revolution, riot, martial law, radioactive contamination, fraud, and nonappearance of individuals critical to the success of the event, unless nonappearance insurance is also purchased. Nonappearance policies come into play if an event's success depends on the appearance of a person, performer, musical group, author, speaker, or any other person or persons and they fail to appear. As with cancellation insurance, there are inclusions and exclusions. Acquisition of a nonappearance

policy may require a medical exam of the individual(s) subject to the policy; exclusions may include preexisting medical conditions, private aircraft travel, self-inflicted hazards, and contract disputes.

It's Serious

The previous sections describe risk, liability, and preventive measures that can be taken to reduce risk and liability. Many nonprofit organizations fail to fully consider risks, do no training, have no policies, have little or no insurance, and take no precautions of any nature to protect against risk—the staff, officers, and volunteers go about in a state of ignorance that could lead to ruin of the organization, their own lives and livelihoods, or others.

Risk management is all about reducing the risk of liability and the consequences of problems. There is no way to eliminate the risk of liability or control all risks. But nonprofit organizations can take a variety of actions to identify and control known risks as well as take steps to avert unknown risks that could create liability for the host organization, its staff, and volunteers. Nonprofit organization leadership that takes no precautions invites devastating consequences, perhaps bankrupting an organization, a staff person, officer, or volunteer. Consider the unthinkable consequences of a person injured in a horrible fashion by the action or inaction of staff or volunteers of an organization, and because the organization or person causing the injury has no assets or insurance, that victim has no means of recovering his or her own loss.

21

Tax Matters

We had been advised by our financial audit firm to get a legal opinion. There was growing concern that some of our fundraising activities might be a better fit for an organization recognized by the Internal Revenue Service (IRS) under a different section of the Tax Code. Not much had changed about the way the organization raised funds, except the scale of fundraising had grown immensely. Fundraising through auctions and consumer trade shows by the parent organization and its chapters provided the base of funds. The organization's original filing for recognition as a charitable organization initially received a rough reception from the IRS. The IRS ultimately agreed to recognize the organization as charitable under Section 501(c)(3) of the IRS Code, which allowed contributors to the organization to receive tax advantages, but a record of concern had been established.

As the organization grew, so did the scale of fundraising and activities that had been of original concern to the IRS. So did the scale of other kinds of fundraising and activities that unmistakably fit with the IRS's definition of a charitable organization. We were at a point at which an unfavorable decision by the IRS about the activities of concern could challenge the charitable status of all the organization's activities since everything the organization did was through a single legal entity.

Earlier I had worked for an organization with an affiliated network of several thousand organizations. We regularly advised our statewide affiliates to split their organizations into two separate legal nonprofit entities to ensure against problems with the IRS. In general these organizations were split between a "charitable entity" so funds could be raised for truly charitable work and allow contributors to take tax deductions, and a "social advocacy entity" so funds could be raised to lobby for improving environmental laws. Social advocacy organizations are recognized by the IRS under Section 501(c)(4) of the IRS Code and face fewer restrictions on lobbying than charitable organizations. Contributions to such organizations are not tax deductible.

So it was familiar ground to me when tax advisers suggested splitting my current employer's organization into two separate entities. We set the stage for splitting the organization. The president and past president of the board were strong supporters of the move. Both were attorneys and played a key role convincing the other 235 or so members of the board that creating two organizations out of one was necessary to protect the whole organization.

Ultimately three legal entities formed the base of operations for the membership, each with advantages of interest to members. One was a charitable organization called the "foundation" that managed the organization's natural history museum, education outreach, humanitarian services, conservation work, and science. That organization accepted tax-deductible donations and could apply for foundation grants and contracts. Another was a social advocacy organization that conducted lobby work and managed the annual fundraising convention, trade show, and auction events. Contributions were not tax deductible. A third organization was an already-existing political action committee that was now attached to the social advocacy entity. This allowed members to lobby through nondeductible political contributions.

Members now had three ways to give and support the organization in three areas of work they felt important. Each entity went about its business in a fashion unquestionably consistent with IRS rules. The organization benefited from increased giving and became much more effective in its work, as each entity could now focus on its legally defined missions without reservation about running afoul of IRS rules.

A HOST ORGANIZATION for a fundraising event is ordinarily a nonprofit group, incorporated as such in a state and qualified by the IRS under one of the sev-

eral sections of IRS Code covering nonprofit "tax-exempt" organizations. For nonprofit organizations chartered and qualified under Section 501(c)(3) of the Code, certain contributions or portions of contributions may proffer tax advantages to contributors. Such organizations are commonly referred to as "charitable" organizations, because the mission of the organization qualifies as a charitable cause. Money given to such organizations is commonly referred to as a "tax-deductible contribution," although personal tax status and form of donation determine the extent to which a donation may be tax deductible.

Nonprofit organizations recognized under other sections of the IRS nonprofit Code may not be qualified to provide tax deductions for gifts. Such organizations may still hold fundraising events, and money raised may go to a worthy cause. Contributions can even go to causes usually associated with charitable giving, such as for animal welfare or medical research, yet provide the donor with no deduction if the organization receiving the contribution is not qualified by the IRS as a charitable organization. It is the status of the receiving organization that determines whether a contribution is or is not tax deductible.

A group not formally incorporated in any fashion may also hold a fundraiser. An example of this is a youth sports team raising money for uniforms and equipment. Donations at the team's fundraiser would not be tax deductible.

In addition, only certain kinds of donations or portions of donations made to an organization at a fundraising event are tax deductible, even if the organization is recognized as a charitable organization. In general, a donation is tax deductible only when, and to the extent, no items or services of value are received in return. Unfortunately, there is considerable misunderstanding about the tax deductibility of giving and charitable events. Some of this confusion may even be perpetuated by host organizations that mistakenly or even purposefully misinform donors about receiving tax benefits for their donations or "purchases" at auctions.

WARNING AND DISCLAIMER: *This section of the book provides information about potential tax benefits, and misconceptions about such benefits, associated with donations or participation in charity fundraising events. This book is not a legal or tax advice text, does not provide legal or tax advice, and is not a substitute for legal or tax advice or professional counsel on matters of tax law. Event planners should seek legal or other professional advice where appropriate. While efforts have been made to ensure the accuracy of information presented, laws and tax rulings may change over time. The author takes no responsibility for any errors or outdated materials and assumes no responsibility for any actions by anyone as a consequence of reading this book, including the actions of anyone who takes action in disregard of this paragraph of warning and disclaimer.*

Tax-Deductible Contributions

Despite the carefully worded hype in advance of and during auction events by host organization representatives, charity auction events offer rather limited tax advantages to donors and buyers of auction items. There is widespread belief that charity auctions are, simply put, "tax deductible." It is not that simple. Donors of auction merchandise often (maybe almost always) believe they can claim a charitable tax deduction for the full amount of the market price of the contributed item. Winning bidders often believe they can claim a tax deduction for the full amount they pay for auction items won. Neither belief is correct.

Although it is understandable that donors and winning bidders may not understand the rules governing tax deductibility of donations and auction-item purchases, it is less understandable when a host organization's leadership fails to understand their responsibilities for informing donors and auction-item buyers about tax matters. Donors and buyers need to rely on their tax consultants to provide relevant advice, but host organizations have legally defined obligations to inform donors and buyers about the potential deductibility of contributions.

The following sections provide an overview of tax matters affecting charity auction events and the people who donate at, participate in, and plan them.

This is an overview only, covering the most typical situations encountered at auction events. In particular, if donations involve gifts of land, appreciated properties, stocks, or high-value items, there are various limitations on tax deductibility that are best explained by tax advisers. This book does not address complicated tax issues. Actual questions about tax implications of giving to charitable organizations should be discussed with personal tax advisers.

The Host Organization's Responsibilities

According to IRS rules, charitable organizations must provide a written disclosure statement to donors of any quid pro quo contributions in excess of $75 (in 2011). A quid pro quo contribution is defined as a "payment made to a charity by a donor partly as a contribution and partly for goods or services provided to the donor by the charity."

If a winning bidder pays $100 for an auction item having a fair market value of $30, the winning bidder has made a quid pro quo contribution, of which the charitable portion of the payment is $70 and the cost of goods or services received is $30 (see "Fair Market Value"). Even though the charitable donation part of the payment did not exceed $75, a disclosure statement is required because the winning bidder's total payment of $100 is considered a quid pro quo contribution that exceeds $75.

The host organization must provide a written disclosure statement to the winning bidder that includes the following information:

- A statement that the amount of the contribution deductible for federal income tax purposes is limited to the amount of money paid by the winning bidder above the fair market value of goods or services received for the payment
- A good-faith estimate based on fair market value of the value of the goods or services that the winning bidder purchased

The charity must provide such statements with the solicitation of goods or services and on receipts for items bought at auction. Whenever a charity receives a quid pro quo contribution in excess of $75, it must provide a receipt that includes a disclosure statement as described. This requirement goes beyond just informing winners of the fair market value of auction items won. Any donor to an event who will receive any goods or services in return for any contribution must receive notice of the good-faith estimate of the value of those goods or services to be received.

Solicitation of Cash, Merchandise, and Services

It is particularly important to provide this information when the host organization is soliciting cash from donors to sponsor or underwrite portions of the event, and when the host organization is soliciting merchandise and service items for auction and as prizes for raffles and games. If these donors are being offered goods or services that are not insubstantial in return for such donations, the host organization is required to provide a disclosure statement to the donor (see "Insubstantial Value").

For example, if a sponsor donates $1,000 in cash to help underwrite the event and in return is to receive recognition during the event through oral announcements and advertising in the auction program along with all other sponsors, the good-faith estimate of these advertising services will be of insubstantial value and will not affect tax deductibility. In this case no disclosure is required because there is no quid pro quo donation. But if that same sponsor donating $1,000 is to be given a table and dinner service for 12 at the event in return for the donation, any tax deduction for the sponsor would be reduced by the value of the 12 meals. Thus, if each meal had a fair market value of $25, the sponsor would be limited to a maximum tax deduction of $700 (12 diners × $25/plate = $300, subtracted from $1,000 sponsor donation).

The host organization is required to disclose to the donor the fair market value of these goods and services to be received in return for the donation and that this may affect the tax deductibility of the donation. The same evaluation would apply to the donor of merchandise. If the host organization is offering an incentive for making a donation, such as a commercially sold book valued at $35, then the prospective donor must be told the value of the book and that the portion of the contribution that is deductible will be limited to the allowable value of the donation above the fair market value of the book ($35) the donor will receive in return for the donation.

If the disclosure statement is furnished in connection with soliciting sponsorships, underwriting, goods, and services, it is not necessary to provide another statement to the solicited donors when the contribution is actually received by the charity (see "Auction-Item Donors").

AT THE AUCTION

A good-faith estimate of the fair market value of each item should be provided to or displayed to bidders. For live auction items, this can be done by listing the fair market values for each item in a printed auction program given to all bidders or by displaying and announcing the fair market value as the item is auctioned off. For silent auction items, a good-faith estimate of the fair market value of each item should be listed directly on the bid sheet. An alternative is to place a placard with the item during bidding that lists the fair market value. See figure 16.1 for an example silent auction bid sheet.

PURCHASE RECEIPT REQUIRED

At the time successful bidders at an auction pay for an item, the organization must provide a receipt listing the fair market value of the item. This receipt must also include the amount actually paid for the item, a description of the item (goods or services purchased), the name of the organization, and a statement that the organization provided no additional goods or services in return for the charitable portion (if any) of the contribution. There is no IRS form or particular format that must be used to provide this information. See figure 15.2 for an example auction-item receipt.

Fair Market Value

IRS rules require charitable organizations to provide bidders with a good-faith estimate of the fair market value of goods or services to be auctioned prior to or at the time of bidding. Fair market value is defined as "the amount of money a person would pay for the goods or services on the open market." This information must also be provided on winning bidders' receipts for any quid pro quo contributions. The host organization is burdened with providing this information, and sometimes it can be challenging to obtain.

For goods or services donated by individuals or corporations for auction (sale) at an event, the host organization should require the donor of the item to provide an estimate of the item's fair market value. This estimate may be fully adequate, but some donors may inflate the value of the donated item, or, for unique items such as artwork or items that are no longer commercially available, donors may not know the fair market value. Although donors of goods or services to a charity must make an accurate determination of the fair market value of the donation for determining their own taxes, there are no requirements for disclosure of this value to the receiving organization. There are no sanctions for the donor who inflates value or simply does not know the value of an item at the time of donation. Regardless, the auction host organization has the burden of determining or verifying fair market value and must make a good-faith effort to do so.

The IRS defines a good-faith estimate as "any reasonable method to estimate the fair market value of goods or services . . . as long as it applies the method in good faith." Here are a few examples of good-faith efforts to determine fair market value:

- For items readily available for purchase, current retail prices can be obtained by looking in stores, using catalogs, or making an Internet search for the list price of the item.
- For items that may no longer be available for sale, it is acceptable to use prices for similar items currently available for sale.
- For goods or services not commercially available, an estimate can be made by determining the value of goods or services that are similar or comparable even if they do not have the unique qualities of the goods or services being valued. An example would be a fly-fishing trip guided by the organization's president, who is not a professional fishing guide. Fair market value could be determined as the value of a fly-fishing trip in the same general location if booked with a professional fishing guide.
- For unique services that have highly variable prices, such as a dinner cooked at the highest bidder's own home by a local chef, it may be possible to find the price of comparable services, or an expert can be consulted for an estimate. For example, an expert may be a local chef. The chef's opinion about the value may vary considerably from the value declared by the donor, but at least the host organization can document a reasonable attempt to obtain a fair market value appropriate for the locality.
- For expensive items that do not have set prices, such as works of art, it may be necessary to obtain the services of a qualified appraiser.

Efforts to obtain the value for each item must be documented to help protect the host organization against risk of liability over the determination. If a donated item has a value greater than $5,000, charitable deductions for the donor require an appraisal supplied by the donor, but since the donor need not provide verified values to the charitable organization, it remains up to the host organization to use good-faith efforts to determine value of high-priced items.

Insubstantial Value

The host organization does not need to provide a disclosure statement if the goods or services given to a donor have insubstantial value. The IRS considers goods and services to be insubstantial if a donor's payment occurs in the context of fundraising where the charitable organization informs the donor of the amount of the contribution that is deductible, and where

- the fair market value of all benefits received in connection with the payment is not more than 2% of the payment, or $97 (in 2011), whichever is less, or

• the payment is at least $48.50 (in 2011; this amount may be adjusted for inflation), and the only benefits received in connection with the payment are token items, such as bookmarks, calendars, key chains, mugs, posters, and T-shirts, that bear the organization's name or logo. The cost (as opposed to fair market value) of all benefits received by a donor in total must be within IRS limits established for "low-cost articles," which was $9.70 for the 2011 tax year.

For current limits, event planners should consult tax or legal advisers or contact IRS Exempt Organizations Customer Account Services for annual inflation adjustment information.

Newspapers, program guides, and other noncommercial low-cost items generally distributed free by the organization to attendees at events are considered to have no measurable fair market value. According to the IRS, if a host organization is providing only insubstantial benefits in return for a payment, such as purchase of an admission ticket, any materials should include a statement similar to this one: "Under Internal Revenue Service guidelines the estimated value of the benefits received is not substantial; therefore, the full amount of payment is a deductible contribution."

Penalty for Noncompliance

A penalty may be imposed on a host organization that does not make the required disclosure in connection with a quid pro quo contribution of more than $75. The penalty is $10 per contribution and is capped at $5,000 per event. The penalty may be avoided if the organization can demonstrate that the failure to provide disclosure was due to reasonable cause. In addition, if the host organization provides a donor an incorrect receipt that leads to the filing of a fraudulent tax return, the charity may be fined up to $1,000 (or more for some types of goods) depending on the amount of error.

General Attendees and Price of Admission

Attendees often believe the ticket price to charitable events is a tax-deductible donation, even if they do not participate in auctions or other fundraising activities. They may or may not be correct. If price of event admission is more than $75, the event host has an obligation to inform the ticket buyer that the admission price is tax deductible only to the extent the price exceeds the fair market value of the goods and services received in return for purchasing the ticket. For example, if the ticket costs $80 and admission to the event includes a $25 dinner, then only $55 of the ticket price is deductible. Thus, the disclosure statement on the ticket could read, for example, "Ticket price is $80, of which $55 is tax deductible." As noted previously, if the attendee will receive only insubstantial benefits in return for buying the admission ticket, the statement on the ticket should read, for example, "Under Internal Revenue Service guidelines the estimated value of the benefits received is not substantial; therefore, the full amount of payment is a deductible contribution."

Sponsored Goods and Services

Event attendees often receive "free" goods or services underwritten by event sponsors, such as the cost of all or part of dinner service. A sponsor can donate a special gift for attendees; for example, all ticket buyers could receive a special leather-bound limited-edition book of photographs of Yellowstone National Park. These underwritten items, although given to attendees at "no cost" to the host organization, qualify as goods and services received by the ticket buyer. Any charitable deduction would need to be reduced by the fair market value of the "free" items or services received.

The disclosure statement on the ticket would need to reflect the fair market value of goods and services received. If ticket buyers received an underwritten dinner and book, the true cost of the meal and retail price of the book would have to be accounted for in the disclosure statement. For example, if the price of the ticket was $80, the dinner

$25, and book $75, then the ticket buyer would receive no tax deduction. The disclosure statement on the ticket could read: "Ticket price is $80, of which $0 is tax deductible." To make it even simpler, the statement could read: "Price of admission to this event is not tax deductible."

Raffle Ticket Buyers

No tax deduction is available for purchase of raffle tickets because the cost of a chance to win is considered the price paid for the tickets. The quid pro quo for raffle tickets is the cost of the ticket. Of course, the "cost of a chance" varies greatly and is set by the organization holding the raffle, but the price has no bearing on deductibility.

Winning Bidders

The IRS allows donors who purchase items at a charity auction to claim a charitable tax deduction for the amount of the purchase price paid for an item over its fair market value. For example, if the winning bid is $80 for an auction item having a fair market value of $50, the tax-deductible portion of the amount paid for the item is $30. That the auction item itself may have been donated fully to the host organization is not relevant. Only the fair market value of the goods or services received by the buyer factor into the valuation of tax deductibility.

Receiving a tax deduction also requires donors to somehow demonstrate that they knew in advance of bidding that the value of the item was less than the amount they paid. The host organization must help event attendees meet this requirement, so it is important for organizations to comply with IRS rules requiring display of fair market values to bidders in advance of and/or during silent and live auction bidding. The IRS rules place a burden on the buyer to prove there was intent to make a charitable contribution if a tax deduction is claimed for the payment. In the absence of proof of such intent, where a transaction involves payment for purchase of an item of value, the IRS presumes that the transaction is not a gift made for charitable contribution purposes. Instead, payment is considered equal to the purchase price and not a gift for charitable purposes.

Ways to ensure adequate display of fair market values to bidders have been discussed earlier. Since values will be clearly displayed to donors and since donors have no reason to doubt the accuracy of values displayed by the host organization, the donor easily meets the IRS requirement of having prior knowledge. Should a winning bidder pay more than the fair market values displayed, the difference between the amount paid and the published value should constitute a justifiable tax-deductible contribution. The host organization must provide auction-item buyers a receipt that discloses the price paid and fair market value of the item.

Auction-Item Donors

Auction events are often dependent on donation of items or services usable for raffles, game prizes, and live and silent auctions. The most commonly donated items are general merchandise and services. Donations can come from individuals or from businesses, many of whom mistakenly believe the fair market value or appreciated value of their donations is tax deductible. That may not be the case, but it is correct that donations will provide for some amount of charitable deduction, the exact nature of which is subject to a number of rules that hinge on the nature of the donation.

Following are a few of the more common kinds of donations made to organizations hosting charity fundraising events for use in auctions or prizes. Other types of donations to charitable organizations may provide tax advantages to donors, but these are less commonly donated as gifts or prizes for charity fundraising events and are not covered in this book. If other types of gifts are considered, please consult a tax adviser.

Merchant's Inventory

Merchandise from merchants and businesses may be the most common items received during solicitations for donations to be used as prizes and in auctions. These are items usually sold in stores to customers. In almost every case the amount of deduction allowed is equal only to the cost of the item to the donor, regardless of the list price or current fair market value. A general rule governing tax deductibility of donations is that if a donor contributes tangible personal property to a charity that is put to an "unrelated use," then the donor's contribution is limited to the donor's cost basis in the contributed item. Tax basis here is the amount the donor originally paid for the item. The term "unrelated use" refers to a use that is unrelated to the charity's exempt purposes or function. The sale of items by a charitable organization at auction events is always considered unrelated, even if the sale raises money for the charity to use in its mission.

Business Services

Donation of services for auction or prize use is generally not deductible for the donor. The IRS considers the gift of a business service to be "lost income," which is not a deductible item. An example of a service is an accountant donating two hours of time to advise a winning bidder how to better manage a home budget. Another example of a nondeductible donated service is free ad space in a newspaper or airtime on TV gifted to a charitable organization to announce a fundraising event.

Donations from Individuals

As for businesses, gifts of services from an individual are not tax deductible. An example of such a gift is the president of the host organization donating personal services as a river guide for a half-day canoe trip. The president would receive no deduction for this donation.

Donations of real property from individuals may qualify for a deduction but are subject to a variety of rules. If an individual donates an item for auction, such as a vintage book on natural history, the donor's charitable deduction is limited to the donor's basis in the item, the amount paid for the item, even if it has greatly appreciated in value. This limitation in deductibility applies because the do-

nated item will be sold at auction, making the donation unrelated to the charity's tax-exempt purpose. This point is often confusing to donors, because that same item donated to the same charitable organization for use in a related purpose would ordinarily provide the donor a tax deduction for the current fair market value. This value would be much greater than the donor's basis. A related purpose would be, for example, a charitable land conservation organization being gifted the book for use in the organization's natural history library.

Donation of use of an individual's property for a period, such as a weekend stay for four at the donor's fishing lodge, is not deductible. This is not a gift of the property. It is simply a limited right to use the property. Such gifts are not ordinarily deductible because they are considered a partial-interest gift, and generally the IRS does not allow deduction of a contribution of less than the donor's entire interest in a property or item. Deductible gifts are usually transfers of an entire asset. If partial-interest donations were deductible, donors could take multiple deductions that could exceed any actual value transferred; thus, specific requirements limit deductibility of partial-interest gifts.

Donor Responsibilities

To be deductible, a donation must be a gift that meets the following conditions:

- The donor must give the item as a contribution or gift for use by the event host organization.
- The gift must be voluntarily given without compensation, goods, services, or benefits received greater than the value of the gift.
- Any goods or services received by the donor in return for the donation reduce the charitable portion of the donation by the value of the goods and services received.

The donor of items used as prizes or auction items for an event is responsible for determining the fair market value of donated items in order to substantiate tax deductions. The donor, not the charitable organization, has the burden of proving to the

IRS how the fair market value of donated items was determined. For a donor to claim a contribution of more than $5,000 for an item, the donor must obtain an appraisal from a qualified appraiser. To claim a deduction for paintings, antiques, or works of art valued at more than $20,000, the donor is required to attach a copy of a signed appraisal to his or her tax return. The charitable organization has no role in determining such values for tax purposes of the donor.

Donors must also meet certain requirements to substantiate donations of cash, property, goods, or services valued at more than $250. According to the IRS, a donor cannot claim a tax deduction for any single contribution of $250 or more unless the donor obtains a written acknowledgment of the contribution from the recipient organization. The recipient organization is not actually required to acknowledge a contribution unless the donation qualifies as a quid pro quo donation, but without a written acknowledgment the donor will be unable to claim a tax deduction. Thus, the event host organization helps a donor meet this requirement by providing a timely written acknowledgment of any gifts. This statement should include the following information:

- The name of organization
- The amount of any cash contribution or a description (but not the value) of items donated or other noncash contributions
- A statement indicating whether any goods or services were provided in return for the gift
- A description and good-faith estimate of the value of goods or services, if any, that the charitable organization provided in return for the contribution (quid pro quo donation)

Notice that the host organization is not required to provide an estimate of fair market value of the item in the acknowledgment because it is the donor's responsibility to determine the fair market value of the gift for the donor's own tax purposes. See figure 13.1 for an example donor-acknowledgment letter.

Sales Tax

Raffle- and auction-item payments at a charity fundraising event are entirely or partially purchases that may be subject to state or local sales tax, depending on state and local laws. Sales tax may apply to the entire amount paid for an item or service or apply only to the fair market value portion of a payment. Sales tax may be applied to only some kinds of items or services. Event planners must consult with local tax advisers or taxing authorities to determine applicable requirements. If sales tax applies, it must be collected and listed on receipts provided to winning bidders and receipts for other applicable transactions.

Tax-Advantaged Volunteering

Volunteers working on events for charitable organizations may be eligible for tax advantages if they incur unreimbursed expenses. For example, unreimbursed car expenses may be tax deductible. Filing for such deductions requires the "donor" to maintain written records of the expense or mileage driven for the charitable organization in the course of volunteering. Records must include date(s) driven, mileage or expenses, and name of the organization. Other travel expenses may also be deductible, as may be unreimbursed cash expenses for items purchased for use at an event or required during event planning.

In general, any unreimbursed expense directly connected with an event or required in the course of working on an event may be deductible, except for personal, living, or family expenses. The volunteer must retain receipts or other records proving amounts spent, and thus "donated" in the course of planning or managing an event. The nonprofit organization should provide a standard acknowledgment letter to the volunteer, stating services provided, the value of the expenses donated, and a declaration that nothing of value was received by the volunteer in return for the donation. No tax deduction is allowable for any time or services performed by the volunteer, including any additional expenses incurred to make his or her time available for volunteering, such as child-care expenses.

22

Ethics and Security

We suspected something was wrong. Thousands of dollar bills—cash paid for entry and parking—were seen changing hands. It's easy for workers handling small bills to pocket a few, and it happens all the time at events where workers, such as parking attendants, are hired locally to provide services. But even pocketing thousands of dollars in cash couldn't explain the poor performance of the event. Tens of thousands of dollars were raised through the sale of exhibit booth space. There were raffles. Virtually the entire workforce, including parking and gate attendants, was volunteer labor.

Why then, did the paid executive director of the organization report so little net income each year from the nonprofit sports show that was the organization's primary annual fundraiser? There were rumors the executive director was burying cash in "coffee cans" in the woods behind his house, but nothing was proven. Instances of organizers siphoning cash off event income are rare, but there are the stories.

After a contentious political and legal battle, executive control of the organization changed hands. The following year's sports show fundraiser—nearly identical to those held earlier—yielded net revenue of almost $100,000, an astonishing increase over previous years. Nothing was proven by the huge upswing in revenue, but an unspoken point about suspected fraud by the old administration was made by the new one.

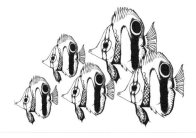

YES, THERE MAY BE crooks among us. As pure and wholesome as most charitable fundraising events are, interest by people with criminal intent must be assumed lurking wherever large amounts of money change hands or valuable merchandise is placed on open display. The advertising that often precedes a major fundraising banquet almost assures there will be advance notice to any criminals looking for a job. The loose security at most charity fundraisers make events an easy mark for the well-informed petty thief. Large amounts of cash in small denominations changing hands, and an almost complete lack of immediate accounting for cash collections, also make fundraisers attractive and vulnerable to thieves, including ones the host organization may inadvertently hire or take on as volunteers. Areas of particular vulnerability include any point where cash is collected in small bills, such as where lot attendants collect parking fees, where attendees register, where cash is collected at raffle and arcade booths, and where roving workers sell raffle tickets.

Although it is not desirable, or perhaps even possible, to avoid collection of cash, it is possible to exert some control over how cash is handled and provide for a reasonably rapid accounting system. There are several ways to reduce the potential for theft. Obviously, the most effective means to avert theft is to have only totally honest and disciplined people handling cash. This is certainly a goal, but it may be impossible to know if people handling cash are honest, even if these people are all member-volunteers of the organization. There are far too many instances of theft by members, and even officers, of charitable organizations to take for granted that all members of the organization are trustworthy. It is unfortunate, but necessary, that event planners ensure that appropriate financial controls are in place before, during, and after the event; security plans are developed; and planned security measures are taken seriously.

Deterring Thieves

Although there may be no sure-fire ways to thwart the most determined and innovative thieves, steps can be taken to make it more difficult for a thief to succeed. There are also ways to put would-be thieves on notice that security measures are in place and working. The best form of protection is to implement policies and procedures that deter would-be thieves from attempting thievery. Perhaps the best form of protection is to demand that event workers use common sense when handling cash. Tell workers to take the same or greater care to ensure against theft as they would with their personal money and valuables. They need to lock doors, not leave cash unattended and in sight, and not carry large amounts of money. Besides cash, auction merchandise is valuable and may be sought by thieves. Again, event workers need to be told to use common sense. Keep all merchandise in locked areas or maintain a security presence when merchandise is in open rooms. Sidebar 22.1 lists ways to reduce the risk of theft.

Accounting systems and procedures need to be designed, tested until workable, put in place, and used to reduce the risk of theft. This includes hiring or selection of workers at an event. Particular caution needs to be exercised if organizers do not know the workers handling money or workers are inexperienced. Sometimes volunteers are solicited from schools or through community-wide notices. Many organizations hire salespeople for a set fee or pay them a percentage of sales. Event planners often hire local people who may have no experience and may be friends or acquaintances of organization members or of the event planners themselves. Without strict controls and training of sellers or cashiers, it is very easy for money handlers to either steal or ineptly handle money, in either case adversely affecting event revenue. Where raffle ticket sellers or cashiers are hired from companies specializing in such services, bonding, company reputation, and other forms of assurance greatly reduce risk of theft or incompetency.

Donors at auctions and fundraising events notice the care with which their money is handled, especially where cash is used. If they suspect cash is being handled carelessly, they may not say anything, but it can greatly affect their willingness to spend money on games and buy various tickets. Event organizers must be alert to the consequences of the appearance of careless handling of money to avert

Sidebar 22.1. Fifteen Ways to Stop a Thief

1. Use common sense! Event workers should use the same safeguards as if cash and merchandise were personal, hard-earned money.

2. Use a lock box or safe to hold cash. The box should be locked and placed out of sight when unattended.

3. Designate an event "banker/accountant" who is responsible for countersigning all cash receipts and deposit forms.

4. Maintain a separate checking account for money used during the course of the event. Require two signatures on checks, for deposits, and for all other transactions.

5. Require people who handle cash, such as sellers of raffle tickets, to sign cash-receipt forms for any cash they receive, such as dollar bills for making change, and sign cash-deposit forms when they hand over cash collected. This is particularly important if people collecting cash are working for pay on a commission basis.

6. Require all volunteers and people hired to work at an event to sign forms that include their name, address, and Social Security number. People unknown to the organization should be required to show a form of identification, such as a driver's license, which should be inspected and copied (for records) to ensure the information on the identification document matches that given by the person.

7. Accept credit cards to reduce use of cash. Ticket sellers can take a credit card and have it processed. Have "credit card runners" on standby whose job is to rapidly move credit cards between attendees and workers who are processing the cards. This allows rapid credit card processing from anywhere on the event floor. Caution must be used to ensure no inappropriate use of cards.

8. Use a money-substitute system to reduce points of cash use to a minimum. Event attendees use cash, credit cards, or checks to purchase money substitutes, such as promissory notes, chips, chits, or tickets, at one or more central locations. Attendees then use the substitute money for playing games of chance and skill, for snacks and drinks, and for other low-cost items. Thus, only a few people handle cash.

9. Control the conditions under which handlers of cash may leave their work sites with cash in hand. Make available volunteer "relief" workers.

10. Require that two people always be present and working together at the accounting booth where event proceeds are collected. Workers there should not be members of the same family (it is less likely for two or more unrelated people to be implicated in theft than members of a close-knit group).

11. Have a reliable person serve as a "runner" collecting cash on a regular basis from booths, ticket sellers, and others receiving small amounts of cash. The runner then transfers cash to the main accounting booth. Cash should be counted upon collection, receipts issued, and records kept.

12. Use reputable, bonded agencies if hiring service agency workers who will handle cash.

13. Assign a reliable staff person or volunteer to observe cash collections.

14. Establish and use security measures.

15. Adapt these general suggestions to meet individual situations.

---

potential loss of donations. Simple things, like keeping bills in the open during speed raffles or allowing placement of cash only in clearly marked pouches or aprons, give donors confidence that their money is being handled with care. Demand that money collectors never place cash directly into their pockets or into what appear to be personal wallets or pocketbooks. Cash should never be handled in a way that makes it appear "pocketed."

Keeping Order

I have seen tables knocked over, people sprawled on the floor, and an executive director of an organization held at bay by a woman screaming obscenities in his face because she had not won a coveted raffle prize. These are only some of the possibilities when people risk money on valuable prizes while drinking unlimited amounts of alcohol. Alcohol has been at the root of every major instance of disorderliness I have witnessed. People can become disruptive and hostile for many reasons, and alcohol is probably the biggest reason of all. An otherwise well-run auction event can be momentarily or totally disrupted by an incident of disorderly conduct by an attendee.

Security needs to be alert to signs of trouble. Sometimes it is obvious that trouble is on the way. This can be seen when a person is becoming progressively obnoxious due to intoxication. Not everyone reacts the same way to intoxication, and the

Sidebar 22.2. Three Levels of Threat and Hostility

1. *Nonviolent.* Protest marches and pickets are a nuisance, but such actions are usually nothing more than an attempt to use the gala event as a convenient platform to advertise a cause in opposition to the host organization's. Protesters with signs may picket the entrance to an event or stage their protest along the public roadway leading to the event location. Sometimes protesters may attempt to enter the event. In some instances, the protest may take place in a separate location, staged as a "counterevent" to attract media attention.

2. *Malevolent.* This kind of threat is not generally planned to harm people, although intentional damage to property can be an objective, and people may be harmed unintentionally. At this level of hostility, perpetrators may attempt to destroy or damage auction merchandise. Other means to create damage include setting off fire alarms, making false bomb threats, writing graffiti, and setting off smoke or stink bombs. Malevolent attacks can take place before or during the event; thus, deterrence may include keeping auction and raffle merchandise and decorations in secure locations prior to the event's opening. Security guards at the event location should be on alert a day or so before the event takes place.

3. *Violent.* This is pure criminal activity that can rapidly cause harm to people and property. Although this is the most difficult form of hostility to anticipate and deter, it is also the threat that must be taken most seriously. Implements used in this form of hostility include bombs, fire, and guns.

Handling a Planned Attack

At an elegant fundraising event held in the north in winter, many of the men arrived in tuxedos and the women wore gowns, and some wore fur. Fur garments had only recently regained desirability after years of being the target of animal rights activists. If an attendee hadn't worn a fur coat or stole to the event, she certainly had opportunity to wear one home, because among live and silent auction items were wearables made of fox, mink, coyote, and leather.

The event took place in a meeting hall on a university campus. Even so, the jeans-clad person who appeared at the event looked out of place to an alert security guard. The guard, who was an off-duty policeman, approached the young man. As the distance closed between the two, the young man fled from the hall through an emergency exit. As he ran, cans of red spray paint fell from his pockets and scattered to the ground.

Splashing blood on and spraying furs with red paint are among forms of intimidation and hostility that extremist members of some animal rights advocacy organizations may wage against people who wear leather or fur. If not for the alert security guard, there is no doubt that some of the expensive furs and leathers on display or worn by women attending the event would have taken on a distinctly blood-red appearance.

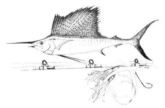

change from normal to disorderly behavior may take only a split second in which an action or words between individuals set a person off. Security is there to deter disorderly conduct and bring trouble to a swift end. There is just no way to predict how far a security matter will escalate. Sometimes hostilities are planned attacks of varied threat levels as described in sidebar 22.2. Most of the time problems just erupt. Keeping order and responding to an unpredictable threat are other important reasons for procuring professional paid security.

If security is left to a member-volunteer who is not an enforcement professional, he or she could easily get into a scuffle with a disorderly person, especially where alcohol is involved. In such instances, one or more people could be injured. Particularly in small organizations, people involved in such an incident could be friends.

ONE PERSON'S CHARITABLE cause may be another's call to arms. Members and supporters involved in nonprofit social advocacy organizations are usually focused on advocating a particular cause. Tactics used in advocacy and promotion of a cause vary by organization, but positions taken by an organization on controversial issues can create opportunity for confrontation.

Issues such as human reproduction, land use, guns, drug use, animal rights, immigration, global warming, and so on are inherently controversial. Advocates of these causes can become zealots, and some become militant. Members of nonprofit social advocacy organizations and anyone who attends a fundraising event for an advocacy organization can suddenly find themselves at the center of a storm of hostility and subjected to acts of terrorism. Event organizers must give consideration to providing adequate security at an event. For organizations with particularly controversial missions, a risk-management plan for fundraising events should be in place and followed to reduce the risk of liability to the organization and harm to attendees from actions of the organization's critics.

Deterrence

Any large event, such as an auction fundraiser, can offer an attractive opportunity for anyone opposed to an organization's mission to stage a protest. After all, many events are well advertised, and the advocacy mission of the organization is often equally well advertised in the publicity surrounding a well-marketed event. Extremists seeking to make a statement, cause harm, and garner press attention may see a fundraising event as the perfect time and place for an act of terrorism. When this happens, it is more than a simple political statement; it is a direct attack on the organization holding the fundraiser and its members. Attendees are intimidated, and contributors are subjected to unwanted publicity. People with extremist views are a fact of life. People are entitled to hold opinions, but extremists with hostile intentions may take action in ways that are not easily anticipated or thwarted. As it was with the activist who appeared intent on disrupting the auction featuring fine furs, an enemy of an event host organization may appear out of nowhere with no warning.

Security Services

Security takes many forms, but if an organization is among the many with missions not universally accepted, security guards must be informed accordingly. The greater the threat, the greater the need to provide security guards with details. Although

security services exist to prevent unwanted intruders from committing unwanted acts, guards will be better prepared if they understand the nature of threats. An alert security force can't guarantee that a fundraiser will be a success, but it could avert an unwanted intruder from making it a failure.

To address security needs, event planners may contract with a security service or hire off-duty police officers. In either case, security services should be handled by uniformed professionals on a paid, not volunteer, basis. Professional uniformed security guards and off-duty police provide a professional and highly visible deterrence to hostilities at events. This alone may be enough to deter would-be thieves, terrorists, or vandals. Contracting for security provides assurance of having a professional-level response and a demonstrated effort by the host organization to reduce risk to attendees. In the event something does happen and security guards must take action or there is harm to people or property, potential liability to the host organization is lessened, because the host was diligent in obtaining trained professional security guards.

EVENT-FACILITY SECURITY SERVICES

Event facilities usually provide security services, either as part of the facility rental contract or as an additional service. When the host organization uses such services, liability for providing adequate and competent security services shifts to the manager of the event facility. Event planners have a duty to let facility managers know if the organization or event might be attractive to protesters, thieves, or people who may cause trouble. Providing advance notice of potential security problems will allow facility managers to warn security personnel, employ additional security workers, and place authorities on alert. Taking such precautions should be part of an organization's risk-management plan and a matter of course in planning an event.

Often a contract with an event facility will include a clause that allows facility management to remove or prohibit persons from the facility at management's discretion. The purpose of this clause is to allow the facility's security personnel to quickly deal with people who are threatening, disruptive, destructive, or in some other way undesirable. Although this may sound like a reasonable provision, consider that the provision allows facility management to remove attendees, including the host organization's own staff, officers, volunteers, and even important donors if facility management deems such persons undesirable. Removing someone from an event may create problems for the host organization if the person removed believes he or she was wrongly accused of bad behavior. On the other hand, removal may be exactly what is in the best interest of the organization, so asking that such language be eliminated from a contract may not be the best solution. An alternative is to negotiate contract language that requires facility management to consult with the host organization's designated representative prior to taking action. Added language could provide for a process in which the organization assumes responsibility for removal of undesirable attendees or provides the organization a role in deciding how the removal takes place.

Although such changes do not restrict facility management from removing people who cause problems, it does give the host organization an opportunity to do damage control. Considering the fact that an event facility is just being rented by the host organization, it is reasonable that the facility's managers have an absolute right to protect the property and people using the facility.

USE OF VOLUNTEER SECURITY

Some organizations recruit members or others who volunteer to perform security services. Volunteers can be effective for some low-level security duties. Volunteers should be used only to supplement uniformed professional security guards in situations that do not carry substantial risk of liability. Volunteer security duties should be limited to nonthreatening situations, such as parking control, keeping order around silent auction tables, and monitoring cash collection. Such duties pose little or no risk, as long as there are ready means to engage professional security if necessary; thus, volunteers should be provided some means to immediately alert uniformed professional security guards if there is an emergency. Volunteers are not equipped to handle hostile situations. They lack official authority. And if a volunteer should take aggressive action against an individual, there could be considerable liability to the volunteer or host organization.

Turning Hostility to Fundraising Advantage

The organization's leadership heard there would be protesters. They were informed by media alerts and notices issued to members of local groups opposed to the work of the organization. There were calls for pickets to peacefully march near the entrance to the convention center at noon the following day. The organization was holding an auction event at the center. Weather was a factor for the protest. The past few days had been cold and a bit snowy, and that would continue. There was a good chance the protesters would still come, although maybe not many. The organization's media expert said it didn't matter that there may not be as many protesters as expected. He added, "We can get pictures and video that makes the crowd look larger than it really is. We can edit as we like, but we really need them to do or say something outrageous to get the most out of it."

The organization's leaders liked what they heard. They assumed many attendees would consider it horrible that there were people trying to ruin the event. The leaders also assumed the angrier attendees became at the protesters, the more they would bid at auction. At least that was the theory.

The protesters came. Not very many. It was cold outside on the picket line, but it really didn't matter. The organization had a video crew and still photographer on the scene filming the dozen or so protesters. Passersby didn't seem to pay much attention to them, except a few members of the press stopped by for a few minutes. It was pretty boring. The big break came when one protester decided to make one very brief obscene gesture. It was captured on film by pure luck.

The event newspaper the next day headlined the protest. Front and center was the photo, with the protester unmistakably showing the organization's members what he thought of them and their beliefs. It was a great day for fundraising.

Nothing generates the drive to give better than a reminder directed personally at donors about why they belong to an organization and contribute to work they believe in. Bless the protesters and their motivational salute to event attendees.

SOME ORGANIZATIONS ARE known for attracting protesters and activists looking for publicity. These are the organizations that take firm positions at one extreme or another in areas of current controversy. The organizations' members and staff tend to be outspoken, forceful advocates and believers in a cause. They also often seek media exposure. Such organizations are particularly good candidates for using auction-event fundraising as a forum for exposure. The spectacle of the auction event provides a ready platform for media attention, generating excitement around funding the organization and flaunting the work of the organization. Besides all the orderly aspects of fundraising, the event offers an opportunity for generating argument and attacking critics if the beliefs of members and event attendees are controversial.

> NOTE: *Although the following discussion itself may be controversial, it is factual and describes an ongoing practice of some groups holding events, including auction events. This makes it worthy of mention in this book. However, the points raised may not be applicable to many organizations, and taking action as described may not produce a desirable outcome for many others.*

The auction event provides a rally point to bait the opposition. Where opponents collide, the media will feed. Protesters marching in front of a convention center are always newsworthy. All involved gain a platform, and in particular, the host organization gets the lion's share of attention should its leaders choose to seize the opportunity. But the real marketing genius of such spectacle is that protesters

and conflict are proof beyond doubt to an organization's members and supporters that the organization they support is, in absolute fact, taken seriously and effective. They will believe this because the opposition's presence proves it. This is of value in the context of an auction event, because there is no better way to demonstrate to event attendees why it is important to give money to fund the organization's work than an active attack on their beliefs. When that attack is going on right outside the event door, the urge to respond permeates the room. The only real outlet event attendees have to counter the attack is to give money.

The event master of ceremonies and auctioneer can readily refer to the protesters during fundraising and the auction. The protesters become the primary motivational element tying the day-to-day work of the organization to the opposition's work. The protesters are most certainly directly attacking the beliefs of the attendees—or at least that's what attendees will hear from the event hosts. Social advocacy organizations often work at odds against other organizations. Here, protesters at the door provide living proof of the strength and persistence of opposition to the advocacy and beliefs of the host organization. What better motivational environment could one have?

Of course, there are degrees of protest and degrees of opposition. Protests that become dangerous, where protesters become physically hostile, require intervention by security or law enforcement. This is rare when protests are widely announced and media are present.

Managing the Perception of Ethics and Integrity

Event attendees and an organization's other supporters and donors are consumers of the nonprofit organization's services. As consumers they need to have confidence that the organization is legitimate, the cause is worthy, and the people running the fundraiser and organization are honest and will properly account for and use funds raised. In my roles managing nonprofit organizations and government regulatory agencies, I regularly heard rumors that cash raised at fundraisers was pocketed or never used for the purposes assumed by the donors. Even the hint of impropriety is anathema to charitable fundraising.

While a high level of ethics cannot be assured, volunteers and paid staff drawn to nonprofit fundraising usually have only the best intentions and go about fundraising in an ethical manner. Exceptions are rare, but those exceptions can become widely publicized and taint the image of fundraising. In particular for large organizations with many subunits, a single incident can be enough to create cynicism toward the entire organization.

Cash Is an Easy Mark

Event fundraising invariably involves taking in cash—usually many small bills—from activities such as raffles and games of chance. As a result of so much cash changing hands, the potential is high for petty theft to occur or for potentially damaging perceptions to arise. Consider that just a single well-executed speed raffle may deliver as many as 100 ten- or twenty- dollar bills in under 60 seconds into the hands of a few people who are moving rapidly about the event floor collecting the cash. Who can keep up with the count of a truly speedy speed raffle?

Nothing really can prevent determined crooks from trying to slip a few bills into their pocket. It can happen virtually anytime: at collection points, as bills change hands on the way to the event "banker," or on the way to the bank. Most serious theft will happen when a large amount of cash is assembled in one place during or after an event. If no accurate and secure accounting is made as small amounts of cash are collected, it is hard to account for loss of a few hundred or even thousands of dollars. Where theft occurs, it is most often done by event workers, event organizers, or workers at the event facility.

Less common in my opinion are occasions when a thief from the outside enters and robs an event, for example, when a cash box is stolen. Considering that many fundraisers are well advertised, they may be held at hotels (where many people come and go), cash depositories are often open tabletops,

and people with little or no experience in security and handling money are handling cash. Where money changes hands in such a visible and free-wheeling fashion, crooks are sure to gather.

If a thief is unknown or barely known to the victim organization's leadership, publicity showing aggressive pursuit of the criminal can help the organization overcome negative perceptions of the organization's care in handling money. Minor theft could even work to an organization's advantage as significant media exposure may publicize the organization's charitable mission, its people, and its need. New funds and funders may result, but this is no reason to invite theft. The opposite effect is just as likely, as any theft will probably at least in some measure be perceived as a result of lax security or money handling on the part of the organization's staff or volunteers. Even if an outside service provider is involved in money handling, the organization can be considered at fault for poor screening of the outside company and failure to require proper bonding. Until money is deposited into a legitimate banking institution, the organization, its staff, and officers can be held at fault to some degree if theft takes place.

Most problematic are instances in which individuals well known to the organization turn out to be thieves. There are examples of long-term staff, officers, or volunteers being charged with fraud and embezzlement. In some instances, minor embezzlement is not reported and never makes the news. Sometimes this secrecy is the result of a legal settlement, but generally it is an attempt to maintain the organization's good image. It is risky to keep internal corruption quiet. If the silence is exposed, the organization now has two matters to address to stunned members, donors, and the public: (1) the theft itself and how it was allowed to happen, and (2) the cover-up of the theft and how that was allowed to happen.

No organization wants the publicity internal corruption brings, even when the victim organization vigorously pursues action against the thieves. It doesn't matter if the theft was by a low-level employee or by the executive director. All staff and officers are held accountable by donors, members, the public, and anyone else who pays attention. An organization's credibility is hurt most when a long-term executive director or volunteer officer is found guilty of a crime. The effect can be irreparable harm to the organization. Vigorous prosecution invariably helps, but recovery can be slow. Sometimes incidents of fraud result in dissolution of the organization.

Who Wins Matters

A wonderful banquet for a well-known statewide environmental organization was thrown into complete chaos when a woman began screaming at the top of her lungs. She apparently had her mind set on winning a particular raffle item and went berserk when the organization's executive director won the item. She claimed the director had fixed the raffle so he could win. I knew the executive director well. At the time of the incident I also knew that he really wanted to win that item. Many others knew he wanted to win, too. I believe his ethical standards were beyond question. He would never rig a raffle, even if it would have been possible for him to do so. But there he was in the middle of the kind of mess that a person in a paid position for a charitable organization cannot afford. Fortunately, he knew exactly what to do. He immediately donated the item back to the organization as an instant surprise auction item, and another ticket was drawn to award the item to someone else.

I was attending the fundraising event as director of a regional office of the parent organization of the statewide chapter holding the event. I had purchased a number of raffle tickets, but these were on a large selection of items of modest value. I had split the tickets up among my three young daughters. Much to my chagrin, one of my daughters was more than just a little lucky that evening. She almost cleaned off the raffle table with her tickets. At her age she didn't even understand why she kept getting "presents" from all these nice people. She won fishing equipment, clothing, art prints, and on it went. Although no one screamed at either me or my very sweet and innocent daughter, I felt all eyes were upon me.

At that meeting, I learned a lesson about perceptions toward employees of nonprofit organizations. I now have a policy, which I also impose on my employees. I make it a rule not to buy raffle tickets or enter events of chance if I am in any way associated with the organization in an employment or consulting capacity. Sometimes you can't avoid buying a raffle ticket, because of pressure and expectations. It happens to me, and when it does, I give it away or leave it in my pocket. In the unlikely event I should win an item of any significant value, my next action is prescribed by my personal policy. The item is immediately donated back to the organization for disposal at their discretion. Just like my dear colleague who faced the screamer, no matter how much I might like a prize, my livelihood is more important.

Continued good relationships with donors require that they have absolute faith in the good intentions and ethical standards of the leadership of the sponsoring organization. Officers and other officials of a charitable organization need to be aware of the perception that winning a major raffle prize may leave with others. This is a problem unique to high-value raffles and other games of chance. Ways to help avoid problems of perception include selecting winning raffle tickets in a very visible way and doing so in a fashion that is obviously and completely random. As a matter of practice, officers and paid employees of sponsoring organizations can get better exposure for their contributions in support of the organization if they restrict giving through bidding on silent or live auction items where the perception of anyone having an unfair advantage is minimal.

Encountering the "Dark Side"

If there is a "dark side" to the business of charity fundraisers, it is manifest in events planned and managed by people seeking to use the event as a means to personally acquire goods and services at cut rates and have a big party doing so. This is not about direct theft of merchandise or cash. Instead, this is a situation in which a group of people use the platform of a charitable organization as a means to receive personal benefits. These benefits are ones well beyond the personal satisfaction of helping a worthy cause.

The "Big Discount"

The "big discount" refers to the entire auction becoming a forum for bargain-based purchase of services and products. This may happen by accident when an organization manages the auction process so poorly that value received for items at auction is consistently very low. But it can also happen by design when the organization's leadership or certain members, such as event planners, purposefully solicit merchandise so they can personally acquire it at below-market prices. This is a scam, or possibly fraud, in which certain members of the organization personally benefit. Access to merchandise desired by the scammers becomes the hidden goal of the "charitable" organization's auction event.

Anyone can form an organization or volunteer for an established organization and work to host a fundraising event. Many large organizations have fundraising chapters, committees, and affiliated organizations through which a group of volunteers holds regular events. Volunteers frequently solicit items for auctions or raffles to benefit well-known and highly respected organizations. This backdrop of volunteers soliciting goods and services provides perfect cover for a group to use the guise of a fundraising event to solicit merchandise or services they personally would like to have.

The scammers canvass merchants, service providers, and other potential donors for donations and then hold an event using the items, ostensibly to benefit the host organization. Since much of the merchandise for a fundraiser may be purchased at a discount, the soliciting individuals can even use anticipated event proceeds to buy what they want. These items are then auctioned or otherwise distributed in a fashion that favors the event organizers or their friends at prices usually well below retail values or virtually free in minimal raffles and as door prizes. Attendance is purposefully kept low. Where such fundraising takes place on behalf of national or umbrella organizations, few people be-

yond the planning group are likely to be "in on the deal." Sometimes merchandise is simply stolen, but there is little difference between that and rigging the event in a way that creates advantages to event organizers.

For this to work, a minimal number of attendees are usually present at auction, and those "in the loop" know not to bid too aggressively. Others may attend who are unaware items are being skimmed and that auctions may be a sham. Actual revenues raised are generally used by the organization on mission-related work. It is much more difficult to hide and pocket actual revenue raised than it is to obscure how merchandise solicited for raffles and auctions may be distributed among event planners. Participants in the scam may even be committed to working for the organization's cause but have found the auction event a way to receive some "repayment" for their effort. "Getting a little payment for volunteer work" is how I have heard persons involved in underperforming events justify taking bargains at auction events.

The "Big Party"

Event planning activities and the event itself can also be twisted to various degrees to provide desirable personal benefits. For example, members of an event planning committee can have free lunch by holding planning meetings—possibly weekly or more often—over lunch at a restaurant and charge meal expenses to the event budget. But why stop at lunch? Planning meetings can be held at restaurants over dinner just as easily. Expenses can be charged against future proceeds of the event, or "meeting" expenses can be paid using revenue retained from previous fundraising events.

There are also entire events that are more party than fundraiser. Some events appear excessive. If the presence of a "three-ring circus" makes you suspicious that your donations might be funding more party than charity, you might be right. As incredible as it may sound, I once ran into a situation where a circus was the major draw at the annual fundraising event—this was a real commercial circus paid to entertain at the event. This event epitomized the big-party event. The event showed a very poor cost-to-revenue ratio. But who cares? It was a circus. Right?

Not everyone expects a circus. Serious fundraising-event attendees and donors expect most of the money raised to fund charitable work. Parties in the guise of fundraising events break faith with donors even more than the party disguised as a fundraiser. At least the bait-and-switch tactic of the latter is for a good cause, assuming fundraising proceeds go to the organization's good works.

If an event looks like, feels like, and has every other semblance of a big party, it may be a big party. It may be a big party for the event organizers. But maybe it is not. For example, if the owner of a three-ring circus donates a performance wholly to the cause, the circus would provide a great draw, and all the hoopla could propel fundraising success into the stratosphere.

The "Big Giveaway"

Another format featuring excess is the "big giveaway." In this situation so many prizes are offered at such low cost to attendees that anyone who plays is very likely to receive prize merchandise or services. Such events provide excessive benefits to event organizers and attendees, but organizers don't necessarily take steps to gain any additional personal individual advantage over anyone else.

Event organizers purposefully overstock the event with prizes, paying little or no attention to earning net revenue for the charitable cause or the organization. The format is distinguished from the "big party" because there may be very little party associated with the "big giveaway." It is used by organizations seeking to boost attendance at an event. There may be a strategic objective, such as introducing more people to an organization, or organizers may just want to attract as large a crowd as possible. The organization that purposefully holds such an event perverts the intent of the charitable fundraiser, which is to raise net revenue for a charitable cause. Attendees at big-giveaway events may be quite happy with everything just the way it is. What's not to like about winning items at an event? Attendees may not even care about the host organization's cause. After all, organizers of such events don't.

The "Big Squeeze"

The final scam, the "big squeeze," takes place when persons who solicit event merchandise also solicit favors for themselves from donors. Personal favors can include discounts on merchandise and services, free products, and free or discounted vacation trips. Such solicitation is most likely to take place when the soliciting person can exert leverage on the donor.

Events may be planned to attract a very unique audience, where attendees share a common passion that may be linked to certain services or products. A donor may see the event as a particularly advantageous opportunity to advertise services or products, especially with a little inside help. For example, an event may draw an elite audience of people who regularly travel to a certain region of the world. An onstage endorsement of a particular destination resort during an event may be of great interest to the person who owns the resort. So when a volunteer soliciting the donor for a donated stay at the resort offers to help the donor receive special treatment, the volunteer may also suggest the donor provide a little something extra for personal efforts in helping promote the resort. Of course, the donor may be the one making the initial offer of a little something extra for the person for extra promotional help. The volunteer has a choice to accept or reject the bribe.

This situation is made particularly probable because volunteers soliciting services and merchandise as prizes at events held for unique audiences, such as the world-travel buffs, are usually enthusiastic members of that audience. The donor seeking help may have many things, services, or contacts the soliciting volunteer would love to have, and often that includes establishing a common interest–related relationship with the donor.

PART 5

Honing to a Fine Edge

23

After the Event

No verbal abuse was too strong for her to direct at staff or volunteers. The highly placed officer of the nonprofit organization didn't really care who was offended. This officer even boasted of her lack of tact. A small corps of people seemed to gain personal benefit in the organization under her shadow, but others were demonized.

Staff or volunteers who did anything the officer didn't like became the subject of attack. In any conversation she was all knowing. Anyone with real knowledge quickly learned to shut up. She knew just enough to sound like she knew what she was talking about, until you listened long enough to realize she really didn't.

None of that may have mattered if it wasn't that this officer also drove away volunteers, donors, and staff. How much her inappropriate actions cost the organization in lost volunteers and investment in staff is hard to say. It's hard to believe some organizations tolerate such toxic influences, but they do. This is not a story about one person. In my time serving nonprofit organizations, I have met several of these venomous people. They have been shes and hes, officers, spouses of officers, and members of the board. Such people persist in influencing nonprofit organizations because the leadership of nonprofits often function much like a family, with members establishing close, long-term relationships with each other. Families tolerate, forgive, and often turn a blind eye to their dysfunctional members. Many nonprofit organizations do, too, large, small, and in between.

Situations, as described, can affect event fundraising because the competently functioning volunteers and staff who plan and host an event must perform competently as a team. Unfortunately, these are the people often most affected by the host organization's dysfunctional members if left unchecked by the organization's leadership. Generally, the most constructively functional people in any organization are the most adversely affected by destructively dysfunctional leadership.

PEOPLE WHO GIVE TIME, money, or services to an auction event are committed to the organization and its cause. These staff and volunteer event planners and workers deserve respect, recognition, thanks, and all the support an organization can muster to ensure their lives have been enriched having done their job at the event. Before, during, and especially after an event there are three groups of people to thank, praise, and keep happy:

- Merchandise and service donors, sponsors, and underwriters
- Attendees and participants in the event's fundraising activities
- Event volunteers and staff event workers

The success of the next auction event starts with the manner in which people who contributed to and helped with the previous event are treated.

Give Thanks

Even though the notion of thanking those who donated, contributed, supported, or worked at an event may seem obvious, not doing so, or not doing so effectively, is a common failing of organizations' leadership. I often hear from event volunteers who feel their hard work went unappreciated. Many say they received no thanks, but many had. They had been thanked, but for reasons hard to understand they had not been thanked often enough or in a fashion they sufficiently appreciated.

Even workers who do relatively little may feel they did a lot and deserve huge recognition. They may be satisfied with a simple acknowledgment unless they also see others receive more praise than

they receive. At that point they may see differential treatment as unfair; thus, they feel undervalued. The organization leadership needs to be sensitive to the unpredictability of human feelings. It takes little added effort to be inclusive, consistent, and sensitive to the emotional nature of people when delivering praise.

At the conclusion of an event, volunteer and staff workers' emotions may be running high, and some people will not be ready for an objective analysis of results, especially if there were problems with the event. Care needs to be taken at that point to ensure that all workers receive equal praise and supportive comments. It is not a time for criticism. A few ill-timed statements at the end of an event by an organization officer or executive staff can make finding help for the next event nearly impossible. It may be necessary to dissect the event to provide insight on how to do it better next time, but that should come days or weeks later.

Donors of merchandise, services, underwriting, and sponsorships must also be recognized and thanked. The level of recognition can vary as desired, based on value or amount of contribution. Differential praise is regularly given, for example, when a host organization creates levels of sponsorship, with differential benefits based on the level of giving. Benefits or recognition should be based on an objective measure (e.g., the dollar amount of support) that donors will accept as a valid basis for differential recognition.

Contributors by means of buying auction items can also be tracked objectively. These contributors can be thanked in a differential fashion if desired, based on the amount spent during the event. One organization created a special "Patron's Club" for auction buyers who spent more than $10,000 at auction. Members of the club received entrance to a special event lounge, exclusive promotions, and more. They could renew membership from year to year simply by spending $10,000 at the annual convention's auctions. People who spent less at the auctions may have contributed a significant amount of money during the event, but if total spending did not amount to $10,000, they were not allowed in the club.

The challenge to organization leadership is to

Sidebar 23.1. **Ten Ways to Thank Donors, Sponsors, and Underwriters**

1. Place the name of each donor, sponsor, and underwriter in the auction program for the event with a statement of appreciation for their contribution. Place the list of names on the host organization's Web site and in its newsletter, magazine, and newspaper.

2. Send each a single-page letter of appreciation, signed by the president of the host organization.

3. Take photographs during the event of each person to be thanked with the president of the host organization and/or with any celebrities that attend the event. Make a determined effort to find each donor, sponsor, and underwriter to conduct this photo opportunity. Then send a framed photo print to each.

4. Give a small gift of appreciation containing the name of the host organization, name of the event, and words to the effect that the item is provided in appreciation for being a supporter of the host organization.

5. Place a large and well-designed announcement in the major local daily newspaper recognizing the donors, sponsors, and underwriters and expressing sincere appreciation for their contributions.

6. Give each a year's free subscription to the host organization's magazine or newspaper.

7. Stage a "donors and sponsors appreciation picnic" several months before the next event but before any deadlines for making contributions to the next auction event.

8. Encourage members to do business with donors and sponsors by placing special advertisements on Web sites and in newsletters, newspapers, and magazines.

9. Create a "special club" for donors, sponsors, and underwriters that includes a gift of regular membership or perhaps a specialized (reduced) benefit membership in the host organization.

10. Publish a special newsletter or e-newsletter, perhaps three or four times a year, for donors and sponsors, providing them with news of the host organization and featuring selected hosts and sponsors, and of course, keeping these very important people informed about upcoming auction events.

Sidebar 23.2. **Ten Ways to Thank Attendees Who Make Significant Contributions to the Organization during the Event**

1. Send a letter of appreciation from the president of the host organization to attendees who made significant contributions through bidding on auction items.

2. Establish a special "benefactors club" for major contributors, with benefits such as a special reception at the next event held by the host or a special side auction of a few unique high-value items.

3. Invite attendees who made significant contributions to special host-sponsored activities during the year. Here are a few examples. For a wildlife-protection organization, this could be a guided tour of a bat cave ordinarily off limits to anyone except researchers. For a water-conservation organization, this could be an private glass-bottom-boat tour of a clear-water spring. For an organization promoting medical research, this could be a private tour of an advanced research facility.

4. Invite attendees who made significant contributions to intimate group discussions with famous people relevant to the host organization's mission. For an organization promoting healthy living, a discussion could be held with a renowned singer known for losing weight through healthful eating. For an organization that promotes pet adoption, a discussion could be held with the host of a TV show about pets.

5. Give major contributors a special gift containing the name of the host organization along with words expressing appreciation for supporting the organization.

6. Give major contributors a series of special low-cost gift reminders throughout the year. These reminders should include the name of the organization and repeat an expression of gratitude from the host organization's leadership.

7. Send major contributors a special invitation to the next event, perhaps including a personal note from the president reminding them of the event and expressing appreciation for their continued support.

8. Send a letter of appreciation from the president of the host organization to all attendees for coming to the event.

9. Feature willing major contributors in short articles about their contributions and commitment to the organization's cause on the host's Web site and in its newspaper and magazine.

10. Form a special "benefactors advisory committee" to the president, and invite major contributors to become members of the committee. The president can meet with members of the committee and ask for guidance on various matters, including funding issues.

design ways to thank the various contributors and volunteers who support the organization through the event. Sidebars 23.1, 23.2, and 23.3 provide 10 winning examples each of how to do that for the three key groups that must be thanked, thanked, and thanked again.

Check the Math

Another seemingly obvious after-event action is to reconcile the balance sheets to account for all money received, in particular all cash received. Event receipts should be reconciled immediately at the completion of an event but is often postponed in the immediate excitement after an event ends. But it is at this exact point when it is most critical for counting and accounting to take place.

The end of an auction event is the time when the bulk of payment for expensive auction items is made. A considerable portion of the event's revenue comes in quickly. Merchandise is distributed, and

there can be a rush to process payment from a crowd of attendees ready to go home. It is a time when mistakes can be made. The time to find and correct mistakes is right then, while all the paperwork is handy and event workers' memories of the event are fresh. One of the key requirements in this accounting is to have at least two people count and double-count cash receipts. Because it is usually not possible to confirm a bank deposit until the day following an event or even later, the amount of cash must be established positively so there is no room for foul play with money raised.

Set Policy on Warranties, Guarantees, and Complaints

The host organization should avoid being placed into the situation of warranting or guaranteeing any of the items sold at auction, raffled, used as prizes, or otherwise distributed to event attendees. Items and services sold at auction may not meet expectations. No host organization is in a position to provide warranties and guarantees, yet after the event is over, it can be difficult to avoid responding to an auction winner who complains about an item that is defective or a service that fails to meet expectations. Many charitable organizations simply offer to refund payment for a defective item or poor service. This may be the simplest way to deal with a defective auction item or poor service. After all, event attendees who actively participate in fundraising activities are generally the organization's most dedicated members and supporters. It is important to keep important people happy.

However, an event host can take steps to reduce the risk of liability. The host organization should establish and follow a policy governing how to deal with winners of auction, raffle, and game prizes who have complaints. The policy should cover auction items, raffle items, and game prizes separately, as attendees acquire each in a different fashion (methods of acquisition and amount of payment differ). In particular, defective raffle items or raffled services that fail to deliver as described may be subject to state or local regulations. Any local legal requirements should be included in the policy.

Policies should address various kinds of failures and defects. For example, a winner of a fishing trip may complain that he or she caught no fish on the fishing trip and wants a refund. The winner of a different fishing trip may complain that the fishing guide never responded to requests to schedule the trip, so the winner of that trip was never provided the fishing trip. Neither winner of the fishing trips caught fish, but one has a real complaint; the other doesn't. The two complainers should receive a different answer from the host organization after complaining, set by policy if possible.

In addition to policies covering the host organization's response to complaints, the organization should provide event attendees a written disclaimer covering the extent to which the host organization warrants or guarantees auction and raffle items and prizes. This disclaimer should be contained in the advance and auction programs and must be written to comply with any state or local regulations. Otherwise, it should be written to absolve the organization of any responsibility for defective items or failed services.

The section titled "Provide Auction Bidding Procedures, Conditions of Sale, and Disclaimers" in chapter 6 provides sample policy language the host organization can use to limit risk of liability. Some organizations may prefer to deal individually with donors, without providing any generally distributed notice. Whichever process is used should be applied fairly and consistently and be based on written guidance or policy.

24 Advanced Techniques

Some people just have to leave their signature on whatever they touch. For some, that signature is a gimmick—a trick. Consider the sleight-of-hand trick used by one veteran volunteer of many auction events. Each year he worked his trick to give the audience the impression of "unparalleled success," even as the event was just getting started. This person had enough experience, or perhaps it was just good advance information, to know approximately how many people would be attending the event banquet.

In making final arrangements for the banquet setup, he made sure the room did not appear excessively large. He said, "Too much empty space makes it look like people forgot to come." He then made sure that too few tables and chairs were set for the number of expected attendees. He had this done on purpose, with the obvious result that when people were seated for dinner, there were not enough place settings. His goal was not to create a standing-room-only event, although that would have been the outcome had he not also made secret accommodation for the "overflow attendance."

His trick was that he had hidden additional tables, fully set up for dinner. These tables were kept behind closed doors and were ready to be carried out and squeezed in among the other tables when needed. He made certain that accommodation could be made quickly when the "unexpectedly" large crowd overflowed the capacity of the room. If the event failed to attract as many people as expected, the extra tables would remain hidden, and the room would appear to have been set to full capacity. Attendees would never notice attendance was less than expected. Instead, they would perceive the event to be a resounding success from the standpoint of attendance.

The magic of the trick came when attendance was better than expected. Then, with fanfare from the MC, extra tables were paraded into the room and squeezed into place with flourish and noisy enthusiasm. The MC would announce, "We are overflowing this year; let's give 'em a hand as we pack them in for charity."

Did the "signature gimmick" add value to the event? It's hard to say. It was part of the show. It caused a slight disruption and put a bit of a spotlight on the "unexpected but welcomed large crowd" of people attending the event. It was a nuisance to the waitstaff and the volunteers who pitched in to bring out the additional tables. It also was a trick that worked. It really made attendees believe that a larger-than-expected crowd came, and to many people that is one true sign of a successful event.

TRICKS, ADVANCED TECHNIQUES, and special options that can improve any event, and risky ventures in fundraising advisable only to ultra-high-performing event planners, are the subjects of this chapter. Presented in no particular order are the secrets behind the phenomenal success of some organizations' fundraisers. These are things event planners do that make the difference between an ordinary event and an unforgettable experience.

Look At Who's Here

An earlier chapter described benefits of having VIPs at an event and making sure attendees know they are there. The MC announces VIPs and has them stand or take a bow onstage. Well-known and famous people are interesting to attendees. Personalities help make the event not just another fundraiser but a real happening. VIPs also attract other VIPs, and their presence entices other people to attend the event. People want to see the VIPs and are curious about what is drawing the VIPs to that particular fundraiser. Some events become known for attracting all the "big names in town."

Why does that happen at some events and not

at others? It is usually no accident but the result of planning, hard work, and experience. Getting VIPs to attend an event is one of the tricks of masterful event planners. Not only do the successful planners work to get VIPs to come but they work hard to get the right VIPs to come. Who attends an event can take on extraordinary importance. For example, consider the impact on a fundraising event held by a small local charity when it has an internationally acclaimed movie star in attendance. Everyone in town will absolutely have to attend. Whether the star has a role in the event or is just there as an attendee does not matter. The presence of the star is enough to set the host organization up for success. Is the star really attending just like everyone else? Maybe, but probably not.

Sometimes a star will just drop in to a charity fundraiser, but that is a rare occurrence. In almost every case the presence of a major personality is the result of a well-planned, lengthy process of solicitation, networking, and very often negotiation over financial considerations. Even if the presence of the star is a direct result of a personal connection to a member of the host organization, the process of getting the star to attend usually goes well beyond a simple phone call or e-mail.

The host wins big when a star agrees to make an appearance free of charge, as a donation to the charitable event. In many cases personalities are paid to attend. This is not about having the star as an entertainer. People understand stars get paid to perform. This is about being paid to play the role of VIP at an event. Attendees may not know about that trick. Payment may be in cash or special services, such as extraordinary trips or unique gifts to which the host organization has access. Stars may be paid to make their role an active one, such as to say a few words or sign a few photos, or they may be paid just to be there—paid to just walk around and be seen. That's really all it takes to turn a humdrum event into an unforgettable evening. And this will be the case for no other reason than the presence of one or more truly memorable VIPs.

My wife and I were attending a charitable event where one of the most famous actors of our parents' generation was signing copies of his autobiography and posing for photographs as he presented the signed book to his admirers. I recall my wife saying she was no big fan of this actor, but she could not resist the attraction. She was unaware the actor was there for a payment arrangement that included all the money he could make selling autographs. She remained unaware right up to the point when he reminded us we owed him $100 for the autographed book and photo. That was a small price to pay for being in the presence of this great actor, receiving his book from him personally, and receiving a photograph commemorating it all.

The host planned the attendance of this actor. Advance materials for the event carried notice of the actor's intent to attend, so his presence was advertised well in advance. Whatever the actor's motivation, his presence surely had an influence on the success of the event. Sometimes host organizations prefer to leak rumors a star will be at an event. If the star does not appear, the host can claim it was all just a rumor. Other times, the event planners may prefer to keep a star's appearance a secret (probably because they are not confident the star will actually show up). When the star appears, they act surprised: "You never know who will show up at our event!"

Choose Sure Winners as High-Value Auction Items

For event planners who plan strategically, it is possible to use specific merchandise or services to entice specific attendees to bid—and to get them to bid high. Conduct research to find out exactly what specific specialty item individual attendees are likely to want to see in an auction and are highly likely to bid on. The key to success is to have at least three potential bidders who will want the same irresistible item; then offer that irresistible item for bid at the live auction. For example, if several people who will attend an event are known to appreciate fine wine from a particular vineyard, the perfect case of wine from that vineyard can be placed into an auction. Make sure these wine lovers know the case of wine will be in the auction.

An even more intensive approach is to enlist potential bidders in acquiring the perfect auction item. As an example, if several people who will

attend an event are known to collect duck decoys from a particular carver, then one of the carver's decoys can be placed in the live auction. Taking this a step further, a discussion can be held individually with each of the decoy collectors about putting one of the carver's decoys up for auction. The collectors can be asked what species of duck they feel would be most attractive to potential bidders. The goal here is not to force the potential bidders into any kind of advance agreement on bidding. Instead, this discussion should be posed as a "consultation" with an expert on collecting decoys to find out what kind of decoy will work best at the host organization's auction. The potential bidders learn event planners think enough of the collectable decoys to place them into the auction and enough of the potential bidder to ask for advice. The carver is then asked to donate fully or on a consignment basis a decoy that is most desirable to the several potential bidders. The collectors can even be asked to help arrange for the donation with the carver, because the collectors probably know the carver personally. The collectors, having been involved in arranging for the item, are likely to be very interested in seeing that the decoy receives a good reception by bidders. That will undoubtedly include their own enthusiastic bidding on the decoy.

This technique can be used in putting together vacation packages, acquiring artwork, and so on. The more participation potential bidders have in acquiring unique high-value items they personally treasure, the more likely those items will command vigorous bidding at auction.

Create Event Web Sites and Branding for Regularly Held Events

Regularly held events can acquire a unique identity when the host organization constantly and over the long term publishes and promotes the event by name in its publications and other media, using a consistently applied special logo or "mark" and making repeated reference to event activities. The name, identifying marks, such as logo, colors, typography, and other visual imagery used in this promotion, must be consistently applied year to year or each time the recurring event is held. The event becomes a continuously promoted topic in both internal and external communications and publicity. This "brands" the event. Its image becomes known by the host organization's members and by people in the communities where the event is held.

A ready means to continue such promotion over time is through an event Web site and other online marketing media, for example, by using simple social-networking media such as Facebook or Twitter to carry an event marketing message. The event Web site can be maintained as a series of pages on the host's main Web site or as an entirely separate Web site. As the date of the event nears, the Web site can carry registration materials and a registration page, the advance program, publicity about special entertainers, descriptions of auction and raffle prizes, hotel accommodation, blogs about the event, and much more. Immediately after the event, photos of people enjoying the event can be posted, along with messages of thanks and comments from attendees about the event. During other periods the Web site continues to deliver information about the event and provides a forum for members, donors, or attendees to communicate with the host or exchange information with each other. See sidebar 12.2 for additional details.

Through a constant presence in media available to members and the community, the event becomes a full-time activity of the host organization. The event establishes a continuity and a life of its own. As for so many other services, products, and activities that are heavily and consistently advertised, a brand is established and maintained over time. Once achieved, such branding provides the host organization with enormous advertising strength, greater community awareness of mission, a tremendous advantage in ticket sales, and a huge increase in potential net fundraising success.

Hold a "Green" Event

In 2004, the state of California passed a law requiring organizations hosting events with more than 2,000 participants and facilities used for such events to develop and implement recycling and waste-reduction plans. California's law deals with only solid waste, such as trash, recyclables, and compostables, but it sets an environmental tone for other aspects of large events held in the state. Several other states and municipalities have recycling laws governing events as well. However, regardless of applicable laws, organizations may hold events of any size using environmentally friendly practices.

Small and large events use energy and water and generate waste. Event planners are in a key position to make choices about supplies, facilities, transportation, waste disposal, suppliers, caterers, and so on that can result in reducing an event's environmental footprint. Numerous guides and Web sites are available to help event planners make choices in environmentally responsible ways. These provide ideas and case studies covering green leadership, such as how to select green event locations, reduce waste and recycle resources, reduce energy use and greenhouse gases, conserve water, and choose food and dinnerware that require less energy to produce.

Hold a green event because people are increasingly conscious about the impact humans are having on the environment. Members are more frequently requesting the organizations to which they belong to practice sustainability. This extends to demanding green practices in events they attend. Some donors are also looking for environmentally conscious actions by charitable organizations' leadership as a guide to future funding decisions. No green action may get as much publicity in the eyes of donors as the host holding an avowed green event.

A green event can be advertised as "helping the environment." For nonprofit organizations working to better society, whether improving habitat for wildlife or feeding the hungry, helping the environment is a positive social-economic action. Taking this step is relatively simple, yet it unmistakably demonstrates the commitment of the host organization's leadership to create a progressive image for the organization by adopting emerging environmental standards and best practices.

Holding a green event helps create positive change outside the normal boundaries of the organization and puts a unique twist on the event that may make it stand out from similar events held in the local community. Truly sincere efforts such as greening of an annual event can enhance relationships with attendees and donors. Many members of nonprofit organizations already demonstrate an aptitude for promoting social and environmental change by virtue of their membership. These people are often looking for avenues to donate their time in a fashion that helps ensure a sustainable future. The green event may provide an added draw to new volunteers.

Given the emphasis in this book on achieving the highest possible net revenue, it may sound counterintuitive to now describe hosting green events. Although hosting a green event at which basic green services are unavailable may result in some increased costs, going green can save time and money. For example, many advance printed materials, such as registration materials and the advance program, can be sent electronically for a green event, avoiding some mail and printing costs.

In summary, besides the value of reducing an event's environmental footprint, the green event can provide a distinct promotional advantage to the host organization. In a community where many organizations host auction events, going green may be one of the few ways to gain an edge in the search for positive event-related publicity and the quest for event volunteers, donors, and attendees.

Find the Magic Bullet

Host organizations in which members have a common interest related to marketable merchandise or services have a unique opportunity to seek out and use a "magic bullet." This is an auction item or category of auction items that elicits high levels of event attendance, extraordinarily high levels of bidding and high net revenue, and strong positive media exposure for the cause (resulting in further donations). A host organization can also stage an event around a common interest and invite only people who share that interest. Even in poor economic times, fundraising interest remains high where there is a magic bullet. Find it, use it, nurture it, promote it, and triumph from it.

For example, while not directly transferable to

most charitable organizations, the wildlife conservation community found a magic bullet long ago and features it repetitively and successfully at event after event. In this case the magic bullet literally holds bullets—a sporting gun. As a raffle item it is a constant draw. High-quality rifles or shotguns are often the subject of special drawings. Sometimes these sporting arms are custom made for the event, bringing tens of thousands of dollars in revenue. In association with that, a subcategory of wildlife organization whose members are somewhat affluent has found success with another seemingly inexhaustible magic bullet—wildlife-associated travel. The double feature of sporting arms and wildlife travel has proven irresistible to people with a common interest in wildlife conservation, outdoor sports, and adventure travel.

Use Advanced Auction Techniques

Advanced techniques are available to increase net revenue from auctions. Following are descriptions of five such techniques.

Pull a Rabbit out of Your Hat

Sometimes bidding on an item is intense, and final bid amounts between two or possibly three bidders are within a few dollars. You can feel it in the air—the runner-up wanted to win but just wouldn't take the next step. The bidder just gave up. Maybe the losing bidder believed that there was no way to outbid the competitor—who knows why, but the disappointment is obvious. Now is the time to pull a rabbit out of your hat. Offer the identical item to the runner-up(s) for exactly the same amount that the winning bidder paid. If the runner-up takes the offer, the host organization instantly doubles net revenue from the auction item.

There are two people involved in this equation who must be handled with care. Neither the winner nor runner-up should be made to feel the slightest bit uncomfortable by this trick—after all, auctions must be fun for all, and in particular, auctions should be fun for bidders. Never offend a bidder. Never break faith with the winning bidder or diminish the value of the auction item by offering an immediate discount. Therefore, the item must be offered for the same price paid by the winning bidder. It is a fair deal as long as the runner-up pays an identical amount. The winning bidder should not be offended.

In making the offer to the runner-up, remember that the losing bidder's adrenaline is still pumping. A few seconds ago the bidder was considering spending a lot of money, bidding and hoping. The bidder lost, but the level of desire is just as high now, or even higher than it was a few moments ago. A few short seconds later, with the offer of a second chance ringing in the bidder's ears, the bidder is back on the hot seat. All eyes in the audience are again turned on the bidder. The losing bidder wanted the item and lost for lack of a few dollars—just a few dollars more! The bidder did not want to go above the winning bid. But the bidder may have been willing to match the winning bid. And with *everyone* watching the action, it's hard not to add a few dollars to the last bid—after all, it's for charity. The bidder is given 30 seconds to decide, while everyone—literally everyone—watches.

Done right, this trick can double net revenue many more times than not. It's impossible to know which, if any, item may elicit the hot bidding that lends to success in doubling up, but the savvy auction team can be prepared for the opportunity should it arise. This is something to do sparingly. Never let bidders think they can get away without vigorous bidding on each and every item. Doubling up once, maybe twice, in an auction is enough, so do it only on items where net revenue is huge to the host organization. Besides, conditions need to be just right for this to work effectively, auction after auction. Here are some points to consider.

Doubling up should not be tried when the winning bid is an outrageous amount over the preceding bid. It does not happen too often, but when it does, forget doubling up. For example, bidding is moving along at a normal pace on an item valued at $750. Bidding is at $800, and bids have been coming in $50 increments. The next bidder announces $1,000, which is $200 above the last bid offered by the runner-up. Bidding stops at the $1,000 offer, and the auctioneer accepts that as the final bid. Offering a second item to the runner up who bid only $800 makes little sense at this point, as it is not just a few dollars but $200 more. There is just not enough information about the runner-up's frame of mind. Why waste time and effort?

A situation in which the winning bid is just a tad higher than the runner-up's is the perfect opportunity to pull a rabbit out of your hat. The best time to do this is after two or three bidders have been fiercely trading bids in relatively small increments. Watch the bidders until the end. Watch the crowd. Listen to the pace of bidding. If the action was hot, really hot, try doubling up.

Prepare for the right moment, and prepare ahead of time. Determine which of the major auction items can be offered to a runner-up, and place the item strategically in the auction lineup, as will be discussed later. For this trick to work, it must be possible to obtain a second, identical item. Maybe an identical deal is not possible. It is critical to know what is possible. Until the point of final bidding, it's impossible to know which items will provide an opportunity to double up, but be prepared for the opportunity when it arises. Know exactly the cost of getting a second identical item. By knowing if a second item can be obtained and the exact price of acquisition, it is possible to decide if it makes financial sense to offer a second chance.

Next, make sure a few items that can be used in this fashion are placed into the auction lineup toward the end of the auction. Some items lend themselves well to this trick, such as vacation packages, major appliances, watches, lawn tractors, or custom-fitted suits. Any item may be offered in this fashion if a second one can be obtained or if there is already an identical second item in hand. If the host organization has purchased an auction item, at cost or for a deeply reduced price, a second item is a simple matter of purchasing two instead of one. Some organizations purposefully purchase two-of-a-kind items to offer a second chance. This second offer then becomes planned, and the auction team hopes bidding is close on the item when the time comes.

Any item that is one of a kind is not appropriate

to use in this manner. In addition, anything advertised as "exclusive" should be maintained as exclusive. After all, the reason for advertising something as unique, exclusive, or one of a kind is to increase its perceived value. Offering a second item or a copy would diminish the value of the item in the mind of the winning bidder and break faith with attendees.

Timing is also important. It may be best to do this rabbit-in-the-hat trick late in the auction, after the halfway point, unless something happens that counters my next point. It is important to get bidders bidding early in the auction to create and maintain momentum. By offering a second item to the runner-up on an item that appears early in the lineup, that offer may effectively take that bidder out of the bidding on an item offered later. This becomes critically important only if there are a limited number of people participating in the bidding, lots of auction items, and bidders with limited ability to spend (or a limited willingness to spend). If a bidder will be bidding only on a single item and loses as runner-up, nothing is lost by doubling up.

If bidders have "unlimited" spending capacity, doubling up just adds to the excitement. There are no timing issues to consider. But few organizations are lucky enough to have members and attendees at their auctions with unlimited spending power. In light of reality, remember, toward the end of any auction there are few opportunities for bidding left, so this provides one way to add one. Besides, by doubling up too early, bidders may anticipate it again and lessen bidding activity. Doubling up on an auction item adds another item to the lineup without using valuable time going through the bidding process. Not only does the host organization double net income on an auction item but it's done in less than 60 seconds.

Hire Two Auctioneers

Sometimes one auctioneer just isn't enough. Auctioning off merchandise is tedious work requiring considerable concentration, especially when high-dollar bidding is under way. Consider that the auctioneer is moving fast, working hard to keep bidders

and bid amounts straight, and all the while there may be considerable commotion in the auction room. Sometimes two auctioneers make more sense than one. For high-dollar items, mistakes by an auctioneer can be costly. Mistakes can be the result of an auctioneer getting tired. Generally, auctioneers take one or two breaks in the course of an auction. Having two auctioneers allows the auction to continue nonstop as they trade off, allowing both to remain fresh and in top form from beginning to end. If the difference between top form and an exhausted auctioneer amounts to several thousand dollars in missed bids or slight errors, a second auctioneer is well worth the added expense.

The main live auction is the pinnacle of fundraising at an event. It is center stage; all eyes and ears are on that stage, hopefully engaged with the nonstop fundraising under way. Every minute must count, and each minute should lead triumphantly into the next until that last item is bid away. If a single auctioneer requires two breaks of 10 minutes each during a 30-item auction, consider the potential consequences. Three things happen:

1. Bidding momentum comes to an immediate halt when bidding stops and the rest break begins. Momentum must be rekindled when bidding resumes. This can sometimes be a challenge, especially late in an event when people are beginning to get tired.

2. Bidders are given an open invitation to get up and leave, turn attention to something else, start up a new conversation that will run on into fundraising when it begins, or otherwise depart mentally or physically.

3. At least 10 minutes of fundraising time is lost to the event during each break. Each of these minutes is the most valuable of all during an event because these minutes take place with everyone's attention focused squarely on center stage. During breaks there is usually some onstage activity, such as drawings for raffle tickets or door prizes. These activities raise no additional funds. They are "housekeeping" chores. There are more efficient ways to announce raffle and door-prize winners, whereas

there is only one way and one stage to conduct the live auction. A highly efficient event can auction off an item every three to four minutes. Neither the break nor drawings raise additional money. Each minute wasted on nonproductive activities during the main live auction represents revenue forgone by the host organization.

The auctioneer, as "key fundraiser" during the live auction, needs to be professionally skilled, be part entertainer, be able to read an audience, look into the minds of bidders, and in other ways serve as the host's superhero. So much rides on the skills and abilities of the auctioneer that if something should happen to this valuable person, the event suffers dearly. For this reason, having a backup plan is a good idea. The best backup plan for an auctioneer who is unable to perform is to have two auctioneers at the event who can assist each other and trade off auctioneering, providing time for rest while allowing the action and momentum to continue. But in the event of a problem with one of the auctioneers, having two allows one to take over for the other for the duration of the event. The host suffers little or no harm in the event of crisis, and if no crisis arises, fundraising efficiency and effectiveness of the live auction are enhanced by having two working auctioneers. This is clearly a fail-safe option that provides the host a win-win.

Hold Multiple Live Auctions

Large day-long events may involve several live auctions if there are a sufficient number of people available to participate. The value and type of merchandise may be varied if several live "side" auctions are held in the afternoon, in addition to a main live auction held in the evening. Side auctions can focus on certain kinds of goods, such as a "children's" auction, a "garden" auction, a "vacation getaway" auction, or a "fishing" auction. Such special auction events help generate added excitement. However, specialty side auctions must be targeted to the interests and income levels of attendees. For example, a "golf" auction in the afternoon, in addition to the

regular main auction in the evening, might sound like a great idea, but if few attendees are golfers, there would be little interest and no value added to the overall event.

Another option is to hold special "value" auctions. For example, one side auction could be advertised as having merchandise valued under a set amount. This could be called an "Under $250 Auction." Carefully determine the limit to set on value auctions by considering the income level of participants and the average value of items in the main live auction. There is little sense holding an "Under $1,000 Auction" if the bulk of items for auction in the main live auction have a value less than $1,000. Also consider that each minute of the event is valuable; thus, auctions must be targeted to deliver a maximum return on the investment in the time it takes to hold them. The value auction allows for participation by people who love live auctions and who want to contribute but may be unable to afford successful bidding in the main live auction. To enable participation, set the maximum value of items in a value auction at the maximum level that will allow a reasonable likelihood of successful bidding by the majority of people who are anticipated to attend the event.

Side auctions are an especially effective addition to large events where attendees enjoy live auctions. With the side auction as an available outlet for bidding and fundraising, attendees have a better chance of winning an auction item than if their only opportunity is the main live auction, in which only 25 to 30 items will be available. Large events supply enough bidders so that bidding on one auction will not affect bidding at others.

Hold a Theme Event

A theme event is one focused on a specific charitable beneficiary or fundraising focus. Theme events can boost excitement, attract new attendees, boost overall attendance, and increase net revenue by adding new events to the host organization's annual fundraising calendar. Here are a few examples.

Food can be made a center of attention and special theme of an event. A gourmet meal itself can be a draw to an event, but a food-theme event takes food and dining to another level. Food in many forms becomes the center of attention at the event, from dining, to raffles, to auctions. The theme can also be further focused on a specific type of food, such as a specific ethnic food, organic foods, desserts only, or foods paired with wines. For fundraising activities, raffles and auctions feature food tours, home cooking demonstrations, cutlery, gift certificates to restaurants, winery tours, hard-to-find spices, and so on. Special speakers can include well-known chefs or TV cooking-show celebrities. Such events can even be done at a modest cost, for example, in an area where fine dining would not be a draw or even affordable. For such an event one could feature several kinds of chili or barbecue made by local cooks as the meal and then carry on a chili or barbecue theme across the event's fundraising opportunities. But if food is made a central theme of an event, beware! All food at the event better be really good and well served.

A few other ideas for theme events include adventure travel, fishing, golfing, ducks, football, baseball, water sports, babies, outdoor youth activities, museums, natural areas, wildlife conservation, medical research, and science education.

Add a "Virtual Auction"

With the now almost universal use of the Internet, some nonprofit organizations have opened virtual auction sites on the Internet. These sites function in a similar fashion to commercial Internet-based auction sites, but the proceeds of nonprofit virtual auctions go to the host organization, and, presumably, any net revenue goes to support the mission of the nonprofit organization and to charitable causes.

As with any auction, items are offered for bid. Virtual auctions generally offer numerous items at any one time, with bidding limited to a set period of time, usually lasting several days for groups of items or for the entire auction. Bidders in virtual auctions simply visit the designated Web site and enter either an opening bid or a bid amount higher than the last previous bid on the items of their choice. Often a minimum opening bid and minimum bid increment are listed. The bidder is prohibited, by virtue of the auction site's programming, from entering a bid outside the set parameters. Thus, a person entering a bid below the minimum opening bid would have his or her bid instantly rejected. Each bid in a virtual auction is considered a contract, and most people familiar with online auctions understand the nature of bidding online.

A virtual auction may be combined with a live auction event on a real-time basis. Thus, it is technically feasible to carry on a live auction via the Internet. Although many of the additional fundraising opportunities associated with a live auction and the drama of "being there" are lost in the virtual environment, live virtual auctions are nonetheless possible. Such auctions are potentially capable of delivering considerable net revenue if the right auction items are offered and sufficient advance notice is provided to attract enough bidders to make the auction competitive.

Employ High-Risk, High-Reward Fundraising

Risk and reward are relative. Determining the level of items to offer at an auction—that is, the value of the items and maximum bid amount that can reasonably be expected from attendees—requires knowledge of who *will* come to the auction. Use of such information can be taken an extra step.

High net revenue and significant excitement can be generated by adding very exclusive, high-value items to an auction. Even a single item of ultra high value can turn an otherwise ordinary affair into the talk of the town. Doing so successfully requires very specific information about attendees. Bringing a vintage sports car to the auction stage and having no one there capable of offering even an opening bid could turn an otherwise successful auction into a loser in the eyes of all who attend. High-risk, high-reward fundraising must be done strategically to ensure success.

The two key ingredients to success are (1) a truly unique, high-value item and (2) at least two or three bidders who will come to the event and will come expressly to bid on the high-value item. The bidders do not even have to be people who ordinarily come to the host organization's auctions—they can come only because they have an interest in the item to be offered at the auction. They can be invited for the express purpose of bidding on that item alone. What kind of item could possibly attract such bidders? It is something to which there is limited access and for which there is limited availability. It is something many people want, few can afford, and even fewer can ever own.

The host organization's access to unique, high-value items for an auction may come through a member or friend. In particular, in an organization whose members have unique but similar interests, one or more members may be collectors of unique items that other members want. Members who own these items may be willing to donate such items for the organization's event. Another way to bring an item of unique stature to an auction is to locate people who can provide items that meet the host organization's goals. It is also possible to conceive of an item and have it made just for the auction. Some examples of unique, high-value items include a vintage restored sports car, a historic document, an original work by a well-known artist, a unique trip, a chance to spend a weekend of fun with a well-known politician or celebrity, a personal performance by a well-known music group or performer, antique furniture built by a well-known craftsman, and skybox seats for four at the Super Bowl.

In virtually every case, the items selected should appeal to collectors or to people who have a passion for the unique qualities of the offering and who see price as no object—to a point. Collectors and aficionados tend to be savvy buyers and know exactly the value of a unique item. In fact, they are the ones who set market values by the amounts they agree to pay. In the specialized category of high-risk, high-reward fundraising, the organization needs to rely on expert guidance in setting values and expectations.

It will be difficult to have such items donated fully to an organization for auction unless there are extenuating circumstances, such as a need for the donor to make a high-value donation or because of a donor's special affinity for an organization or cause.

If full donation of a special item is not possible, a prospective donor may be receptive to a split of the amount received at auction, with a minimum bid level set to ensure a minimum return to the donor. The minimum bid level, in effect, means the item comes to the auction on a consignment basis.

The next ingredient to success is to attract two to three—or more—bidders to the auction specifically to bid on the item. Many auction experts recommend three bidders to ensure strong bidding, but it really comes down to two at the end of bidding. This is the point at which one bidder outbids one other bidder. Then it's over. There should be at least three bidders on-site and ready to bid. I have been present at events where one or more people expected to bid on an item simply did not participate in the bidding at all. It is a good idea to identify prospective bidders before seeking a specific unique auction item. Fortunately, collectors are often easy to identify. Artists, collectors' associations, and collectors know other collectors and may offer assistance.

An organization is best positioned to succeed in using this kind of auction item when its members already have an existing association with collectors and the people who can provide unique high-value items of interest to collectors. An example is an association of car buffs that have a relationship with firms that restore, and people who collect, vintage automobiles.

Once an appropriate item is located and a preliminary agreement is reached with the potential donor, it is time to assess the likelihood that the potential bidders will attend the auction. For an organization whose members already have a history of collecting high-value items, there may be little to do beyond telling known collectors about the auction and providing them with personalized invitations, special seating, or other modest incentives to attend. Where no prior history or association exists with collectors, advance contact with the collectors can be used to determine the likelihood of two or more collectors attending. Special invitations, seating, and so on may be necessary to encourage attendance. Collectors will show interest on the basis of the quality of the items offered and the status of their existing collections. They already know the value of the items.

It doesn't hurt for the host organization to have a cause that also relates to the collector's interests, but if not, it won't matter to the potential bidder, if the auction item is just right.

Include an Exhibition or "Trade Show" for Added Net Revenue

Events may attract large crowds from a local community or large groups having common interests from across a region, the country, or even throughout the world. Businesses, industry representatives, and merchandise vendors may find it beneficial to their interests to "exhibit" or otherwise set up a booth at an event. These booths or exhibits can simply display wares, services, or information or actually sell products or contract for business. Whatever the opportunities for businesses to sell or display their wares, exhibitors are often very willing to pay a fee for such privilege. Many events have a trade show or exhibition area where such booth space is provided as a benefit of event sponsorship. Other events charge a fee for such privilege, with the size or placement of the booth determining the fee paid. Sometimes a combination of payments is required, such as both paying a set fee for booth space and making a donation of an item or service to the event as an auction or raffle prize.

Exhibitions require added management attention and organizing by the event planning team, but they can add significantly to net revenue. Done well, an exhibition or trade show can underwrite a major portion or all of an event's fixed costs. Trade shows and exhibitions are one of the key ways some organizations consistently make so much money by holding events.

Cut Costs for Success

One of the examples of personal experience used in this book refers to a time when event planners felt a need to reduce costs, and they cut the cost of food and service. Although the event was not food oriented and ordinarily had what was only good food and service, attendees reacted strongly when food and service were cut. The food quality and service

were just lousy the year planners cut food costs, and some attendees didn't even get served. Attendees noticed that, and suddenly they started talking about how great the food had been prior to the cost cutting. Of course, attendees didn't know the reason for the bad food was an attempt at cost cutting. All they knew was that the food and service were bad.

The lesson learned was that food quality and quantity were the wrong places for cost cutting. Even though the food was not spectacular at the event in past years, it was good and attendees had learned to expect a good meal. Had food quality and service been variable in the past, with some bad years and some good, the event planners may have gotten away with the cost cutting because the lower-quality food and service may not have been as noticeable.

The same applies to anything else an event becomes known for. Anything attendees expect and appreciate needs to be treated with care in the course of attempts to cut costs. If an event is known for musical entertainment, and every year attendees have enjoyed live entertainment, cutting costs by bringing in a DJ may not go over well. Worse yet would be no musical entertainment. However, if the event had a mixed past regarding entertainment, cutting it out completely might go unnoticed or might even be welcomed by regular attendees.

Thus, the key to successful cost cutting is to cut what is least likely to be missed by regular attendees. First-time attendees won't know the difference if something is missing, but they as well as the regulars will notice things like poor entertainment, substandard food, and a dirty, smelly facility, especially if the restrooms are unclean. Substandard anything will be noticed. Hence, it may be better to do without some things than "make do" on a low budget, and other things, such as a clean event room, cannot be compromised for the sake of saving a few dollars.

Make Everyone a Winner

People like to win, but not all attendees can win a raffle prize or buy an auction item, can they? Sure they can. At many events everyone walks away with something. Savvy event planners know exactly what that something should be. One sure way to make certain attendees remember an event is to remind them of the event and host organization on a daily basis. Make sure attendees take that reminder home with them as they leave the event.

Give each attendee a special gift that will be used and in the course of its use will be placed in a position of visibility. This item should be very tasteful and have the organization's name in plain view (or some other notation or logo that reminds a person who sees the item of the event or the organization). This item should not appear extravagant, but it has to be of sufficient quality, stature, and usefulness that it is used. This means really used and not immediately thrown away. In one instance each donor coming to an event received a nice fountain pen made by a well-known manufacturer. The pen's brand name had become a status symbol. The pens had the name of the host organization very tastefully lettered in gold on the side. I still have mine. Other options are very nice mugs and glassware, high-quality tote bags, and nice wearable apparel. Donors or underwriters may help in acquiring such items. This is not about baseball caps, plastic water bottles, and T-shirts. That kind of stuff has no life after an event. It often gets thrown away.

One company I have worked with does specialty original, nature-related artwork, customized for the organization or event. The art can be applied to wearables, bags, mugs, posters, and many other items. This is actually original art, which makes for a very unique gift and an everlasting impression. This works well for some organizations but is not appropriate for others. There are many specialty-gift retail companies that offer a wide range of gifts. The key to success is finding the perfect quality item that will be used and seen over time, with a price within the range of expectation of the donor.

Dress for Success

Location and ambience can greatly influence bid amounts received, in the sense that events held in expensive-looking facilities where attendees dress up, even to the extent of wearing tuxedos and evening gowns, may impart a higher level of giving. An air of affluence in the surroundings and the influence of dress on giving are areas in need of objective evaluation. However, it is my belief that setting and attire do affect giving. I have no statistics to prove this, just observation of bidding patterns at auctions where the attendees had similar demographic characteristics but where attire differed. Overall raffle sales and auction bid-to-value ratios are higher when setting and dress are more formal given the same group of attendees or attendees having similar characteristics, such as demographic attributes and interests.

Some people simply will not attend an event if they must wear a tie, but others will wear a tie even to events where the tickets are stamped "casual dress." Consideration of dress relative to event ambience needs to be taken into account. Also, some locations lend themselves to more formal attire, whereas others virtually demand casual clothing. Increasing the formality of the dress and location in a relative and appropriate manner that does not deter any attendees may add revenue.

Event planners can set a desired mood given setting and dress, which can affect bottom-line fundraising revenue. Consider that even tents can be made comfortable for a formal event, as is often the case for large weddings. One I attended was a high-dollar fundraising tribute to a benefactor of conservation causes, where the 200 or so dark suit-, tie-, and dress-clad attendees sat on a platform on the beach under a large tent. The tables and chairs were strictly the common folding outdoor catering variety, but the linens, place settings, and table decor were the equal of what one would expect at any fine restaurant. What made the event most remarkable was the serving and service area. It was large and built to the same standards and with the same look as a fine bar and grill, with dark woods and deep rich colors to embody traditional ambience, uniquely designed to create an inviting, original, and relaxed atmosphere. It was like being in a fine downtown restaurant, yet there we were, on the beach. To top it off, it started to rain heavily, and the wind began to blow. None of that affected us, as the tent and "indoor restaurant" structure were even designed to weather a storm.

Thus, lack of a formal event hall need not preclude people dressing up for an auction event. An overriding concern is to ensure that attendees feel comfortable, and that includes feeling comfortable with how they look. In some communities, the annual auction event is a highlight of the year. Families attend and have fun. At an evening event a dress-up affair is often an eventful couples gala. On the other hand, the annual fundraising picnic, where the whole family can enjoy the arcade, the raffles, and auction, is a very comfortable tradition that can work just as well as an evening formal. When the event becomes a true "event," the host organization's event planners will have succeeded in establishing a group of devotees. Financial success, if not already attained, is now only a simple matter of effective fundraising the minute attendees walk through the door.

Use the "Auction in a Box"

Several large national/international ("parent") organizations have turned auction events into consistent moneymakers for their chapters by providing a highly specialized auction service. These parent organizations offer their chapters what is effectively an "auction in a box." A full selection of auction, raffle, and other prize merchandise is preselected, manufactured (or purchased from vendors), assembled, packaged, and sent to the host chapter or event committee in advance of the event. It contains almost everything needed for an event.

These event packages can be tailored to some degree, based on the number of attendees expected and regional variations. The chapter or committee either pays for the merchandise and materials in advance or makes a down payment followed by full payment upon completion of the event. Sometimes minimum bid amounts are set for some higher-value items in the package where failure to attract sufficient bidding could seriously affect net revenue. Rather than

risk financial loss should bidding fail to meet the minimum, the organization can return such items for a refund or credit.

Although only chapters of a few organizations have access to such auction services, there are companies that can provide any organization wishing to host an auction with a selection of products and services at a single price. One such company started out as a supplier to these "auction-in-a-box" organizations. In addition to providing a selection of products and services, this company does custom work to personalize various products to the specifications of the host organization, such as applying a logo or text to every kind of apparel imaginable, briefcases, golf bags, pens, wines, and so on. In addition, this company does original artwork that can be woven into the theme of the event.

Speed Up Payment Processing

If there are large numbers of items that need processing for payment, use a bar-coding system to facilitate payment, credit card processing, and receipt processing. This provides a quick way to process auction-item payment. At many events, people wait until the event ends to pay for auction items. This is good because event planners want attendees to enjoy the entire event, but it can create quite a traffic jam at the payment booth and delay departure of attendees for hours. There are usually only one or two credit card processing machines, and only a limited number of people can work at a payment booth at the same time without getting in each other's way. Bar coding can make payment processing fly. Software programs and hardware are readily available to set up bar-code processing. In effect, the auction is set up like a small store. Buyer's agreements for items, receipts, and even mailing labels are all processed using the codes. This also lends itself well to accounting and maintaining records.

25

Where to Go from Here

I was in a meeting with various department heads and faculty. Among the group was one of the most respected deans on campus, a particularly learned professor who had built the college she represented into one of the most prestigious in the entire university system. I was pitching a start-up initiative based on the idea that university students should have an opportunity to take course work while in school that prepares them to enter the nonprofit sector of employment with relevant practical skills and training. The initiative would consist of at least one introductory course on nonprofit organizations, and for students who chose to make nonprofit work a career, there would be a series of advanced courses in various aspects of nonprofit organization management and administration.

As we spoke, I told of recent graduates of the university who were working in local nonprofit organizations who found themselves ill prepared for the jobs they now held. They had recently formed a group with the objective of asking for continuing education course work to get training they felt they should have received while in school. Another student knew about nonprofit jobs available, wanted employment, yet found no relevant course work that would provide training and skills that would set him apart from any other applicant after he graduated.

The conversation came to a rather abrupt end when the dean declared I needed to visit with faculty in the business school who teach public administration, because that was where students wanting to enter the nonprofit field needed to be going for course work. End of story? It would be if the dean were correct. Truth is that in many critical areas nonprofit organization management and administration are unlike that of for-profit businesses or public agencies. How money is raised—

holding events—is one among many areas that sets the nonprofit sector apart from other businesses, but if I had to choose, I would say managing a nonprofit is more closely aligned with managing a for-profit business than a public agency.

The nonprofit sector has become a very distinct and important "third leg" of employment in the United States today. My university is not unique in missing the growing importance of the nonprofit sector to the economy and employment. Moreover, the nonprofit world is outpacing all other sectors in growth and influence. Students who aspire to manage and administer nonprofit organizations deserve training opportunities at least as rigorous in areas of specialization as training for entry into the public and for-profit sectors.

THE STATISTICS ARE sending a clear message: nonprofit organizations are a major and growing force in the economy and today's sociopolitical landscape. The number of charities and foundations in the United States reached nearly 1.3 million in 2010, representing a 150% growth over the last 20 years, and there are now 1.96 million tax-exempt organizations according to *The Chronicle of Philanthropy*.[1] Even in times of economic downturn, the number of nonprofit organizations and employment in the nonprofit field have increased, with about an average 44,000 new charities added each year between 2005 and 2009.[2]

The situation at the university was not unique to that school. Although students interested in careers in the nonprofit field have a seemingly ever-expanding universe of opportunity for employment, today they have little or no opportunity in many

universities to prepare for these jobs. Most universities offer courses in public administration and for-profit management, but of the nearly 4,500 US degree-granting colleges and universities,[3] fewer than 300 have at least one course in nonprofit management.[4] Most universities have yet to recognize and seize the growing challenge of preparing students for work within this huge sector of employment. Yet it is in this sector where professionals who are committed to mission-driven work are most needed and where their skills can benefit society most.

Nonprofit organizations represent 13% of the US economy, employ 1 in 10 workers, and raise nearly $1.9 trillion in revenue each year.[5] In the state of Texas where I now teach nonprofit organization management skills to university students, the payroll for people employed in the nonprofit industry exceeds the payroll for all of Texas' state government.[6] By any account, this represents a lot of fundraising conducted by a large and constantly growing number of staff and volunteers.

This expansion is a direct reflection of increasing numbers of people who are forming organizations to address missions and causes. Each new organization will have members, and as new and old organizations grow, more people become involved. Staff may be hired or volunteers may continue to serve in all roles as growth continues, but either way, as more people become involved in more nonprofit organizations, more people will become workers and par-

1. "Charting the Tax-Exempt World," *The Chronicle of Philanthropy*, April 5, 2011, http://philanthropy.com/article/Charting-the-Tax-Exempt-World/127014/.

2. "How Many Charities Were Created in America," *The Chronicle of Philanthropy*, April 18, 2010, http://philanthropy.com/article/How-Many-Charities-Were/65144/.

3. National Center for Education Statistics, US Department of Education, *Digest of Education Statistics*, 2010, Washington, DC, April 2011, http://nces.ed.gov/pubsearch/pubsinfo.asp?pubid=2011015.

4. Roseanne M. Mirabella, "Nonprofit Management Education: Current Offerings in University-Based Programs," Seaton Hall University, South Orange, NJ, http://academic.shu.edu/npo/.

5. S. Stannard-Stockton, "In the Down Economy, Let's Not Ignore the Value of Creating Nonprofit Jobs," *The Chronicle of Philanthropy*, December 2, 2010, page 39, http://philanthropy.com/article/Don-t-Ignore-the-Economic/125504/.

6. L. M. Salamon and S. L. Gellere, *Texas Nonprofit Employment Update*, Nonprofit Employment Bulletin 35 (Baltimore, MD: Johns Hopkins Center for Civil Society Studies and OneStar Foundation: Texas Center for Social Impact, Johns Hopkins University, 2010).

ticipants in nonprofit organizations' fundraising activities and supporting mission-driven work. Well-managed events that produce healthy net revenue are among the forces that have powered this increase in the nonprofit sector.

New Technology Is Driving Change

New technology is helping drive this growth as it becomes easier to spread messages among many people quickly and at low to no cost. It is also easier to find people of like minds by using technologies like the Internet and e-mail and then forming a group around the interest. Web sites and networks of friends can be formed to work on missions covering broad interests such as protection of the environment, medical research, or education. Most challenging in the past has been locating people with narrow mutual interests, but that is no more or less challenging now than seeking people with broad interests. For example, it is easy to locate people whose interest in the environment is specific to water pollution or even pollution caused by a certain contaminant, or even that contaminant from a specific polluting industry or chemical plant. In the area of medical research, there are means to locate people interested in a specific disease or in a specific research team working on that disease. Entire organizations can be formed, funds raised, and missions funded around such narrow interests.

New Fundraising

Online fundraising has been celebrated as a tool that will revolutionize fundraising for nonprofit organizations. Although it started slowly because of donors' initial apprehension about giving money over the Internet, several disasters jump-started giving, and disasters continue to produce the greatest surges in online giving.[7] Even during economic downturns, online giving has grown. *The Chronicle of Philanthropy* has tracked online giving for the

Sidebar 25.1. **Top Social-Media Tools Used in 2009**	
Social-media tool	**% use**
Facebook	58
Twitter	42
YouTube	36
Blogging	18
Text messaging	15

Source: *The Chronicle of Philanthropy*'s annual survey of online fundraising, "Top Social Media Tools Used by Charities for Online Fund Raising," April 18, 2010, http://philanthropy.com/article/Top-Social-Media-Tools-Used-by/65151/.

Note: The tools were used by 176 of the top nonprofit organizations for online fundraising (percentages represent percentage of organizations surveyed that used that tool).

past 12 years, with the survey for 2009 showing 5% growth but also the first indication growth in online giving may be slowing down.[8] Sidebar 25.1 displays key means to raise funds using new technology by 176 of the largest nonprofit organizations in the United States. Not included in the survey were online auctions, which have become popular as a result of the success of for-profit, Internet-based companies, but some nonprofit organizations also use online auctions to augment funds.

A Marriage of Old and New

Although online fundraising has been a successful tool, reducing costs of fundraising and reaching new donors, it can go only so far in replacing traditional means of fundraising, such as the gala event. However, a marriage of new technology with the old has a solid place in today's fundraising repertoire, and in particular the planning and holding of a major event. Here are a few examples:

- Event registration (ticketing) can be driven almost completely through a Web site–based registration process on an event Web site. For event

---

7. Noelle Barton, "How the Chronicle's Annual Survey of Online Fund Raising Was Compiled," *The Chronicle of Philanthropy*, April 18, 2010, http://philanthropy.com/article/How-the-Chronicle-s-Survey/65088.

---

8. Noelle Barton and Nicole Wallace, "Online Giving Continues to Grow but at a Slower Pace, Chronicle Survey Finds," *The Chronicle of Philanthropy*, April 18, 2010, http://philanthropy.com/article/Online-Giving-Grows-but-at-a/65089/.

planners not computer savvy, turnkey Internet services are available for hire.

• Social-media tools can be used to advertise an event and invite potential attendees.

• Videos showing an organization's mission accomplishments and projects to be funded can be displayed through Internet sites, eliminating dependency on commercial news media for placement of publicity.

• The auction program listing all live and silent auction items can be posted on the event Web site in advance of the event, with links to video and other information about each item.

• Potential event sites, caterers, and other service providers can be surveyed, satisfaction ratings reviewed, and contact made in hours instead of days.

• Rules governing raffles and games of chance, local requirements, and permit needs can be quickly assembled and reviewed for applicability to a planned event.

• Virtual bidders can be hosted online to participate in the event's auctions.

Events offer a powerful means to bring people of like mind together. New technology and social media can help form and organize like-minded people, but it takes direct social interaction at an event to fully cement those relationships into place. The host can use an event to create meaningful personal experiences for attendees regarding the organization and its accomplishments. Done well, the connection becomes personal and the cause emotionally compelling.

The Event: Past, Present, and Future?

Some may wonder if the event is a creature of the past, present, or future. It's all three. Savvy event planners have always embraced change as a means to more effectively and efficiently raise funds. They have always welcomed new technology and techniques as a means to increase net income and accomplish other objectives of events, such as to gain greater publicity for an organization and its mission and increase its membership. That has been true in the past and will remain true into the future. New technology can help reduce the cost of planning an event as well as invite potential attendees. The Internet and availability of service-vendor Web sites and e-mail make it much easier today than yesterday to do many of the tasks necessary to host a major event. Social media is an incredibly efficient means to invite the entire world to an event, or at least that portion of the world's people who may be willing to give.

In the for-profit sector, planners of business conventions, professional meetings, and other business gatherings have wondered if "virtual event technology" will replace the standard large-scale convention. Such replacement has not yet taken place. Instead, a hybrid of sorts has evolved in which business and professional conventions are planned and held with a strong online and technology-based presence. Virtual involvement of individuals and groups merges within the convention, on the convention floor, and in various specialized meetings. Done right, this virtual involvement enhances the overall experience for convention attendees, without detracting from the personal and social benefits of "being there." And it is this personal, social presence that cannot be fully duplicated by a virtual presence alone.

And so it is with people who attend local, statewide, national, or international fundraising events: the social and personal interactions make the fundraising event (or business convention) as fresh and vital today and tomorrow as it was yesterday. Human beings are social creatures. Events are social affairs. People with common interests enjoy each other's company. People give to people. People who join together for a purpose need a way to express that commitment, and the event provides just that opportunity. The major event, full of raffles, good food, auctions, fun games, rockin' music, and compelling speeches, is now and will remain relevant. Even though technology changes and will continue to change and be used as appropriate to improve event effectiveness and efficiency, people will remain basically the same. They will remain social and will seek reasons to be with others who share common interests.

Nonprofit organizations by design form around people who share a common interest in achieving a goal. The number of nonprofit organizations hovers around 2 million, a number that continues to grow, with some individual organizations having several million members and supporters, and many having tens of thousands. Each of those organizations has a purpose—a mission. Achieving that mission gen- erally involves financing projects. The modern fundraising event has evolved with the growth in nonprofit organizations and the need to fund their missions. That evolution continues. This book is dedicated to furthering that evolution and to those members of organizations committed to making the world a better place for humanity.

Nonprofit Resources
for Nonprofits

The following nonprofit organizations, media, and agencies provide support and offer resources such as books and training to support nonprofit organizations' fundraising and other essential functions, for example, board support, membership, administration, and general management.

Alliance for Nonprofit Management, San Francisco, CA
http://www.allianceonline.org

American Society of Association Executives, Washington, DC
http://www.asaecenter.org

Association for Research on Nonprofit Organizations and Voluntary Action, Indianapolis, IN
http://www.arnova.org

Association of Fundraising Professionals, Arlington, VA
http://www.afpnet.org/

The Center on Philanthropy & Public Policy, University of Southern California, Los Angeles, CA
http://cppp.usc.edu

Center on Philanthropy at Indiana University, Indianapolis, IN
http://www.philanthropy.iupui.edu

The Chronicle of Philanthropy, Washington, DC
http://philanthropy.com

Council on Foundations, Arlington, VA
http://www.cof.org

Dorothy A. Johnson Center for Philanthropy, Grand Valley State University, Allendale, MI
http://www.gvsu.edu/jcp/home-45.htm

Foundation Center, New York, NY
http://foundationcenter.org

The Hauser Center for Nonprofit Organizations at Harvard University, Cambridge, MA
http://www.hks.harvard.edu/hauser

idealist, New York, NY
http://www.idealist.org

Institute for Nonprofit Management, Portland State University, Portland, OR
http://www.inpm.pdx.edu

Internal Revenue Service, Charities & Non-Profits, Washington, DC
http://www.irs.gov/charities/index.html

Lodestar Center for Philanthropy & Nonprofit Innovation, Arizona State University, Phoenix, AZ
http://lodestar.asu.edu

Midwest Center for Nonprofit Leadership, University of Missouri, Kansas City, MO
http://bloch.umkc.edu/mwcnl/

National Council of Nonprofits, Washington, DC
http://www.councilofnonprofits.org

Nonprofit and Public Management Center, University of Michigan, Ann Arbor, MI
http://nonprofit.umich.edu

Philanthropy Journal, North Carolina State University, Raleigh, NC
http://www.philanthropyjournal.org

Rollins College Philanthropy & Nonprofit Leadership Center, Winter Park, FL
http://www.rollins.edu/pnlc/index.html

Society for Nonprofit Organizations, Lavinia, MI
http://www.snpo.org

TechSoup, San Francisco, CA
http://www.techsoup.org

TheNonProfitTimes, Morris Plains, NJ
http://www.nptimes.com

Young Nonprofit Professionals Network (online only)
http://ynpn.org

Index

Entries denoted with *f* indicate photographs or other images.